Sacred Spaces and Transnational Networks in American Sufism

Islam of the Global West

Series editors: Kambiz GhaneaBassiri and Frank Peter

Islam of the Global West is a pioneering series that examines Islamic beliefs, practices, discourses, communities, and institutions that have emerged from "the Global West." The geographical and intellectual framing of the Global West reflects both the role played by the interactions between people from diverse religions and cultures in the development of Western ideals and institutions in the modern era, and the globalization of these very ideals and institutions.

In creating an intellectual space where works of scholarship on European and North American Muslims enter into conversation with one another, the series promotes the publication of theoretically informed and empirically grounded research in these areas. By bringing the rapidly growing research on Muslims in European and North American societies, ranging from the United States and France to Portugal and Albania, into conversation with the conceptual framing of the Global West, this ambitious series aims to reimagine the modern world and develop new analytical categories and historical narratives that highlight the complex relationships and rivalries that have shaped the multicultural, poly-religious character of Europe and North America, as evidenced, by way of example, in such economically and culturally dynamic urban centres as Los Angeles, New York, Paris, Madrid, Toronto, Sarajevo, London, Berlin, and Amsterdam where there is a significant Muslim presence.

Amplifying Islam in the European Soundscape: Religious Pluralism and Secularism in the Netherlands, Pooyan Tamimi Arab
Islam and Nationhood in Bosnia-Herzegovina: Surviving Empires, Xavier Bougarel

Sacred Spaces and Transnational Networks in American Sufism

Bawa Muhaiyaddeen and Contemporary Shrine Cultures

Merin Shobhana Xavier

BLOOMSBURY ACADEMIC

LONDON • NEW YORK • OXFORD • NEW DELHI • SYDNEY

BLOOMSBURY ACADEMIC
Bloomsbury Publishing Plc
50 Bedford Square, London, WC1B 3DP, UK

**BLOOMSBURY, BLOOMSBURY ACADEMIC and the Diana logo are trademarks of
Bloomsbury Publishing Plc**

First published in Great Britain 2018

Series design by Dani Leigh
Cover image © Brian Stablyk / gettyimages.co.uk

A catalogue record for this book is available from the British Library.

Library of Congress Cataloging-in-Publication Data
Names: Shobhana Xavier, Merin, author.
Title: Sacred spaces and transnational networks in American sufism : Bawa
Muhaiyaddeen and contemporary shrine cultures / Merin Shobhana Xavier.
Description: New York : Bloomsbury Academic, 2018. |
Includes bibliographical references and index.
Identifiers: LCCN 2017046920 | ISBN 9781350024458 (hardback) |
ISBN 9781350026698 (epdf)
Subjects: LCSH: Sufism–United States. | Islamic shrines–United States. |
Muhaiyaddeen, M. R. Bawa.
Classification: LCC BP188.8.U6 S46 2018 | DDC 297.40973–dc23
LC record available at https://lccn.loc.gov/2017046920

ISBN: HB: 978-1-3500-2445-8
ePDF: 978-1-3500-2669-8
ePub: 978-1-3500-2670-4

Series: Islam of the Global West

Typeset by Newgen KnowledgeWorks Pvt. Ltd., Chennai, India
Printed and bound in Great Britain

To find out more about our authors and books visit www.bloomsbury.com and
sign up for our newsletters.

To Thatha and Bawa

Contents

Figures

Acknowledgments

In 2011, while living in London, England, I had a sudden urge to travel to Sri Lanka, where I was born but had left as a child because a civil war was brewing. At the time, I had just been accepted into a PhD program at Wilfrid Laurier University in Waterloo, Ontario, Canada, to study M. R. Bawa Muhaiyaddeen and his community known as the Bawa Muhaiyaddeen Fellowship. I knew Bawa was a Tamil spiritual teacher from Sri Lanka, but I did not know details about his origins in the country. Still my impulse to visit Sri Lanka had nothing to do with Bawa, or so I thought, but rather I wanted to learn more about my own homeland. I could not articulate this desire to return to Sri Lanka to my mother, who lived in Toronto; however, when she found out about my plans she pleaded desperately with me not to return because she was worried about the instability of the region. Against all my mother's wishes, I, stubbornly and, I might add, naively, arrived in Colombo after twenty-one years.

Upon my arrival, my cousin, thinking that this would be my only visit to Sri Lanka, was adamant that I go to our *sonta ur* ("ancestral village" in Kayts [also known as Velanai Island]) in Jaffna, where I was born and where my grandfather's (Thatha) house was situated. My mother at this point was irate, and rightly so. One of her last memories of Kayts was of clinging to her three young children (me only a month old), and her father and siblings, as they were held at gunpoint by the military while they attempted to escape the violence in the region. And here I was willingly returning to that postwar land because of an urge to discover more about my homeland and identity. Despite my mother's pleas, I followed my cousin to Jaffna.

I arrived in Jaffna from Colombo on the overnight bus just as dawn broke over the horizon. This sunrise remains one of the most sombering experiences I have ever had. The civil war ended in Sri Lanka in May 2009, but even in June 2011, the remnants of this war decorated the arid landscape in Jaffna and was etched on the bodies and faces of Tamils who survived a long and devastating conflict. Immediately, I felt guilt-ridden because I escaped that war and many did not.

My cousin eventually took me to my Thatha's house, who lived in Toronto at the time. I was the first family member to step into our ancestral house in nearly three decades. As I walked through the house, my cousin explained what life had been like before the war. He took me into what used to be my mother's kitchen, where I was surrounded by an abundance of bullet holes on the walls and bullet casings on the floor. I became ever more paralyzed with each family story my cousin relayed, as I stood amid a residue of violence and conflict. My cousin, realizing that I was fading, took me out of the village to another village nearby and then to Chaddy Beach.

As we stood on the shore with our feet deeply planted in the seaweed-filled cool water, he explained the history of the sacred spaces on this beach. He pointed to a Roman Catholic church further inland dedicated to the Virgin Mary, which my mother regularly visited. Closer to the shore were two mosques, one of which, however, looked familiar. I knew I had seen it before but could not quite figure out from where. It took a few minutes, but it occurred to me that I had seen a photograph of the same mosque in the Fellowship in Philadelphia. It was the mosque Bawa built. It was not until my return to Kayts that I found out that Bawa, who I first heard of in an Islamic Mysticism course at York University and on whose American movement I had proposed to write my PhD thesis, started his ministry in Jaffna, where I was born. I instantly knew I had to ask my Thatha about Bawa when I returned to Toronto, as I was certain he would have heard of him or perhaps they had even met. A couple of days later, I was in Chennai, India, and my mother called from Toronto to let me know that my Thatha had just died. My return to Jaffna and my Thatha's house coincided not only with the loss of my Thatha but the recovery of a complex ancestral history, which, I imagine, will take a lifetime to process. At the same time, though, this homeland and history also belonged to Bawa, a figure who played a formative role in the development of American Sufism. Both my Thatha's and Bawa's histories stirred my academic journey and have inevitably led to the book you are holding.

This project would not have been possible without all the members of the Bawa Muhaiyaddeen Fellowship and the Serendib Sufi Study Circle from Sri Lanka (the matron and the president of the Jaffna branch) to Toronto (Roshan Jamal and Nur Sharon Marcus) to Philadelphia (Imam Muhammad Abdur-Razzaq Miller, Hamzabibi Applebaum Dale, Janie Posner, Michael Green, Sitti Fatima, Dr Ganesan, Kelly Hayden, Mary-Fatima Weening, Chuck Ginty, and John Barnett) and many many more who welcomed me into their homes and shared meals with me and allowed me to accompany them on their pilgrimages. In so doing you entrusted me with carrying your stories of Bawa. I thank you for this trust and I hope I have done your story some justice.

Friends along the way have kept me grounded and took care of me in so many ways: Maxie Bai Martin, Shane Bai Martin, Zabeen Khamisa, Rachel Brown, Jason Ellsworth, Sahir Dewji, Leanne Roncolato, Alex Roomets, Mike Martell, Tehseen Thaver, SherAli Tareen, and Irfaan Ishan Jaffer, thank you so much. William Rory Dickson readied the path with his own study of Sufi leaders in North America and was a constant conversation partner during the writing of this book—without him I would not have been able to easily enter this world as I did. I also extend my gratitude to my friend and colleague Amarnath Amarasingam, who helped me navigate the daunting terrain of our *sonta ur* in Sri Lanka during my fieldwork. Thank you also to my family in Sri Lanka who took care of me throughout my fieldwork, especially Dilip-anna, who brought me to Jaffna for the first time and visited Sufi shrines with me, as well as his family (Maureen-akka, Stephanie, and Damian) for being gracious hosts. A special thank you also to Sarah Morgan and Shanelle Kandiah for your help with the interview transcriptions, and to Maxie Bai Martin for your help during the manuscript revision process.

I extend my heartfelt gratitude to Professor Amila Buturovic at York University, who first introduced me to Islamic Mysticism in her undergraduate seminar and was my master's supervisor. Thank you to all the faculty members in the joint Religious Diversity in North America Program at Wilfrid Laurier and Waterloo University, especially Janet McLellan, Michel Desjardins, David Seljak, and Carol Duncan. I specially thank Doris Jakobsh, Jason Neelis, Nathan Funk, and Gisela Webb, the members of my dissertation committee, who supported me with kindness and encouragement, and read earlier iterations of this project. I would also like to thank the Religious Studies Department at Franklin & Marshall College for their support during my two years as a visiting assistant professor, and all the students in my Islam and Sufism classes, especially those who participated in field trips to Bawa's *mazar*—your questions, reflections, and insights on Bawa, the Fellowship, and the *mazar* were so valuable to me during the writing of this book.

I am most grateful to *Islam of the Global West* series editors Kambiz GhaneaBassiri and Frank Peter. Thank you so much for your sustained interest in this project and for your gracious effort and time in refining this manuscript; thanks as well to the editors at Bloomsbury Press, Lalle Pursglove, Amy Jordon, Lucy Carroll and Kalyani. Funding from the Department of Religion and Culture, the Faculty of Arts Deans Office, the Graduate and Post Graduate Studies at Wilfrid Laurier University, and the Canadian Corporation for Studies of Religion Doctoral Scholarship, along with the Ontario Graduate Scholarship (OGS), made this research possible. Thank you also to Wade Clark and Ithaca College's Centre for Faculty Excellence.

Last but most certainly not the least, this project is what it is due to my doctoral supervisor and mentor, Professor Meena Sharify-Funk. Professor Sharify-Funk stood by me and guided me with encouragement, love, and support from the moment I arrived in Waterloo. She realized before I did that this project was more than just an academic enterprise—it was riddled with my own memory, loss, homeland, and return, and in spite of it all, she patiently helped me find my way back home, all the while ensuring that I completed my dissertation.

It was the collective legacies of my Thatha and Bawa that gave me a new story of my homeland, one that was not drenched in the blood of violence and hate that tore a country apart, but one that moved beyond difference to honor a shared humanity. I dedicate this to them. In the end, however, any errors in this book are mine alone.

Introduction

In the rolling hills of Pennsylvania Amish farm country stands a curious structure. It has a large white dome and four doors angled toward each of the cardinal directions. The presence of this building evokes a Mughal past, albeit one that would be imaginary. This structure is a *mazar* (place of visitation) and it contains the remains of Muhammad Raheem Bawa Muhaiyaddeen (d. 1986), a teacher who arrived in Philadelphia in October 1971 from Jaffna, Sri Lanka. In Philadelphia, his charismatic leadership and teachings formed the foundation of the Bawa Muhaiyaddeen Fellowship. When he died, he was entombed in Coatesville, Pennsylvania, where a cemetery already existed for the burial of members of the Fellowship, as did a farm. This shrine, however, has gained fame beyond the immediate Fellowship. It has become a site of pilgrimage for diaspora Muslims living in North America who seek to replicate the practice of *ziyara*, or visitation to graves of Sufi saints, as a means to access God.

In Sufi parlance graves of saints are understood as being transformative. The blessing sought by a devotee who approaches a tomb of a Sufi saint is based on the belief that she/he is partaking of the charisma or blessing (*baraka*) released by the holy figure's union with God. Though communities of following have formed in the living presence of Sufi figures, it is in their death that they are solidified as saintly beings who emit blessings. It is understood that saints supplicate prayers on behalf of the adherent. Tombs of saints, then, are the epicenters of ritual performances and acts of personal piety by the diverse religious supplicants who engage them. With the construction of Bawa's burial tomb in Pennsylvania, tomb practices historically associated with Sufism and Islam in regions such as the Middle East, North Africa, and South Asia now form a central thread of Sufism in the global west.

For the members of the Bawa Muhaiyaddeen Fellowship, the practice of shrine visitation is also institutionalized in Sri Lanka, where Bawa began his first institution. Bawa's *mazar* in Pennsylvania is linked to a mosque and shrine known as Mankumban in Jaffna. Mankumban sits amid the archipelago of islands off the northern tip of Sri Lanka on Velanai Island (also known as Kayts). Situated within the shore of Chaddy Beach, this *masjid-mazar* (mosque-shrine) complex was dedicated to Maryam, the mother of Jesus ('Isa) by Bawa. It was the first institution established by Bawa. This complex is known variously as "God's House" and a mosque (*palli*), in addition to being treated as a memorial for Maryam and Bawa. There are varying interpretations associated with Maryam and Bawa's relationship to this particular shrine. In Bawa's case, his presence is memorialized by his Tamil adherents because he is associated with the building of the shrine, whereas Bawa taught his students that Maryam visited this location when she was alive, presumably centuries ago, and so she is believed to be spiritually present here. In Islam, Maryam is viewed as an exemplary and holy figure, on par with other females such as the wife of the Prophet Muhammad, Khadija, or their daughter Fatima.

Bawa's death and subsequent burial in 1986 was a time when his first institutions in Sri Lanka, and especially in the region of Jaffna, were embroiled in ethnic violence between the majority Sinhala and minority Tamil and Muslim populations. Ethnolinguistic conflicts unfolded in Sri Lanka for nearly three decades and only subsided in 2009. In America though, Bawa's physical passing and burial led to the institutionalization of Sufism in ways unimagined by his immediate disciples. Bawa joined Jaffna with Coatesville both physically and metaphysically, for his disciples and pilgrims from all walks of life for years to come. The case study of the Bawa Muhaiyaddeen Fellowship, and its parallel institutional developments in Sri Lanka, known as the Serendib Sufi Study Circle (SSSC), is an example of the historical precedent of Sufism and its contemporary manifestations in the global West. It is one that captures local dynamics of Islam and Sufism, and global renditions of these practices into new regions where they are further transformed and retranslated. Mankumban in Jaffna is also linked to Bawa's *mazar* in Coatesville and highlights the nuances of shrine culture and networks within transnational Sufi communities as this one in particular is deeply rooted in Sri Lankan and American Sufism. The story of Bawa in Coatesville illustrates Sufi traditions' particular and universal trajectories, as the shrine expands out into new spaces and epicenters in the transnational community of the Fellowship, while Bawa's legacy also draws to itself new stories of diasporic Muslim pilgrims from North America and beyond.

Transnational religions are usually framed within immigrant and diasporic contexts; such is not the case for the origins of the Fellowship in America. The Fellowship did not begin in South Asia and migrate to the United States. It developed as an American spiritual movement, and over the years its mosque and *mazar* in Pennsylvania have gained traction among immigrant Muslims. The Fellowship is a part of a broader network, with two distinctive poles,

one Sri Lankan and the other American. As such, it is shaped by ongoing negotiations of movements and performances that are distinct but interconnected.[1]
The Fellowship thus serves as a formative case study to comprehending Sufism's
development in the global West. This book is motivated by the following questions: what is the Fellowship and its counterpart Sri Lankan institutions, known
as the Serendib Sufi Study Circle? What subspaces have developed around these
transnational nodes? How are these spaces and institutions connected to a global
reality? And who is Bawa? What is the story of the figure buried in Coatesville
with origins in Jaffna?

Toward a Sufism of the Global West

In his historical study of Sufism from classical periods to the twenty-first
century, Nile Green maps the mystical tradition of Islam as it developed in
Mesopotamian, Arabian, and Persian regions, and then as it continued to spread
throughout South, Central, and East Asia, North and Sub-Saharan Africa. Green
does not frame Sufism solely as a phenomenological or textual tradition, like the
early Orientalist scholars who surmised that Sufism was waning. Rather, he situates it as a tradition embedded across different cultures, disseminated by living
teachers (*shuyukh*) who enacted particular institutions, spaces, and rituals that
transformed and maintained continuity into new epochs and regions.[2] As Sufism
spread, it took on the vernacular tendencies of the local culture while maintaining continuities through ritual practices, cosmological principles, and theologies. Sufism also traveled into Europe and North America during the colonial
and postcolonial global period (1800–2000).[3] The transmission of Sufism to the
West, namely Northwestern Europe, unfolded through waves of cross-cultural
textual and itinerant exchanges over the past two centuries. Sufi poetry, such as
the work of the fourteenth-century Persian poet Hafiz, influenced the German
writer Johann Wolfgang von Goethe (d. 1832). Such examples of literary encounters proved to be popular among European audiences in the nineteenth-century
era of colonization, and even influenced literary output of European Romantics.[4]
The latter poetic and literary reception of Sufism played a role in universalizing
the tradition as a perennial one rather than a particularly Islamic one. In the
colonial period, Muslims were represented in Orientalist scholarship as "fanat-
ics" while Sufis were placed on par with Hindu yogis and Buddhist masters, in
effect emphasizing their universality while relegating their Islamic particularity.[5]
These comparative approaches set the course for the spread of Sufism into the

West, primarily via the literary figures that dominated European Romanticism, which laid the foundation for the westward expansion of Sufism beyond Muslim majority countries—especially through migration.

Where Green maps the broader historical spread of Sufism through Islamic empires, wandering mendicants, and Sufi orders, Mark Sedgwick highlights the philosophical and ideological exchanges led by philosophers, leaders, and students from hermetic and Neoplatonic traditions in the premodern era to Islamic and non-Islamic esoteric and perennial schools of thought in the modern era. The circulation of these ideas led to the development of Sufi orders and movements, such as Traditionalism, in the West.[6] These cross-cultural exchanges of spiritual ideologies were further compelled by the migration of Sufi teachers and practitioners to the West. Both Green and Sedgwick frame the globalization of Sufism as a model of spirituality that appealed, and continues to appeal, to Western culture beyond Muslim majority regions. And thus, it developed outside of the framework of Islam, while simultaneously maintaining an Islamic cultural and religious register for Muslim practitioners. This broader and modern context is the backdrop to *global Sufism*.[7] The complexity of globalization is the "tensile interplay between time-space compression and distanciation."[8] The "flows" resulting from globalization, of cultures, capitals, ideas, and peoples led to efforts to preserve and protect nation-states and borders but also transcends territorialized conceptualizations of the world.[9] It has forced the removal of the "shackles" of "boundary-oriented" concepts of cultural and religious manifestations— particularly as they are oriented around ethnic, racial, or cultural identities— such as it has unfolded with global Sufism, in that Sufism is not just an Arab, Persian, or South Asian religious and spiritual preserve, but has become an European and American one too.[10] The "global West," as a conceptual framework, is defined by connections and exchanges that traverse multiple directions. Perhaps America is one of the most porous regions where these transmissions and transformations are unfolding.

American Sufism

Within the discussions of "Western Sufism," there has emerged a subfield dedicated to "American Sufism."[11] During the early twentieth century, the enthusiasm for all things occult, spiritual, and "metaphysical" led to new spiritual movements, such as the Theosophical Society.[12] Interests in non-Christian Eastern traditions led to the presence of Buddhism, Hinduism, and Sufism in literary networks. For instance, figures in the Transcendentalist movement like

Ralph Waldo Emerson (d. 1882) were significant in the diffusion of Sufi poetry in America, which led to widespread popularity of the poems of Hafiz, Omar Khayyam (d. 1131), and Jalaluddin Rumi (d. 1273) among a new American audience.[13]

The earliest known Muslim-Sufi teacher to arrive in America was Hazrat Inayat Khan (d. 1927). By the time Khan arrived in New York City from India in 1910, Sufi literary traditions had already been transmitted into a new cultural landscape wherein they appealed to a spiritually and esoterically inclined American audience.[14] Khan's arrival benefited from the Parliament of the World's Religions held in Chicago in 1893 that welcomed other teachers from Asia, such as Swami Vivekananda (d. 1902). Khan's visit is the first known instance of a Sufi teacher who disembarked to America to disseminate Sufi teachings to an American audience. He did not remain in America long due to his experiences of racism, this likely led to his universalizing of Sufi teachings to his early American students. He also initiated an American female student, Rabia Ada Martin (d. 1947), in effect institutionalizing Sufism in America through the *murshid-murid* (master-disciple) relationship that has been the quintessence of Sufi institutions across space and time. Decades later, after the relaxing of immigration policies in America during the 1960s, the spread and diversification of Sufism was accelerated by migration, as both Sufi practitioners and teachers from Muslim-majority countries established a significant number of Sufi orders in American urban centers, which, of course, coincided with the further development of Islam in America.[15] Teachers arrived from Senegal, Turkey, Bosnia, Iran, and Sri Lanka, each establishing their own Sufi communities and teachings. These teachers institutionalized Sufi traditions across America's permeable religious and spiritual landscape.[16]

Early scholarship on American Sufism attempted to theorize these broad movements that emerged regionally across the eastern and western seaboards. Aside from providing important historical analysis on these movements, some scholars developed taxonomies to qualify these movements (i.e. "quasi," "Islamic," or "non-Islamic").[17] Groupings were organized according to types of practices, ethnic, religious, and racial composition of the movements themselves, and the method of the movements' transmission into America. Using these qualifications, early investigations were devoted to determining whether the Sufi movements developing in America maintained continuity with the "traditions" of Muslim-majority societies where they originated or transplanted from or whether they were an American "innovation."[18] For instance, was Khan's movement, whose members were predominantly non-Muslim American students, a new religious and spiritual tradition or a continuation of Sufism from India, especially given that he initiated a non-Muslim female student as its leader in America? If it was a complete innovation, can it still be labeled Sufism? Two broader concerns seemed to be implicitly evoked with the creation of categories and labels in the study of Sufi communities in America. First, there was an inference that the Sufism forming in America was not only *innovative* but its novelty was due to its *Americanness*. Here *Americanness* alluded to modernization, represented by principles of liberal democracy, egalitarian gender norms, pluralism, and diversity, which seemed to have influenced the development of Sufism for the *better* in America.[19] This American Sufism was positioned against the stereotypes attributed to Islam: puritanical rigidity, social conservatism, and legalism. Binaries, which were, for instance, concretized in the colonial and imperial encounters of Islam by the West. Second, early categories of the nature of American Sufism were consistently concerned with its relationship to Islam or lack thereof. Most of the labels that appeared in the categorization of Sufi communities attempted to ascertain its proximity to Islam, the closer it was to Islam (i.e. ritually and legally), the more legitimate the order and thus the Sufi teacher. This rationale of course presumes that there is a monolithic and pure Islam to achieve proximity to and that *a Sufism* could easily be defined.[20] In the early iterations of the charting of Sufi communities in America, there has been a disregard of the historical processes and dynamics that have led to the development of Sufism and Islam.

For instance, the question of Islam's relationship with Sufism is one that has followed the rise of Sufism from its earliest occurrence among the immediate generations of the followers of Prophet Muhammad and it continues nearly a millennia later—Is Sufism authentically Islamic and/or does Sufism presuppose Islamic law and practice (i.e. *shari'a*)? As Shahab Ahmed explains, when it comes to the treatment of Sufism in Islam "Sufism is in the dock and the discourse of law is invariably the ultimate judge and jury of the contest."[21] The answers to these questions have been a point of theological and legal debates in premodern and modern periods, as Ahmed's work shows.[22] This question of the authenticity of Sufism raised in discussions of Sufism in America, then, is not unique to the American context but rather it has been, and continues to be, deliberated within Islamic communities globally.[23] Further complicating these assumptions in scholarship was the premise that a supposed authentic Sufism was preserved by Muslims who were ethnically South Asian or Arabs, for instance, and not European American (White) Sufis, who presumably were not Islamic enough. This study problematizes these presumptions that American Sufism somehow embodies critical innovations, which impact its legitimacy or distinguish it as more modern (and thus less traditional), while challenging easy racial, cultural, and religious taxonomies of those who identify as Sufis. Tendencies toward pluralism, universalism, and egalitarianism found in modern forms of Sufism are not solely a by-product of American (or Western) modernism. The dynamic history of Sufism challenges the narrative of its unilateral reception into any region into which it has spread. Sufism has taken on the vernacular form of its locality but it has also maintained continuity. In order to nuance the current discourse on American Sufism, which sees the vernacularization of Sufism in America as a by-product of American values and morals, this book offers an in-depth analysis of a case study of a global Sufi community—with Sri Lankan and American roots— known as the Bawa Muhaiyaddeen Fellowship.

The Bawa Muhaiyaddeen Fellowship

What is the Bawa Muhaiyaddeen Fellowship? This question is a difficult one to answer because its members themselves disagree about the nature of their community beyond their central devotion to Bawa and his teachings. The question of whether the Fellowship is an Islamic, Sufi, or spiritual movement was deliberated when Bawa was alive and has only further intensified after his death. Bawa maintained a plural religious system, one that reflected Islamic-Sufi ritual tendencies, and he repeatedly defied these religious labels himself. What added further complexity to the movement was that Bawa appointed no successor to his community prior to his death in 1986. The uncertainty of whether the Fellowship is solely a Muslim community and/or a Sufi/universalist one is a deep-rooted discussion unfolding among the students of Bawa with numerous senior disciples positioning themselves on different ends of the spectrum of these approaches, both in Sri Lanka and America, without a living *shaykh* (master) to forge the way. The core of the concern unfolding for Bawa's Sri Lankan and American institutions, then, is similar to long-held theological and metaphysical debates found in Islam with respect to Sufism historically: Is Sufism predicated on the performance of Islamic traditions and rituals—such as ritual prayer five times a day and fasting during Ramadan—or are Sufi metaphysical and philosophical orientations toward universality, as founded in the Qur'an, enough to be authentically Muslim/Sufi? There is no single answer to these questions for the students of Bawa.

Despite these internal negotiations, the Bawa Muhaiyaddeen Fellowship is often presented as a quintessential example of American Sufism in scholarship.

This illustrative capacity of the Fellowship as a model of Sufism in America is important to interrogate because beyond the fact that scholars cite the Fellowship regularly, there has been no uniform consensus as to what the Fellowship actually is and what makes it American, if that. Discussions of the Fellowship have resulted in its divergent categorization as a New Religious Movement (New Age), an American Sufi movement, and a diaspora South Asian Muslim community.[24] The earliest study to be completed was by a member of the Fellowship named Mohamed Mauroof. He was a graduate student at the University of Pennsylvania and also a Muslim, Sri Lankan disciple of Bawa. He described Bawa's ministry as Islamic in nature with "syncretistic and ecumenical" tendencies.[25] Gisela Webb also engaged in years of focused analysis on the Fellowship. She understood the Fellowship as an example of "the process of transmission of Islamic belief and practice in the contemporary American context."[26] But she also examined whether the Fellowship was "conserving . . . the tradition" or departing "from traditional Islamic values and practice."[27] Other scholars have been intrigued by Bawa's community and added other labels to it. For instance, Marcia Hermansen placed the Fellowship within the category of "Islamic sharia" with South Asian flavor, in effect highlighting the Fellowship as religiously Muslim and culturally South Asian, while in an earlier study, she categorized the Fellowship as a "hybrid" movement (i.e. Islamic and non-Islamic).[28] Frank Korom was the first scholar to historically situate Bawa in Sri Lanka. In so doing, he wrote, "Bawa was highly skilled at contextualizing and adapting his teachings to his immediate surroundings. To succeed in the United States, he created a form of what we might tentatively call 'protestant Islam' which emphasized similarity in difference by borrowing Christian social structures and congregational practices while simultaneously developing a linguistic discourse on distinctness."[29] He added further that in America (as opposed to in Sri Lanka) the Fellowship underwent "Islamization . . . [resulting] in the establishment of a distinctly American form of Islamic practice based on civility, democracy and transparency."[30] For Korom, then, the Fellowship was consciously defined by Bawa's engagement with his American Protestant context. Additionally, when the Fellowship is not accepted as a Sufi community, even if the kind of Sufi community it is perceived as varies (i.e. South Asian or American), then it is described as a community that is either a New Religious Movement (New Age) or an alternative form of Islamic spirituality that bourgeoned in America. An example of this framing of the Fellowship is found in Jane Smith's analysis on Islam in America, where she described the Fellowship as a "blend of New Age influences with more institutional tradition-based Islamic orders."[31]

In a 2013 chapter contribution, Webb turned to engaging with varying identity politics and institutional processes within the Fellowship, which led to a
productive analytical shift, one that has informed my approach to Bawa's transnational community as a whole.[32] She writes that the Fellowship emerged out
of the 1970s American counterculture era and shifted to "'normative' Islam in
the 1980s and 1990s."[33] This provided the context for the Fellowship's "multiethnic" makeup and the variety of "interpretations of Sufism's relation to Islam—
'Sufi-Muslim,' [Sufi approach to Islam] 'Sufi-not Muslim,' [Sufi without practice
of Islamic rituals] and 'Muslim-not Sufi' [Muslim with no interest in Sufism]—
under the umbrella of the 'Bawa Muhaiyaddeen Fellowship and Mosque."[34] Due
to these differing religious and cultural dynamics, Webb framed Bawa's teachings as not only "wisdom teachings" but also as an example of the "dynamics of
the transmission of Sufism in the context of developments of Islam, diaspora
religion as well as interfaith and intrafaith relations in the United States."[35] For
Webb, then, the Fellowship was both a community space for local Muslims in
the Philadelphia area and a movement that developed out of the countercultural tendencies in a specific era in American religious history. Instead of labeling the Fellowship within one typology, as early scholarship on this community
had done, Webb demonstrated the religious intricacies unfolding within the
Fellowship. She showcased that different currents of Sufism *coexisted* within one
institution and this coexistent nature of the Fellowship may in fact be representative of the coexistences of Sufism in America.[36]

It is the paradigm of coexistence within the Fellowship, first proposed by
Webb, that I build upon in this study. However, I further this paradigm by
exploring the ways in which these coexistences of Sufism in the Fellowship are
maintained, while introducing the context of Bawa's Sri Lankan institution, the
Serendib Sufi Study Circle, to illustrate that the patterns found in America are
also apparent in Sri Lanka. The Fellowship in Philadelphia is often noted for
its religious pluralism, including Jewish and Christian practitioners, while the
question of their relationship with Islam and Sufism vary immensely from
member to member. However, this is apparent not just in the American context. Bawa's first community in Jaffna also functions at a similar level of religious
diversity. The Sri Lankan milieu further indicates the role that particular cultural forms of Sufism have upon American Sufism. The Fellowship is a reflection of a specific South Asian (viz., Sri Lankan) Sufism that institutionalized in
America particularly through the ritual and the liturgical languages that Bawa
taught, which his followers adopted and continue to use to relate to one another
despite their differences. The two nodes in the communities of Bawa, therefore,

reveal the mutual crossings between Sri Lankan and American worlds, regions that have not been historically associated with the "Muslim World." To map the transnational context of this Sri Lankan and American movement, I employ a spatial focus throughout this study.

Embodiment and American Sufism: A Spatial Turn

Pnina Werbner and Robert Geaves in their respective studies employed a spatial focus to chart migration and diasporic patterns of Sufism in Britain.[37] Werbner, for instance, mapped the "charisma" (in Weberian terms) of a Sufi teacher (Zindapir) as a means to plot global and local manifestations of his Sufi cults. In a more recent chapter contribution, Werbner provides a "comparative" outline "to differentiate Sufi cults or shrine-focused orders from one another" as well as from other groups, such as Salafis or Reformists groups (i.e. Deobandi).[38] I have employed Werbner's use of "embodied traditions" for this comparative framework, including ideas such as "ritual performances" (i.e. *'urs* or a Sufi saint's death anniversary) and "religious organizations" (i.e. branches), but where Werbner compared different Sufi "cults" across regions (e.g. Indonesia with Pakistan), I focus on comparisons within one movement with a singular teacher that has institutionalized in two different localities. Additionally, I do not frame the Fellowship or the Serendib Sufi Study Circle as "regional cults." There are several reasons for this. First, "cults" carries pejorative connotations in discussions of New Religious Movements the Fellowship is embedded within, which can become problematic. Second, the members of the Fellowship do not understand their movement as a shrine or solely a spatial movement. According to the members of the Fellowship, their movement is Bawa and his teachings, whereas the spaces (e.g. shrines, mosques, and centers) exist as a by-product of Bawa and his teachings. I, then, have chosen to focus on sacred spaces exclusively for the purposes of my research questions, and hence my attention to spatiality.

In Sufi traditions, spaces are often centralized around the authority of a *shaykh*. It is the spiritual and charismatic authority of the *shaykh* that enables him or her to transmit *baraka*, or blessings, both in life and more so in death. When a *shaykh* dies, they are usually entombed, and structures, such as shrines or mausoleums, are built around their entombment as a memorial and legacy. Some of these tombs transform over time and become part of larger complexes that include schools (*madrasa*), mosques, and lodges, in effect becoming seminal social and religious institutions.[39] They also become sites associated with miracles and centers for retreats, due to the emission of *baraka* as channeled through the physical remains or associated memory of the deceased teacher. The blessing sought by a devotee who approaches a shrine is based on the understanding that she/he is partaking of the grace from the union achieved by the saint with God.[40] Saints, both living and dead, are epicenters of ritual and devotional activities; they "shape and reshape a sacred landscape."[41] They attract adherents because those who beseech the saints believe that the saint supplicates prayers on behalf of the adherent.[42] This practice may be compared to approaching an "inaccessible emperor" by way of his ministers (e.g. the saints) or "transposing them [saint] into a devotional setting, in which one could approach a transcendent God through immanent mediators who have been granted intimate proximity to the divine."[43] It is due to the intermediary (*tawassul*) capacity of Sufi saints that communities of veneration have formed in the living presence of saints but have solidified in their death, which results in a culture of devotion surrounding their remains, such as the construction of burial tombs that then attract pilgrims.

Pilgrimages to Sufi shrines are known as *ziyara*. For some Sunni Muslims, nonobligatory pilgrimage, or *ziyara*, is contrasted to the obligatory pilgrimage to Mecca, or *hajj*. Some Muslims view *ziyara* as theologically incompatible with the teaching of monotheism (*tawhid*) found in Islam, as the practice may be interpreted as associating partners to God (*shirk*). Despite such contentions, praying, meditating, and celebrating at a *mazar* form an important and, in some cases, central part of many Muslims' lives. These spaces were not only centers through, and in, which Islam proliferated, but they were also sites for inter- and intra-religious interactions, as has been documented of Sufi shrines in South Asia, which are noted for their religious pluralism (i.e. Hindu and Sikh participants).[44]

In his *The Sacred and the Profane*, a survey of sacred spaces across civilizations, Mircea Eliade writes, "Every sacred space implies a hierophany, an eruption of the sacred that results in detaching from the surrounding milieu, making it qualitatively different."[45] In this understanding, the Sufi shrine is a hierophanic sign of the sacred and hence it is "worshipped."[46] In the Eliadian sense, space is not "homogenous" though the sacred is static, and thus fissures or breaks in these spaces reveal "absolute reality," such as the body of a deceased Sufi teacher.[47] These spaces are separated by what Eliade calls the "threshold" which establishes a "boundary" or "frontier that distinguishes and opposes two worlds."[48] Eliade also frames space as intimately tied to sacred time, wherein time is not homogenous either. Sacred time, in the Eliadian sense, is "reversible" from primordial time; it is "recoverable" and "repeatable" in the "now" and is made possible by partaking in festivals, a central component of Bawa's communities from Jaffna to Pennsylvania, be it through the commemoration of the *mawlid* (celebration of birthdays of holy figures), the *'urs* (literally meaning "marriage" and is understood as the death anniversary), or daily *poosai* (*puja* or prayer service).[49] While the language used by many of the followers of the Bawa in America to explain the spatial and temporal framework of the Fellowship resonates with these notions of the sacred and profane that Eliade popularized, this study adopts a comparative approach to sacred space and thus relies on Michel Foucault's discussion of "heterotopia" as the dynamic space of practice and relations through which notions of the sacred and profane could be imagined and enacted socially or politically.

In Foucault's *"Des Espace Autres"* ("Of Other Spaces: Utopias and Heterotopias"), he develops the heuristic framework of "heterotopia." Spatially, a heterotopia is placed between utopia (sacred) and its opposite, dystopia (profane), as a space of otherness which might contain utopian features and aspirations, or indeed, dystopian ones. Foucault understands that heterotopias are part of "a network that connects points and intersects with its own skein."[50] They can be found in "every culture, [and] in every civilization."[51] They are "effectively enacted" and reflect an imagined ideal.[52] Foucault's category of heterotopias and the principles he attributes to describe these "simultaneously mythic and real" spaces are more useful than Eliade's notion of sacred spaces as hierophanies because it allows for engaging with the parallel and contested spaces found in Bawa's communities, especially his shrines.[53] Bawa's shrines, such as the *mazar* in Coatesville or Mankumban, are "three-dimensional space" that maintain "contradictory" meanings while keeping to "symmetry" (and not homogeneity); they are also part of networks and connections.[54] It is both the mythic and the contested that enables parallel shrines to function in the particular global network. It results in diverse manifestations of practices, such as personal rituals of devotion, pilgrimages, and communal prayers, at the same time that a shared myth of Bawa or Maryam is persevered. Further, even within these spaces, subspaces or "parallel congregations" emerge.[55]

Paul Numrich first coined the phrase "parallel congregation" in his study of two Buddhist temples in Chicago and Los Angeles, and its congregations, which included parallel memberships of immigrant (Asian American) and nonimmigrant (American) converts. Numrich framed "congregation" as "two largely distinct, face-to-face (i.e. personally known) memberships within a local religious institution, since the members in either group typically do not personally know temple members outside that group."[56] Like Numrich, my use of "congregation" in this study is fluid and stresses the "continuum of religious adherents" to Islam, Sufism, and Bawa within his spaces (e.g. mosque in Philadelphia). Throughout my discussion of ritual activities at Bawa's sites in Jaffna and Philadelphia, tendencies of "parallelism" are evident, not only as it unfolds through "building occupancy" but more importantly during the performance of rituals and the subsequent "interactions" and/or "intersections" among members, nonmembers, pilgrims, and visitors at Bawa's spaces.[57] Importantly, Numrich expressed that these parallel congregations within a space are in no way hermetically sealed, as cultural, ethnic, and religious fluidities abound and shift, not only through movements but in beliefs and understandings.[58] For instance, an example of parallelism in the Fellowship community is found especially in the Fellowship mosque in terms of the racial and religious compositions (Chapter 2). Despite maintaining congregational parallel presence during rituals, members, nonmembers, pilgrims, and visitors to Bawa's spaces shared a mutual understanding of the myth or symbol enshrined in the space they employed, be it Maryam in Mankumban or Bawa at the *mazar*. Foucault's attention to spaces as heterotopias provides a productive structure to situate these complex movements and their different meanings as they unfold at the *mazar* in Coatesville and at Mankumban. For instance, rituals at the shrine may "surge and subside, ebb and flow" as the space changes and becomes created and recreated.[59] However, these rituals are not always in agreement among practitioners who utilize the space or those who perceive the space as antithetical to their understanding of Islam and Bawa's teachings. Since Sufi shrines could be found in various parts of the world, the myths, etiquette, and rituals surrounding shrines change from locality to locality, despite their shared beliefs that the religious significance of the shrine lies in the deceased holy figures' remains entombed within it. Thus, the spaces under consideration are not contested at the level of the nation-state or as a result of colonialism; rather what is being negotiated are culture, ethnicity, identity, gender, and practice as a means to establish the shrine as either an "Islamic" (orthodox) space or not.

Due to the diversity of the adherents who utilize the shrine, shrines are a "nexus of contradictions."[60] Shrines, then, are *multidimensional spaces* that illustrate facets of embodied and contested Sufism and Islam. The interactions that result in these moments of contestations and affirmations of conceptions of orthodoxy at Sufi shrines illuminate the broader questions prompting this study, such as how is Sufism unfolding in Pennsylvania, especially when compared to its parallel site in Jaffna? What do shrine activities reveal about Sufism in the Fellowship and in America at large? In examining these sites as heterotopias one can begin to map the spatial and ritual transmissions of Bawa's traditions from Sri Lanka to America and its localized variations. Though Sufi leaders have been foundational to the spread of Sufism in America and globally, the spaces they have instituted and left behind are also representative of the ways in which Sufism develops nationally, culturally, and globally. Muslims' and non-Muslims' relation to these spaces (shrines, pilgrimage sites, and centers of worship) has changed in the modern era, primarily in nations such as Sri Lanka where modern ethno-political and (inter- and intra-) religious conflicts have unfolded over territory, thus affecting uses and conceptions of religious spaces and practices. In this regard, the Sri Lankan context highlights the complex position of Sufi spaces, against which we may understand its American counterpart.

The Ethno-political Landscape of Sri Lankan Sufism

For most people, Sri Lanka is not immediately imagined as part of the "Muslim world"; it is usually treated on the periphery of South Asian Islam.[61] Studies of South Asian Islam have tended to privilege official linguistic canons and traditions of Urdu, Arabic, and Persian, while "marginalizing" Tamil, Malay, Telugu, and Bengali.[62] Emerging scholarship on the latter linguistic Muslim traditions in South Asia have demonstrated various networks of travel, trade, and Sufi orders, and their role in reimagining new borders and contacts in the "transregional Muslim world" of South and Southeast Asia.[63] Capturing these localized and marginalized histories, such as of Tamil Sufi traditions, decentralize South Asian Islam, and the Muslim world as monolithic enterprises, which then provides a more realistic landscape against which to measure the emergence of Sufism and Islam in new terrains, such as America.

Sri Lanka, historically known as Ceylon, gained independence from the British in 1948. Leading up to independence and the power shift to indigenous inhabitant's self-rule, fault lines emerged between ethnic and linguistic groups (the majority Sinhala and the minority Tamil). Muslim identity was framed as distinct during this period, even though Muslims spoke Tamil. Sri Lankan Muslims, who self-identify as Moors due to the label that their Portuguese colonizers gave them during their rule from 1505 to 1658, traced their lineage to Arab and Persian traders and sailors in South Indian and Sri Lankan coastal regions. These Arab and Persian traders and seafarers visited Serendib, or *Jazirat al-Yaqut* (the island of rubies), as it was known among the Arabs.[64] The history of the origins of Islam in Sri Lanka is one of "migration" and "conversion" especially as it was enabled through sea trade,[65] though there is still a popular perception among some Sinhala communities that Muslims "entered the country as invaders."[66] The varying interpretations of the origins of Islam in Sri Lanka have been evoked during the political and ethnic crisis on the island. For instance, in the late nineteenth century, some Muslim elites from the west coast of Sri Lanka deliberately used the label of "Ceylon Moors" to claim "seats in the colonial system of communal (i.e. racial) representation" established by the British.[67] The rhetoric of claiming Muslims under the umbrella of a Tamil ethnic block for a national agenda by the Tamils further led Muslim communities to consciously represent themselves as distinctively ethnic, altering identity politics in Sri Lanka. In his 1885 speech, the Tamil Hindu political leader Ponnambalam Ramanathan (d. 1930) stated that aside from religion, the Moors (i.e. Muslims) shared the same "cultural and linguistic" affinity as the Tamils, but Muslims disagreed with this assertion, emphasizing their Arab origins as a distinct ethnic and cultural marker.[68]

After independence, the Tamil minority felt marginalized by the new state policies that favored the Sinhala majority. For instance, Sinhala was deemed the official language in 1956 and further constitutional reforms of the 1970s prioritized the majority group by privileging Sinhala applicants for civil service jobs or Sinhala language in the administration of university entrance examinations. Muslim political leaders, ethnically speaking, were not unified in their responses to these new policies, but they were also affected by the pro-Sinhala policies as Tamil-speaking Muslims. When the new constitution was officially passed on May 22, 1972, violent riots and protests erupted in the northern and eastern provinces. During this period, many different Tamil nationalist groups, some militant, slowly emerged as a reaction to governmental and societal marginalization. Some of the concerns of these movements were addressed when the constitution was amended again in 1978 but by then the tensions had boiled over.[69]

The most successful militant organization that led the Tamil nationalist cause by seeking a separate nation was the Tamil New Tigers (TNT), who later became known as the Liberation Tigers of Tamil Eelam (LTTE or Tigers). Led by Velupillai Prabhakaran (d. 2009), the LTTE was the dominant militant movement during the civil war against the state, which emerged due to the Tamil minority's dissatisfaction with self-determination. LTTE led attacks across the island, utilizing methods such as suicide bombers. In the north, violence escalated in the 1980s, leading to assassinations of political candidates by Tamil militants during the height of critical district elections, as well as police officers. Riots and arson became the norm, which culminated in the attack of the historic

Jaffna Public Library from May 31 to June 1, 1981. The loss of close to a hundred thousand historical books as a result of this attack left Tamils feeling unsupported by the Sri Lankan government, which further solidified their support for the Tamil Tigers. The majority of these conflicts unfolded in the Jaffna Peninsula, known as the Tamil Heartland, where Bawa's ministries first took root.

There were various phases to the nearly three-decade civil conflict, the details of which are beyond the scope of this brief introduction, but religious spaces became one focus of violent assaults and retaliations in the name of nationalism from the different ethnic parties. Tamil militants attacked Sinhala communities and spaces (i.e. the sacred Buddhist pilgrimage site of Anuradhapura in 1985) as the state, army, and Sinhala nationalists retaliated. As vicious attacks between the LTTE and the Sri Lankan government continued, the LTTE believed that the Muslims in the north and east were covertly sharing information about them to the government. Some Muslim youth were said to have joined the Tamil militants freely while others joined by force. As a result, on August 3, 1990, 140 Muslims were killed in a mosque in Kattankudy by the LTTE and days later 122 Muslims were killed in Eravur. These attacks against Muslims and their places of worship culminated in the expulsion of all Muslims from Jaffna on November 30, 1990. Some Muslim communities were given two hours to evacuate, while other districts were given one to two days to vacate Tamil strongholds. These mass expulsions led to the internal displacement of nearly 65,000 Muslims.[70] The expulsion of the Muslims from the north was a seminal moment that altered the trajectory of Muslim-Tamil relations throughout the remainder of the conflict.

The civil war, which began in 1983, ended in May 2009 with the demise of the LTTE by the Sri Lankan government. Investigations—such as those led by the United Nations Human Rights Commission—resulted in reports of war crimes and torture committed by the Sri Lankan government. There were also reports of governmental torture after the war. From a religious perspective, Sinhala nationalism's claim is that Sri Lanka was (is) a Buddhist space.[71] The majority population on the island is predominately Sinhala (75 percent), of whom 90 percent are Buddhist, while others are Christian Sinhalese. Tamils form 11.2 percent of the population and are religiously Hindu with smaller groups of Christian communities. The island also consists of Indian Tamils who make up 4.2 percent of the population. The Moor Muslims who speak Tamil form 9 percent of the population, while Muslim communities of Burghers (those who trace their lineage to European settlers) and Malays and indigenous people of the island, known as Vedas, comprise the remaining 1 percent.[72] Furthermore, religion in Sri Lanka varies by region. For instance, the east has a rich array of Muslims, Christians, and Buddhists, while the north is mainly Tamil Hindus. Due to trade and Sufi pilgrimage sites and their patrons (i.e. *pirs* and *bawas* [wandering mendicants]), Sri Lankan Moorish settlements can be found historically in Beruwala, Kalpitiya, Jaffna, and other coastal settlements.[73] These religious traditions are themselves immensely diverse. Not all Buddhist adhere to the strict militant nationalist tendency that has arisen post war. Christian communities are further divided into various denominations that include Catholics and Protestants (i.e. Methodists, Pentecostals, and more).[74]

Muslim identity politics in Sri Lanka has been dominated by the island's historical Sinhala-Tamil conflicts. Muslims are perceived as "historical latecomers" and "not ancient primordial stakeholders in the future of the island."[75] Thus, they have not been granted an equal voice in the larger political situation in Sri Lanka, which was evident during the heights of the Eelam Wars when Muslims experienced violence and discrimination from both the state and the LTTE. Currently, postwar realities showcase that in order to speak about Muslim presence on the island one must not only engage with the political and ethnic category of Muslims and their relationship with Sinhala and Tamil groups, but also account for the dynamic realities of intra-Muslim negotiations that have been introduced with revivalist and reformist movements in addition to Sufi traditions on the island.

Contestations at Sufi Shrines in Sri Lanka

For some Muslims, Sri Lanka is believed to be the land where Adam, the patriarch of humanity according Abrahamic traditions, was expelled to from paradise.[76] These narratives attracted Muslim seafaring traders, itinerant Sufis, and colonialists to partake in pilgrimages to Adam's Peak, or Baba Adam-*malai* (mountain of father Adam), as it is known historically by Muslims. The historian and qur'anic exegete Abu Ja'far Muhammad ibn Jarir al-Tabari (d. 923) writes that "Adam was hurled into Hindustan. In this land, there is a mountain called Serandib, and it is reported that there is no higher mountain in all the universe. Adam landed on this mountain."[77] Tabari describes that it was the leaves that Adam carried with him from paradise that brought perfume to Ceylon, while it was his tears, because of his separation from God and Eve (Hawwa), that cultivated vegetation cross the island.[78] He continues in his chronicle:

> It is said that he [Adam] remained in prayer for a hundred years. Tears streamed down his face and rolled across the mountain of Serandib; to this day, it is the tears streaming down Adam's face that cause large trees to grow, such as the

various myrobalan and other similar shoots that have medicinal properties. Their medicines are used even now, and are brought to us from the mountains of Hindustan.[79]

In South Asian hagiographical tales, Adam and Eve were expelled from the seventh level of heaven, when Adam landed in Sri Lanka leaving a footprint in the rock attributed to this mountain. Adam stayed in Sri Lanka repenting for his sins for a thousand years, when the Archangel Jibril (Gabriel) led him to Arafat to reunite with Eve. After they met in Arafat, Adam and Eve returned to Ceylon where they began the human race.[80] Some sources, such as Ghulam ʿAli of Bilgram (1704–86), add that Adam made regular pilgrimages to Mecca, but remained in India ("Serendip"), concluding:

> Among them is the point that the land of India was honored with the descent of the viceregent of God, his Pure One [Adam] (on whom be peace). And therefore Serendip [the ancient name of Ceylon] is known as the "realm of viceregency." And no one before me has applied this term to it, though it was well-deserved, for God Most High inspired me to do so.[81]

Not only is Adam said to have made pilgrimages from Serendib (Sri Lanka, but generally India) to Mecca, the tradition of Adam's fall leads many believers to make pilgrimages to Adam's Peak, specifically to his footprint on the summit. As pilgrimages to Adam's Peak grew, new sacred spaces became linked to Adam's Peak. Dafter Jailani, or the Rock Cave Mosque, near Balangoda, is an example.

Dafter Jailani receives its name from the Baghdadi saint ʿAbdul Qadir al-Jilani (d. 1166) the namesake of the Qadiriyya. Popular Tamil Islamic tradition holds that al-Jilani sojourned in Serendib and mediated in a cave hermitage in the mountainous jungles of Balangoda. The site of his meditation led to the formation of a shrine complex known as Dafter Jailani. It includes a cave mosque and numerous tombs to male and female Sufi saints (most of whose names have now been lost).[82] Historically, many pilgrims used to walk from Adam's Peak to Dafter Jailani. The third major site that forms the larger network is dedicated to the perennial mystic Khidr at Kataragama.[83] Kataragama, located in southeastern Sri Lanka, is a Sufi and Hindu pilgrimage site.[84] It is associated with both the Hindu deity Murukan and Islam's perennial mystic Khidr.[85] Collectively Adam's Peak, Dafter Jailani, and Kataragama form a pilgrimage network in Sri Lanka. As indicated in Chapter 1, these were the sites that Bawa spent his early years meditating in and in effect, I argue, Bawa's spaces both in Sri Lanka and America may be viewed as extensions of these sacred traditions and spaces in Tamil Sri Lankan Sufism. In fact, the shrine-keepers at Dafter Jailani have photographs of Bawa and his *mazar* in Coatesville in the main complex, while Mankumban contains photographs of Dafter Jailani in its meeting room. Material culture alone indicates the deep connections between these ancient and new spaces.

Subsequently, many minor Sufi shrines, especially in close proximity to mosques, proliferated to honor Sufi saints. Also known as "friends of God" or *Awliya allah* (sing. *wali allah*) in Arabic, Sufi saints and their shrines are central to much of the early history of Sufism in Sri Lanka. Sufi masters (*pirs* in Persian or *shuyukh* in Arabic) are also known locally as "bawas."[86] There are many different Sufi *tariqa*s or orders, though the Qadiriyya associated with al-Jilani is the most prominent in Tamil regions. However, other orders also exist, such as Shadhiliyya, Chishtiyya, and Naqshabandiyya.[87] The Rifa'iyya is another popular Sufi order on the island, though more associated with *fakir*s, or wandering mendicants, who arrive during special festivals.[88] Travel, trade, and Sufi tendencies influenced the development of Islam in Sri Lanka in its early years, though the identity politics of Sri Lanka's religious and ethnic communities have become further politicized, especially spatially, as ethnolinguistic tensions festered throughout the modern period.

With the rising threat against Muslim communities, both during the war and after, Islamic spaces and Muslim communities across the island have been facing threat due to growing Sinhala-Buddhist extremism. Historically shared spaces were and continue to be caught in the crossfire of these nationalistic politics. For instance, Adam's Peak became a site of conflict due to contestations over its provenance. Adam's Peak holds an alternative significance for Buddhists on the island who believe that it is Buddha's footprint on the mountain; hence it is known as *Sri Pada* in Sinhala, "the Auspicious Foot."[89] The Sri Pada Temple at the summit of Adam's Peak is currently maintained by Buddhist authority.[90] Those who perform pilgrimages to Adam's Peak today are mainly Buddhists and Hindus. Even between Hindus and Buddhists there are tensions about the use of the space; this is seen in the various Hindu shrines and altars to deities at the foot of the trails that are at times desecrated by opposing religious communities. Muslims also perform this pilgrimage, but their presence has diminished. Those from Muslim communities who perform this pilgrimage have conveyed a general sentiment of uneasiness due to lack of hospitality toward them by non-Muslims. This historically shared religious space has homogenized in recent years due to the state's nationalistic Buddhization, but some of the earliest records showcase a pluralistic view of Adam's Peak, as seen during the fourteenth-century Moroccan traveler Muhammad ibn Abdullah ibn Battuta's pilgrimage to Adam's Peak in 1344, which includes mention of "jogees" (yogis) and "Brahmins" as well as Muslims.[91]

Dafter Jailani is another example of a Sufi site that is caught between Buddhist and Muslim communities and disputes over land ownership. The Sinhala Buddhist and Tamil Muslim communities both attribute different religious significances to this space.[92] Buddhists understand this space as Kuruagala, an ancient hermitage for Buddhist monks, while Sufi Muslims treat it as a hermitage for Sufis due to its association with al-Jilani.[93] The ongoing disputes have been captured by Dennis McGilvray, who explains the situation is in "renewed jeopardy" for Muslims who utilize the sacred cave complex.[94] This mountain shrine contained a sanctuary for Khidr and al-Jilani, along with various unmarked tombs and a *masjid* (mosque).[95] I visited this shrine twice, first in 2013 and then in 2016. During my first visit to Dafter Jailani in August 2013, the Defense Ministry, authorized by Gotabhaya Rajapakse, the brother of the then Sri Lankan president, removed all of the structures (except one of the mosques) and dismantled some tombs of Sufis in the complex.[96] This practice of desecration followed similar trends that emerged during the postwar period, led primarily by militant Buddhist movements, such as by Bodu Bala Sena (BBS), against Muslim spaces across the island.[97] It was daunting to see all the flags removed from the large mountain top complex. Reputedly, an elephant was brought up the mountain to remove the sacred flagpole that used to be on top of the mountain peak, which I later saw lying twisted on my climb up to Soragam Cave.[98] Demolished building complexes with debris were left to the local community of devotees to clean and sort through. The main mosque complex remained, however. Notable amid this deconstruction of a sacred Islamic site were Muslim and non-Muslim women from the nearby village, who were dispersed around the cave mosque, some with their infant children in their arms, either praying or just being in the space. One of the buildings that were removed was Khidr's sanctuary, which was in the cave beside the main complex. The main sanctuary itself contains a tomb for a Darwesh Mohiyaddeen Oliuallah, a saint from Yemen reputedly dated to 1478 (Figure I.1).

These sanctuaries have been shared across different religious communities, but they have also been sites of tension at varying levels (state, religious, and communal). Beyond the religious significance of these spaces, incidences such as those at Dafter Jailani described above emphasize the ongoing conflicts in (and through) land and geography in the name of sacred capital in an effort to

Figure I.1 The tomb for Darwesh Mohiyaddeen Oliuallah, a saint from Yemen, dated to 1478.

narrate a particular national past and preserve a pure national future. Sufi spaces on the island that have been sites of pilgrimage are not only caught in between extreme nationalistic violence, they are also wedged in the middle of reform tendencies of some Muslims with anti-Sufi beliefs,[99] a trend that is seen throughout this study, especially in Jaffna.

Scholars have posited that it is likely that reformist influences are appearing from both Saudi Arabia and India (foreign effects), due to economic ties and labor migration between these regions, especially as migrant labor and workers from Sri Lanka have moved to Saudi Arabia and other Arab countries in hopes of upward economic mobility. In the current landscape of Islamic movements in Sri Lanka, groups such as Tablighi Jama'at, a pietist movement, and Jamaat-i-Islam, an Islamist movement, are active and are attempting to disseminate "orthodox" practices of Islam, who then oppose shrines and the practices that unfold at them.[100] Though external factors have influenced reformist movements in Sri Lanka, it is a rather simplistic and limited portrayal of the complex exchanges that have unfolded and continue to unfold in Tamil Islamic revival and reform movements.

Many studies capture the negotiations that arose among prominent South Asian intellectuals, such as the North Indian Muslim reformer Sayyid Ahmad Khan (1817–98), who responded to colonial presence and negotiated Islam's relationship to westernization and modernization. Missing from these discourses of Islamic reformism in South Asia are the voices of Tamil Muslim intellectuals from Sri Lanka. Noteworthy here are figures like I. L. M. Abdul Azeez (1867–1915) and Muhammad Cassim Sidde Lebbe (1838–98), whose ideas of reform and revival were bred in a Tamil Sri Lankan Muslim context under British colonial power. Lebbe, for instance, insisted on the preservation of Tamil and Arabic for the Muslim communities in Sri Lanka (then Ceylon), while Azeez, who headed the Moor Union, was critical of practices, such as the *mawlid* (birthday celebration of prophets and saints) and *'urs* (the death anniversary or *kanturi* in Tamil), which led his opponents to label him a "Wahhabi."[101] Lebbe, like Azeez, was an activist and a reformer, but Lebbe was far more steeped in Sufism, even writing a seminal Sufi treatise, *Asrar al-'alam* ("Mysteries of the Universe") that ignited controversy because it was deemed heretical, not only in Sri Lanka but also in Tamil Nadu.[102] Though more research needs to be completed on the dynamics between "tawhid people" (Salafi groups) and "tariqah movements" (Sufi groups), labels used by indigenous Muslims in Sri Lanka, both historically and in modern periods, it is safe to say these intra-Muslim theological and philosophical dynamics are multifaceted, and were implicated by both internal and external factors on the island, which then unfold in and around Sufi shrines.[103]

In Sri Lanka, then, the "national identity" of Muslims is constructed in response to Sinhala Buddhist and Tamil Hindu and Christian identities while simultaneously the "local" identity is entrenched between the Sufi and what has at times been represented as the "orthodox" rendition of Islam and its reformist proponents, which is influenced by the transnational Muslim *ummah*.[104]

These identities are far more complex than can be captured in simple dualisms of orthodox and Sufi, or even rural and urban. Despite these historic ties to the island, especially through Sufi narratives, Sufis remain a minority group within a minority (Muslims), or are a double minority, in Sri Lanka's overall religious and ethnic landscape. And as such, shrines and spaces associated with Sufism in Sri Lanka face a *double marginalization*. On the one hand, the state and majority groups with nationalistic leanings discriminate against Muslim populations on the island and direct their views by dismantling Sufi shrines, because they are viewed as Muslim spaces. On the other hand, the same space also receives negative opposition (sometimes violent) from certain fractions of the Muslim community, who view Sufi spaces as theologically heretical, and thus as non-Islamic. For many, however, Muslim and non-Muslim, Sufi shrines are exemplary spaces of sacrality and are central to their religious identity, be it Islamic or otherwise. These multiple paradigms constitute the legacies of Sufi shrines and associated saints in Sri Lanka. It is in this landscape that we experience the roots of the Bawa Muhaiyaddeen Fellowship and the sites of Bawa's first ever ministries.

Overview of Field Research

In 2008 during my undergraduate studies at York University I was introduced to the Bawa for the first time in my Sufism Seminar. I became curious about this Tamil Sufi in America, contacted the Fellowship, and learned that there was a branch in Toronto. I was then connected to a fellow student at York University, a member of the Fellowship, who invited me to my first Fellowship meeting in Toronto. This first encounter planted the seed of interest in Bawa and the Fellowship, but I was not able to pursue it further until I began my doctoral work in 2011. I first visited the headquarters of the Fellowship in Philadelphia in early July 2012. Since my first visit I intermittently visited the Fellowship throughout my doctoral studies, especially during holy days, such as Bawa's death anniversary (*'urs*) or birthday commemorations for the Prophet Muhammad or al-Jilani (*mawlid al-nabi and mawlid al-Jilani*). I also partook in the Boston Retreats held by the Boston Fellowship branch in Deerfield, Massachusetts, in 2013 and 2014, while continuing to maintain regular attendance at the Toronto branch.

My early visits to the Fellowship prompted interest in the Serendib Sufi Study Circle, the Sri Lankan institution first formed by Bawa. As a result, I conducted field work in Sri Lanka from July to August 2013 as a part of my doctoral thesis. When in Sri Lanka, I divided my time between Colombo, where the center of the

Serendib Sufi Study Circle is located, and Jaffna, in the north. In Jaffna, I concentrated most of my time in the *ashram* (residence) of Bawa and Mankumban. I did this first at the beginning of my trip in early July for Ramadan and then I also joined a pilgrimage group that consisted of disciples of Bawa from North America, Saudi Arabia, and Sri Lanka as they traveled to Jaffna. I also visited Matale, another branch of the Serendib Sufi Study Circle, which is located in central Kandy, and the newly refurbished farm of Bawa in Puliyankulam twice during my time in Jaffna. I did not travel to Puttalam where the majority of the Muslims displaced from Jaffna live in internally displaced camps. I met some of these displaced Muslim disciples of Bawa at *dhikr* (ritual of divine remembrance) at the end of August 2013 in Colombo. In the Colombo and Matale sites, the members were mainly Muslim Sri Lankans, while in Jaffna and Puliyankulam members were mainly Tamil Hindus, with a few Tamil Catholics.

Overall, in Sri Lanka, the political and social climate and the spaces I was engaged in necessitated participant engagement as my main form of data gathering. Though I spoke with varying senior disciples of Bawa in Colombo, Jaffna, Matale, and Puliyankulam, these interviews were not recorded, as they were in North America. I avoided recording interviews primarily for the safety of the members of the community, as tensions remained high with growing persecution of Muslim communities in the postwar period. Jaffna also had a heavy military presence despite the end of the war, and I did not want to attract unwarranted attention to the community or myself. As such, I kept detailed field journals for the whole duration of my time in Sri Lanka, which I utilized throughout this study. Due to the limitations I faced in Sri Lanka, my discussions of my research in Sri Lanka in the following chapters tend to be more descriptive than my discussion of my research in the United States and Canada.

Upon my return to Toronto from my fieldwork in Sri Lanka, I conducted interviews with members of the Toronto branch, while continuing to study Bawa's discourses in Tamil. Thereafter, I concentrated my time at the Fellowship in Philadelphia, immersing myself in the institutional life of the Fellowship by participating in all the activities, from weeknight meetings to congregational or *jum'a* prayers in April 2013. Members of the Fellowship graciously invited me to their homes for dinner or shared tea with me. They spoke openly and passionately about Bawa at length.

During 2013–14 of my fieldwork year, I completed twenty-three recorded semi-structured interviews in Philadelphia. I also finished nine semi-structured interviews in Toronto and one interview via Skype with a member of the Fellowship who lives in Florida. I maintained several email correspondences with leaders and members of the Fellowship in Boston, Toronto, and Philadelphia.[105] Of the recorded interviews, twenty of my participants were European American from Judeo-Christian backgrounds. Two were African Americans from Christian backgrounds. Three were Iranian Muslim Canadians (of whom two identified as Shi'a Muslims). One was a Sri Lankan Muslim living in Saudi Arabia. Two were Tamil Sri Lankans who were originally Hindu but now identified as Muslim, while one was an Indian Tamil Muslim. Finally, one Pakistani Sunni Muslim living in Saudi Arabia was interviewed as well as a Pakistani Canadian living in Toronto and an East African Indian Sunni Muslim in Toronto. In terms of gender composition of my interviewees it was a split of sixteen males and sixteen females (this was not intentional). In spite of all these various ethnic, cultural, racial, national, religious (sectarian), and gender identities, all of them identified as being Sufi or found affinity to Sufism through Bawa, the Fellowship, and the Circle, though, as I discuss later, the ways in which they articulated this varied. Some of my conversations were strictly off the record as per the wishes of those who shared their experiences of Bawa and the Fellowship with me and so requested that they not be recorded or mentioned in my research. I have respected the wishes of these individuals and have not included them in the official count of interviewees, though I am mindful of their perspectives throughout my analysis. When referring to my recorded interview responses in this text, where I have been given permission from my interlocutors, I use their real name. Some of my interviewees requested that I use the Arabic names or nicknames Bawa gave them when they arrived at the Fellowship and others requested that they be given pseudonyms. Though this does result in inconsistencies in referencing my interviews, I have honored the individual requests of the members of the Fellowship and have noted these specificities of their names in the footnote that follows their interview.[106] For Bawa's Sri Lankan disciples, I only use pseudonyms for their protection, unless they are deceased.

Where I was able to complete recorded interviews with members of the Fellowship, this was not entirely possible with non-Fellowship visitors and pilgrims whom I encountered at the Fellowship house or at the *mazar* in Coatesville. It was not possible to pull out my recorder and ask for an interview when pilgrims drove hours to come to the *mazar* from the Eastern Seaboard, other states, or abroad. These were usually one-time visitors that I met while eating a meal in the meeting hall, sometimes language was a barrier, but between their broken English and my lack of Urdu (or several other languages) we attempted to converse. At other times gender was a barrier. So, my encounters with those who were making a pilgrimage to the *mazar* were recorded solely in my field notes.

Once I completed my dissertation in the fall of 2015, I was employed as a visiting assistant professor at Franklin & Marshall College in Lancaster, Pennsylvania, which is about thirty miles from Bawa's *mazar* in Coatesville. From the fall of 2015 to early 2017, at the time of revision of this book, I maintained regular field work at the *mazar* and I arranged field trips for students in my Islam-related courses. These visits with students furthered my engagement with the *mazar*, the Fellowship, and Sufism in America. I also revisited my field sites in Sri Lanka during the summer of 2016. So, from 2008 to 2017, I have been studying the Fellowship, the Circle, and Bawa's teachings at different iterations of my academic career. Even as I write this book, there remains an overwhelming feeling that I still have not fully comprehended the depth and diversity of this transnational organization, and thus as all academic projects go, this book is only an introduction and by no means a conclusion.

The multisited nature of this study meant that my position and relationship with my project and those whom I regularly interacted with from Toronto to Philadelphia to Jaffna required constant negotiation. As George E. Marcus writes, "In practice, multi-sited fieldwork is thus always conducted with a keen awareness of being within the landscape, and as the landscape changes across sites, the identity of the ethnographer requires renegotiation."[107] This negotiation meant that my interlocutors perceived me through different identities depending on their own backgrounds. The Bawa Muhaiyaddeen Fellowship and the Serendib Sufi Study Circle are open spaces where people with diverse religious and cultural identities are welcomed. This inclusivity is a reality in both contexts, as Bawa's teachings and spaces were freely given and not restricted to "initiated" members, or initiated Muslim members, as some Sufi *tariqa*s are. As such, I was eagerly welcomed. Most students of Bawa were, however, critical of my attempt to "academize" Bawa, because for Bawa's students the intellectual and the rational needed to be abandoned before one could grasp what Bawa taught— a truth which required "heart knowledge" according to senior disciples. A few welcomed my academic interests in Bawa and the Fellowship, but where my academic pursuits were perceived as a limitation for me to "experience" Bawa, it was my Tamil identity that seemed to remedy the fact that I was a researcher. Many followers felt that my shared ethnic and cultural ancestry of their spiritual teacher was not coincidental but seemingly signaled to Bawa's "hand" in the completion of my research project. Initially I was happy with sharing an ancestry with this community's spiritual teacher if it meant that I could directly access Bawa's followers, but when this significance was interpreted in spiritual ways, I did become overwhelmed and tried to downplay my Tamil identity in North America. That being said, in Sri Lanka, the significance of my Tamil identity was far more intricate. As a diasporic, female Tamil Canadian and a researcher, my presence in the larger social political milieu of Sri Lanka was challenging to navigate in a postwar zone. Incidences such as the attack of the Grandpass Mosque in Colombo on August 11, 2013, created heightened security concerns among Muslims in Sri Lanka, but also worry for a researcher who may be interested in documenting it. However, once I arrived at the *ashram* (residence of Bawa), being Tamil was invaluable. As a Jaffna female-Tamil the Matron and I were able to connect directly without translators. She welcomed me and adjusted to my regular presence at the *ashram* to the extent that I was cutting vegetables in the kitchen, a task usually given to the local women who assist in the *ashram*.

In Philadelphia though, my gender played a more immediate role than it did in Jaffna in shaping how I experienced the spaces of the Fellowship. Here, the *masjid* was a gender-segregated space and Bawa's room also became gendered because it was accessible to females mostly during particular rituals, such as the *mawlid*. If special events did take place in Bawa's room, gender boundaries were created, modesty was maintained, and veiling (however loosely) was expected. As such, the movements I meticulously capture in this book in and around spaces also mirror the methodological movements maneuvered by myself as a researcher. Similar to Zareena Grewal, I viewed ethnography as "a process of reflective participation rather than participant-observation" which "undid anthropology's oxymoron of fieldwork, in which participation involves communication and emotional investment and observation requires detachment and objectivity."[108] My access to the Fellowship and its networks of communities is dependent on the foundational premise that it is a "multilayered" movement, and I as an institutional outsider to this community have been given access to certain historical and lived archives and in the process experienced "episodes and events" via members' perceptions and my own experiences of certain rituals and spaces.[109] What is captured in the pages that follow is dependent on a journey that I experienced of the Bawa Muhaiyaddeen Fellowship and the Serendib Sufi Study Circle.

Outline of the Present Study

The first chapter provides a history of Bawa's community from Sri Lanka to America through the use of oral histories of senior disciples along with archival research. Then, the study is stylistically divided. Chapters 2 and 3 are purposefully descriptive in nature. They chart the transnational spaces and ritual activities in Bawa's communities from Sri Lanka to America and are fundamentally ethnographically driven. Chapters 4 and 5 then build upon the ethnographic data of the previous chapters and shifts to the *symbols and myths* constituted as sacred in the previous chapters. Chapter 4 engages Maryam at Mankumban, and then situates the role of female presence in Bawa's space in Sri Lanka and Pennsylvania. Chapter 5 frames Bawa as *al-insan al-kamil* or "the perfected human being." Throughout the chapters spatial (and trans-spatial) and trans-temporal features of Bawa's heterotopias lead to a comparative examination of culture, religion, and gender and its impact on ritual embodiment, which are far more similar than different considering their respective Sri Lankan and American localities.

Chapter 1 provides a historical survey of Bawa's early institutions in Sri Lanka and his migration to America. It introduces all the spaces in the transnational communities of Bawa. I employ interviews from senior members of Bawa's community to provide a window into the early formation of Bawa's institutions. There are many spaces (branches) in Bawa's movements, and an examination of them all is beyond the scope of the present project. So, the subsequent chapters focus on nodes that are seminal in the transnational movement, around which branches and sub-branches have formed.

Chapter 2 situates one of the seminal nodes in the Sri Lankan context of the Serendib Sufi Study Circle. Though the SSSC would be the legal and official label under which Bawa's institutions developed in Sri Lanka, Chapter 2 frames Bawa's earliest and first space, his residence (*ashram*) in Jaffna, as one of the important sites for daily ritual activity, which ritually and spatially parallels his American headquarters in Philadelphia. Daily prayers, breaking the fast during Ramadan, and personal acts of devotion are a common feature at Bawa's *ashram*, which presently serves as a memorial shrine of sorts to those who utilize the space. The *ashram* is tended by a female shrine-keeper, the Matron, who leads all the rituals and prayers. The Matron also hosts international pilgrims and visitors. These international pilgrims, however, are not only coming to visit the *ashram*, but rather, their eyes are set on Mankumban, on Velanai Island. This *masjid-mazar* complex was completed by Bawa's Tamil and American disciples. According to some senior disciples, Bawa was to be buried here upon his death. Since he died in America, leaders of the SSSC built a memorial shrine in 2003, which is the center of devotion in Mankumban. I discuss this *masjid-mazar* space in Chapter 2 by highlighting the ritual activities that unfold in it, but I also illustrate some of the many interpretations of its significance, for both local devotees of Bawa and for pilgrims from North America. I conclude that though this sacred heterotopia hosts a vibrant Hindu and Muslim demographic, the multiple meanings that have evolved about Mankumban can also be traced to practices emerging at Bawa's *mazar* in Pennsylvania.

Chapter 3 contextualizes the Bawa Muhaiyaddeen Fellowship in Philadelphia, which contains numerous subspaces, such as Bawa's room, the meeting hall, a bookstore, and publication house, a kitchen and a *masjid*. Often the mosque of the Fellowship draws the most attention, both within the community and in the scholarship of the Fellowship. However, my research indicates that the mosque is just one facet of the larger complex that is the Fellowship, wherein various ritual activities unfold. These include the commemoration of birthdays (*mawlid*) of the Prophet Muhammad or al-Jilani and the death anniversary (*'urs*) of Bawa.

In the second half of Chapter 3, I shift to the comparable space of Mankumban in America, the *mazar* in Coatesville. I argue that Bawa's *mazar* is the most notable site, especially as it has gained popularity beyond the Fellowship among immigrant Muslims in America and American Muslims. I situate the various spaces that form the *mazar* complex, which includes a welcome center, a prayer pavilion, cemetery, and a farm. The Fellowship members utilize this space for ritual purposes, such as to perform daily *dhikr* and for funerals of community members. In this chapter I also capture the narratives of non-Fellowship pilgrims who travel to the *mazar* from across North America. In my analysis of this distinct sacred site, I illustrate the diverse approaches to the uses of the *mazar*, specifically for members of the Bawa Muhaiyaddeen Fellowship and, in recent development, for non-Fellowship members who seek *baraka* from a Sufi teacher. The arrival of new Muslim pilgrims to the *mazar* of Bawa has transformed the Tamil Sufi teacher from Sri Lanka to the Pennsylvania Sufi of America.

Chapter 4 examines the role, authority, and presence of women in the transnational movements of the Fellowship. Early scholarship of Sufism in America has suggested that Sufism is more egalitarian in terms of gender practices and leadership than its counterparts in Muslim-majority societies. The long-standing institutionalization of devotion to Maryam in Jaffna along with female roles and presences contests this hypothesis. Additionally, this chapter engages with the authority of women in the Fellowship, especially in light of the *masjid*. I conclude that though women are active in the Fellowship and maintain an engaged presence, be it through the leading of discourse meetings or the holding of executive positions in America, active female engagement is not unique to Sufi institutions in America. Rather closer analysis on gender dynamics in the Fellowship elucidates the complex negotiations and varying factors (i.e. *shaykh*'s directives) which implicate the performance of Sufism for women in Bawa's movement.

In most Sufi orders, teachings become transportable through a *shaykh*-disciple relationship. In the Fellowship and the Circle, however, the *shaykh* (i.e. Bawa) is not physically present, nor did he authorize anyone to replace him. The institutionalization of his teachings and its dissemination is related to him as a figure who transcends time. He is always present and thus the way to connect with him in everyday life gets centered around the places he touched and formed. Chapter 5 seeks to understand this living presence of Bawa following his physical demise; it explores his metaphysical state as interpreted by his diverse disciples. I examine responses from the disciples of Bawa according to varying honorifics or titles given to Bawa. These include *swami* (lord), *guru, shaykh, qutb* (axial pole), and *al-insan al-kamil*. These epithets suggest that Bawa is now a timeless figure in this movement, and it is his presence that students, pilgrims, and many more come to access when they arrive at the *mazar* in Coatesville. The living authority of Bawa is then to be found at his tomb in Coatesville.

The Bawa Muhaiyaddeen Fellowship and its parallel institution of the Serendib Sufi Study Circle not only accentuate the global diversity of a Sufi community from Sri Lanka to the United States but they also emphasize the fluidity of a singular Sufi community which contains distinct followers of Muslims, Hindus, Jews, and Christians. By illustrating the flows and networks of people between the sacred spaces of the Fellowship and the Circle, which includes mosques, burial shrines, farms, and community centers, this book elucidates the diverse manifestations of Sufism, not only in North America and South Asia, but also in a global context. This study highlights historical Sufism and its contemporary reality as a tradition where there have been dialogical encounters between Sufism in the non-creedal form of universalism and as a spiritual ethos that was and is uniquely Islamic. These internal negotiations, dynamisms, and fluidities of Sufism sometimes are positioned against questions of Islamic authenticity, even more so in the American landscape. Although scholarship and those in the community contend with these questions of authority, legitimacy, and orthodoxy, this inherent plurality has been a feature of Sufism in its historical and formative periods across Islamic civilizations. Thinking of Sufism through this trajectory of both expansive and subtle continuities and discontinuities, especially through transnational sacred spaces and rituals, captures the fluidity and dynamic formations of Sufism. This framework moves away from approaching Sufism as a reified and static entity. These findings not only challenge scholars to reconsider how Sufism is developing in the modern American landscape, but also globally.

Charting Bawa's Spaces from Jaffna to Pennsylvania

Introduction

Kambiz GhaneaBassiri posits that American Islam is not an "exceptionally unique or adulterated form of Islam."[1] Muslim history in America, explains GhaneaBassiri, is defined by the encounters between Muslim American and non-Muslim Americans and their exchanges—it has been a relational and reciprocal experience.[2] They are not "mutually exclusive" but as "lived traditions" they "have been varyingly thought and re-thought in relation to one another and to their respective historical contexts."[3] The same relational approach has unfolded with American Sufism, and the Fellowship is one such example where such a relational process is evident. The Fellowship then can help us understand the "relational nature" of Sufism in American religious and Islamic history.[4]

To provide a history of Bawa and his ministries, I begin in Jaffna and shift to Colombo and then Matale, in Sri Lanka, where the Serendib Sufi Study Circle (SSSC) originated. I capture the Hindu and Muslim students of Bawa's first spaces in the Circle. The second half of this chapter turns to America and maps the development of the Fellowship in Philadelphia. This historical emphasis on Bawa's early ministry in Sri Lanka further nuances the growth of the Fellowship in Philadelphia with particular attention to the racial, cultural, and religious dynamics during the early institutional development of the Fellowship. For example, the initial interested seekers who visited Bawa in Philadelphia were mainly African Americans. This racial trend shifted to encompass more European American members and visitors during much of the late 1970s and 1980s. Currently, the Fellowship has a prominent Muslim diasporic presence, especially from South Asia and the Middle East. These trends in the Fellowship reflect the broader historical development of American Islam at large, which includes the rise of race-based Muslim organizations, such as the Nation of Islam, conversion to Islam, and the arrival of more immigrants to America from Muslim-majority nations with the relaxation of national immigration quotas after 1965.

Bawa's Early Ministry

Bawa's Early Life and His *Ashram*

In Jaffna, if one were to ask any of Bawa's senior disciples to recount the story of Bawa's origins, the answer would be the same: he came from the jungles. The stories became more hagiographic in character the more I probed into this common oral narrative of Bawa's origins. Bawa himself remained mute about much of his early history. When asked, he always replied that his story was not the one he was here to share; instead he was to share "His story," or the story of God. In a few of Bawa's discourses, or oral lectures, he speaks of his pilgrimages to Sufi and Hindu shrines in South India, such as in Tripathy. In the rare instances that he does share something of his early history, the stories signal to a life of mendicancy and wandering. In a collected anthology of Bawa's discourses, compiled and published by early disciples in Sri Lanka entitled *Guru Mani* (*Teacher's Jewel*) in 1961, Bawa is quoted as saying:

> I lived for eighteen years on the slopes of the Silver Mountain in Kataragama. After that I spent twelve years in the caves near Jailani. Then I spent about eight years on the slopes of the mountain called Adam's Peak. I spent four and a half years after this in Nurwara Eliya in the cave in which Sita was presumed to have been kept in captivity by Ravanna, the King of Lanka.[5]

Bawa lived as an ascetic in holy sites across Sri Lanka. Above he lists Adam's Peak, Dafter Jailani, and Kataragama, which form a historically significant pilgrimage network in Sri Lanka for Muslims (see Introduction), as places where he spent time in spiritual retreat. Bawa also mentions spending time in Hindu spaces, such as ones associated with Sita, the wife of Rama and the avatar of Vishnu in Hindu cosmology. In relaying these stories of his travels, it is evident that Bawa emerged from a cultural and religious landscape in Sri Lanka where shared sacred spaces were the norm, particularly between Hindus and Muslims.

Bawa's senior disciples can agree that Bawa was first spotted by two Tamil Hindu pilgrims in Kataragama sometime in the 1940s or 1950s. Brothers and Hindu pilgrims, Pariyari and Kumarasami from Nallur, Jaffna, were on a pilgrimage to Kataragama when they encountered Bawa in the jungles. Reputedly, they were not able to communicate easily with Bawa as his dialect of Tamil was too classic, or regionally variant. It was not until a few years later that Bawa's Tamil is believed to have become more decipherable to his early Tamil disciples in Jaffna. Hence, theories emerged that he may have come from South India. The two pilgrims, and later disciples of Bawa, asked him to return with them to Jaffna but Bawa told them to go ahead and promised to arrive forty days later. He kept his promise and arrived on the eleventh day of the Nallur Kovil (temple) festival for Murukan in 1944 and stayed with the brothers. For about seven years, Bawa lived at Pariyari's house in Kokuvil, a village outside Jaffna, after which he moved to another village called Kondavil before finally moving to Jaffna Town. There he purchased a worn-down, formerly Dutch warehouse and began using it as his *ashram*, or place of residence, sometime in the 1950s.[6] Slowly, local people started to visit Bawa. Initially, many came to see him at his *ashram* to heal their complaints of physical ailments and demonic possessions. Other times, visitors came to seek counsel to help settle minor family, or land, disputes. Some of these visitors slowly became regulars and stayed on to become dedicated students. In Jaffna today, many of Bawa's most committed students originate from this early period and still participate regularly in the communal and individual venera- tion of Bawa at the *ashram*. It was during this early period that Ahamed Kabeer, who later served as one of the two *imam*s at the mosque built in Philadelphia, first met Bawa. Kabeer was a pearl diver from South India who moved to the Mannar region of Sri Lanka to dive with his uncle, who introduced Kabeer to Bawa sometime in the 1950s. In 1962, Bawa asked Kabeer to move into the *ash- ram* and started training him to make *du'a*s (intercessory prayers) and amu- lets using Arabic alphabets and numerology, a practice that formed the basis of Bawa's healing ministry.[7] From the earliest days of his public ministry in Jaffna, Bawa was known as a healer and performer of exorcisms, a practice which he then taught select students, such as Kabeer.[8]

The Matron, who is the caretaker of the *ashram*, is another early student of Bawa.[9] Initially a Tamil Hindu, she met Bawa in the 1970s. She was a school teacher and had chronic stomach pain. She visited numerous doctors and local healers but no one was able to provide any remedies for her. She heard about Bawa's abilities to heal and visited him at his *ashram* and he cured her. Though she initially visited for a healing, she found herself drawn to his presence and remained as a disciple. At the time, Periya Teacher and Aachi, two other Tamil women, were the caretakers of the *ashram*. Since the passing of the previous two female caretakers, the current Matron believes that she was appointed by Bawa to continue their role. The *ashram* has always been under the care of a "matron" and the current custodian has continued this tradition of maintaining it as the female custodians before her have done. The Matron also holds the position of the treasurer of the Jaffna branch.

Working closely with the Matron is another senior disciple in Jaffna, named Priya Thambi, the current president of the Jaffna branch, who also acts as the prayer leader at Mankumban and the *ashram*.[10] He met Bawa when he was hired to work on the electrical wiring at the *ashram*. During his work, he became curious about Bawa and inquired about him to some of his students, who then encouraged him to visit Bawa during one of his public lectures. Priya Thambi self-identified as a Hindu, but was also interested in philosophy and spirituality more generally. He read works by Ramakrishna Paramahamsa (d. 1886), an Indian mystic and yogi. He also heard of other gurus, saints, and Sufis locally, and thus when he met Bawa he felt that he was "the one" he was looking for and stayed on as a dedicated student. Both Priya Thambi and the Matron are the main institutional leaders of the *ashram* and Mankumban in Jaffna. Priya Thambi resides with his family, while the Matron resides at the *ashram*.

Dr Ganesan, another early student of Bawa, was a Tamil Hindu student of Satya Sai Baba, a religious movement centered on a living guru who also embodies Hindu and Islamic tendencies.[11] As a practicing medical doctor at a hospital in Jaffna, Dr Ganesan heard about Bawa and went to hear him speak. Here, he describes his experience of visiting Bawa in Jaffna during the 1970s:

He would sit at the table . . ., he had a sarong, sometime[s he was] bare bodied . . . you know . . . [he was an] old . . . ordinary person. He'd sit on the bed and . . . all [the] poor people in that area, a man or family, would go and sit next to him and relay their problems. And he would talk to them . . . very attentively [and] listen to every word; ask questions. It could be something simple as "so and so borrowed fifty rupees from me and haven't returned it to me." Or, "so and so was re-fencing the border and they've taken some part of our land"; something like that. Worldly things. They would come to him about many things but he would listen very carefully, attentively and nobody can disturb you at that time. And he didn't say I didn't come here to do these things, my business, my mission is different, no [nothing] like that, [he offered] a lot of love. And then at the end he would . . . give them a solution about what to do. And I would see them and they'd . . . come back and he'd go "you are all God." He said "I worship the same God you worship. You ask God and I also ask God" . . . The thing that I noticed was poor or rich it [didn't] matter, he treated them all the same way. And . . . you can call it love [which led to his . . .], full attention to them. [He was] completely dedicated to their wishes and their wants, and this was what I saw, I was a Hindu; he was supposed to be a Muslim. No difference, that was very well. And then at the end of it all, he'd tell a small story ... which was wisdom based. As much as to say, if you had this wisdom, you wouldn't need to come here. You would be able to solve it your own way [and with] your own mind on your own.[12]

Dr Ganesan and his family moved to Philadelphia, due to the growing ethnic unrest in Sri Lanka, where I met him during my fieldwork. When we met, he prayed five times a day and fasted during Ramadan. Still, conversion to Islam by Hindus was not a common trend among students of Bawa in Jaffna. Bawa did not require religious conversion. As a result, especially in Jaffna, most of Bawa's followers were Hindus in those early years of his ministry, and they remain as such today. Dr Ganesan and the Matron are examples of two individuals who made the personal decision to adopt more outward Islamic practices, as was the case among his American students, albeit far more gradually.

As early as the 1960s and onward, Bawa attracted Hindus and Muslims (with the occasional Christian and Buddhist visitors) to his *ashram* for a variety of reasons. He provided counsel, healing, and food to his visitors, lectured on the indivisibility of God, and organized *mawlid*s for Prophet Muhammad and al-Jilani. He himself did not lead the recitations of the *mawlid*s and he did not institute or lead daily ritual prayers. In fact, most expressed that they did not see him completing the five daily prayers at all. The main rules and practices of the *ashram* were posted on the entrance way, as found in Mohamed Mauroof's dissertation. These rules highlighted that there was a "non-sectarian attitude toward religion and gods," and that "the matron of the ashram was the final authority in regard to conduct."[13] If Bawa was not present "patients and students were to sit silently and make their requests within their selves" while any activity seen at the *ashram* was not allowed to be relayed to "outsiders."[14] From the early days, the *ashram* was already a space wherein affiliation with a specific religious tradition was avoided, though tendencies of Hinduism and Islam were notable and the early visitors and students were predominately Hindus. Some of Bawa's Hindu followers felt that he was a reincarnation of Murukan, the Hindu deity. Some also alluded that Bawa named his two deer, his pets, Theivanai and Valli, the names of Murukan's wives. The epithets given to Bawa by his followers in Jaffna, most of whom were Hindu in this period, was *swami* (lord) and guru (teacher), labels that were particularly Hindu Tamil in nature.[15]

According to some oral accounts relayed to me, sometime in the 1940s or 1950s, Bawa also sought out property in northern Jaffna, based on a vision and mystical relationship to Maryam, the mother of 'Isa. Some senior disciples who helped during this early period shared their memories of this time. Ragavan, whose mother was one of Bawa's early disciples, recalls frequently traveling with Bawa as a child; and he was with Bawa when they arrived at the village known as Mankumpan on Velanai Island, on the northern tip of Sri Lanka. Now, one can travel on a causeway to get to the island, but when they first found the land, they used to take a small row boat across the Palk Strait. The complex built on this property came to be known as a mosque or "God's House," although the name "Mankumban" (taken from the mis-transliterated name of the village, Mankumpan, it is located within) is also used interchangeably. In 1954, Bawa began the construction of God's House, which was to be dedicated to Maryam, but it was not completed until the arrival of American disciples to Jaffna in the 1970s. Mankumban transformed into a shrine once a memorial tomb was built inside the mosque in 2003 by Bawa's disciples in Sri Lanka (Chapter 2).[16]

Bawa was also a farmer and he cultivated two to three farms (with different sources giving differing accounts). The location of these first farms also shifts depending on the source. Those, like Ragavan, who claim that Bawa was from Tripathy, South India, believe that he had a farm while he lived there; while one of the farms was in Puliyankulam, in Vavuniya district in northeastern Sri Lanka, which is still in use today. Details aside, Bawa's initial reason for acquiring the land in Puliyankulam was to feed his growing community, including the visitors, who sought out his *ashram*. He used the crops from his farm to sell to the local market to acquire money for his *ashram* in addition to using the crops to cook vegetarian meals, a diet he advocated.[17] His abilities to cultivate land and cook formed the basis of some of his discourses and teachings, especially as they taught the importance of self-sustainability and environmental consciousness. He also used farming and cooking as metaphors for spiritual development. This model was replicated in America with the property purchased in Coatesville, Pennsylvania.[18] As his spaces began to expand, he also instituted ritual practices.

Ritual Practices in Jaffna: The Beginning of the *Mawlid* and General Meetings

Mawlid (birthday) celebrations (also *milad*) honor the birth day of a holy figure, such as Prophet Muhammad or Sufi saints. Marion Holmes Katz writes that the *mawlid* celebrations that were noted centuries after the death of Prophet Muhammad were viewed as *bid'a*, or a heretical innovation. The tradition itself was attributed at its earliest to the Fatimid Shi'a dynasty, who ruled Egypt from 969 to 1171, during which Prophet Muhammad's birthday was celebrated as a "state occasion."[19] These "festivals" hosted by the Fatimid Dynasty "involved the distribution of sweets to state and religious functionaries and a brief ceremonial viewing of the ruling Fatimid Imam."[20] Some of the earliest *mawlid* literature, for instance, dated to a Medinan judge by the name of Wahb ibn 'Abd Allah ibn Zam'a Abu'l-Bukhturi (815), was not for Prophet Muhammad, but rather for his son-in-law and cousin 'Ali ibn Abi Talib.[21] *Mawlid* literature for Fatima, Prophet Muhammad's daughter and Ali's wife, along with their sons Hasan and Husayn, also developed. This "devotional literature" then extended to include Sufi teachers, like al-Jilani, by specific Sufi communities.[22] Sunnis also commemorated this festival for the Prophet Muhammad during the end of the Fatimid Dynasty but focused on the commemoration of Prophet Muhammad's life, unlike their Shi'a counterparts, but shared in the "combined feasting and sufi audition (*sama'*) with various kinds of literary production."[23] It was likely Sufis, such as the early Persian figure Sahl al-Tustari (d. 896 CE), who used the light verse of the Qur'an (24:35) to develop teachings about "the light of Muhammad" or the primordial Muhammad, which comprises a formative theme in the literature recited during the *mawlid* celebration.[24] These narratives and the *mawlid* practices are a central trend among the Tamil Muslim society (in Sri Lanka and South India), the backdrop of Bawa's communities in Jaffna.[25] The *mawlid* is commonly celebrated at a tomb of a Sufi saint or her/his relic, and often unfolds over the span of weeks or days.[26] This celebration speaks to the belief that God's grace and blessings can be accessed through his holy servants.

In a pamphlet entitled *Why We Recite Maulids* [sic], published by the Fellowship on February 7, 1982, based on a discourse given in Tamil by Bawa and translated by senior students, Bawa explains why celebrating the *mawlid* is a duty:

> What is this month that has been set aside for Muhammad (*Sal.*)?[27] It is a month in which we honour Muhammad (*Sal.*) and give praise to Allah. We thank Muhammad (*Sal.*) and praise Allah. This is why we observe the *maulid* [sic], like we did today. This is not wrong. We are not making a comparison, even though some people may claim that this is what is [sic] we are doing. But you, children who are true believers [*mu'min*] if you have absolute faith [*iman*], then it is your right and privilege to honour resplendent beings, the *qutbs*, the friends of God [*awliya*] and the prophets who came to help us and show us the right path. And it is your right and privilege to give praise to Allah, the One who sent them. It is our duty to do this. This is what we have to do.[28]

For Bawa recitation of the *mawlid* is an act of gratitude toward God who sent these divine figures to help humanity. Bawa's communities do not only celebrate the *mawlid* for Prophet Muhammad alone but Bawa also instituted the *mawlid* for al-Jilani, the lineage that Bawa associated his authority and movement with.[29] Bawa hosted *mawlid*s for al-Jilani as early as 1962 at his *ashram*. Singers and reciters were invited for the special festival, which attracted hundreds of participants. A vegetarian meal was served after the recitation of the *mawlid*, and gifts, in the form of fruits or coins, were distributed by students of Bawa and sometimes by Bawa himself, to the visitors. The same was done for the *mawlid* for Prophet Muhammad. The *mawlid* was an annual holy celebration, which coincided with the yearly general meeting for all of Bawa's students. The annual general meeting was held in the town hall in Jaffna. Locals from Jaffna and across the island attended in order to hear prominent speakers that were invited by Bawa. Some of Bawa's followers attended both celebrations.[30] During these large public gatherings, those in attendance viewed Bawa according to their religious identities. Thus, though Bawa was known as a Muslim teacher, Hindus related to Bawa as a guru/*swami* and Muslims viewed him as a *shaykh* (teacher), while Christians and Buddhist respected him as a holy sage.

Mauroof, a Sri Lankan Muslim disciple of Bawa and graduate student who completed his dissertation on the Fellowship and Bawa, describes his experience of the annual meetings and *mawlid*s of al-Jilani, which he attended in August 1967, 1968, and 1970. The event attracted many students, visitors, and friends of Bawa from all over the island. He writes:

> The event was announced in the town of Nallur [in Jaffna] and a great many people from that community also participated in the feast. The *ashram* was painted and decorated for the event. The formal proceedings would start about 5:00pm. At that time about a dozen persons could recite the mowlood [*mawlid*]- the Arabic songs are sung during these occasions . . . This went on for about three hours. The crowds of people would be seated around, respectfully listening to the chants. Bawa did not participate in the singing . . . Singing the Muhaiyaddeen mowlood [*mawlid*] was a religious act for them [Sri Lankan Muslims] which they would have performed in many a household during that month. They were now performing it in Bawa's household.[31]

Several important details emerge from Mauroof's early documentation of the *mawlid* for al-Jilani at the *ashram*. First, the *mawlid* celebrations held at the *ashram* are similar to the practice of the *mawlid* held by Muslims across Sri Lanka, who have historically hosted *mawlid*s at their homes or Sufi shrines, a practice which continues today. The popularity of this tradition in the Tamil Muslim world likely led to its wide traction that Mauroof describes above. Second, Bawa did not lead the recitation of the *mawlid*. He was the host and participant in the event, while singers and reciters were invited to lead the celebrations, including the recitation of the stories and verses from the Qur'an during the event. Finally, those who attended the *mawlid*s were not only Muslims, but Hindus as well. In his study, Mauroof adds that there was some ambiguity among some of those in attendance (perhaps the Hindus) as to Bawa's authority during such rituals. He explained that the "trance-like state" of Bawa led some of those in attendance to believe that Bawa was, in some capacity, the "*Qutb* Muhaiyaddeen" (the "pole" or "axis" Muhaiyaddeen, a referent to al-Jilani). This fluid interpretation of Bawa's identity and authority created challenges for the diverse individuals who participated in such rituals (see Chapter 5). After the recitation, Bawa gave a public lecture and then a vegetarian meal was served to all those in attendance.[32]

Jaffna to Colombo and the Formation of the Serendib Sufi Study Circle

The spread of Bawa's ministry further south into Colombo from Jaffna was precipitated by a fortuitous meeting between Bawa and two separate families. While in Jaffna, Bawa's fame began to spread and he became known to a prominent Muslim family in Colombo by the name of Macan-Markar. Although the Macan-Markars met Bawa in the 1960s, Ameen (the wife of Ajwad Macan-Markar) explained that Bawa knew her father-in-law nearly three decades earlier, when her father-in-law had gone to look for a healer for her sick son. Years later, a second connection emerged when Ameen's sister-in-law Araby Macan-Markar (Gnaniar) invited Bawa to their house in Colombo. During this time Ajwad and Ameen's son, who also became unwell, was in need of a healer. Reputedly, it happened to be the same holy figure encountered by Ameen's father-in-law. Ameen describes these early events:

> My husband, Dr. Ajwad-Macan-Markar, and I met Bawangal [honorific for Bawa] in 1962 at one of these meetings at Gnanier's (my other sister-in-law) house in Colombo. After hearing Bawangal speak several times there, we spent ten days in the ashram in Jaffna with him. When we visited Bawangal in Jaffna, between 1962–1971 . . ., we and our five children and others from Colombo, as well as Fuard's family from Wattala, would travel to Jaffna in one carriage (train) full of people every year to attend the maulids [*mawlid*s]. If Bawangal was in Colombo at that time, he too, would be in the carriage with everyone else, making the journey to Jaffna. When the maulids [*mawlid*s] ended, everyone

would proceed to Mankumban bringing pots and pans and cooking supplies from Jaffna in a van that they had rented . . . Whether in Mankumban or Jaffna, Bawangal would talk, cook and serve food each day.[33]

The second family that formed an important center in Colombo was the Udumans. Fuard Uduman, mentioned above in Ameen's recollection, was a Muslim from Colombo who had also found Bawa while searching for a holy man to follow during the late 1950s.[34] When he arrived in Jaffna looking for Bawa whom he had heard about, he found a disciple of Bawa waiting for him in the hotel lobby with orders to bring Fuard to Bawa's *ashram*. This encounter with Bawa led Fuard to be a dedicated student of Bawa. In addition to visiting the Macan-Markars in Colombo, Bawa would also visit the Udumans at their home in Colombo, where Bawa held *mawlid* celebrations and public lectures. Eventually, the Macan-Markars requested that Bawa stay with them in Colombo, and after some resistance, because his home was in Jaffna, he agreed.[35] Due to these new dedicated disciples, Bawa's ministry branched out into Colombo. Nevertheless, Bawa spent most of his time in Jaffna at his *ashram*, while the Macan-Markars' home became one of the principal meeting houses in Colombo. Later, it served as the home where Americans who would visit Bawa in the 1970s and 1980s stayed.

To further cement this as the organizational center, Bawa's students in Colombo founded the Serendib Sufi Study Circle (SSSC) in 1963. It was the first time that Bawa and his students formed an official organization, and the impulse to do so came from Bawa's students, and not Bawa himself. In the legal documents, Bawa was listed as the official "patron" and subsequent committees and trustees were formed to help run the institution, through meetings and voting privileges, as a means to diffuse any other form of authority beyond Bawa. The incorporation of the SSSC was one of the final stages in the formal establishment of Bawa's community in Sri Lanka, as the *ashram* and Mankumban in Jaffna were incorporated into the SSSC.

The Sri Lankan government officially recognized the group on November 27, 1974. The SSSC charter indicates the objective of the incorporation in clause 3 to include:

A. the promotion and study and understanding of Sufism (mysticism) among all persons seeking knowledge of Sufism (mysticism), including the teaching of the principles and practices of Sufism (mysticism) as expounded by His Holiness Sheikh Muhammad Muhiyadeen Guru Bawa during his lifetime;

B. the compilation, translation, publication and dissemination of the principles and practices of Sufism (mysticism) as are or may be expounded by His Holiness Sheikh Muhammad Muhiyadeen Guru Bawa and the research works, reports and material pertaining to Sufism (mysticism) as are or may be forthcoming from the scholarship of any member for the public good;

C. the establishment and maintenance of voluntary charitable organizations for any one or more of the following purposes:

   (ii) the relief of poverty,

   (ii) the care of widows and orphans, the aged and the destitute, by establishment of homes, orphanages, dispensaries, medical care, and

   (iii) the relief of hunger, disease and sickness by the provision of sustenance and nourishment and medical care to the needy, the orphans, the indigent and the sick.[36]

The objective of the SSSC was to propagate mysticism, or Sufism. This was the first time a religious label was placed on Bawa's ministry, at least in official documentation. As I indicated above, the codes of conduct found at the *ashram* evaded any particular religious label. Even in the name of the organization, the Serendib Sufi Study Circle, one begins to see how the members of the Colombo branch, majority of whom were Muslims, framed Bawa and his teachings within mysticism and Sufism. Bawa was understood as the *shaykh* and guru of the organization. His followers did not frame themselves as a *tariqa*, or a Sufi order, as is often found with communities that form around a Sufi *shaykh*. Rather, the SSSC was a corporation of sorts, with trustees and operating committees. This legal document specified that Bawa would have the power to nominate members to an elected committee as well as summarily remove them during his lifetime. The committee would bear responsibility of managing the SSSC both during Bawa's lifetime and after his death, according to the "Committee of Management" in Section 4 of the charter:

1. The affirms of the Corporation shall, subject to the rules in the force for the time being of the Corporation, be administered

   A. during the lifetime of His Holiness Sheikh Muhammad Muhiyaddeen Guru Bawa, by a Committee of Management nominated by Him and elected by the members; and

   B. after the lifetime of His Holiness Sheikh Muhammad Muhiyaddeen Guru Bawa, by a Committee of Management to be elected by the members,

2. The Patron, His Holiness Sheikh Muhammad Muhiyaddeen Guru Bawa, shall have the right during his lifetime to remove from office, on the recommendation of the Committee of Management, any member of the Committee of Management and nominate any other person to fill the vacant post.[37]

Although the institutional power of Bawa's communities remained in Jaffna, this written legal document and its registration with the Sri Lankan government meant that it was regionally controlled in Colombo by a Muslim contingent, even though Bawa had a greater number of Hindu followers in the north, a trend that continues today. Additionally, the movement was framed as a corporation, rather than a *tariqa* or religious community.

The Macan-Markar home continues to serve as the headquarters of the SSSC, where Bawa's former room is treated as a memorial shrine. And to further the contrast, while the *ashram* in Jaffna focused on the performance of exorcisms and healing, the wealthy and socially endowed Muslim followers in Colombo were more attentive to Bawa's teachings and made a concerted effort to disseminate it through book publications and recordings of his lectures.[38] In Colombo, the members also continued to serve and help those who were less fortunate and poor, as well as facilitate some forms of healing, but the overall focus in Colombo was more heavily weighted toward spreading Bawa's teachings along with the commemoration of *mawlids*, a practice that began in Jaffna and continued throughout Bawa's spaces in Sri Lanka.

A Jungle Shrine: The Branch in Matale

The final branch that developed under the SSSC is in Matale. This branch is located in the mountainous regions near Kandy in central Sri Lanka. The Matale branch is composed of local Malay Muslims, but this particular shrine dedicated to Bawa and his student has also started to attract Muslims from across the island, including Tamil Muslims.[39] The Matale branch developed as a result of a relationship between Bawa and T. K. B. Rahman (d. 2004), who was nicknamed Customs Rahman Thambi (younger brother) by Bawa because he worked as a customs officer at the airport. The Matale branch is the home of Rahman and his relatives. In the 1970s, Rahman dedicated a bedroom for Bawa, which included his photographs and his articles, and this room was treated as a shrine to Bawa. The home was not used for hosting meetings, as it was too small. Then gradually over the 1980s, Rahman started to build a jungle garden in the back of his house, containing areas to congregate, which included a flag pole (for the *qutb*), a library for Bawa's book, and a special prayer room. Rahman also dedicated his living room to regular prayer meetings, as well as spiritual and qur'anic classes for the local youth. He also hosted *mawlids*. Since his death, Rahman's family (which includes his brothers, his sisters, and now their children) are the shrine keepers in Matale. They also constructed a memorial room for Rahman as an addition to the complex he constructed. The shrine complex does not include a tomb or sarcophagus in the traditional sense, but it serves as a memorial for Bawa and his student Rahman. And like the *ashram* and Mankumban, *mawlids* are hosted at this shrine. The shrine complex has been transformed to serve as a retreat (*chilla*) space after Rahman's death, although less and less American disciples visit this shrine.

During his lifetime, Rahman emerged as a spiritual leader in his own right in Matale, and he commented on Bawa's teachings, especially in the form of pamphlets and newsletters, which he distributed to interested students in Matale. In one such pamphlet entitled "In Loving Memory of Our Beloved Shaikh Muhammad Raheem Bawa Muhaiyaddeen May Allah be pleased with him," he wrote:

> You and I [who] have been blessed to be in the presence of our late Sufi Sheikh during his life time for many decades[;] will undoubtedly bear testimony that he fulfilled for those in his presence a triple role, i.e. as Teacher, as Prophetic Preacher, and a Pastor (Healer). Through his discourses which he so eloquently delivered, he prophetically preached with fervor, conviction and authority. In personal situation [*sic*] he ministered to the needs of the individuals in a pastoral way.[40]

The Making of the Bawa Muhaiyaddeen Fellowship

Bawa's Arrival in America: 1971–72

The catalyst for Bawa's arrival in Philadelphia was Mauroof, a student from Sri Lanka who was completing his graduate studies in the Anthropology Department at the University of Pennsylvania.[41] Mauroof was distraught by the racial rioting taking place in Philadelphia (e.g. the Columbia Avenue Riots in 1964 in north Philadelphia), and he felt that Bawa, whom he had known in Jaffna to engage diverse religious and ethnic followers, could quell this racial unrest with his message of peace and unity.[42] Another important thread to this narrative is the story of Carolyn Andrews, who is the current executive secretary of the Fellowship. Andrews was a student of Mauroof's in 1968. Andrews had a peculiar mystical experience early in life when all things "disappeared"—there was an absence of light, sound, smell, touch, and body—and she came to recognize a reality of oneness.[43] She struggled with this event for years, until her connection with Mauroof led her to Bawa. Andrews started writing letters to Bawa. In his letters to Andrews, Bawa interpreted her experience as mystical and, for Andrews, this exchange confirmed Bawa's spiritual abilities. She wanted to visit him in Sri Lanka, but lacked the financial resources to travel and so helped Mauroof mobilize support to bring Bawa to America.

To sponsor Bawa's visit to America, Mauroof is said to have initially approached the Moorish Science Temple (MST), an African American Muslim movement. After consulting with their headquarters in Chicago, the proposal was declined but they suggested that Mauroof contact the Dembys, particularly Robert (Bob) Demby, an African American, who was at the time involved in Hindu and yoga movements in Philadelphia, but prior to which had affiliations with the Nation of Islam and Malcolm X (d. 1965), as well as other African American Muslim communities. Robert, and his then wife Virginia, were leading a yoga group in Philadelphia from which many students would later join the Fellowship. Zahra Williams, who is also African American, remembers taking a yoga class taught by Virginia Demby when Mauroof visited to speak about Bawa.[44] He sought signatures from them to procure a visa for Bawa's visit to America. Mauroof brought with him photographs of Bawa, along with some pamphlets of Bawa's teachings in English.[45] With the efforts of Mauroof and Andrews, along with the signatures of the early members, such as the Dembys and Williams, Mauroof was able to procure a visa for Bawa to visit the United States. Demby would become one of the senior presidents of the Fellowship, and take the name Khwaja Muhaiyaddeen. When Bawa arrived in Philadelphia on October 11, 1971, Williams was among the approximately one dozen visitors who went to the airport to greet him during his first visit to America.[46] From the airport, they all went to Mauroof's home in West Philadelphia and listened to Bawa discourse for the first time.

In the earliest days, Bawa's talks were primarily attended by locals from the immediate neighborhood, and they included many members of the African American community in Philadelphia. Khair ul-Nissa, an African American Muslim female disciple of Bawa, who also knew Mauroof, explained that her mother, who used to work at a recreation center in West Philadelphia, was approached by Robert in order to use the recreation center to host a discourse by Bawa.[47] Soon, local cooperative shops and grocery stores in Philadelphia displayed posters and advertised him as a "mystical guru" here to help the "poor, the African-American [and] the downtrodden."[48] Soon after he arrived in 1971, Khair ul-Nissa went to visit Bawa and noted right away that most of the visitors were African Americans and many were from the MST, whose members she recognized because of their fez caps.[49]

In order to accommodate the growing number of visitors, and not disturb Mauroof who was lecturing and trying to complete his dissertation at the time, Bawa moved to a new house in the suburbs in January of 1972.[50] In the first few months of Bawa's arrival to America, Mauroof counted twenty-eight regular members and sixty-nine interested members of the Fellowship.[51] By March of the same year meetings began to attract more than a hundred people, sometimes even two hundred, while paid membership increased as well.[52] Mauroof distinguished between "regular members" (those who were heavily involved in the life of the early Fellowship and performed tasks such as publishing) and "interested members" who were not actively engaged and only occasionally visited but were key to publicizing news of Bawa through word of mouth. He also indicates a gender imbalance. There was a larger female presence than male, but visitors and members were religiously diverse coming from Catholic, Hindu, Islamic, Jewish, and Protestant faith backgrounds.[53] Additionally, the institutional network that formed in Sri Lanka—centers around Bawa (e.g. his *ashram* or Mankumban) and smaller branches based in homes of disciples—was slowly being expanded and replicated in the Fellowship in America.

Dhikr, Kalima, and Meetings in the Early Fellowship

During his early stay in Philadelphia, Bawa taught silent *dhikr* (remembrance of Allah).[54] The instructions included the repetition of *la illaha illa llah* (there is no god but God), the first part of the testament of faith in Islam, or the *shahadah*. He paralleled it to the Tamil statement *unni tavira verru onrum illai* (except for you, there is nothing). His discourses on *dhikr* were meticulous. They detailed inhalation of breaths and movements from the toe of one's foot through the "4448 nerves and vessels and also the pore of the skin" that vibrate with the sound of *Allahu*, while it rises to the top of the head, which Bawa explained was the *'arsh*, or throne of Allah.[55] Eventually, *dhikr* instruction changed from silent to out loud, in order to accommodate American disciples who struggled with silent *dhikr* due to its practice in the dawn hours. The aloud *dhikr* manifested in variations of litanies and eventually became standardized in the 1980s in Sri Lanka by Bawa.

He instructed some students in the *kalimah*, or "the word."[56] Farida Nur Parker was born into a Catholic family and was one of the members of the Demby yoga group. When the Dembys stopped the yoga group, Farida inquired as to their whereabouts and found out that they had become members of the Fellowship. Curious, she went to visit but she did hesitantly as she was studying yoga with a Hindu teacher, who had already given her a "mantra" and she did not want to "guru hop." Eventually her experiences of Bawa and his teachings confirmed that she was to be a part of the Fellowship too. So Bawa invited her to receive the *kalimah*.[57] Farida explained her experience of this "initiation":

> I just remember he had me recite *la illaha illa llah*. And the [Hindu] mantra completely went out of my head and [was replaced by Bawa's] mantra, the new mantra so to speak—*la illaha illa llah*. [During the "initiation"] he took his thumb and put his hand here and wrote on my forehead. I later came to understand that the *nasib* [destiny] is written with the *qalam* [pen]. It's called the pen of destiny, [and . . .] even the angel that brings it doesn't know what it will write and the pen itself doesn't know what it will write. And Bawa said that its *nasib* [destiny] which Allah alone knows. And it can only be changed by a divinely wise guru and I thought he has changed my destiny by writing there. I don't know what he wrote. Some people say that it was the *kalima* [word] but that's what I was given.[58]

These practices, such as Farida's initiation, which is how she understood the experience (instead of it as a conversion), usually took place in private or in smaller groups. Markedly, the second part of the *shahadah* is not included in this initiation process described by Farida (e.g. *muhammadan rasul allah*). Though Prophet Muhammad is evoked in *dhikr* and other ritual events at the Fellowship, Bawa taught that the essence of reality is only the existence of God, everything else was secondary. This is likely why he had his students recite the first part of the *shahadah* and not the second. Bawa also handed out *du'as* in Arabic or protective amulets, similar to the practices he performed in Jaffna but he did not institute the *salat* or the five daily prayers.[59] The only regular Islamic practices that took place annually were *mawlids*, as they had in Jaffna, and daily *dhikr*, which did not take place communally in Jaffna.

For Bawa's students, meetings formed another critical facet of the regular Fellowship communal activity. Meetings were held in the evenings about four times a week, and though the number of visitors varied, some estimations suggest that about sixty people regularly came to hear Bawa discourse during the first year of his stay.[60] Bawa's teachings and songs began to be translated into English immediately once he arrived in Philadelphia. They were recorded on audio and film footage (which are all stored in the Fellowship archives) and books of his discourses were published (initially in the form of pamphlets).[61] These meetings continued with recorded discourses played or read when Bawa left for Sri Lanka, and even at this early stage there were disagreements over how to interpret Bawa's teachings in his absence.[62] Despite these disagreements over interpretation, Mauroof felt that the "unity was based on everybody's belief in Bawa whom they had all seen and accepted. That is why it is possible to surmise that Bawa represented to them, in visible form, something that each of the individuals had believed in all the time—even before they had met Bawa."[63]

When Bawa was present at the meetings, he lectured and took questions from those who visited him. As in Jaffna, in Philadelphia, students and visitors came to Bawa with a variety of questions, be they personal matters (e.g. marital or health related) or broader philosophical queries. These early meetings set the precedent for how meetings were held after Bawa died. Today, at the Fellowship or any branch location, Bawa's recorded discourses are the center of meetings. There were differences of interpretation and application of Bawa's teachings when Bawa was alive, and this would be even more the case in his death.

The Shifting of Racial and Religious Composition of the Early Fellowship: 1972–84

In June of 1972, Bawa returned to Philadelphia from his first trip back to Sri Lanka and recommended that a new house be purchased. By late 1973 a Jewish community center on Overbook Road was acquired.[64] The Fellowship House on Overbrook Road became Bawa's home as well as the headquarters for the Fellowship. As his immediate followers began institutionalizing at the Fellowship House, Bawa's popularity spread further and his disciples arranged lecture tours for him, especially at universities, and on radio and television programs. For instance, Mitchell Gilbert, a radio personality and a popular disc jockey in Philadelphia, advertised Bawa's teachings along with the schedule of the Fellowship with invitations for all to visit.[65] Lex Hixon, later known as the Sufi Shaykh Nur al-Anwar al-Jerrahi (d. 1995), hosted a radio program called *In the Spirit*. It ran on WBAI in New York City (from 1972 to 1989) and regularly hosted Bawa as a guest speaker.[66] Bawa's students also arranged numerous speaking engagements across the United States and Canada, including regular trips to San Francisco, New York, Iowa, California, Boston (Harvard University), and Toronto (University of Toronto and York University). Students from nearby universities, such as St. Joseph's University, Villanova College, and Temple University, came to visit the Fellowship. Visitors were not limited to North America. Spiritual seekers visited from European countries as well, such as Finland.

These speaking tours and guest appearances on radio shows, along with the press attention, helped spread Bawa's message and attracted students from many different parts of the United States, Canada, and Europe. Bawa's visits to different American cities and the homes of interested disciples resulted in the establishment of smaller branches, or gathering places where students would meet and listen to Bawa's discourses. Some of these branches are located in Boston (Massachusetts), Stamford (Connecticut), Woodstock (New York), San Francisco and Los Angeles (California), and Toronto (Ontario, Canada).[67] Bawa also spoke with many different religious and spiritual groups, including other Sufi groups that were forming in America, such as the Turkish Sufi group—the Jerrahis—and their teacher Muzzafer Ozak (d. 1985). He spoke to the students of Georges Ivanovitch Gurdieff (d. 1949)[68] and Swami Muktananda (d. 1982).[69] The 1970s in America particularly saw the arrival of many wisdom teachers or "gurus" from the "East." It was in reaction to the proliferation of "gurus" who were both becoming common across the United States and associated with charlatanism that the title "guru" was dropped from "Guru Bawa."

These speaking tours diversified Bawa's followers. The initial African American following slowly transitioned to become a predominately Jewish, Christian, and European American audience, inclined toward spiritual rather than institutional religions.[70] The Fellowship's location in Overbrook Road, a predominately Jewish and affluent neighborhood in Philadelphia, started becoming known as a Jewish Sufi group. According to Mauroof, Bawa's relocation was one factor that led to the shift in the racial and cultural demographic of the group. Many of the early African Americans with affiliations with black Muslim organizations were unable to cope with the shifts in the racial and cultural make-up of the Fellowship community, even though the nature of Bawa's teaching did not change. Philadelphia was still steeped in racial tensions and black power movements; black Muslim movements, in particular, created racial tensions among members within the Fellowship. Despite Bawa's continued efforts to work toward unity and peace, early African American Muslim and non-Muslim members slowly left the community, although some, such as Robert Demby, Williams, and Khair ul-Nissa, remained and maintained significant leadership positions and service. Williams spoke about these early racial dynamics:

> Bawa would come down from his bedroom, and just sort of seemingly do some alchemical, invisible stuff to calm the . . . animosity. But people would actually be shoving because you know, maybe some of the real Black Nationalists types, the Nation of Islam types, they didn't want a white person sitting next to them or touching them. "Don't touch my child" it was you know "you devils" and this kind of vibration and speech . . . But what happened basically was that . . . most of the black people left, and never came back. So, over time it then became predominantly white. And there were those of us who were there from day one . . . I remember saying this to somebody who was getting on [my case . . .] saying "are you still going there with all those white people?" And I said "look, there can be lions and tigers in there and if Bawa could keep them from eating me, I would still be there."[71]

Williams's comments above signal to the intersection of race, culture, and, ultimately, class in the early development of the Fellowship. Though scholars of American Islam have engaged race dynamics within Muslim communities in America, they have not focused as much on these dynamics within the study of American Sufism.[72] In particular, this early historical narrative of race dynamics in Philadelphia is absent in discussions of the Fellowship's development, especially as African American students of Bawa were pivotal to the institutional development of the Fellowship, such as the Dembys and Williams. The framing of the Fellowship by some scholars as a purely South Asian immigrant movement overlooks African American experiences in the early history of the Fellowship in America.[73]

Sri Lanka and America: Continuities in Bawa's Ministries

During Bawa's fifteen years in the United States, he returned to Sri Lanka four times; the first from 1972 to 1973. He returned to Sri Lanka again from February 1974 to July 1975, and then again on November 1976 where he remained until August 1978. During these visits, many projects were being completed. Mankumban, known as God's House, was completed on February 17, 1975, and under Bawa's direction, the building was constructed by both Sri Lankan (Tamil) and American disciples. Bawa's American and Tamil disciples also built the second floor of the *ashram* in 1977. Those who visited Sri Lanka with Bawa also immediately noticed that he seemed to feel more comfortable in his *ashram*, his own domain, than in any other space including Philadelphia. American disciples traveling with Bawa were exposed to life in Sri Lanka, and the differences were significant and startling. Bawa's healings and exorcisms—the work that gained him fame in Sri Lanka—were not commonly performed in America, or at least not as publicly as in Jaffna. And when he returned to Jaffna, he continued them. For example, Bawa was known to have used a cane to try to negotiate with "demons" and "spirits" to willingly leave their hosts, but other times he would literally "beat" the spirits out of the possessed. This experience of other aspects of Bawa's work shocked many of the American disciples. In Jaffna, he continued to tend to the needs of the local Tamils, who came to him for healing and advice. In Colombo and Philadelphia, he discoursed and spoke about God. In both contexts, he catered to the needs of his students, regardless of racial or religious identities.

Aside from the differences mentioned, Bawa's method of teaching did not vary too much between the Sri Lankan and American contexts. He continued to give lectures in Sri Lanka, albeit without the need for translators as he did in America. Michael Toomey, originally from Kanas City, recalls traveling to Philadelphia to meet Bawa on April 11, 1972, at the age of 24.[74] Bawa and his teachings resonated with him and he eventually moved into the Fellowship house in Philadelphia. He also traveled to Sri Lanka with Bawa and he shared with me some of his experiences from his first visit:

> He would give public talks; he'd give a talk in Colombo and annually he gave a public [talk] in Jaffna. On the radio, he would talk and then he would speak in the main town hall in Jaffna, and then he'd invite everybody to come to the *ashram* in all of Jaffna . . . So, we would spend three or four days cutting things, and he had big cauldrons [*laughs*] and the woodmen would come, the woodchopper, and [they would] chop wood and the people of the jungle, they speak Tamil. They lived in caves until the mid-eighties I think [. . . and] they would bring special things to Bawa from the jungle . . . We spent days cutting banana leaves [. . . into] squares and so we would have like a thousand people . . . in the *ashram*, we'd feed them all . . . and they had little coins with colored paper wrapped into them each as a gift . . ., because there was a lot of grace [in] coming to get something from Bawa . . . And then Bawa when he did talk, [even in a] formal meeting of the Serendib Sufi Study Circle in Colombo, he would ask us [to deliver a speech too]. He'd say "okay you just have to speak for five minutes so write it, write something and talk, and speak wisdom, say what you're learning."[75]

As he had done from the beginning, Bawa continued to give public discourses in Jaffna and Colombo, and provide food to his visitors, but now he had his

American students helping and serving in this process, particularly during public talks and *mawlid* celebrations. These, in effect, were notable continuities from Bawa's ministries from Jaffna to Philadelphia.

An Engaged Sufi: Bawa and Social Activism

While in Philadelphia during the height of the Iranian hostage crisis, Bawa also caught the attention of various newsprint outlets such as the *Philadelphia Inquirer* and *Pittsburg Press*. From 1978 to 1980, Bawa began a letter writing campaign to Iran's Ayatollah Khomeini, Prime Minister of Israel Menachem Begin (d. 1992), Egyptian President Anwar al-Sadat (d. 1981), and President of the United States Jimmy Carter. Distraught by the association of Islam with violence in the news media, Bawa provided an Abrahamic prophetic lineage and history that reflected a precedent of peaceful coexistence in the regions of Mesopotamia and Arabia in his letters to the world leaders.[76] He reminded the recipients of the letters that Islam was about peace and unity, not violence and discord. This letter writing campaign resulted in Bawa being featured in *Time Magazine* in 1980. At Bawa's insistence that the West needed it, the campaign also led to the first publication by the Fellowship Press of Bawa's *Islam and World Peace: Explanations of a Sufi*. Bawa's social activism was not limited to Philadelphia, however.

In Sri Lanka, Bawa's counsel was sought by Ranasinghe Premadasa (d. 1993), the future prime minister of Sri Lanka, early during his election campaign. Premadasa was a Sinhalese Buddhist and Bawa was known as a Tamil Muslim; so, due to the intensifying ethnic and political conflicts during the 1970s, Premadasa's visits with Bawa were kept secret.[77] Amina, who was present during the first visit by Premadasa, shared the following:

> [Premadasa] had a dream . . ., that there was a holy man on the island who could help him with this problem that he saw looming but he wasn't Buddhist. So, he searched [and] he had his people search and search and they found Bawa. He came at midnight very secretly to the *ashram* to meet Bawa, it was this big thing we were all preparing for like we knew but we had to keep a secret. And he and Bawa would talk and he would be escorted out at 2am or something. This happened over and over. And then with the elections . . . approaching I guess I don't . . . understand what was going on with the elections, but it was a big deal. It was like a big deal of how it would work out in terms of the country . . . and Bawa was really into it. I mean he was like watching TV for every election results and like praying but you know it didn't come out the way he would have liked . . . and it was a disappointment. Bawa saw what was coming down the pipe and he

was in pain. You know it was hard, because Sri Lanka was really going to be hurt and his people were going to be hurt and everybody was going to be hurt . . . So, that was a big thing to be present for that was really interesting.[78]

Personal involvement in politics and hosting visits from state officials, as exemplified by the stories of Premadasa in Sri Lanka or Bawa's letter writing campaigns in Philadelphia during the Iranian hostage crisis, formed a consistent facet of Bawa's broader ministry. Bawa attempted to counteract the misrepresentation of Islam in popular media by political and religious leaders in America, while in Sri Lanka, he worked to calm ethnic riots. Bawa tended to work toward peace and justice through activism in his immediate surroundings and he keenly promoted nonviolence and dialogue as a means to create understanding and respect within members of God's family (i.e. people's religious and ethnic identities). Bawa lived and ministered in two climates; one place that was torn by ethnolinguistic nationalisms that led to communal and governmental violence, and ended in a full-out war after Bawa's death. In America and the broader Western imagination, there was growing fear and demonization of Islam with which he contended. Bawa responded to both situations. For instance, when youth in Jaffna visited Bawa and expressed interest in the growing rebellion of militant organization that came to be known as the Liberation Tigers of Tamil Eelam (LTTE), Bawa challenged the disenfranchised Tamil youth to avoid violence and seek other means for upward mobility and peace with one another. Many of those who chose the path of armed resistance did not return to the *ashram* or to Bawa, but this did not stop Bawa from trying to guide them. Bawa's stance on peace as the essence of Islam, and his application of this framework in situations such as Sri Lanka and America, has led scholar-activists, such as Scott Kugle and Sa'diyya Shaikh, to associate the tradition of "engaged Sufism" with Bawa; and Bawa's model has also been invoked in Peace and Conflict Studies in Islam.[79]

Due to the rising civil conflict in Sri Lanka, Bawa was unable to return to Sri Lanka before his death. His final trip to Sri Lanka took place in December 1980 and he returned to Philadelphia in November 1982. The year 1982 was a formative period in modern Sri Lankan history, as it marked the beginning of the ethnic riots that led up to the Eelam Wars, or civil wars. The circumstance in Jaffna, where Bawa's first institutions were formed, became increasingly difficult and it was no longer safe to travel to Colombo and Jaffna. In spite of these broader political and ethnolinguistic conflicts across the island, it was in Colombo that the members of the Fellowship who remained with Bawa experienced their own transformative moment; this in turn, would lead to the construction of Bawa's final project in Philadelphia, his *masjid* (mosque).

The Building of the *Masjid*: 1984–86

During Bawa's final visit in Colombo, at the request of a female Muslim convert to Islam, female American students of Bawa began performing *salat* for the first time communally. (I describe the details of this process in Chapter 4, where I engage with the role of women in the Fellowship further.) This practice of *salat* continued when the group returned to Philadelphia. Some of the members had begun to take part in this prayer, in addition to *dhikr* that was already taking place regularly, but it was not without some anxiety. Williams recounts feeling trepidatious the first time she saw *salat* performed at the Fellowship:

> So, I remember going into Overbrook Avenue and seeing people making *salat*, and I said, "What are they doing" to somebody who was sitting there, not up there doing *salat* with them. And they said, "They're making *salat*." And I said, "Well what's *salat*?" And they said, "Those are the Muslim prayers." And I said, "Why are they doing it?" They said, "I don't know." So, you know, it was kind of like, slowly beginning to dawn on me that . . . some people were very interested in associating with the Islamic tradition, and believing that there was no way to be . . . on a Sufi path, unless you were Muslim. So, I didn't necessarily agree with that, but I was looking and observing. And then if Bawa told me to do something, there was no way I wasn't going to do it because by that time you know my faith in him was complete. But I was concerned because like many people in the West, . . . I've heard very negative things about Islam, particularly as it related to women.[80]

The performance of Islamic prayers led to the start of the construction of the mosque as the final addition to the Fellowship in Philadelphia, which now included a small carriage house at the back of the Fellowship house, which was used as a printing press, a large meeting hall, a public kitchen, classrooms, as well as rooms for Bawa and other students who lived in the house. Even before the addition of the *masjid*, the Fellowship house in Philadelphia was a multidimensional space. Despite his fading health, the construction of the mosque was directed entirely by Bawa, with funds raised by the community, and built by the volunteer efforts of Bawa's students. Those who were part of the building of the *masjid*, such as Sarah, spoke about their experience as a "labor of love."[81]

This "labor of love" was also riddled with internal challenges for some members who were struggling to associate the Fellowship with a religion. Sarah goes on to describe this further:

> It was difficult because this was going to be an outer establishment of a religion to those people. Even though Bawa had given us this very esoteric and more mystical explanation of what Islam was, building an actual mosque represented to them [an outward association with Islam] and they said now people won't come to the Fellowship because people will think we're exclusively Islamic. But this was Bawa's intention to build this mosque.[82]

As concerns continued to grow in terms of the relationship of the Fellowship to Islam and the *masjid*, Bawa discoursed on this topic to address his students' growing anxieties. Some members of the community as well as Bawa's students who were not content with this direction, nor the emphasis in outward association with Islam and religion, left the Fellowship during this time. And yet, despite the growing uneasiness from some members of the Fellowship, many remember Bawa's commencement of this new project as spiritually profound:

> And so then Bawa at this one point just very suddenly he ... had cleared the area and ... outlined the foundation line. He said, "Bring me a brick" one morning, and he said, "Call the executives and tell them I'm having a brick laying ceremony ...." So ... we had this brick brought up to his room and he became very, very serious and went into this like sort of state of meditation ... And some people were there, not a large group of people. And he said, "Alright now every one of you should say *bismillah ar rahman ar rahim* [in the name of God the most compassionate, the most merciful], and say a prayer over this brick." And he had the brick passed around to every single person in the room, and it was a rainy day. And Bawa wasn't really well enough to go outside himself, but they had a camera down there so he was viewing it on his TV in the room and he had Kabir and some Sri Lankans were here, [such as] Gnaniar ... And they had dug the corner stone which is right outside of here actually, in this corner I believe right here [*outside the classroom*]. It is also this place that they designated as the *qiblah* [direction of prayer]. ... Bawa sat in absolute silence and deep meditation while that ceremony was taking place. And you just knew that it was very significant what was happening.[83]

Because of the building of the *masjid* some early members left; others who did not agree with building a *masjid*, but were dedicated to Bawa, stayed but chose not to engage with the *masjid* project; and some committed to this new venture of adopting outward Islamic practices fully.

Figure 1.1 The Bawa Muhaiyaddeen *Masjid* completed on May 27, 1984, by Bawa and some Fellowship members. It is a Sunni Qadiri Hanafi mosque.

The Bawa Muhaiyaddeen *Masjid* was completed on May 27, 1984, just in time for Ramadan and the celebration of *Eid al-Fitr* (end of Ramadan), cementing fasting as another Islamic practice maintained at the Fellowship, in addition to the observance of *mawlid* and *dhikr* (Figure 1.1). The Bawa Muhaiyaddeen *Masjid* in Philadelphia was the first *masjid* in the city to be built from ground up, as most mosques at the time were converted spaces, such as storefront properties. Bawa's own understanding of the *masjid* was that it was "God's House," the same name that was given to the *masjid* he had constructed for Maryam in Mankumban. In the transcription of a discourse titled by his students as "Talk to Executive Committee: As One Family, Look for the Truth. This is God's House," and dated May 1, 1984, Bawa explained that the Fellowship house is a house, but the *masjid*

is God's House. Now, we have two houses, God's House and Country House. Now we look at it like a people's house. We are looking at it as a people's house. Wisdom's mother, wisdom's children, wisdom's son, wisdom's brothers; what should you see? As mother and father, those duties to the God's House or the Fellowship House, you must do your duties as mothers and

fathers of wisdom. Tell them what needs to be done. Tell them to do your
duty. Suppose we form a committee of five or ten people, but the major society is here, in the Fellowship. This is the main [center], the president and
everybody is here. We go look [after the mosque/God's House] in the same
way that a mother and father goes and sees how the children are doing their
duty, the main Fellowship should go and cover the duties of the children who
are looking after there, just as they are looking after duties here. There should
be no difference . . . People do *dhikr* here. They do the five times prayer there.
They do this. But when you go there, you have to take off your shoes, your
slippers, do your ablutions, wash your hands, legs and face, and go up. And
then do the duties that you can do there.[84]

In Bawa's discourse to the executive members of the Fellowship, he explained
that the Fellowship ("Country House") and "God's House" were meant to coexist
with each other. The Fellowship was presented as the main center of the institution beyond God's House (since the president and executive members were
established in the Fellowship House), and it was the members of the Fellowship
who were supposed to be caretakers of "God's House," but not necessarily bound
or limited by it. If they wanted to, they could go and pray in "God's House," albeit
with some prerequisites prior to entering it (i.e. ablutions and dress code). In the
same discourse, Bawa elaborated further:

You cannot beat someone into that place of prayer [such as] through anger or
compulsion. If each one wants to go with a willing heart, then they can go. Those
who want to do *dhikr*, they can do *dhikr*. Those who want to do *salat*, they can do
salat. Those who want to study, they can study. Wherever you want to go, there
is a *palli* [mosque] here, there is synagogue there, there is a church there. If not,
let's sit here and learn the *dhikr* . . . It is we who have to close the door when we
go out . . . We are the ones who open the door and we are the ones who close the
door. It is we who are the ones who open our hearts (*qalb*), we are the ones who
close the heart (*qalb*) we are the ones who make our heart beautiful. It is not the
fault of anyone else outside of us. Whose fault is it? The fault is in us; we are the
ones who are responsible. Closing and opening is with us, it is our responsibility.
So, if we open the door, the fresh air will come, if we close the door, the fresh air
cannot come in and breathing will be difficult . . . Whatever you can do with a
loving heart, do that, whatever you wish to do.[85]

God's House, or the mosque in Philadelphia, was a challenge not only for members of the Fellowship who struggled with the new addition to an already thriving community, but also for those who were outsiders seeking to label Bawa's

community. For outsiders who found this new building and its religious association difficult, he explained:

> They will criticize you. "Oh, you have built a mosque, you are all Jews, you are
> all Christians. Now you have become Islam, have you? Yes, we are Islam. Are
> you Jews? Yes, we are Jews. Are you Christians? Yes, we are Christians. Are you
> all three? Yes, we are all three." Just nod your head. If you nod your head to any-
> thing they say they will think that you are crazy and leave you in peace and go
> away.[86]

For Bawa, any confusion brought forth by the addition of God's House, or the
masjid, appears to be beyond the confines of creedal exclusivity; the Fellowship
aimed to be inclusive of all religious identities, and "God's House" was seen as an
addition to the diverse Abrahamic composition of the community in America.
According to Bawa's teachings, the *masjid* was to be viewed more as an effort
to complete the diversity of the Fellowship, than as an effort to embrace Islam
exclusively. It should be mentioned that Mankumban, or God's House, was
understood as a *masjid* in Jaffna during Bawa's lifetime, as the tomb dedicated
to Maryam and Bawa was not added till after Bawa's death by his students in
Jaffna. Despite Mankumban's dominant spatial and ritual presence in Jaffna,
the construction of a *masjid* in Philadelphia still created anxiety for the young
American community.

Many other members of the Fellowship also point out that Bawa always
intended to build a *masjid* at the farm property he purchased in Coatesville. This
property was purchased to be used as a cemetery for members who had died in
the Fellowship, as burying the dead in Philadelphia was deemed very expensive
by Bawa. Some members explained to me that Bawa suggested that a mosque be
built in Coatesville, but he was also aware that the distance between Philadelphia
and Coatesville made it difficult to build and take care of this mosque properly.
So he opted to build the mosque as an addition to the Fellowship in Philadelphia
instead.

The Professor of Religious Studies Gisela Webb writes:

> The building of the mosque was a public articulation of Islam that brought into
> high relief the question of the relationship of Bawa's teachings to Islamic prac-
> tice. Did Bawa intend a gradual movement toward Islamic religious practices
> (such as salat) as an outer manifestation of inner maturity and discipline, or did
> he intend it as a concession to the human need for unifying cultural forms and
> rituals, despite the "illusory" quality of religious distinction, or was it both?[87]

The question of whether Bawa began with the highest teaching (i.e. silent *dhikr*) and built the *masjid* to provide the primary foundations which could be "bypassed" to reach the ultimate goal of union with God, or whether the institution of *salat* was the highest teaching that Bawa was priming his disciples for from the beginning, is an ongoing debate for members of the Fellowship. Does *dhikr* supersede Islamic ritual practice (i.e. five daily prayers), and if it does, does one who fails to keep the ritual daily prayers still qualify as a Muslim? This debate about whether Sufi practices supersede Islamic ritual injunctions is not particular to the Fellowship, but rather one that has followed Sufism throughout its history. Many Sufis and non-Sufi Muslim scholars have discussed the relationship between *tariqa* (the inward Sufi path) and *shari'a* (the outward revealed law). The responses by Fellowship members, such as one must practice *shari'a* to follow *tariqa* or the former is not required for the latter, to the question (articulated by Webb) highlights a pluralistic understanding of Sufism, Islam, and spirituality by those affiliated with Bawa and his Fellowship in America. But this plurality was not limited only to his American context, as it is becoming more and more apparent.

The Preamble to the Bylaws of the Bawa Muhaiyaddeen Fellowship of Philadelphia

By the time the *masjid* was under construction, the Fellowship already institutionalized formal bylaws. The bylaws of the Bawa Muhaiyaddeen Fellowship, originally known as the Guru Bawa Fellowship of Philadelphia, state that the founder and chief executive of the Fellowship is Bawa and he is referred to as "His Holiness" in this document. In "Article III: Purpose and Function," there are three prominent sections that express the institutional purpose and administrative function of the Fellowship. Two types of objectives are listed: one that applies to those within the Fellowship and another that concerns relations with non-Fellowship communities and members. This article's "Section I: Internal Objective" states:

> The purpose of this Fellowship is to inculcate in man the Wisdom of teachings and the example of His Holiness, which reveals the purpose of the creation of man, makes known the birthright of True man, discloses the present conditions of man, and answers the fundamental questions: Who is Man? Who is God? What is the relationship between God and Man? The goal of the True Man shall be to know his Self through Divine Wisdom, to discover the Secrets that are

within the Self, to know the nature of the Soul within, to know God Who is Life within life, and to merge in God and become God-Man, Man-God.[88]

This statement of "Internal Objective" of the Fellowship encapsulates Bawa's essential teachings of *al-insan al-kamil* (perfected human being) or "God-Man, Man-God" in an official document. The formal directive of the Fellowship is not the forwarding or maintaining of a particular religion (i.e. Islam or Sufism) but rather a wisdom teaching about human perfection. Many disciples of Bawa see him as the example of this state of being, a state of being he encouraged all of his followers to achieve (Chapter 5).

If the internal purpose of the Fellowship is to cultivate wisdom through Bawa's teachings, the external objectives differ in terms of administrative function. "External Objectives" are outlined in a subsection of Article III as follows:

A. Promotion of the study, understanding, and realization of God's Truth among all who seek Truth through the teachings and example of His Holiness.

B. The compilation, translation, publication, and dissemination of the principles and practices of Truth as are or may be expounded by His Holiness. (The publication of research works, reports, or material pertaining to the Truth as expounded by His Holiness as are or may be forthcoming from the scholarship or personal insight of any member of the Fellowship may only be carried out with the prior permission of His Holiness or the successor(s). The emphasis on these writings should be confined to God and the Guru's teachings.)

C. Generally, the carrying out of all such works, matters, or things as may be necessary to attain the aforesaid objectives, including raising moneys to defray costs and expenses encountered in accomplishing those objectives.

D. Helping all Human Beings to embrace all of mankind with Love and Compassion without any separations or distinctions.[89]

The "External Objectives" promote the "study" and "research" of both "God's Truth," and of the teachings of Bawa (i.e. "His Holiness"). They also dictate the process of the translation and publication of sources, along with the promotion of activities to alleviate the incursion of debts or costs. And finally, there is a directive to welcome all individuals without discrimination and with "Love and Compassion." This mandate was reportedly authorized by Bawa to form the formal and legal constitution of the Fellowship; as such, it is notable that there is no specific mention of religious or spiritual orientations. The document suggests, in contrast to the spaces Bawa built (e.g. mosque and Fellowship house), that the distinction is not between Sufism and Islam, but rather universal wisdom and Sufi Islam. The promotion of "the study of wisdom" (i.e. Bawa's teachings), as it is written and included in the constitution, is the ultimate purpose of the Fellowship.

The bylaws also detail administrative roles and responsibilities for senior leaders in the Fellowship. In "Article IV: Administration" the structure of the governing body is listed as follows:

The Chief Executive (Bawa Muhaiyaddeen)
The Executive Committee
The Board of Trustees
The General Council[90]

According to some members, Bawa used his chief executive powers to disband this particular structure of the Fellowship in Philadelphia with hopes of revising the bylaws. He wanted to restructure it to address ongoing tensions in the Fellowship that developed between some of the governing bodies, particularly in terms of the official practices and religious identity of the Fellowship but Bawa was never able to do so; his health declined and he passed away leaving no formal mandate for the Fellowship. After Bawa's death, the members reinstituted the original structure. With the reinstitution of the Fellowship structure after Bawa's death, and no living chief executive appointed by Bawa, the Executive Committee now bears the entire weight of leading the Fellowship, at least legally and administratively. In the description of the role of the "chief executive," or Bawa's role, the constitution does allow for the possibility of Bawa appointing a "successor(s) for this task."[91] Bawa could have chosen a successor(s) to take his place upon his death, but he did not. Thus, Bawa still remains the sole authority in the Fellowship.

The Executive Committee consists of a "certain number of Presidents, Secretaries and Treasurers," and all who were appointed by Bawa to these positions prior to his death were unseated and then reinstated after his passing, by those who held the positions. The Executive Committee consists of three presidents, three secretaries, and three treasurers; and among these positions, the senior president, secretary, and treasurer are all legally required to sign official documents. If a senior committee member of a position is not available, then the second (or subsequently the third) appointee assumes the responsibilities. The Executive Committee forms the core group, and together with the board of trustees, and the general council, it forms the administrative authority of the Fellowship.[92] The original bylaws, "By-Laws of the Bawa Muhaiyaddeen Fellowship of Philadelphia," were signed by Bawa (as chief executive), Robert F. Demby (senior president), Carolyn Pessolano (executive secretary), and F. Richard Miller, Jr. (or *Imam* Abdur-Razzaq, executive treasurer) on March 15, 1973.[93] Of these individuals, both Bawa and the first senior president, Robert F. Demby (Khwaja Muhaiyaddeen), have passed away; and while Bawa remains listed as the chief executive, the current senior president is now Musa Muhaiyaddeen, an American Jewish lawyer. He was appointed after the death of Mitchell Gilbert (d. 1986), who also held the position as president. Branches of the Fellowship also function using a hierarchy of committees with appointed branch presidents, treasurers, and secretaries; and there are numerous branches of the Fellowship throughout North America, Sri Lanka, and Europe.[94] As the sites of Bawa's homes, Philadelphia remains the central site of activity and authority in the United States, as Jaffna remains the most active site in Sri Lanka.[95]

Comparing both the bylaws of the Circle and the Fellowship, it appears that both organizations emphasize the dissemination of Bawa's teachings as their central function and purpose; that said, the Fellowship categorizes these teachings as related to "wisdom," and the Circle aligns Bawa's teachings specifically within Sufism (as mysticism). There is a shared sense that future publications and recordings (any medium of productions) should focus on Bawa's teachings and a call to serve beyond the Fellowship, or the Circle, by helping those in need (e.g. orphans or the sick). It is Bawa's teachings, the publication of those teachings, and service to those in need that remain the primary emphasis in both documents in Colombo and Philadelphia. Organizational differences, as outlined by the bylaws, also exist. Not present in the document of the SSSC are any references to particular titles of presidents, secretaries, and treasurers as noted in Philadelphia. There is also no mention of specific instructions for branches (including voting rights) in Sri Lanka, as there is in Philadelphia. Based on the SSSC bylaws, it appears that administrative control over Bawa's teachings maintained in Colombo, without mention of other centers such as Jaffna or Matale. Still despite the institutionalization of the Fellowship in Philadelphia, in a lecture Bawa explained:

> They [Mauroof, Demby, and Andrews] formed a society for that purpose, to invite me here. I did not come to Philadelphia with the idea of establishing a fellowship. There is only one Fellowship and that is Allah's. There is only one family and only one Fellowship. The whole world is one Fellowship. We are all the children of Adam (AS), and Allah is in charge of that Fellowship. I did not come here to establish a fellowship, I came here to see my brothers and sisters, to see my children, this is the reason why I came.[96]

With Bawa's passing in 1986, he was buried in the Fellowship farm and ceme-tery located in Coatesville, known as the Unionville branch (farm) (Chapter 3). Soon after his death, students of Bawa constructed a shrine (*mazar*) over his burial spot to honor their teacher. Since Bawa did not appoint a successor to lead his community, it is understood that he remains the authority and thus his tomb is one way through which his students may access him. During its early years, the farm and *mazar* was initially a site for private visitation for the Fellowship members and a community space. In the past two decades, the *mazar* has transformed into a far more public space as diaspora Muslims have begun to search it out as a site of pilgrimage (*ziyara*) to acquire *baraka* (charisma) from a Sufi saint.

Conclusion

This chapter mapped the history of Bawa's influence and documented the development of sacred spaces from the *ashram* and Mankumban in Jaffna to the jungle shrine in Matale, and then from Philadelphia to Coatesville. From Sri Lanka to America, Bawa attracted religiously, culturally, and ethnically diverse followers. Many came to hear him speak, to receive food and aid from a spiritual teacher and to seek his spiritual and personal advice. In Jaffna, this first took place in his *ashram*, while in Philadelphia, his home became the Fellowship house. Bawa's final trip to Sri Lanka took place from December 1980 to November 1982; this is significant because the civil unrests of 1982 led to the Eelam Wars (civil wars) in Sri Lanka. As riots and communal unrest ensued throughout Sri Lanka, circumstances in Jaffna—where Bawa's *ashram* and Mankumban are located—proved to be precarious. This limited travel between Colombo and Jaffna for Bawa and his disciples, and Bawa never returned to Sri Lanka.

In Philadelphia, the Fellowship headquarters was a multidimensional space, but the final addition to the already thriving center was a *masjid*. Bawa's disciples were divided in their response to this new sacred space and the introduction of Islamic prayers. There were members of the Fellowship who followed the teach-ings of their *shaykh* (Bawa) without question and participated wholeheartedly in the *masjid* project; there were those who loved the *shaykh* and his teachings but choose not to partake in this new venture and the outward religion; and last there were those who left the Fellowship, stating that they had not sought Bawa to find religion, especially not Islam.

At a time of serious confusion about the religious nature of the Fellowship, Bawa meticulously fostered diversity, and by the time of his death in 1986, it appeared that he ministered specifically to parallel religious communities in America, while in Sri Lanka he tended to Hindus, Muslims, and at times Christians and Buddhists. In both localities, Bawa presented his teachings, or perhaps Sufism and Islam, in esoteric ways wherein some of the traditions of Hinduism, Christianity, and Judaism were incorporated into his framework alongside central teachings regarding the indivisibility of God and stories about the prophets, including the Prophet Muhammad, found in the Islamic tradition.

After his death, Bawa was buried in the Fellowship's cemetery, on the farm located one hour outside of Philadelphia. Initially, there was no building around his tomb, but after several meetings were held to determine how best to honor the legacy of their teacher, a shrine was constructed on top of his burial spot (Chapter 3). Bawa remains the spiritual authority of his Sri Lankan and American communities. In what follows, I take up the question of how these institutions constructed by and around Bawa have continued since his passing. How have Bawa's Sri Lankan institutions developed in a post-charismatic era? Is it similar or different to what was experienced in Bawa's spaces in America, or by his students? What practices are commemorated and who attends the daily prayers and annual celebrations? Who utilizes and maintains his sacred spaces? The next two chapters explore these questions by engaging with the parallel spaces and ritual activities in Jaffna and Philadelphia, such as the pilgrimage practices to the *mazar* in Mankumban and Coatesville. The official discourse of an institution (i.e. bylaws) is not always reflected in the lived reality. The dissonance between lived reality and official rhetoric, or praxis, are powerful signifiers of the complexities of identity and community formation. As such, the next two chapters focus on lived practices unfolding in Bawa's spaces from Jaffna to Philadelphia.

2

From the *Ashram* to Mankumban: Everyday Practices among Bawa's Sri Lankan Followers

Introduction

The first sites developed by Bawa in his ministry are in Jaffna. His community in Jaffna remains active around two essential spaces: (1) the *ashram* and (2) Mankumban. This chapter provides focused descriptions of these two specific sites in Jaffna. In discussing these spaces, I provide explanations of the features of the spaces themselves, followed by an analysis of the ritual and devotive activities that unfold in and around these sacred spaces. These accounts also consider the lives of the leaders of these spaces, as well as members who attend the ritual activities explained.

The latter half of the chapter shifts to emphasize the postwar realities of these sites, particularly by highlighting the relationship of Tamil Hindus and Muslims to Bawa and his *ashram* and Mankumban, as well as accounting for the visitations performed by foreign pilgrims (e.g. Americans and Canadians) to Jaffna, who seek to reaffirm their ties to Bawa. The chapter captures examples of Hindu, Islamic, and Sufi pieties in Jaffna. I do this not only to illustrate the legacy of Bawa's spaces in Sri Lanka, but also to set up Bawa's Jaffna sites for a comparative analysis of his Pennsylvania spaces in the subsequent chapter. The latter allows us to trace the trajectory of Bawa's communities in a transnational context, while also providing the opportunity to determine the continuities and transformations that are unfolding between the Sri Lankan and American contexts.

The *Ashram* and Its Subspaces: Bawa's First Institution

The main space in the *ashram* is the open meditation hall. Those who visit offer *du'a*s and venerate Bawa's empty bed, which sits at the center of the hall. For Hindu members, this may entail circumambulating Bawa's bed with lit incense sticks. They also venerate photographs of Bawa, positioned behind the bed, by kissing it or running their hands over it and then wiping their face or placing their hand over their heart. Afterward, members stand at the end of the bed and pray with their hands open. They offer personal prayers of devotion. Bawa's beds appear to contain the presence or *baraka* (charisma) of Bawa.

The main floor of the *ashram* opens into a courtyard that contains large coconut, mango, and lime trees, along with a small building with two bathrooms, one of which is finished in Western-style for the comfort of visiting American disciples. This veranda area also contains two small kitchen fires that are used to cook for large events. To the left of the veranda is one of the two kitchen areas of the *ashram*. Over the kitchen door in faded font is "786," the value of *bismillah* or "In the name of God, the Compassionate and Merciful" in the traditions of Muslim numerology. To the left of the kitchen door is a framed picture of Bawa cooking over a large cauldron, taken from one of the Fellowship calendars printed in Philadelphia.

A well near the second kitchen, at the back of the *ashram*, is the main water source for the property. Bawa is reputed to have dug the well himself. In many of his teachings, Bawa stressed the significance of water and all of the spaces that he created contain a source of water, such as through a well (at the Fellowship headquarters in Philadelphia and the *mazar* in Coatesville, the *ashram*, and Mankumban). The female custodian of the *ashram*, the Matron, expressed that only well water is used in the cooking that she does at the *ashram*. According to the Matron, the wells in Mankumban, the *ashram*, and the Coatesville *mazar*, all maintain mystical connections to the spring of Zamzam in Mecca that contributes to rendering the spaces holy. This mystical linkage was affirmed during one potent incident. During Ramadan when I was at the *ashram*, one of the members opened a package delivered from a disciple in Saudi Arabia that contained fresh dates and bottles of water reputedly from Zamzam. Members were trying to sort out how to distribute the water and dates between the *ashram* and Mankumban for breaking the fast (*iftar*). While sitting next to me, the Matron quietly reprimanded them and asked, "Why do you need that water when you have the Zamzam water in the well?" They looked at each other and smiled, then pleasantly retorted that as "the devotee sent it to Bawa, it [was their] obligation to distribute it." The Matron felt slighted by their excitement over the package delivered to the *ashram* from a disciple who journeyed to Mecca because she believed that the same source fed the *ashram* well. When the fast was broken at the *ashram*, it was done with the water from the well. Nur Sharon Marcus, a Canadian senior disciple of Bawa, from a Jewish heritage, and an executive member of the Toronto branch, also held, similar to the Matron, that the water found at the well at the *ashram* is sacred. On one occasion, Marcus was amazed and shocked that water from the well at Mankumban was used for ablutions, instead of curative purposes. This practice of treating the water as holy is further demonstrated by the pilgrims who travel to the *mazar* in Coatesville and fill up empty water jugs at the water pump in front of the *mazar* to take home. From the perspective of the Matron, all of Bawa's spaces, such as the *ashram*, are associated or even directly connected to other holy sites, such as Mecca.

The *ashram* contains numerous sub-rooms where particular rituals unfold. For instance, behind the stairs on the main floor of the *ashram*, there is a smaller sanctuary for Bawa. Some devotees claim that this room is especially sacrosanct. This prayer room displays a large painting of Bawa, an altar with incense stick, and a *kuthu-velaku* (an oil lamp) (Figure 2.1). There were also photographs of Bawa on the wall, as well as a banner with an image of Bawa superimposed over a green-glittered gold mosque. According to the narratives of Hindu Tamil disciples, during the height of the civil war, the LTTE and the Sri Lankan army occupied the *ashram* in turn. Reputedly, in both cases, the occupiers were scared away from the *ashram* after seeing snakes (particularly albino snakes) in this sanctuary. For this reason, this room plays a central role in the performance of varying rituals at the *ashram*. Members and devotees who regularly visit the *ashram* make sure to venerate Bawa and pay obeisance in this room; fast is broken in this room during Ramadan. The cauldron in which *kanji* (rice soup), the traditional meal with which Muslims break the fast in Sri Lanka, is placed in front of the altar of Bawa as an offering before it is distributed to those present.

The *ashram* consisted of two storys. The top floor contained two large rooms with more beds, one of which was used by Bawa. The rooms also included his personal items, such as his shoes and his walking sticks, including the infamous walking stick that Bawa used as a curative by physically striking away illness or spirits from those who came to visit. Bawa's bed is similar to all other beds at the *ashram*. They also are draped with green bedding and had a *tasbih* (prayer bead) hanging on one of the poles. A yellow toque and two small footstools with Bawa's brown shoes are also placed near the bed. All the beds have prayer rugs in front of them and a silver cup that is always filled with water to indicate Bawa's presence in these rooms. In a room upstairs, there is a window that faces the lagoon across from the *ashram* and a bed. Opposite to the bed, there is a side table with a framed *ta'widh*, a talisman for protection that is inscribed with qur'anic verses or a symbolic numerical formula; this *ta'widh*, in particular,

Figure 2.1 An ancillary room in the *ashram* used regularly for ritual activity, such as breaking the fast (Ramadan) but also for private devotion.

was made by Bawa but there are many other protective talismans that are hung around the *ashram*, including the one above the main entrance to the *ashram* to ensure its protection.

Poosai at Bawa's *Ashram*

Poosai is a Tamil word, and a variation of the Sanskrit *puja*, which means to honor and pay homage. As such, it is a word used to describe ritual performed by Hindus, Jains, and Buddhists in South Asia. Generally the *poosai*, a series of ritual acts to commemorate a deity or the divine, can be done individually at one's home, or communally in a temple. Tamil Hindus, for instance, use this word to refer to the Hindu prayers in the temple, while Tamil Christians employ this term to refer to prayer liturgies at a church. This tradition is not typically associated with the Muslim community but it is the name used for the daily prayers at the *ashram*. Daily communal prayers, or *poosai*, take place at the *ashram* twice a day. During my visit, throughout Ramadan, they occurred once in the afternoon and again just prior to the breaking of the fast. Typically, the Matron leads the daily rituals at the *ashram* and during my visit she led the *poosai* and the breaking of the fast. She began the afternoon prayers by walking through all the rooms in the *ashram* to complete her personal devotion, while tending to Bawa's room and details like ensuring that the oil lamps had sufficient oil. Completing her devotion, the Matron moved to the main prayer hall where two mats were laid out in front of Bawa's bed; one placed directly in front of Bawa's bed and meant for use only by females. (This was where the Matron stood during prayers.) In front of this mat there was also a silver pot with burning incense that slowly released smoke around Bawa's bed. Against the pillar near Bawa's bed was a separate prayer carpet near the cassette player, which was meant to symbolically mark Bawa's presence during the *poosai*. On the right side of Bawa's bed, against the wall, was another mat laid out for males. Once the Matron was ready, she played an audiocassette, the poor quality of which showed its prolonged use. The sound from the audiocassette filled the air with Bawa reciting the *Surah al-Fatiha* ("The Opening") and *Surah al-Ikhlas* ("Sincerity") in Arabic. At the completion of these two qur'anic recitations, a further recording was played of Bawa reciting a *du'a* in Tamil asking for protection and guidance. Given the poor quality of the cassette my repeated attempts to transcribe the *du'a* were not very successful. From the fragments that I was able to translate, Bawa invoked Allah's names of *ya Rahim* (the Merciful) and *ya Rahman* (the Compassionate), and concluded by calling to "the Lord of the universes" (*Rabbil alamin*). Once the recording was finished, the Matron led those present in the singing of the Tamil and Arabic lyrics of "*Engal* Bawa" or "Our Bawa":

> Precious Bawa, Golden One, our *Sheikh* of *Gnanam* (wisdom), Muhaiyaddeen,
> Let us meet together with love and praise as the Virtuous One.
> *La ilaha ill Allahu, La ilaha ill Allah* (there is no god but God, there is no god but God)
> *La ilaha, ill Allahu, Muhammadun-Rasulullah* (there is no god, but God and Muhammad is his messenger)
> As the Guru, lacking nothing, as the one complete and good,
> You show the Treasure without equal, O *Sheikh* of *Gnanam*, Muhaiyaddeen
> Chorus
> To swim the roiling sea of birth, to cross with the *Kalimah* (word) boat,
> You're the rudder, which guides us to shore, O *Sheikh* of *Gnanam*, Muhaiyaddeen.
> Chorus
> As the stag, as the doe, as the Limitless Ray of Light,
> As pure honey, as the *Deen*, you're the *Sheikh* of *Gnanam*, Muhaiyadddeen.
> Chorus

As pure gold, as precious jewels, as ruby, as pearl, and emerald,
As jeweled light within the eye, you're mingled with effulgent light.
Remain forever in our hearts, O *Sheikh* of *Gnanam* Muhaiyaddeen.
Chorus
As the grace, as the wisdom, as the Guru within wisdom,
You're the effulgence mingled with the Guru, spreading
Everywhere O Allahu.[1]

At the *ashram*, this song is one of the central features of the *poosai*. This song is also sung in the Fellowship in Philadelphia—and read via handouts with transliterated lyrics—but only during annual commemorative events for Bawa. Those who participate in this daily ritual showcase their devotion to Bawa, who, as the song expresses, is the guru of wisdom. The invocation of *la ilaha, ill Allahu, Muhammadun-Rasulullah,* in Arabic in the chorus, also highlights the focus of Allah and Prophet Muhammad in close proximity to the guru of wisdom, Bawa. At the *ashram*, then, the three figures of Allah, Prophet Muhammad, and Bawa formed the objects of veneration and devotion. This focused piety is further affirmed after singing "*Engal* Bawa" when the Matron led everyone in the singing of the *salawat* (blessings) to the Prophet Muhammad in Arabic: "*Salla llahu 'ala Muhammad; sallallahu 'alayhi wa sallam salla llahu 'ala Muhammad; ya Rabbi salli 'alaihi wa sallim*" (May God bless Muhammad; May God bless him and grant him peace. May God bless Muhammad; O my Lord. Bless him and grant him peace).[2] The *tasilya, as-salah 'ala Muhammad* (plural *salawat sharifa*), or the invocation of blessings for the Prophet Muhammad, forms one of the central invocations in Islamic communities and "pious Muslims will never mention the Prophet's name or refer to him without adding those words."[3] This practice was often documented in Sufi communities as they recited the *tasilya* hundreds of times during *dhikr*. The recitation of blessings to the Prophet Muhammad is connected to prophetic traditions, such as the *hadith qudsi*, which are sayings outside of the Qur'an that were attributed to God by Prophet Muhammad, "Do you approve, O Muhammad, that nobody from your community utters the formula of blessing for you [even] once but I bless him ten times, and nobody from your community greets you [even] but once I greet him ten times."[4] Historically, these traditions led to the understanding that the invocation of blessings upon Prophet Muhammad, through the *salawat*, meant one could gain "good credits" or seek intercession from Prophet Muhammad.[5] It consists of the "blessing formula" *salla Allahu 'alaihi wa sallam* (God bless him and give him peace), which is recited in unison by the Matron and those present at the *ashram*, at the end of all prayers. This tradition of recitation originated from Bawa himself as he ended his discourses by reciting the *salawat*. This devotion to the Prophet Muhammad, especially through the reciting of the *salawat* and the commemoration of the *mawlid*, remains one of the most critical shared ritual practices connecting the ministries of Bawa from Jaffna to Philadelphia, and all the subsequent branches of Bawa's ministry (see Chapter 3).

As I heard Tamil Hindu students of Bawa reciting the *salawat* at the *ashram*, I became intrigued and wondered if those present understood the "Muhammad" invoked in the *salawat* to be the Prophet of Islam or his namesake, Muhammad Raheem Bawa Muhaiyaddeen. The placement of a separate prayer carpet for Bawa by the pillar during the *poosai*, while the focus of the *poosai*, which was directed toward Bawa's bed, also raised more questions about who was being particularly beseeched. When I asked the Matron if she was praying to Bawa, Prophet Muhammad, or *Andavan* (God), she replied with a smile, "They are the same." Fascinated by her response even more, I enquired further about her conversion to Islam; I wondered, for example, if she attended a mosque or prayed the five daily prayers regularly. She explained that Bawa never told anyone to convert to any religion. She added that she did not attend another mosque in town, but only Mankumban. Her Islam was defined specifically by her service and prayers to Bawa at the *ashram* and Mankumban. The Matron's perceptions of Bawa, the Prophet Muhammad, and God as one and the same formed the basis of her devotion and leadership at the *ashram*. The notion that Bawa, the Prophet Muhammad, and God were all one and the same sources of divinity was expressed by the many Tamil disciples, both Hindu and Muslim, whom I met regularly in Jaffna.

Iftar at Bawa's *Ashram*

During Ramadan and immediately after the afternoon prayers described above, meal preparations began for the breaking of the fast. The preparation was a communal effort by all those present, who happened to be mostly female. Depending on who was at the *ashram* to help, tasks were assigned for the cooking of *kanji* (rice soup). As my presence became routine, the Matron eventually assigned me to the back kitchen to help the other females chop the vegetables. Initially, the four to five women preparing the vegetables were apprehensive of my presence and my attempts to cut vegetables without a proper cutting board, sometimes while squatting on the floor. By successfully cutting the vegetables without injuring myself, a minor feat, the women at the *ashram* began to trust me to complete more difficult tasks and we all slowly relaxed around each other. We began to converse regularly with each other during the *kanji* preparation. In the beginning, the topics were broad, and they were interested in why I was at the *ashram*: they enquired about my religion, my relationship status, and details about my family, which allowed me the opportunity to ask them the same questions. Through these conversations, I discovered that most of them were Hindu students of Bawa. Two of the females were siblings, and had grown up with Bawa after he healed their mother, who had a heart condition (she was also at the *ashram*, but did not help with preparations because of her old age). This was a common narrative among the regular students; they had grown up in the *ashram* after Bawa had cured someone in their family of some illness, which resulted in complete devotion to him as their guru. During the *kanji* preparations, a cassette of Bawa—reciting *dhikr*, discoursing, or singing songs—played in the background. The use of Bawa's discourses to summon his presence throughout daily activities and preparation of food was a constant. Throughout my time in Jaffna, I repeatedly found that Bawa and his teachings formed the basis of all activity in the *ashram*. Sometimes, while cutting vegetables, these women (most of whom self-identified as Hindu) joined in the *dhikr* with Bawa and repeated the Arabic names of God.

At some point, during the evenings in Ramadan, the outdoor fire-pit would be set alight near the front kitchen in the verandah area, and a large cauldron would be placed on top. The Matron would cup three handfuls of rice into the cauldron while looking at the picture of Bawa that was located in the prayer hall but was visible from the courtyard; then all those present in the *ashram* would do the same. Before beginning the sunset prayers, the Matron and the others would go into the small ancillary shrine and break their fast by drinking water from the well and eating dates in front of the painting of Bawa. Finally, everyone would take their place, either in the women's or men's section on the mats, and the prayers began. The Matron started by sprinkling incense three times into the fire pot in front of Bawa's bed; the smoke rose again and those present did the same. Some members also performed personal acts of devotions by venerating Bawa's bed, or photographs of Bawa (e.g. bowed to or kissed the bed). Then, the same cassette of Bawa used during the morning *poosai* was played, followed by the singing of "*Engal* Bawa," and then the *salawat* to the Prophet Muhammad. After the *salawat*, some of those present prostrated themselves fully and touched their forehead to the ground toward Bawa's bed. Those who prostrated themselves, including the Matron, were women. None of the males who were gathered followed this practice and it never became clear to me why this was the case.

Thereafter, the Matron went into the ancillary shrine and poured the *kanji* into bowls that were distributed to everyone present. By this point, the front gates to the *ashram* were opened so that all the waiting children, who live on the main street, rushed in to receive *kanji*. These young children were mischievous. When they repeatedly came running into the *ashram*, the Matron reprimanded them for running in a holy place. Once they calmed down, they assembled in a line, received a bowl of *kanji* from the female disciples serving it, and sat in rows to eat it. Some went for seconds and thirds. When they finished, they also took some home in a bowl or plastic bag.

Langar (free kitchen), wherein food blessed through service or worship is distributed, is a common trend in South Asia especially in Sikh *gurdwaras* as well as at Sufi shrines. The practice has been said to originate with Sufi saints as "an organized step for the welfare of the people" but those who participate in it, either via the preparation or the distribution of food, do so "to gain personal and spiritual satisfaction by making a symbolic sacrifice of a part of themselves, or they may seek the saint's supernatural assistance through these acts."[6] It is a trend that is found at the heart of communal activities at the shrine of Bawa, one which was transmitted to America. The women in Jaffna who prepared and dis- tributed the food saw their act as one of service to Bawa. The distribution of only vegetarian food, not only in Jaffna but also in Pennsylvania, is also reflective of the inclusivity maintained at Sufi spaces, such as the *ashram* and Mankumban, where, for instance, distribution of meat (e.g. beef) would exclude some Hindus.

I stayed at the *ashram* for two weeks during Ramadan, and this was the regular practice that I both observed and participated in. Women were at the forefront of the ritual activities taking place at the *ashram*. The Matron led all the prayers and broke the fast, while the other female students came afterward (from work or from tending to their immediate families) to assist and partici- pate in rituals. The dominant presence of women in the *ashram* is rather telling, as women, be they Hindu or Muslim, have limited access to Hindu temples and mosques in Sri Lanka. Since Bawa did not prevent women from being present or participating in the *ashram*, women are actively present and involved in devo- tional practices at the *ashram*. The large female presence, especially in leadership roles, is discussed further in Chapter 4 but suffice it to say here that studies of shrines or *dargah*s in South Asia have similarly noticed the significant role and presence of women.[7]

The *ashram* is also noteworthy for the way in which it houses religious diver- sity. In 1990, the Tamil Tigers forcibly expelled Muslims from the region and stripped Muslims of their land titles in the process. At this time, the land deed to the *ashram* was also on the verge of being handed over to the militants as it was understood to be a property of Muslims. Members of Bawa's community, especially those at the *ashram*, collected signatures from all of its members and brought them to the rebel leaders, explaining to them that they would not give over the land deed or leave because they were not a Muslim community. They explained that the *ashram* was a place that was frequented by all people, including Christians and Hindus. During the time of mass expulsion of Muslims from the north, it was the diversity of this small community that prevented it from falling into the hands of the LTTE. Although the *ashram* remained unscathed, Bawa's Muslim disciples were expelled during the 1990s. Many of them were displaced to camps in Puttalam. Some visited Colombo regularly, where the Serendib Sufi Study Circle (SSSC) offered them financial assistance and food.

Since the 1990s, when Muslims were expelled from Jaffna, Hindus have become the majority of the Tamils living in Jaffna and as such they have formed the main faction of Bawa's following in Jaffna. One cannot, however, conclude that this Hindu majority was strictly due to civil unrest or the expulsion, especially when considered in light of Mauroof's study. He indicated that during the 1960s attendees at *mawlid* celebrations at the *ashram* came from different religious backgrounds, but the majority were Hindu. Today in Jaffna, Hindu students break the fast during Ramadan, participate in daily prayers by reciting prayers of blessings to the Prophet Muhammad, and even recite *dhikr* individually. They do not deny that Bawa was a Muslim teacher, and they do not consider their devotion to him theologically contradictory to their Hindu identity. Sufism, Islam, and Hinduism, as they are embodied frequently share spaces, rituals, and beliefs in Sri Lanka in general and in relation to Bawa in particular. The way Bawa's teachings have been experienced and lived out in different localities, then, is varied based on the predominant religious following of a particular space and its demographic. As the *ashram* forms a central site of Bawa's network in Jaffna, it is connected to a second site across the Palk Strait. Via the Jaffna-Pannai-Kayts road to Velanai Island sits Mankumban, or "God's House," which was built by Bawa and his Tamil and American students for Maryam and later dedicated to Bawa by his students.

Mankumban: A *Masjid-Mazar* Complex in Jaffna

The Jaffna-Pannai-Kayts road is a narrow road that runs across the Palk Strait to Velanai Island (sometimes referred to as Leiden in Dutch or Kayts Island, after the main village on the island), which is located off the coast of Jaffna Peninsula in northern Sri Lanka. Velanai Island consists of several smaller villages and towns, including the major town of Kayts and Mankumpan from which the *masjid-mazar* complex, or Mankumban, receives its name. This road to the island, which runs across the Palk Strait, was reconstructed after the end of the civil war. As you drive on this road, fishermen and women can often be seen tending to their nets as they dabble in the knee-deep water, wading through the strait, or sometimes diving into the strait for seafood. Motorcyclists occasionally pull over to take a quick break during a long drive, and might even dip into the strait to cool off from the heat of the searing sun. The end of this narrow road is signaled by a military checkpoint. Now that the war has ended, this military checkpoint serves more as a symbolic presence than a means to prevent possible threats or uprising. I crossed this narrow road several times as I traveled on tour buses with pilgrims from North America, in vans rented by visitors from Colombo, or on a rackety auto-rickshaw; neither I nor the company I was traveling with were ever stopped and questioned by any military personnel.

Beyond the checkpoint, the island appears as barren land interwoven with lagoons and palm trees waving in the dry wind; cows meander aimlessly, and Hindu temples and Catholic churches are dotted throughout the landscape. This main road leads directly into Kayts, the largest of the small towns on this island. Prior to this town, an immediate left on the road takes you down a rough path, and at the end of this road is another path that veers directly onto the village of Mankumpan.

The building constructed by Bawa (Mankumban) sits across from a Sri Lankan army base on Chaddy Beach. Chaddy Beach is famous and most outsiders who come down this path do so to visit the pot-shaped shoreline from which it received its name. This local beach—with fresh seaweed mingling in the water along the shoreline of white sand—is popular among the locals and hosts a series of religious communities. For instance, tucked in further from the shoreline is a Roman Catholic church that is dedicated to the Virgin Mary. Popular narratives among locals, including my own family from this island, informed me of the church's special proximity to Mary (Mariyaa in Tamil). Some have even claimed to see apparitions of her. A few miles away, seated right on the shoreline, is another mosque-shrine complex dedicated to *Shaykh* Sultan Abdul Qadir Voliyyullah (*awliya* or friend of God) (spelling based on vernacular pronunciation and death date unknown); little is known about him except that he's dated to 1598 by locals.[8] Ahamed Kabeer relayed a story of when Bawa visited this mosque-shrine and its ancient *oli* in Tamil (saint or *wali* in Arabic pronunciation), whose tomb formed part of the *masjid*.[9] According to Kabeer's account, when Bawa walked into the *masjid*, the grave started to rumble. At the disquiet, Bawa reputedly put out his right hand and motioned the saint to rest, uttering "*thambi, thambi*" (or "younger brother, younger brother") as though the rumbling was the saint's attempt to pay obeisance to Bawa. Those present, including Kabeer, were shocked that Bawa was addressing this ancient saint as "*thambi*." According to Kabeer, after the news spread of what took place between Bawa and this saint entombed in this *masjid*, Bawa's fame began to grow in the region.[10]

This hagiographic narrative conveys that the *masjid-mazar* as an institution played an important role in this region. Saints, such as *Shaykh* Sultan Abdul Qadir Voliyyullah, appear to be seminal figures through which Islam developed in Sri Lanka historically.[11] As illustrated in the Introduction, Sufi, Hindu, and Buddhist spaces in Sri Lanka have had historical linkages, which have led to their contestations during heightened ethnolinguistic conflicts on the island. Still, Adam's Peak, Dafter Jailani, and Kataragama were sacred spaces where Bawa embedded himself and his institutions. Bawa is part of this broader sacro-spatial legacy in Sri Lanka, which was later transmitted to North America.

Bawa purchased this property on Velanai Island in 1954 because of his understanding of the geographic (i.e. land/shore) proximity to Maryam. Some of the senior disciples of Bawa explained that the proximity to the shore (e.g. water) may be the reason why Bawa selected this particular site for the construction of "God's House" or Mankumban. Some narratives relayed to me by students of Bawa expressed that Maryam's actual tomb was in the ocean, and this shore was the closest site to it. For instance, Rizwan Ali, a senior disciple of Bawa and a Sri Lankan Muslim, recalls a time when Bawa described how Maryam ended up near this island while she was attempting to run away from the verbal persecution after the death of 'Isa (Jesus); Bawa met her, offered her shelter, and promised to build her a home when he was able.[12] Mankumban was then built to fulfill this promise that Bawa made to Maryam in a different lifetime. (This understanding that Bawa's essence has existed in other forms is discussed further in Chapter 5.) Amir Khwaja, the former president of the SSSC and a Sri Lankan Muslim, gave me a similar explanation.[13] According to him, Maryam was suffering and ridiculed because people called her "mother of God" in her own land of Rūm (Byzantine Empire). She left her home and ended up in northern Sri Lanka, where she met Bawa who offered her protection and shelter. Similar to Ali, Khwaja explained that this Bawa was not the same physical Bawa of his time; rather, it was Bawa's essence, referring to a timeless *qutb* (axial pole), that later became embodied in the figure Bawa, who promised to provide shelter for Maryam. Bawa kept his promise to Maryam and built her a shrine.

Priya Thambi, the president of the Jaffna branch, also added another dimension to the sacred myth associated with Mankumban, especially as it related to Bawa. During the construction of Mankumban, Bawa laid the foundation and dug a grave, and while he lay in the grave, he seemed to fall unconscious for ten minutes. When Bawa awoke from his "sleep," he reportedly exclaimed, "This is a good place," which led to the construction of the building itself. Bawa did not construct the tomb inside Mankumban himself. Rather it was constructed by senior Hindu and Muslim leaders of the SSSC in 2003. According to some part of the reason for the construction of the tomb after Bawa's death was the possibility that this site was intended for Bawa's burial had he died in Sri Lanka. Since he died in the United States, this space has transformed into a spiritual tomb for Bawa. There is no physical body entombed at this site but the tomb honors the spiritual legacy of Maryam and Bawa. During my fieldwork, Mankumban served as a *palli*, or prayer house, that included a tomb. It was used by both Muslims and Hindu students of Bawa, especially those in the immediate region (Figure 2.2). Hence the label "mosque-shrine" which I have given to this space.

Figure 2.2 Mankumban, a mosque and shrine dedicated to Maryam and Bawa, in Jaffna, Sri Lanka.

The classification of Mankumban as a *palli* by the local Hindu members and devotees is noteworthy because *palli* in local Tamil parlance refers to a mosque, while American disciples of Bawa call it "God's House"; thus varied visitors, members, devotees, and pilgrims designate different descriptors to this place of veneration. Some disciples of Bawa believe that Maryam is buried there and therefore the tomb in the inner sanctuary becomes the focus of their devotion and veneration. Others believe that Bawa wanted to be buried here and but left something of his presence here via the grave that he laid in (over which a tomb was constructed).[14] Many of his disciples in Sri Lanka—and now America, Canada, and Saudi Arabia—recognize Mankumban to be a sacred shrine dedicated to Maryam and a place of intimate proximity to Bawa, while for the Tamil members it is also revered as a memorial for Bawa.[15] Numerous members and devotees express ideas that angels and *jinn*s (spirits) visit the *masjid* to pray at night, while others believe that the presence of spirits (even of Bawa or Maryam) will grant the requests of all prayers.[16]

Some of the local members and devotees indicated that Maryam dwells in this space and has appeared before sincere seekers as a beautiful woman. One of those who claim to have seen Maryam is Ahamed Kabeer. Kabeer describes an evening when Bawa told him to spend the night at Mankumban and that night Kabeer saw a vision of a woman. At first, he was horrified and thought that perhaps it was an evil spirit. But the figure slowly walked toward him and gently touched his forehead. Startled, Kabeer stayed awake all night (as he was too frightened to sleep) because he could not return to the *ashram* without breaking Bawa's directive that he must spend the full night on site. The next morning, he took the earliest bus back to Jaffna and rushed into the *ashram* where he found Bawa sitting on his bed. Struggling to put sentences together, Kabeer explained to Bawa that he had had a vision of a lady, wearing a white gown and of good height (she was very tall as Kabeer is also very tall). Bawa started to laugh. Kabeer was genuinely frustrated with Bawa. Then Bawa explained to Kabeer that since he had seen Maryam, he was now prepared to complete the work that Bawa needed from him. Kabeer understood this work to be focused on healing and producing *du'a*s, as Bawa had begun training him to do.[17]

The Subspaces of the Mankumban Complex

The gated property that includes Mankumban consists of several subspaces. There is a two-story building that was added after the passing of Bawa to serve as accommodation for visitors, mainly for followers of Bawa from abroad. There is also an outdoor cooking area and pavilion with an indoor wood kitchen similar to the *ashram*; these are important areas as cooking and serving food are crucial to events that take place at Mankumban. There is also a smaller complex that consists of an open hall in which people are served food after *jum'a* services on Friday and for special celebrations, such as the *mawlid*, where everyone is served a plantain leaf (as is the local custom) with a meal laid out on top. At the end of the hall, there is another room which contains Bawa's resting chair along with other personal items; this small room functions as an ancillary shrine analogous to shrines to Bawa seen in the *ashram*. Right outside Mankumban is a flagpole (*koti*) with a green flag and adjacent to it is the well from which water is drawn and used by visitors to perform ablutions before entering Mankumban. A paved path is also visible and it leads from the main *masjid-mazar* complex to the gates that open directly onto Chaddy Beach.

Like the *ashram*, the large open hall inside this *masjid-mazar* complex contains an oil lamp near the inner sanctuary. The top of the oil lamp is designed with a crescent moon. Oil lamps are a regular feature at Hindu temples and Catholic churches in Sri Lanka, and its presence in Mankumban indicates a Hindu influence. There was also a holder for incense sticks near the oil lamp. There are three smaller rooms inside Mankumban: the *imam* at Mankumban used the room to the left for his ritual prayers (*salat*) and the one on the far right was used as a storage room or for food preparation, especially for weekly congregational prayers or for the *mawlid*.[18] The center room is the main sanctuary that contained a large and elevated tomb for Maryam. (This is the "grave" that Bawa laid in, as explained by Priya Thambi above.) The tomb was draped over with a green suede *chaddor* (cloth) with golden embroidery and a red and gold border. There was also another oil lamp here. This tomb was under an engraved canopy made of wood with four poles that occupies most of the space in the room with just barely enough space for the tomb. In front of the tomb is a Qur'an on a Qur'an-stand and some Fellowship newsletters from Philadelphia. Those who visit Mankumban for private devotion go up to the front of this room and, usually, fully prostrate themselves and touch their forehead to the ground in front of the tomb. They also light incense sticks and circumambulate the tomb.

Poosui, Jum'a, and *Iftar* at Mankumban

The SSSC Colombo committee maintains legal authority of this property. It appointed a Muslim prayer leader named Bagoos (d. 2016) to Mankumban to perform the five-times-prayers and demonstrate Muslim etiquette or *adab*.

Bagoos was a strikingly tall and clean-shaven man. When I first met him, he wore a long white tunic, white pants, and a white *kufi* (brimless cap) with a white shawl draped over his shoulders, and he informed me that Mankumban was beyond any particular religious tradition. Still, over time, I found that he was often uncomfortable during daily and weekly prayers when the focus of the activities was on ritual devotion toward the tomb rather than the Islamic five-times-prayers. In fact, he was the only one who kept *salat* at Mankumban regularly.

Jum'a at Mankumban does not follow conventional *jum'a*, which consists of a sermon (*khutbah*) and communal performance of *salat*. And the reason for this was not poor attendance. During one of my visits, there were over fifty people, both male and female, gathered in the main hall of Mankumban patiently waiting for Bagoos and an East African Indian Muslim who was visiting from Toronto, to finish their prayers. Once they completed their prayers, the Matron and Priya Thambi began their portion of the liturgy, or *poosai*, which was similar to the ritual that takes place at the *ashram* daily. They played the same audio of Bawa reciting the *Surah al-Fatiha* and recited the *salawat* to the Prophet Muhammad and "*Engal* Bawa." The service also included the lighting of incense, a ritual that was not practiced at the *ashram* in Jaffna nor in Philadelphia. In this ritual, some of those present circumambulated the inner sanctuary of the tomb with lit incense sticks and continued back to Bawa's room (in the separate complex adjacent to the shrine) making sure to wave the incense stick near objects associated with Bawa (i.e. his beds or chairs). They then made their way to the flagpole outside Mankumban where those participating finally placed the incense sticks at the base of the flagpole.

Priya Thambi and another male member were in the inner sanctuary of Mankumban during the ritual but everyone else, including the Matron, remained in the large hall. The Matron stood in front of all the devotees leading the recitations as men and women sat separately in side-by-side sections. The women, who were mostly Hindu, participated in the singing and the circumambulations, as did most of the men. In addition to Hindus, there were also a couple of Christian members and devotees of Bawa in attendance along with a few children from the local village, who restlessly waited for the food to be distributed. Bawa's disciples who live near Mankumban arrived early in the morning to prepare the vegetarian meal that is served after the *poosai*.

Muslim women were also present but not Muslim men. The Muslim women did not participate in all the rituals (especially the circumambulations), but they recited the *salawat* with their hands cupped in front of their faces. They were distinguishable by their long gowns and their loosely covered hair, while the Hindu women wore ankle- or knee-length skirts with t-shirts and only some covered their hair with a shawl. Practices of covering and modesty were loosely maintained by the women at Mankumban. Female presence at, and female access to, Mankumban is generally meaningful as *masjid*s in the local region do not permit women to enter at all. But at Mankumban, females have full access to the space except for when they are menstruating at which point, just like the *ashram*, they are considered to be in a state of impurity and not permitted to enter.

Yet, this trend of female presence in Sufi spaces is not consistently maintained in all Sufi shrines in Jaffna. For instance, local Muslim men tend to attend the mosque (though it was a shrine and has a historically Sufi lineage, this is not emphasized now, as this is now a non-Sufi community) of *Shaykh* Sultan Abdul Qadir Voliyyullah, next to Mankumban, for Friday prayers. Women are not permitted to enter this mosque, so the wives of some of these men attend Mankumban. Afterward these men meet their wives at Mankumban and partake of the free meal offered. The access offered to women meant that they were at the forefront of all the activities that took place at Mankumban, especially the preparation of meals even though some men assisted with cooking. Once the main *poosai* is completed, food is served on plantain leaves in the food hall. All the males were served first and then all the females. There seems to be no religious reason for this, and it was more likely a reflection of a gendered practice of the dominant culture. Then fruit, cookies, and sweets were presented as offerings in front of the tomb, and then they were distributed to those present as small bags of *prasad* (blessed food) to take home.[19]

Iftar was also kept at Mankumban, just as it was at the *ashram*. Compared to those who attended the weekly Friday meetings, *iftar* was attended by a much smaller group of locals (around ten), mostly Tamil Hindus and women. Bagoos was present but, as usual, he did not participate in the acts of veneration, such as the lighting of incense, which were completed by the Tamil Hindus. However, Bagoos led the recitations of prayers during *iftar*. The same ritual acts described during the Friday *poosai* unfolded to mark the end of fasting during Ramadan. After the completion of the *salawat*, dates were passed out to everyone present to break the fast. Thereafter, those gathered walked over to the pavilion near the outdoor kitchen where *kanji* was prepared and served by local female disciples of Bawa.

Typically, a large cauldron of *kanji* was placed in front of the tomb in Mankumban, just as it was taken to the *ashram*'s smaller ancillary shrine in front of the altar for Bawa. In both instances, the cooked *kanji* was first offered to the holy figures prior to distribution; at the *ashram*, it was first offered

Figure 2.3 The memorial tomb for Bawa and Maryam in Mankumban, taken June 2016.

to Bawa, and at Mankumban, it was offered to Maryam and Bawa. One can equate this offering and distribution to the practice of *prasad* at Hindu temples, a tradition that would be familiar to many of the Hindu participants. The serving of *kanji* at Mankumban and the *ashram* is similar in that it only takes place during Ramadan, whereas at the Fellowship in Philadelphia, *kanji* is cooked during Ramadan to break the fast daily. Otherwise, at Mankumban, meal preparation and distribution takes place only on Friday at lunch time for *jumʿa*, or during the *mawlid* for Prophet Muhammad and al-Jilani (Figure 2.3).

Between Hindus, Muslims, and Christians: Sharing Spaces at the *Ashram* and Mankumban

In postwar Jaffna, both the *ashram* and Mankumban experienced a revival in ritual activity including visitations from foreign pilgrims as discussed below. Both Priya Thambi and the Matron explained that their practice of Friday afternoon prayers began after the war had ended in the region. Bawa did not institute this weekly practice when he was alive. Instead it commenced as a means to reinvigorate this particular site and to discourage squatters. This was a real concern at the time as the army had attempted to move onto this property but leaders quickly moved to advertise weekly events to ensure that a regular presence of devotees would indicate that the space was being utilized. Due to this relatively new practice of weekly prayers and the greater presence of Hindu participants after the war, the SSSC in Colombo appointed Bagoos to Mankumban in the hopes of instituting communal Islamic prayers and traditions. However, the SSSC was not quite successful in "Islamicizing" Mankumban. Rather Bagoos led Islamic practices, while Hindus members attended commemorations (i.e. *mawlid*) or implemented their own practices in the same space. Bagoos did not participate in the *poosai*. When he completed his *salat*, he retired to his room. Once when we connected after the *poosai*, Bagoos explained that he was uncertain about many of the rituals taking place at Mankumban, adding that they were not Islamic in nature. The neighboring mosque, which had been a *masjid-mazar* complex, regularly complained about the "heretical" or "idolatrous" practices that were unfolding at Mankumban. These sentiments came from some local Muslims, disgruntled about the predominant presence of Hindus and the ritualistic practices such as the lighting of the incense and circumambulations, and they left Bagoos feeling unsettled: to him this was not Islam. These internal tensions between the *imam*, the institutional leader of the Mankumban, and leaders of ancillary spaces, such as the Matron and Priya Thambi, demonstrate the vast interpretative legacy of Bawa's teachings and ministry. Bagoos, the Matron, and Priya Thambi were and are all senior students of Bawa. Bagoos's comments highlight the negotiations that take place between vanguards of authentic Islam and devotees whose ritual enactments are at the forefront of devotional practice to Bawa.

Historically, studies of Islam in India proposed that Sufi saints' presence and proselytization generally was responsible for Indians' conversion to Islam.[20] However, more recent studies suggest that this was not the only way to explain the spread of Islam. Kelly Pemberton, for instance, has submitted that "most Sufi saints in the subcontinent did not actively try to convert people" and instead coexisted with other religions.[21] An oft-cited example is that of *Shaykh* Nizam ud-din Auliya (d. 1325), a Sufi teacher of the Chishti lineage who did not encourage his Christian, Sikh, and Hindu followers to convert to Islam.[22] Bawa followed a similar approach with his Hindu followers, particularly in Jaffna. Since Bawa did not require conversion, his followers in Sri Lanka are Hindus, while his Colombo followers are Muslim. These questions of conversion also depend on one's interpretation of whether Bawa was Muslim, or not. For example, the Hindus I met in Jaffna accepted that he was Muslim but the same cannot be said of all of his followers in America, as discussed in Chapter 5.

Mankumban functions via the work of the *imam*, a senior student of Bawa who identified with Islamic practices (i.e. praying five times a day), Hindu members and devotees who cooked all morning, or leaders of the ancillary spaces like the Matron or Priya Thambi, who showcased their commitment to Bawa by leading the *poosai* and preparing food to be distributed (*langar* and/or *prasad*). They all serve the religiously diverse visitors, some of whom do not even know Bawa, such as the young children, as they also do at the *ashram*. These visitors come to share in the *baraka* (and/or *darsan*, viewing the divine) they perceive at the place or to partake in a free meal. Despite their differences, the leaders, members, and the devotees share in their faith (*nambikai*) in Bawa, which drives their participation in the ritual and commemorative practices, forming parallel congregations while maintaining uniform adherence to Bawa and his legacy, a pattern that is evident in Pennsylvania as well (Chapter 3).

The way their faith in Bawa manifests in rituals and religious identities is similar to the tendency that Afsar Mohammad found in his study of Shi'i and Hindu communities in Andhra Pradesh, where devotees stressed "total surrender to the *pir*" as "*prapatti or iman*" or in Tamil as *nambikai* through "*bhakti* and *ibadat*," or devotion as central to their participation in Sufi communities.[23] This belief led to the "combining" of "devotional traditions." In Mohammad's study, these actions of devotion included the "local and localized manifestations of Islam, South Indian Hindu temple practices, devotion to Islamic holy persons, [and] the idea of shared pilgrimage between Muslims and Hindus."[24] Dominique-Sila Khan further challenges these plural identities in the South Asian milieu in her case study of Ismaili communities, another Muslim tradition that has been influenced heavily in its South Asian context by Hindu linguistic, mythic, and ritual traditions.[25] Khan writes that "faith will certainly always remain a strictly personal matter that no material power can ultimately manipulate" and it is this faith that forms the basis of shared spaces and rituals among diverse religious followers, similar to Mohammad's study.[26]

The centrality of faith (*iman* or *nambikai*), and not religious identity, in shaping acts of veneration was represented to me in the field during an emotionally charged conversation with another of Bawa's Tamil Hindu followers. Nayani and I were sitting in the small room beside the inner sanctuary in Mankumban seeding pomegranates when I asked her how she had heard about Bawa.[27] As we sat there working, she nonchalantly relayed that during the height of the ethnolinguistic conflicts in Jaffna, there was an incident when the army had come searching the area for Tamil males who might be affiliated with the rebel movement, the LTTE. She explained that this *palli* (Mankumban) was one of the spaces that many locals used as a hideout for safety. On this occasion, during a search for rebels, her family hid at Mankumban. She expressed that there were so many people that individuals were piling up on top of each other in an effort to hide from the incoming raid. But the army came into the mosque, took all the men, and slaughtered them including some male members of her own family. As she unearthed herself from the pile of bodies and regained some sense of what had happened, she realized that she was still alive. It was at this moment that she started having *nambikai* in Bawa, a holy figure she never physically met.

This story of Nayani captures a far different narrative of the reality of Bawa's community in Jaffna in contrast to the experience of Bawa's American followers who encountered their teacher with the luxury of spiritual experimentation and seeking. She felt that she was dependent on his grace to survive the violence of a civil war, and so she committed herself to this guru who protected her. These narratives only begin to capture the far more traumatic stories of the members who form this contingent of Bawa's communities in Sri Lanka. Their survival, as they understand it, was granted because of Bawa's protection. It is this that forms a part of their understanding of Bawa as a figure with close proximity to God. In contrast to Bawa's American students (not necessarily non-Fellowship pilgrims or visitors who do not make such a pilgrimage to Jaffna), these experiences of war and survival pave a radically dissimilar path of devotion for the followers of Bawa in Jaffna or in Sri Lanka at large. The otherness of the *ashram* and Mankumban is validated by the experiences of these students of Bawa. They view the sacrality of the spaces as originating from their connection to Bawa, who serves as their conduit to the divine; the same divinity that protected them during a war. The war in Sri Lanka led to the transformation of Bawa's spaces for his followers. They evolved within the same culture in different ways and integrated different dimensions of the wider culture into singular spaces. These multidimensional aspects of Mankumban are both suffering and salvation, both death and new life.

The predominant presence of Hindus at Mankumban has also led to the institutionalization of new Hindu practices. For instance, at Mankumban, local Hindus commemorate Hindu religious holidays according to the Tamil calendar. During *karthigai deepam*, or the festival of the lights, small clay oil lamps are lit and used to decorate homes or temples in Tamil Hindu tradition. This event usually falls in the Tamil month of *karthigai* (mid-November–mid-December) and takes place when the moon aligns with a series of auspicious constellations that signify Lord Murukan, who is in turn associated with Bawa whose

Hindu followers gave him the title "*Qutb* Murukan." In December 2014, Bawa's Hindu devotees decorated Mankumban for this festival. It is these moments of embodied and negotiated religiosity that captures the complex ways of being Sufi, Hindu, and Muslim in Sri Lanka, especially at the crossroad of local culture. In the context of the American Fellowship, it is pertinent to highlight that the diversity and pluralism that has traditionally been viewed in scholarship as a general feature of American Sufism is well rooted in the tradition of Bawa's first spaces in South Asia. It thus behooves us to ask how much of the Fellowship's religious diversity in the American context is a reflection of Bawa's ministry, which was formed in Sri Lanka?

Pilgrimages to Bawa's Spaces in Sri Lanka by the Members of the Fellowship

A revival of Bawa's institutions has also been aided by increased pilgrimages to Sri Lanka since the end of the civil war with pilgrims visiting from the United States, Canada, England, and Saudi Arabia. Although I speak mainly of pilgrimages made by North Americans and Sri Lankan Muslims who live in Saudi Arabia in the sections below, there are also instances of Muslims from Colombo and followers from Jaffna who travel to Philadelphia. Some pilgrims visit because they have family members who live in cities close to Philadelphia. Others go to honor Bawa's grave in Coatesville. This movement from Sri Lanka to North America is far less the norm due to financial constraints and the difficulty of acquiring visas to the United States, but Sri Lankans who reside in other countries such as Saudi Arabia or England tend to visit sacred sites associated with Bawa in Jaffna and Pennsylvania, annually or biannually. On the other hand, many members of the Fellowship take individual trips to Sri Lanka that usually involve a visit to the *ashram* and Mankumban. Some even stay at the *ashram*, or the lodging spaces that are available at Mankumban, while others stay at nearby hotels depending on personal preferences. The aim of these visits is to spiritually reconnect with Bawa through his spaces.

In August 2013, there was a group of Fellowship members who were participating in a pilgrimage to Sri Lanka. The group consisted of members of the Fellowship from various branches, such as Toronto and New York, but also included members from Saudi Arabia and Colombo. This particular group consisted of about twenty members including families with young children and those traveling individually; some had traveled to Sri Lanka previously on a similar itinerary, while for others it was their first visit. Those who were traveling to

Sri Lanka for the first time made sure to stop and visit tourist sites (such as the beach) as part of their pilgrimage route, but their trip was mostly centered on the places associated with Bawa including the SSSC center in Colombo for their Sunday morning meetings and a stopover in Jaffna for a few days to visit both the *ashram* and Mankumban.

On the first day of visiting the *ashram*, the pilgrims were greeted with *salaam*s and handshakes by Bawa's Hindu students who were at the *ashram*. Upon their arrival at the *ashram* most of the pilgrims went directly to Bawa's rooms upstairs and spent time in private devotions; some running the *tasbih* through their fingers while others embraced the bed of Bawa, or leaned against it, for the entirety of their time there. Hussein, a Pakistani Canadian Muslim, was one of the pilgrims present during this trip. Hussein's father came to the Fellowship through his connections to one of Bawa's senior disciples who now resides in Saudi Arabia. They met each other in Toronto while Hussein's father was visiting and eventually Hussein's family was introduced to Bawa. This was Hussein's first time traveling to Sri Lanka. I did not get a chance to speak with him during our travels as a group. However, we reconnected in Toronto, and he shared his experiences:

> The real experiences began as we headed to Mankumban and Jaffna. This was in the North of the country where we [went] to see Bawa's first Fellowship. The area of Jaffna was where the heaviest and most brutal of the fighting occurred during the thirty years or so of civil war. I'm speaking of bombed out buildings and bullet holes all over every building. You'll see whole swathes of land where buildings were completely erased with just a hint of their foundations left. It was in this area where we found Bawa's Fellowship. Untouched. This was a miracle in and upon itself as literally next door was a home that had been shelled and fired upon. It was blackened from fire and shrapnel. The green colour of Bawa's Fellowship stood in stark contrast to its surroundings. Inside, it was cool and refreshing which was also a difference from outside where the weather was hot and humid. Bawa's Fellowship was an amazing and beautiful place to see with one's eyes.[28]

Hussein was obviously taken by the contrast between the residue of war and his immediate surroundings. Once he and the rest of his group arrived at the *ashram*, Hussein continued to explain what he felt once he entered Bawa's room on the second floor:

> It had a peacefulness that was astounding and a constant breeze blew through one of Bawa's rooms . . . . The members of the fellowship [*ashram*] were amazingly sweet and generous. Always smiling and had a spark of happiness with whatever

they did or say [*sic*]. I spent a good amount of my time sitting in Bawa's room giving my *salaams* and repeating the *du'a* of: "Ya Baghdadiy Shaykh Sultan Faqir Muhaiyaddeen, Abdul-Qadiril-Jilani *radiyallahu 'anhu'*"—or "O' Baghdadi, King of Shaykhs, Pauper Muhaiyaddeen, slave of the Almighty, Abdul-Qadiril-Jilani, may Allah be pleased with him." I did not know why I repeated this as this is part of the morning *dhikr* that I do, however, it felt right to be in that hallowed room with its light and giving my blessings and *salaams* to Bawa. Bawa is my Father, my Master, and my *Shaykh*. The Emerald jewel of my Heart and the Emerald light of my Eyes. He who pulled me out of the Fire, wrote upon my hands, and took me under his protection . . . This is my mantra and my belief and my connection to Bawa and for this *du'a* to pop into my head was what felt right.[29]

Both Nayani, who survived a raid at Mankumban, and Hussein, in crossing of the threshold into the *ashram*, felt that time was altered. For Hussein, his time in Bawa's room was climatic, and an experience that was set apart from those he had at the Fellowship in Philadelphia. He was also moved by the disciples he met in the *ashram* but it was his time in Bawa's room that served as the superlative moment for him; he recited portions of the morning *dhikr* that was completed by the Fellowship in Philadelphia. In doing so, he reaffirmed his relationship with Bawa, who was not only his master and *shaykh*, but something far more personal, the "Emerald jewel of my Heart and the Emerald light of my Eyes." For Hussein, Bawa was the source of continual guidance and with Bawa's presence in the "hallowed ground" of the *ashram*, this intimate relationship with Bawa was solidified. Such examples of personal devotion at the *ashram* by pilgrims capture the purpose and practice of visiting the *ashram*. Each individual pilgrim set their own protocol in how they navigated the space, but it is the reorientation of time that was a fundamental aspect of the experience of that space.

Once most of the pilgrims finished their personal rituals of veneration in Bawa's room, they came downstairs and headed back onto the tour bus to Mankumban. On my way out with these Fellowship pilgrims, I noticed that it was time for *poosai* at the *ashram*. Those at the *ashram* laid extra mats on the floor in the main meditation hall (where Bawa's bed is ornamented) and were standing and waiting for the pilgrims to join them for prayers but the pilgrims all rushed out without taking notice. The pilgrims generally do not partake in the prayer practice of the locals. In such a moment, it becomes evident that spaces like the *ashram* and Mankumban are simultaneously "mythic" spaces for pilgrims and "real" everyday spaces for the Hindu students who tend to it on a daily basis and as such, these groups form parallel congregations.[30] Heterotopias, such as the *ashram* or Mankumban, are "effectively enacted" and functionally reflect an imagined ideal; and like Foucault's mirror wherein the real and mythic are inverted, the heterotopia of the *ashram* or Mankumban became spaces in which the inversion of realities and myths are actually dissonant and parallel to one another, even though they both occupy the same space.[31] North Americans who came from a particular Muslim understanding of Bawa did not unite together in prayer with Hindu students of Bawa in Jaffna. This group of pilgrims, who were students of Bawa and mostly South Asian Muslims, did not perform *salat* together, as they traveled on their pilgrimage (although they might have completed their required prayers on their own time). These parallel dynamics are best captured by Sarah's comments.

Sarah, a senior member of the Fellowship in Philadelphia, who converted to Islam, described her own trips to Mankumban and her experience of their *jum'a* prayers, which had "the Islamic flavor and the Hindu flavor," but she negotiated these flavors based on Bawa's teaching that Mankumban was an "open space of prayer" or "God's House."[32] Sarah was also quick to indicate that other travelers had trouble with these "flavors" of ritual:

> So, if you were a Muslim going there expecting it to be like [here in Philadelphia . . .] you might find fault or you might not. I don't know. Some Muslims do go out there and maybe I think if they understand Bawa and they love Bawa then they know the value and the purity of what exists there. And they would just do their prayers and have that understanding but I think if there is a more fundamental sort of trend in Sri Lanka that they would probably find fault with that and they are trying to protect Mankumban from that actually.[33]

Sarah highlights the dynamic between Bawa's North American and Sri Lankan followers and their varied perceptions of Mankumban, especially as it is associated with Islamic etiquette or *adab*. Sarah, despite the diversity of the practices and devotees, negotiates these propensities based on the personage of Bawa himself, who personified this diversity, but this has not been the case for everyone who visits these sites regularly.

When the pilgrims arrived at Mankumban, Bagoos waited by the gates to the complex. The pilgrims were solemn and soaked in the pilgrimage experience, as Mankumban was the main site that they longed to visit due to its signification of both Bawa and Maryam. After entering the complex, the pilgrims went directly to the well outside the main building and used the well water to wash their feet and faces, while others drank it. Then they took off their shoes and walked into "God's House." In the inner sanctuary of the tomb, the pilgrims again performed individual acts of piety and devotion. Everyone also stood around the tomb for Maryam and Bagoos led the recitation of *Surah al-Fatiha* and the singing of the *salawat* to the Prophet Muhammad. Many of the pilgrims were emotional. Some wept in response to what they claimed was the state of being overwhelmed, whereas others wept at the realization of their prayer to visit this sacred space. They meticulously planned this journey and, in some respects, they endured many challenges to travel to and through this unfamiliar land. Thus, crossing the threshold at Mankumban was the pivotal moment of effort, success, answered prayers, and special graces for a journey fulfilled. Most of those gathered bent down, kissed, and hugged the tomb covered in the green-gold embroidered *chaddor*. Some of the female pilgrims kissed it repeatedly on all ends as they circumambulated the tomb and hugged the pillars of the canopy that rose above the tomb. Hussein, who described being in a state of deep elation and contemplation wherein time was intensified, remembered that

> the drive to Mother Mary was amazing at night as it felt like we were crossing a different land one that was untouched and removed from the world. We passed through army checkpoints and finally we got to edge of the ocean where Mother Mary is. Filled with trees and an unusually cooling breeze, throughout Jaffna I only felt this breeze when in Bawa's room and then in Mother Mary's *mazar*. I tasted the sweet miraculous waters that filter from the ground. It was amazingly sweet. I gave my *salaams* and greeted Mother Mary and kissed the four corners of her grave and thanked Ya Allah, the Rasul, and Bawa for giving me permission to see Mother Mary. I smelled oud and a flower that I can't remember its name on her grave and in the room . . . It felt like redemption. It felt like a thousand bricks were being lifted off of my back and it felt as if Mother Mary herself was saying, "It's gonna be okay. It's gonna be alright. I love you."[34]

Hussein's journey began with a visit to Bawa's *ashram* and ended with "redemption" at the tomb of Maryam, wherein he felt that Maryam was personally lessening his burden for a journey he took a vow to complete.

The pilgrimage group traveled to the *mazar* several times together during this particular trip. Most times, pilgrims who spent time in the inner sanctuary were emotional and often tearful. And although there were moments of communal prayers, such as the singing of the *salawat* to Prophet Muhammad or the recitation of *Surah al-Fatiha*, most of the devotions were individual. At times, the children of the group would go to the beach in front of Mankumban and frolic in the water while the adults in the group were praying. During these visits, the Hindu members and the *imam* of Mankumban served pilgrims water and fruit. The locals thought of the pilgrims as visitors to Bawa's home, which meant that

Bawa's followers in Jaffna and Mankumban—who are mainly Hindu with the exception of Bagoos and the Matron—were the caretakers of these spaces. And as host to these visitors, they believed that serving Bawa's guests was like serving Bawa himself.

For some of the pilgrims, visiting the shrines inspired much individual and collective self-examination. During downtime, some members would gather on the verandah of the hotel near the garden and informally discuss their experiences of the trip. They also used this time to engage in dialogue on Sufism and their purpose for participating in this particular pilgrimage. Some of this informal discussion touched upon the difficulty of explaining to family members why travel to such places was a part of their Islamic faith. Some even had to explain Bawa's significance to their immediate relations. Most of the members on this trip were predominately South Asians who had come to Bawa and the Fellowship after his passing. They were Muslims prior to encountering Bawa. New disciples interested in the Fellowship are not Hindu, but mainly Muslims and Christians, who are culturally East African Indians, Indians, and Pakistanis. As such, their new understanding of Islam and spirituality through Sufism was difficult for some families of new devotees to grasp. In this regard, their expedition went beyond the physical and emotional acts of veneration at sacred spaces; it included gatherings across numerous hotel lobbies and penthouse roof tops for collective contemplation and discussion. Some of these conversations consisted of trying to fathom what being a Sufi really entailed and the role of shrines such as Mankumban.

One pilgrim suggested that going to places like Mankumban was based on a wish to receive inspiration, while others expressed that it was in order to receive graces or blessings. Another pilgrim even quoted the South Asian mystic and poet Kabir, "Not *mandir*, church or mosque your temple is within you."[35] But if this was truly the case, why did they travel physically when the journey should be within? In response to this query, another quoted the famous *hadith qudsi* in which God states, "Take one step towards me, I will take ten steps towards you. Walk towards me, I will run towards you." This was an allusion to the fact that their presence here was indicative of the step that they were taking in order to get closer to God. Throughout their travel, pilgrims were concerned with their spiritual state and trying to understand Sufism while negotiating the clash between their own inherited sense of Islam with the newfound teachings of Bawa, one which was preserved mostly by Hindus in his homeland. As seekers, they were deeply engaged with the endeavor to grasp Sufism and the classic Sufi question, how should one be practically absorbed in God? In this regard, they were not too different from their Hindu counterparts who share their space and also seek Bawa's grace through their everyday devotion.

Since John Eade and Michael Sallnow suggested that shrines do not have inherent meanings but rather are sites upon which competing meanings are projected, scholars have turned toward understanding sites of pilgrimage in terms of contestation and convergence rather than in terms of Victor Turner's notion of collective feeling or *communitas*.[36] Anthropological studies have heavily gleaned from Victor Turner's theories of "communitas" and "liminality" in the study of ritual and pilgrimage. Collective experience and passage from the mundane world to the sacred through structure and ritual has been challenged by pilgrimage studies in regions of South Asia, where "interconfessional" rituals and pilgrimages contest the homogenous experience of communitas. Eade and Sallnow contend that it is the "universalistic character: its capacity to absorb and reflect a multiplicity of religious discourses, to be able to offer a variety of clients what each of them desires" that enables a shrine to function.[37] This capacity to absorb multiple religious narratives is evident at the *ashram* and Mankumban in Jaffna. The variety of Bawa's followers who share his spaces include Tamil Hindu followers as well as American Muslim and non-Muslim pilgrims, and this trend of parallel congregation is evident in Bawa's *mazar* in Coatesville, the topic of the next chapter.

Conclusion

Similar to the *ashram*, the prayer leaders at Mankumban were direct disciples of Bawa at some point in time. Some people who attended the prayers were also students of Bawa when he was alive, but most attendees were devotees from two or more generations after a grandparent or parent was healed by Bawa. These disciples with familial connections to Bawa are the ones who attended most regularly and maintained active devotion to their guru as they helped with preparation for *jum'a, poosai, iftar,* and other regular events, such as the *mawlid*. For them, Bawa's spaces are the only spaces through which they can maintain access to his presence. The narratives of some of these members who form the Jaffna communities of Bawa differ noticeably from the North American community but both of these groups experience a reorientation of time at Bawa's spaces (for example, Nayani and Hussein).

The consistent activity in the overall rituals at the *ashram* and Mankumban is the singing of the *salawat* to Prophet Muhammad, a pattern that appears at the

Fellowship in Philadelphia as well. The recitation of the *tasliya*, or the blessing upon the Prophet Muhammad, is a meaningful form of piety among Sufi communities. It was sung by all those who attended, as was the song "*Engal* Bawa," in honor of their teacher, Bawa. In northern Sri Lanka, unlike in Philadelphia and in the other branches of Bawa's communities such as Colombo, Bawa's discourses do not form the center of everyday ritual activity. But Bawa is the key and center of veneration as is evident from the reverence and attention that his personal items (e.g. beds and shoes) receive both in acts of piety by devotees and during institutional/communal rituals. Spiritual activity is still directed and guided by Bawa, as recordings of Bawa reciting *Surah al-Fatiha* and *Surah al-Ikhlas* form the core of the ritual activity at the *ashram* and Mankumban. Aside from God, Prophet Muhammad, and Bawa, devotion in Jaffna, especially Mankumban, is also concentrated in the idea of Maryam about which more is said in Chapter 4.

In spite of major differences in terms of cultural and political experiences of Sri Lanka, among Bawa's senior students, such as the Matron, Priya Thambi, and Bagoos, there are still similar struggles as it relates to questions of authentically following the teachings of Bawa be it through the performance of Islamic practices (Bagoos) or through the performance of devotion (*poosai* by the Matron and Priya Thambi). The ways in which students and followers of Bawa in Jaffna perform devotion to Bawa and/or God may also define the performer's respective identification with Islam and/or Hinduism. Among the immediate leaders there are certain disagreements about interpretations and performances of ritual activity. For instance, the *imam* at Mankumban, Bagoos, did not approve of many of the rituals that took place among Hindu students. Yet for other leaders like the Matron and Priya Thambi, these activities formed the core of the service that they had performed for Bawa while he was alive, as well as after his death. Their faith in Bawa and/or God drove them to volunteerism, like distributing food to gain blessings from the guru (*langar* and *prasad*) or to address the dire need of the food in a region where people are still recovering from nearly three decades of war.

Most of the disciples of Bawa that I met in Jaffna are contending with a postwar reality. Throughout the height of the civil conflict, both the *ashram* and Mankumban were, each in turn, abandoned or used as a place of refuge for families immobilized by the war. In their survival stories, Bawa's students marvel at the fact that his spaces remained untouched when the homes around the *ashram* and Mankumban were destroyed. They attributed this marvel to Bawa's protection. For these students, their survival after years of war, trauma, and poverty is attributed to their devotion to Bawa.[38] This was also a consistent narrative among Bawa's Jaffna followers, but a reality that is not a part of the experiences of the students from Philadelphia. At the same time, since the end of the civil conflict, many more of Bawa's disciples from Canada, the United States, and Saudi Arabia are making pilgrimages to these centers to experience the origins of Bawa's ministry. This trend increases the interaction between non-Tamils and Tamils, who usually do not pray together, leading to the formation of parallel congregations, because of the localized nature of the veneration of Bawa, especially in contrast to the typical Islamic practice of North American pilgrims. These interactions could, and did, lead to moments of discomfort or obvious difference. For example, the incense, oil lamps, and *poosai* are alienating to those not culturally and religiously familiar with them. And the pilgrims and the locals present at the *ashram* came together for meals but language was a severe barrier for any interaction even though, during my time there, I could serve as a translator between the Tamil- and English-speaking groups. This difficulty aside, the reality is that the visits, presence, and efforts of North American disciples have always been part of the narrative of Bawa's communities in Jaffna, from helping to build the *ashram* and Mankumban in the first place to their regular visits now.

Accordingly, local Sufism in Jaffna is particularly intertwined with the development of Sufism in North America. These intersections at Mankumban, and Bawa's spaces in Jaffna, are a part of broader complex networks of practices, rituals, and interpretations. These heterotopias, such as the *ashram* and Mankumban, have gained further sacred capital with Bawa's death. Most of the spaces have ancillary leaders who tend to the day-to-day activities of the spaces, such as the *ashram* in Jaffna. And as each space attracts diverse members and visitors, a spatial analysis of this community illustrates the depth of religious diversity and the ways in which Sufism and Islam, and other localized religious traditions, such as Hinduism, are framed through the spaces and its ritual activities. Given the transnational networks evident in the Sri Lankan context, the following chapter asks, how have these spaces transformed or been preserved from Jaffna to Pennsylvania? This question is prompted by Foucault's useful observation that the same heterotopias exist across different cultures but their utility and meaning change from one culture to the next. By mapping the changes in spatiality from one region to the next, one is better able to understand how the Fellowship emerged in America, particularly in terms of how the American students of Bawa are constructing an American shrine culture.

3

From the *Masjid* to the *Mazar*: Rituals and Spaces in the American Fellowship

Introduction

The Fellowship was initially conceived as Bawa's American *ashram* and his place of residence but since his death, it has become another center for ritual activity and veneration. His room in Philadelphia, as it is in Jaffna, has become a memorial and functions as an ancillary shrine. Though some transnational similarities exist spatially, there are also significant differences in terms of, for example, ritual activities. Following the structure of Chapter 2, in this chapter I provide detailed descriptions of rituals that unfold at the Fellowship. In the second half of this chapter, I shift focus from Philadelphia to Coatesville, Pennsylvania, to the *mazar* of Bawa, a site that parallels Mankumban. I situate the diverse facets of the *mazar* both as a vital space for the Fellowship and as a site of pilgrimage for non-Fellowship Muslims. As communities of Muslims and non-Muslims alike complete pilgrimages to Bawa's shrine in Coatesville, members of the Fellowship must negotiate the presence of these new visitors to the *mazar*, who introduce their own ritual practices when they come for the blessing of their saint. Aside from pilgrimage practices, I also describe my observation of the *'urs*, which literally means "marriage," an event that marks the death anniversary of Bawa, at the *mazar*.

The Spaces of the Bawa Muhaiyaddeen Fellowship in Philadelphia

Embodied Practices in Bawa's Room at the Fellowship

School groups from nearby universities and colleges regularly visit the Fellowship. When these students enter Bawa's room, they often ask what the purpose of this particular space might be and the responses vary depending on which member of the Fellowship is leading the tour. Some express that this room is a "museum" of sorts preserving objects associated with Bawa, such as his bed, paintings, and his recorded lectures, while others explain that this is a meditation room. The different information given to the visitors by various Fellowship members is indicative of the diverse purposes of Bawa's room (I describe the female-specific purposes of Bawa's room in Chapter 4). Bawa's room is used for Fellowship meetings and on Fridays at 8:00 p.m., silent *dhikr* (remembrance) is held here and it is mixed-gender. *Dhikr* is a central practice in Philadelphia among Bawa's disciples. It was adopted by his disciples at its earliest stages of the community's formation, even by those who did not identify with Islam or practice *salat* (prayers).[1] *Dhikr* is recited daily in the *masjid* and the *mazar* at 4:30 a.m. and it remains an essential institutional as well as personal practice for the members of the North American communities of Bawa. *Dhikr* is also recited weekly in different local branches.[2] In contrast, *dhikr* is not communally recited in Jaffna (with the exception of Colombo where *dhikr* is recited once a month) as it is in North America, though as noted audiocassettes of Bawa reciting *dhikr* are played while members cook or perform other preparatory work. Many at the Fellowship understand the *dhikr* to be central to Bawa's teachings (Chapter 5).

During his tenure in Philadelphia, and in contrast to the public discourses he gave in the meeting hall, Bawa's room served as one of the central spaces of activity where his students met with him privately, either individually or in small groups. Today, Bawa's room contains a television set that is used during events to play video recordings of Bawa's discourses. There is also a bowl that contains an assortment of candies set atop a bookcase. When Bawa was alive, he would end his discourses by distributing chocolate, fruit, or some similar food item first to the children and then to the adults. In order to preserve this practice of receiving a token or a blessing from the guru (e.g. *prasad*), a bowl of treats is always kept in the room. Today, when children come to the house, they often jet straight to Bawa's room, step up upon the small stepstool by the bookcase and search through the bowl to find their favorite confectionary treasure, only to then jet out of the room.

The central focus of Bawa's room is his bed, as was the case in his spaces in Sri Lanka. Older members venerate Bawa's bed or sit beside it, in meditation, before leaving with a candy. Many walk out of the room backward to avoid having their backs toward Bawa's bed, which is seen as a sign of disrespect. As with Bawa's bed and other personal effects in the *ashram*, his bed in Philadelphia is also understood to retain something of his presence. This room thus remains a significant space for private devotions throughout the day. When there are no rituals or celebrations, Bawa's room is the most accessible and fluid space in the Fellowship house, similar to the *ashram* in Jaffna. Many members of the Fellowship come and sit beside Bawa's bed, especially during times of trial and tribulation. Some South Asian members of the community even spend nights by Bawa's bed, similar to the practice of *istikhara* (a divinatory form of prayer or supplication) that is, coincidentally, discouraged by some senior members of the Fellowship as it is thought to signal an attachment to the earthly Bawa.[3] Others sit beside Bawa's bed and read a book from the shelf or the nightstand.[4] Family commemorations, such as blessings for a baby or wedding, are also held in this room.[5]

Bawa's room, then, is a vital space wherein activities that unfolded during his life continue to take place in his physical absence. The lack of Bawa's physical presence does not negate his spiritual presence, as evident in the way Bawa's room, especially his bed, is treated by members of the Fellowship. Bawa's room is a space in which he is believed to be accessible as he was when alive. His students gathered in Bawa's room and spent most of their time with Bawa in this room, especially as he became less well. Bawa's room was where his students, who he treated as his family, gathered. As Bawa seemed to suggest, when he called the Fellowship a "funny family," he was not only a spiritual leader but also the father of this community. As previously seen, reverential treatment of Bawa's bed was also found in Jaffna, Colombo, and Matale. These acts of veneration and communal celebrations (e.g. baby blessings) are limited to followers of Bawa and not practiced by pilgrims. In fact, for first-time, non-Fellowship visitors, especially those with inherited Muslim identities, the memorialization of Bawa's personal things, such as his bed, and the devotion to them is rather peculiar.

The Fellowship is home for some members of the community. There are several rooms located on both the second (adjacent to Bawa's room) and the third floors. The main administrative and archival office, where Bawa's discourses are stored and archived, is also on the third floor. Here, members can complete translations, transcribe, and type out work that is then published by the Fellowship Press, which is located in the carriage house in the backyard. The house next to the Fellowship was purchased in 2014 and now serves as an additional administrative and archival center. Most of Bawa's discourses, including those on video, are now on a digitized database that members can subscribe to via a weekly or monthly email list where discourses are sent out based on members' preferences. This day-to-day work of administration, organization, and dissemination of Bawa's teachings is maintained by his followers. Volunteers from the Fellowship consider it their "duty" to Bawa, and to God, to complete this work.

This systematic process of publishing is not evident in Sri Lanka, nor was this level of organization ever the case.

The main floor also contains several rooms where members reside and a bookshop that sells only copies of Bawa's books, CDs, DVDs, and paintings. There are two kitchens in the house. One is an industrial kitchen on the main floor where meals are regularly prepared, and another is on the second floor, which is referred to as the "Ceylonese kitchen" (Sri Lankan), as it was frequently used by the Tamil students of Bawa who resided in the house, and continues to be used by the Tamil members who live in the Fellowship house currently. Breakfast and dinner are a daily feature of the Fellowship, although these daily meals are not as elaborate as they are on special commemorative days, such as the *mawlid*. During weekday evenings, anyone interested in Bawa's teachings may come to the Fellowship, fix a plate of food, and sit in on an evening meeting in which a video recording of Bawa's discourse is played. Weekends and Muslim holy days—such as *iftar*, *Eid*, and *mawlid*—prove to be the busiest time in the kitchen when different families volunteer to prepare vegetarian meals. Given the cultural diversity of the members of the Fellowship, meals inevitably vary culturally from Sri Lankan to Syrian to Moroccan to many more. Families who own restaurants in Philadelphia also donate food for these events.[6]

Bawa frequently utilized the kitchens. He cooked for his disciples regularly. When Bawa was physically unable to make it to the downstairs kitchen, due to his waning health, his students brought the ingredients and materials to his room and the feast was prepared there. When he completed his preparations, he personally served his disciples. These moments spent preparing meals were teaching moments for Bawa. Cooking and providing meals to all the visitors was also a significant part of Bawa's ministry from Jaffna to Pennsylvania (*langar*) and, fundamentally, a testament to his own personage as a farmer and cook. Cooking food at the Fellowship is still understood as an act of service to Bawa, as it was for the members in Jaffna. This is evident in Philadelphia, similar to the *ashram*, where some followers of Bawa prepare meals while playing recordings of his discourses or songs in the background. Thus, for some Fellowship members, their service along with their performance of their Fellowship and/or Sufi identity may be restricted to cooking and serving in the kitchen.

Gatherings at the Meeting Hall

In the early days of the Fellowship, the meeting room served as the primary space for the congregation to hear Bawa's teachings. Bawa lectured on Wednesday,

Thursday, and Saturday evenings, and on Sunday mornings; this is a weekly schedule that the Fellowship follows even today when a member plays an audio or video
recording of one of his discourses. These weekday meetings appear to have the
fewest in attendance, sometimes averaging only about five people but those numbers may be misleading as these meetings are also streamed online via Shoutcast,
where listeners log in online from across America, Canada, and (occasionally) Sri
Lanka (a map on the server page indicates where users are logging in from).

The largest numbers of people are drawn to Sunday morning meetings, the
end of which overlaps with the noon prayers at the *masjid*. A member of the
executive committee usually leads the Sunday meeting wherein they play or read
a discourse, to which commentary is added, and discussion unfolds. Those present then share personal anecdotes of Bawa as they relate to the topic under
discussion. The extent to which the facilitator of the meeting may prompt or add
commentary is a topic of debate in the Fellowship. This contestation of how the
meetings are to unfold in the absence of Bawa is part of a trend that Mauroof
noticed when Bawa first left Philadelphia to travel to Sri Lanka. It is during
such moments of dialogue that differing approaches to Bawa's legacy, and their
impact on Fellowship practices, emerge among members of the Fellowship. The
framework for Bawa's teachings varies depending on the member who is leading
the meetings. For instance, some members have more universalistic orientations
in their understanding of the Fellowship and Bawa's teachings, which leads to
the belief that all religions—even Islam and Sufism—need to be abandoned to
comprehend his teachings. Other students feel that Islamic practices and traditions are the pillars of Bawa's message.

On Saturday mornings, there are separate meetings hosted for the young
people of the Fellowship. Children, sometimes as young as a year old and up
to 7 or 8 years old, attend the children's meetings that are led by a parent member designated for the session. Grandparents (members who are among the first
generation of students of Bawa in America) also bring their grandchildren to
the meetings. The facilitator reads a story from one of Bawa's children's stories
published by the Fellowship and then starts a discussion by providing prompts
and/or questions; this is followed by activities, such as arts or crafts. At the same
time, in Bawa's room, a separate meeting occurs for teenagers although others,
such as older members or young adults, also sit in on the meetings to share
their personal experiences or interpretation of a selected discourse. The meeting
concludes with a pop quiz, game, or activity. In terms of attendance, the youth
meetings usually consist of about five or less people, and the number of children
varies although it is often less than ten. These meetings, like all the Fellowship

meetings and the prayers at the *masjid*, end with the singing of the *salawat* to Prophet Muhammad.

Saturday morning meetings are followed by lunch, which are very popular with young members of the Fellowship as the menu specifically caters to them (i.e. vegetarian tacos and hotdogs). Members who live in the neighborhood also drop in to socialize and connect with one another. Other times, if a baby or young member of the Fellowship has a birthday, families bring a cake and celebrate with the larger "Fellowship family." The Fellowship provides community space for families of immediate members that in turn encourages many members, of all ages, to play an active role in the Fellowship. The communal space reveals that the Fellowship is a generationally inherited space, similar to Bawa's spaces in Sri Lanka. However, Jaffna did not have the sustained presence of young people as seen in Philadelphia. The presence of young people in Philadelphia is additionally evident during summer events, such as the Fellowship Summer Camp ("Funny Family Day Camp") which runs from late July to early August and takes place both at the Fellowship house and the *mazar*/farm.

Finally, for larger events, such as the anniversary of Bawa's arrival to Philadelphia, which is commemorated yearly in October, bazars are set up outside the Fellowship, traditional vegetarian South Asian and Middle Eastern food vendors are arranged along with book stalls, resulting in a large outdoor festival. The children of the Fellowship perform a play to highlight an aspect of Bawa's teachings with costumes, singing, and music. In such instances, the Fellowship becomes the site for a neighborhood and community gathering, where all are welcome from the neighborhood and many members from branches across North America travel to participate in special meetings. These meetings include special discourse sessions, as well as official business meetings, all of which are held throughout the weekend-long commemoration.

The *Masjid* of Bawa Muhaiyaddeen

At the Fellowship, ritual activity on a Friday afternoon centers on the prayers that take place at the *masjid*. *Jum'a* prayers are attended by local Muslims from across Philadelphia, who attend the Fellowship *masjid* to complete their Islamic obligation of keeping the Friday congregational prayer, without much interest in Bawa. Friday afternoons and the weekend *salat* also attract the largest numbers at the mosque in contrast to the five daily prayers during weekdays. After *jum'a* prayers, a South Asian meal is served that consists of rice and an assortment of vegetarian sides (e.g. *dhal*, or lentils, and potato curry). Most attendees pack food to take home or back to work. Those who have time to socialize do so in the Fellowship meeting hall where they sit and eat.

At the conclusion of communal prayers, during moments of formal socialization centered around food, one begins to observe racial and cultural stratification in the Fellowship. Members of the Fellowship who observe Islamic practices are mostly European American and African American converts to Islam. Looking around at those who sit and eat together, it is clear that groups tend to be racially and culturally similar: African American Muslims are gathered among themselves, as are the South Asians, and so on. The historical reality of racial demographics of the Fellowship has changed throughout the past forty-three years; it has gone from being predominately African American to European American and now hosts Muslims with immigrant backgrounds. Despite these changes, there are still undertones of racial segregation within the Fellowship, especially after Friday afternoon prayers which attract Muslims from Philadelphia. These subtle racial dynamics, particularly between African American Muslims and other Muslim groups, reflect a broader reality that includes other mosques in America. Williams, a female, African American Muslim convert and senior member of the Fellowship, shared her thoughts on racial and cultural dynamics in the Fellowship:

> You know, it's really a lesson for me, as a person who since I was—18, was involved in the Civil Rights movement, and fighting against Jim Crow or racial discrimination and segregation and all of that, and [being in] the Fellowship . . . I have very informally, sort of studied how persistent race is. And . . . it's not only race . . . in case of the Fellowship . . . it's economics too, because many of the African Americans who have stayed are poor people. And you have some very wealthy white people. So, . . . it's class as well as race, that often operates. And I know there are people who really tried to bridge those . . . gaps. And you know when I've taken African Americans there, often they cannot get past the racial composition to even stay long enough to hear what is being taught. So, it becomes . . . difficult to change the population demographics, because race is still such a prominent factor in American culture . . . As Martin Luther King once said, the most segregated hour in America is eleven o'clock on a Sunday. So, even in a place like Philadelphia, you have predominantly black mosque, very separate from the other groups—you know—be they Asian, or Turkish . . ., the mosque [are] very racially divided there also.[7]

As Williams mentions above, the cultural and racial dynamics of those who attend the Fellowship *masjid* are not based on a singular cultural or ethnic group, as may be the trend in other *masjid*s in the Philadelphia region. The congregation at the Fellowship *masjid* is racially, culturally, and socioeconomically diverse, and it is a part of a community at-large that is religiously diverse. The differing socioeconomic makeup of those who attend the *masjid*, along with their diverse racial backgrounds, are also evident within the Fellowship mosque community and have existed, broadly, within the Fellowship since its early development, as explained in Chapter 1. If one were to visit the Fellowship only during *jum'a*, one's perception of this community would be that it is an Islamic *umma* (community) with a strong South Asian and African American Muslim presence, along with a few European American (white) Muslims. Notably not present on Fridays are members of the Fellowship who are not connected with the *masjid* (and do not perform Muslim prayers).

The mosque community at the Fellowship, with non-Fellowship Muslims, Fellowship-Muslims, and Fellowship non-Muslims may be viewed as a "parallel congregation" (see Introduction).[8] The Fellowship congregation ranges from a continuum of Muslim to non-Muslim members in the Fellowship and/or attendees of the *masjid*; of the latter, some venerate Bawa and others do not.[9] The existence of parallel congregations was also evident among the Hindus and Muslims who shared spaces in Jaffna. Despite regional and cultural variation between Jaffna and Philadelphia, Bawa's spaces were consistently used by parallel congregations primarily due to the traction of Bawa's message among religiously, racially, and culturally diverse members. These parallel congregations also facilitate further networks beyond the Fellowship. For example, Muslims who use the *masjid* may be a part of the larger Philadelphia Muslim community and are not necessarily part of the institution of the Fellowship. It is at this juncture that the *imam* of the Fellowship *masjid* becomes central to catering to these parallel congregations.

Diverging Voices Ranging from Leaders of the Fellowship *Masjid* to Non-Muslim Students of Bawa

Ahamed Kabeer was one of the first two *imam*s appointed to the Fellowship *masjid*. He shared responsibility with a Syrian *imam* (Abu A'la) who eventually left the Fellowship over a dispute with Bawa. Richard Miller (Muhammad Abdur-Razzaq) or Dick Thambi (younger brother) as Bawa called him, was the executive treasurer at the time and was appointed as the head *imam* at the occasion of the fight, which occurred several months before Abu A'la left the community. There was thus a brief period when there were three *imam*s at the Fellowship *masjid*.[10] *Imam* Abdur-Razzaq was a young man who came from an American

Christian background. He told me, "I never thought of being an *imam* because I could see that was a position that entitled one to a lot of abuse."[11] Nonetheless, he felt that Bawa was slowly training him to become an *imam* from the day they met in the early 1970s.[12] Bawa taught Abdur-Razzaq the essence of the Qur'an and *Sunnah*:

> That's the whole thing . . . Bawa didn't want me to just use the same words as him because everything has to be based on Qur'an and *Sunnah*. So what you do is you take that and then you explain them in the same way Bawa did. Almost everything Bawa did was from the Qur'an and *Sunnah* but he didn't say it was from that. He'd take a point and he would explain that but once you become familiar with it you say oh that's what he was explaining.[13]

Bawa's discourses, for Abdur-Razzaq, were wisdoms derived from Islam packaged in a way that would be accessible to a wider non-Muslim audience. *Imam* Abdur-Razzaq went on to express what he understood of the relationship of the Fellowship to Sufism and Islam:

> I call it the Medina principle. In Medina, everyone was there. There were Christians, there were Jews, there were pagans, there were . . . idol worshipers and so on. So they all came to listen to the *rasul* [Messenger], there was a restriction. If they wanted to follow him that was fine, if not they did what they did and they have a pact for mutual defense of the city. And that's sort of the way it is here. I mean, the main thing is in building the community you can't reject anyone. So everyone's welcome, come, come, come, come. That's what Bawa's discourse said. Don't exclude anyone. But then people naturally started excluding themselves. He [Bawa] said at one time "over 100 000 people have come and left because they couldn't accept what I was saying." So there's a natural selection process. The same thing that happened with the mosque here. There is a selection. The people that come to this mosque are selected because the hot heads come and their feed isn't there, you know [*laughs*], they think "That was boring. They didn't talk about *jihad* and that sort of thing!" Not that I don't touch on those subjects but they are explained in the sense of classical Islam, which is basically not far from Sufism.
>
> And in Islam, it's called the *tazkirah* [reminder] of purification. The idea that there's a society of people that are Sufis without the concept of purification is a very misguided concept. So really Sufis are more restrictive in their behavior than regular Muslims.[14]

Abdur-Razzaq draws a comparison between the authority and leadership of Prophet Muhammad during his tenure in Medina, where the Prophet migrated (*hijra*) with his young community, and the dynamics unfolding within the Fellowship after Bawa migrated to the United States. During the Medinan period of Prophet Muhammad's spiritual and political leadership, Abdur-Razzaq notes that Prophet Muhammad welcomed everyone—Christians, Jews, and Pagans (however, historically, Prophet Muhammad actively proselytized to Pagans, who according to his new movement, were committing the worst sin, that of polytheism). If they choose not to accept the message of Prophet Muhammad, they still remained under his protection. The Fellowship similarly does not exclude anyone. As Abdur-Razzaq perceives it, individuals exclude themselves from the Fellowship, for example, during the construction of the *masjid*, some of Bawa's students did not want to participate in the *masjid* activities, a trend they continue today. He places Sufism within Islam while at the same time holding the notion that Islam is not an exclusionary religion. For Abdur-Razzaq, those who disassociate Sufism from Islam are excluding themselves from the Muslim community. Sufis who try to put into practice Islamic injunctions are not being exclusionary because Sufism involves Islamic practices. At the same time, however, those who take this approach to Sufism (Islamic-Sufism) do not impose their method on everyone, especially Sufis with universal inclinations. Still, for Abdur-Razzaq, the path of Sufism requires far more rigor in acts of purity (i.e. Islamic *adab* of prayer and fasting, as well as living an ethically and morally upright life), even more so than being a Muslim. When I asked whether one has to be a Muslim to be a Sufi, he replied, "No, I would say not. But perhaps to reach the highest stage of Sufism you would have to be a Muslim. Now I'm basing that not on what Bawa said but 'Abdul Qadir Jilani, who was the *qutb* . . . the highest saint."[15]

Abdur-Razzaq *khutbah*s (sermons) attract many from the Muslim community in Philadelphia. He recites from Sufi commentaries on the Qur'an, relying heavily on al-Jilani's writings and Bawa's discourses. When I asked people why they attend the Fellowship mosque and not another mosque in Philadelphia, they often exclaimed that "he [Abdur-Razzaq] recites Qur'an beautifully," adding that Abdur-Razzaq's sermons along with the overall atmosphere of the Fellowship community are the reason for their mosque preference. His popularity among the mosque community is also due to him being an American convert to Islam and the head *imam* of a known Sufi mosque in Philadelphia. The formalization of the *masjid* was not without its challenges in the early years, as Williams explained:

> It's kind of interesting how you know . . . you probably have heard that for the longest [time . . .] the Muslim Association there in Delaware, what do they call themselves? I don't know if they still even exist, but it was like an association of mosques . . . that were from Philadelphia, Delaware, and South Jersey and they would not let the Fellowship join, because they said we weren't real Muslims,

that we were worshipping a man, Bawa. You know so, for the longest [time] we were not accepted. But that's all changed, and of course the *imam* [Abdur-Razzaq] from the Fellowship is an active part of . . . associations of Muslim, *imam*s and all that there are.[16]

Abdur-Razzaq has worked not only to develop but also maintain the standards of the *masjid* of the Fellowship within the greater Sunni Muslim community in Philadelphia. He has also played an active role in the community through interfaith activities. He is a founding member of the Interfaith Center of Greater Philadelphia and serves on its board of directors. He has also functioned as a Muslim chaplain (Widener University, 2007), worked as a police chaplain with the Philadelphia police department, and is still a member of the Fellowship's Broad of Trustees. When schools visit the Fellowship, Abdur-Razzaq is usually present to speak with students in the Fellowship classroom or in Bawa's room. Abdur-Razzaq is sometimes dressed in his regalia white robe with Arab-style head covering, other times in a pant and suit, with a *kufi* (brimless cap). Because of his immensely tall presence, his meditated strides and his long white beard, which includes a walking staff during the *khutbah*, some young Muslim Fellowship and non-Fellowship members have enthusiastically nicknamed him "Gandalf the White."

Abdur-Razzaq's leadership straddles a fine line between the varying contingents in the Fellowship, just as Bagoos found himself overlapping a fine line in between the practices of Hindu followers of Bawa in Mankumban and his own upkeep of Islamic rituals. Those who hold administrative positions may only have to contend with the Fellowship in terms of its mandate to propagate the "universal truths and wisdoms" that Bawa taught. Abdur-Razzaq, though, must not only maintain this perennial framework of Bawa's traditions when he leads the Fellowship discourse meetings, but also uphold his public position as an *imam* of a *masjid* that is open to all Muslims. For Abdur-Razzaq, Bawa's teachings and the practices of the *masjid* are not contradictory. Abdur-Razzaq acts as a spiritual counselor to many non-Fellowship Muslim members of the *masjid* who attend from varying backgrounds—university students, recent immigrants, African Americans, and new converts. He must be a role model of the teachings of Prophet Muhammad and Bawa Muhaiyaddeen and a keeper of the *shariʿa*. His fulfillment of the obligations of an *imam* has solidified his position as an *imam* among the Muslims in the Fellowship and beyond.

His upkeep of Islamic precepts has at the same time marginalized him, as it did Bagoos in Jaffna, from those within the Fellowship who do not see the teachings of Bawa solely confined to Islam. Still, unlike Bagoos, who did not have a Muslim congregation but a Hindu one, Abdur-Razzaq has a thriving mosque community that parallels and, at times, intersects with the Fellowship community. It is Abdur-Razzaq's devotion to Bawa that informs his need to fulfill this position and to serve both contingents within the *masjid*. A devotion shared by the leaders and Fellowship members depicted thus far.

Abdur-Razzaq has ensured that the Fellowship *masjid* adheres to certain norms per Bawa's instructions. For example, in Philadelphia, males and females use separate entrances, and there are signs at the women's entrance that list detailed instructions on *hijab* and appropriate attire required to enter the *masjid* for prayers. There were no such rules posted at the *masjid-mazar* complex in Mankumban, where women are freely able to access the space (in a region where women are generally not permitted to enter mosques at all). For the first time, it can be said that the Fellowship community has experienced a process of *Islamization* that has not necessarily unfolded at Bawa's Jaffna sites, though attempts were made by Bagoos and the executive leaders in Colombo to take those sites in a similar direction. The characteristics that a lay observer may associate with "orthodox" Islam is far more present at the Fellowship in Philadelphia than in Jaffna: these characteristics include the keeping of daily prayers and the rules of dress and attire adhered to by males and females. In Philadelphia, during the *jum'a* prayer, I did not witness the same divergences in observance to Islamic precepts among Bawa's follower as I did in Mankumban. Although I observed a variety of attendees at the *mawlid*, *'urs*, and discourse meetings at the Fellowship, this was not necessarily the case with Friday prayers in the *masjid*, which includes Muslim members of the Fellowship as well as Muslims from the larger Philadelphia community.[17]

The Fellowship in Philadelphia encompasses the spaces of Bawa's room, the Fellowship meeting hall, and the *masjid*. As discussed in Chapter 1, the addition of the *masjid* created some resistance as some students of Bawa viewed it as marking the Fellowship as a Muslim community. This relationship with Islam and the Fellowship continues to be questioned and, even in this period of contestation, the *masjid* continues to attract Muslims who are not interested in Bawa but who need a Muslim community to complete their Islamic ritual obligations. There is a continuous presence of Muslims, most of whom happen to be new immigrants with varying ethnic and cultural backgrounds, such as Pakistani, Punjabi, Bengali, and Syrian. The *masjid* attracts large crowds on special occasions such as Ramadan, the *mawlid*, and *jum'a* prayers. The disparity in the number of Muslims who attend these events and the non-Muslim members of the

Fellowship has raised concerns about the future of the institution among some Fellowship members. Members who align on the end of the spectrum that identifies the Fellowship with a form of universal spirituality argue that Bawa did not identify the practice of Islamic rituals as a central component of his teachings. This sentiment is captured in the comments of Jane, a European American from a Christian heritage and a senior student who met Bawa in Philadelphia in 1972.

> Well . . . we don't claim to have a religion. I mean there are people here who have made it into Muslim, but it's far beyond Muslim [*sic*]. It's beyond any form. I don't have to go into that mosque, I don't. I don't have to go in there. And God knows I can sit here and say that because I'm not saying anything against [Bawa]. That's for people who need to go. People who need to go and do that five-times-prayer, the prayer has to be on a moment-to-moment basis. We're doing prayer. There is not a moment when the prayer is not going on.[18]

Jane's comment demonstrates one approach among disciples of Bawa who interpret Bawa's teaching as transcending religious forms, even Islam. Interpretations of Bawa's teachings as beyond Islam is further complicated by the arrival of immigrant Muslims who attend the Fellowship and infuse it with their cultural experience of Islam.

Sarah, a European American from a Jewish Christian heritage, is a member of the Fellowship who came to Bawa and the Fellowship in 1978 and converted to Islam. She describes the interaction between these parallel congregations when those who attend the *masjid* do not take an interest in the Fellowship activities, such as meetings on Bawa's teachings:

> Some of them do. Not as much I would say because you know there are a lot of people who come here specifically because . . . we observe the five-time-prayers and then for the two festivals, you know the *Eidis*. So, we have a huge crowd of people that comes for that. But I'd say there's a lot of them that do come specifically because they love our mosque and they respect that we have Bawa, but maybe . . . they wouldn't come in like the members who are really here seriously to study Bawa's teachings.[19]

Abdur-Razzaq, Jane, and Sarah are all senior members of the Fellowship. Even though all of them come from European American Christian and/or Jewish cultural and religious backgrounds and encountered Bawa personally during the same time, they have different relations with Bawa and his teachings. For Abdur-Razzaq and Sarah, this relationship manifested into an adoption of Muslim identity, while Jane does not identify as a Muslim and does not engage with the *masjid*. These perceptions of what Bawa's teachings are and subsequently what the Fellowship is has only become further complicated with the growth of the mosque community. Activities that once centered on Bawa prior to the institutionalization of the *masjid* were not aborted after the construction of the *masjid*. Rather they continued to thrive and did so concurrently with the *masjid* activities after it was completed in 1984, suggesting that, at least until now, one has not superseded the other.

Piety and Devotion at the Fellowship: *Mawlid al-Nabi*—Birthday Celebrations for the Prophet Muhammad

Similar to the description of rituals and activities in Bawa's Jaffna spaces in Chapter 2, in the following section, I provide details of rituals and gatherings at the Fellowship in Philadelphia. I illustrate two types of Fellowship events: Muslim rituals and prayers (i.e. the *mawlid*) and rituals that focus on Bawa's teachings and the commemoration of his life. For the first example, I provide a more descriptive analysis of my experience of the *mawlid*. The *mawlid* is a long-standing Muslim practice that Bawa celebrated with his followers as early as 1962 in Jaffna, long before the building of the Fellowship's *masjid*, which brought forth anxiety about whether or not the Fellowship was becoming outwardly Islamic. As such, it is a seminal example of a Sufi practice transmitted to Philadelphia from Jaffna. Additionally, its observance institutionally ties Bawa's legacy both to classical Islamic forms of piety and to Sri Lankan forms of devotional spirituality that surrounded his ministry.[20] The *mawlid* celebrations for both the Prophet (*nabi*) and al-Jilani, whom Bawa's followers recognize as the *qutb* (axial pole), follow the same ritual framework. For the sake of space, I only describe the *mawlid al-nabi* below.

During my fieldwork, the recitation of *mawlid* literature (e.g. poems and narratives) for the Prophet Muhammad took place from January 2 to January 13, 2014, twelve days in advance of the birthday of the Prophet Muhammad, which according to the Julian calendar that year, fell on January 14. The recitations commenced after midafternoon (*'asr*) prayers. Attendance was influenced by several factors but, in general, *mawlid* attendance is larger during weekends and Friday evenings. In 2014, the *mawlid* for Prophet Muhammad occurred in winter and many found it difficult to physically travel to the Fellowship so many listened to the recitation online via Shoutcast. At the Fellowship, males gathered and led the recitation from the Fellowship classroom on the main floor, and females listened to the recitation of poems and narratives via a television screen in Bawa's room. The meeting hall, a mixed-gender space, also projected the recitation on a large screen. That year the text presented was *The Subhana Maulid: Maulidun-Nabi (Sal.)*, which was translated by Abdur-Razzaq and Ruqaiyyah E. R. Lee-Hood, a member of the Boston branch of the Fellowship and a PhD student at Harvard University.[21] The recitation began with chapters from the Qur'an (i.e. *al-Fatiha, al-Iklas, al-Falaq,* and *an-Nas*). The first half of the *mawlid* recitations weaved narratives that emphasized the celestial light of Prophet Muhammad, which eventually manifested into the human Muhammad through Aminah, his mother. After each reading of the narrative, the attendees sang a song of blessing or praise for the Prophet Muhammad and then sang the *salawat* before the next narrative. These narratives are all recited in Arabic by males and those present followed along by reading booklets that have the Arabic, Arabic transliteration, and English. The *mawlid* recitation paused for the completion of *maghrib* prayers at sunset. Not everyone went to the *masjid* to complete *salat*. Some females completed their *salat* in Bawa's room, while others took a break and visited the kitchen or socialized in the meeting hall downstairs.

After the sunset prayers, the recitation continued. The second half of the recitation of the *mawlid* was attended by many more people than the first half as it is deemed the ritually climatic moment of the *mawlid* due to the recitation of the *du'a*, or prayers of intercession, to the Prophet Muhammad. Numerous songs praising Muhammad are sung, such as "*Hubbu n-Nabi*" (loving the prophet). Then Abdur-Razzaq read a discourse given by Bawa that related to Prophet Muhammad. After, Ahamed Kabeer led the singing of the Tamil song "*Engal Nabi Natha*" (our prophet lord) as non-Tamil speakers in attendance used transliterated lyrics to join the singing. The climactic moment occurs when everyone stands and sings "*Ya Nabi*" (O Prophet) in Arabic:

O Prophet, may peace be upon you!
O Messenger, may peace be upon you!
O Beloved, may peace be upon you!
May the blessings of Allah be upon you!
The Full Moon rose, radiant upon us,
the other moons hidden by it,
the equal to your perfect beauty we have never seen,
O, Countenance of Bliss!
You are the sun! You are a moon!
You are a Light above Light!
You are an elixir, dearly beloved!
You are the Lamps of the Hearts!

O Beloved! O Muhammad!
O Bridegroom of the East and West!
O one supported and extolled,
O *Imam* of two *Qiblahs* [direction of the Kaaba]!
One who has seen your face is blissful,
O Benefactor of Parents!
May your pure pond, serene and cool,
On the day of Resurrection be our oasis!
O Allah, Forgiver of mistakes,
and even of mortal sins,
You are the Veiler from what corrupts us,
and veil our stumblings from the gossips.
O Patron of good deeds,
and Exalter to high degrees,
Forgive me my sins,
And wipe away my evil actions!
O Knower of the secret and most hidden,
O Answerer of prayers,
O my Lord grace us every one.
With all of the pious deeds.
O Prophet, may peace be upon you!
O Messenger, may peace be upon you!
O Beloved, may peace be upon you!
May the blessings of Allah be upon you![22]

When members of the Fellowship were asked why they stood to sing this song, many explained that according to Bawa, Prophet Muhammad was present during the song. Hence attendees stand as a sign of respect to the spiritual presence of the Prophet. During this song for the Prophet Muhammad, a young child, often at the request of one of the female elders, retrieved the water sprinkler from Bawa's table and went to each person in the room. Eventually the child moved through the meeting hall and the classroom, sprinkling rose water into the palms of attendee's hands or dabbed some on their heads. Those who have the rose water sprinkled onto their hands brushed it on their face. The recitation culminated in the invocation of the *du'a*. Due to its importance, it was read twice, first in English and then in Arabic.[23] At the completion of the *mawlid* literature, the females in Bawa's room embraced one another and greeted each other with *as-salaamu alaykum* (peace be upon you). Then it was time for *'isha* prayers. Some females went into the mosque for the *'isha* prayers while others completed their evening prayers in Bawa's room. The festivities and socializing then commenced as all attendees gathered in the meeting hall to partake in food and company.

Food, again, was central to the *mawlid* at the Philadelphia Fellowship. Throughout the evening, as the *mawlid* literature was being recited, trays of food were set as an offering in Bawa's room and in the classroom where the males congregated. At the end of the *mawlid* literature recitation, this food was distributed. As attendees partook of the sweet and savory items displayed in Bawa's room, it was understood that the food had been graced with blessings from Bawa and Prophet Muhammad. Dinner is also served every night of the *mawlid*.

The *mawlid* attracts a more multiethnic Muslim (predominantly South Asian and Middle Eastern) crowd to the Fellowship, most of whom do not regularly participate in the Fellowship events that focus on Bawa's teachings. Members who are part of the Fellowship but do not observe the five daily prayers also partake in the *mawlid* as they relate to it as a practice instituted by Bawa. Their association of the *mawlid* with Bawa, rather than Islam, precisely demonstrates the manner in which these differently oriented members of parallel congregations intersect with one another. There are those who understand the *mawlid*, and other Islamic events such as Ramadan, as practices that Bawa taught and are not necessarily associated with Islam; and there are others, especially non-Fellowship Muslim immigrants, who know of events like the *mawlid* for Prophet Muhammad from an Islamic cultural and religious experience via an inherited Muslim identity and Old World Islam.

Bawa instituted the *mawlid* at his *ashram* in Jaffna and this tradition is maintained by Sufi Muslims in Sri Lanka, especially those with affiliations with the Qadiriyya. Hindu disciples and devotees of Bawa participated in the *mawlid* at his *ashram* because of their devotion to Bawa and the ritual's ability to grant access to the (a) divine grace. This practice traveled with Bawa to Philadelphia and was further instituted as a core ritual within the Fellowship. Now American disciples of Bawa host the *mawlid* yearly in Philadelphia, and welcome predominately Muslim immigrants and American-born Muslims, who bring their own understandings of the *mawlid* with them. In the scholarship of Sufism in America, at times, the Fellowship has been treated as an alternative form of Islamic spirituality or as a non-Islamic Sufi community. However, these labels are reductive and fail to capture the nuances of religious experiences in the Fellowship, particularly during rituals such as the *mawlid*. During the *mawlid* described above, non-Muslim Fellowship members and non-Fellowship Muslim members all participate in the commemoration of the Prophet Muhammad's life. Their participation may appear contradictory but their parallel presence has actually been cultivated by Bawa in Philadelphia as in Jaffna.

One member of the Fellowship pointedly commented to me during a *mawlid* recitation that "Bawa did not speak Arabic." This was one example of growing critique of how Arabic was used to Islamize the Fellowship, a critique that was held by those with far more universal approaches to the teachings of Bawa. They felt that the Fellowship had become more Islamic with Bawa's passing. Even though Bawa was not versed in Arabic, early members noticed that Bawa readily used Arabic phrases and words.[24] Bawa did not lead the recitation of the *mawlid*, just as he did not lead it in Sri Lanka. He participated as the reciters who were able to read Arabic led the *mawlid*. Bawa taught the *kalimah* to his followers and most importantly the *salawat*, which was praise and blessings sung to Prophet Muhammad. The growth of the Muslim presence after the death of Bawa has been a point of tension for students of Bawa who frame the Fellowship as transcendent of all religious labels. Events like the *mawlid*, as one example of the Islamic holy day that Bawa commemorated at the Fellowship, complicate the issue as members in the early days did not necessarily associate the event with Islamic traditions per se, but with Bawa himself. But the *mawlid*, a long-standing pious practice in Islam, is familiar to many Muslims who visit the Fellowship from Syria, Somalia, Morocco, Pakistan, or Iran. They are familiar with the ritual of the *mawlid* and the literature and narratives used for the event, as well as the devotion to holy figures like Prophet Muhammad, from their own cultural and familial contexts and so are readily able to connect with it in the Fellowship. With Bawa's death, the celebration of his death anniversary has become another central ritual for the Fellowship.

At the Grave of Bawa: The Making of a *Mazar* in America

The *mazar* in Coatesville is a principal site of memorialization for the Fellowship as it contains Bawa's body. It is also the place that maintains the authority of Bawa as a living *shaykh*. Bawa's *mazar* is not the first of its kind in America. Samuel Lewis, or "Sufi Sam" (d. 1971), a student of Hazrat Inayat Khan (d. 1927) and the creator of the Dances of Universal Peace, was the first known Sufi leader to be buried in America.[25] Sufi Sam was buried in San Cristobal, New Mexico, where the Lama Foundation, which oversees his *maqbara* (mausoleum), has constructed a *dargah* (shrine) for his tomb.[26] The mystic Hazrat Shah Maghsoud (d. 1980), of the Ovesyse Gharan Order from Iran, is buried in a cemetery in Novato, California, where a memorial is maintained for him.[27] Interring practices of Sufi leaders are developing across America but no research has been completed specifically on the significance of these spaces in relation to Islam and Sufism in America (Figure 3.1).

After the construction of the *masjid*, Bawa's health diminished drastically. When he passed away on December 8, 1986, Bawa was given an Islamic burial on the plot purchased by the Fellowship in Coatesville, an hour west of Philadelphia that now comprises over a hundred acres of property. This property was purchased on September 18, 1980. At the time the property was just over fifty acres but it has since expanded to over a hundred acres and it includes a cemetery, a farm, a garden, and a wisdom center, the latter is the site of weekend discourse meetings and meals for Fellowship members. The farm property had been previously purchased when a Fellowship member died and Bawa was dismayed at the cost of burying people in America. As a solution to the staggering funeral costs, Bawa prompted his students to find some property that could be used as a cemetery to enable the practice of Islamic burials without the overwhelming cost. When Bawa died, no plans were in place for his burial, and so the community agreed that the farm would be the most practical place to inter him. Originally, Bawa's burial ground was marked by a simple iron fence. Soon after

Figure 3.1 The *mazar* of Bawa Muhaiyaddeen in Coatesville, Pennsylvania.

his entombment, his senior disciples held meetings and debated whether they should raise a memorial for their teacher and eventually, after much deliberation, members agreed to erect an architectural design proposed by Michael Green. An American artist and senior member of the Fellowship, Green explained this process further:

> But [. . . his] body died and suddenly it was very important that we have a cemetery [for him] and we picked that little highest place. And we simply dug the grave and put him [Bawa] in. And, there were meetings, I'm not sure how long they went on. Dick Thambi [the *imam* of the mosque of Bawa Muhaiyaddeen in Philadelphia] naturally said that in Islam you don't build an edifice, that *hadith*, or whatever, said the best monument is the footprints of people walking around the burial. But people did want something. And so, we began a series of meetings which actually were utterly bizarre because they were open [to everyone in the Fellowship]. I went to every one [of the meetings . . .]. And I was trying to shape something, so what I finally did is I drew up this [design . . .]. It's based on fairly classical designs, except that I had [. . . it] completely symmetrical and the idea [of the design] was . . . the four doors. Bawa talked about the four archetypal religions . . .; the four doors faced the four religions [Zoroastrianism, Christianity, Judaism, and Islam] to the place inside where they call, meet, and transcend. It's all based on the sacred geometry [. . . and] is based on the golden mean [. . . which] is something like 62 [or] 61.3267, it's irrational, it's like pi, it's considered one of the basic numbers of the universe like pi. It's leaves [and] you [can] find it in a . . . sea shell . . . So, this proportion is all throughout this [shrine].[28]

Green explained that there was a long process wherein numerous meetings were held in order to determine what sort of memorial was to be constructed for Bawa. The meetings were open to everyone in the Fellowship and those who attended had differing thoughts on how to proceed. Green eventually proposed a design based on Bawa's teachings of the four religions (Islam, Judaism, Christianity, and Zoroastrianism) as the four doors of the shrine and his design was accepted.

The structure of the shrine at the *mazar* now stands ten feet above Bawa's tomb and was completed within three days with the help of Bawa's students. Subsequently, the actualization of the internal design took a year to complete. The shrine itself resembles the Taj Mahal in India and this is a deliberate feature as the image is supposed to be representative of Bawa's South Asian origins while the white coating throughout the space symbolizes his purity. The shrine was the final addition to an existing cemetery for members of the Fellowship, which also included a garden project and a center for meetings. Successively, some members of the Fellowship moved to be near the tomb (i.e. Bawa) and maintained weekly activities that paralleled the schedule of prayers and meetings held in the Fellowship house in Philadelphia, which is known as the Unionville branch.[29] The transformation of the farm in Coatesville with the new addition of the shrine captures how the sacred associated with a space is not static but rather transforms over time.

The building of the shrine, unlike the building of *masjid*, was a project actively aided by the efforts of virtually the entire Fellowship. Kabir, a European American and former Catholic, was the senior student of Bawa who led much of the construction efforts of the mosque in Philadelphia, and informed Bawa about the property in Coatesville when Bawa and the Fellowship were searching for an initial site for a cemetery.[30] Kabir spoke with me further about the construction process of the *mazar*, outside the *mazar*:

> That was another very incredibly beautiful experience in a way different and beautiful in that all the children [Bawa's students] came. Not all the children of Bawa's family [not biological family but Fellowship based family] came to help in the mosque, some people didn't feel that they wanted to help or weren't able to. But when we built this, everybody showed up. Mrs. G was stuccoing, you know, and Amin was stuccoing. And Gnainar and Araby, they were all working on this and Dr. G, you know. Everybody took part of it and even in the top, around the perimeter there is, you see the little ledge that sticks out on the top [*pointing to mazar behind us*], the little cap on the corners that you can see sticking out a little bit? . . . That was the roof that was poured on top of the walls and on top of the walls, written in the top of the concrete, before it dried, all of the children [disciples] were brought up to write little notes to Bawa all along the perimeter . . . It was so much, you know, love and yearning and sadness but it was like reconnecting in a certain way. This was something that everyone could get together and do with their [spiritual] father . . . to build this place to protect this grave.[31]

Kabir's words are poignant as he describes how the efforts to build a tomb to honor Bawa's legacy, as a teacher and father, brought his disciples together for a purpose even if it was momentary.

Members of the Unionville branch, the name of the farm/*mazar* branch, became particularly active in cultivating the farm project.[32] According to the researcher Eleanor Finnegan, in the summer of 2009, this branch consisted of about twelve families and an estimated total of thirty to forty members.[33] Finnegan was also told that by 2010, approximately twenty to twenty-two families lived within a fifteen-mile radius of the farm, wherein most members had moved closer to the farm after Bawa's passing.[34]

Daily *dhikr* is held at the *mazar* in the mornings at 4:30 a.m. (as it is in the *masjid* in Philadelphia) and, depending on the time of the year, *fajr* (dawn prayers) are also completed before, in between, or after *dhikr*. Members also perform *salat* in a prayer pavilion across from the *mazar*. This prayer pavilion serves as the community *masjid*, until a proposed mosque is completed (more on this in the following section). This prayer pavilion is also used by visiting groups, such as college students or pilgrimage groups, to gather so as not to disturb the silence maintained in the *mazar*. The *mazar* is also the site where the *mawlid* for the Prophet Muhammad and al-Jilani are celebrated concurrently with the recitations that are held in Philadelphia. These commemorations begin with the raising of the flag and end with its lowering in Coatesville, as Bawa instructed (similar flag raising ceremonies are held at Mankumban). Those who live close to the *mazar* complete these rituals concurrently with the *mawlid* ceremonies in Philadelphia.[35]

The *'Urs* of Bawa Muhaiyaddeen

Bawa's death anniversary, or the *'urs*, is by far the most significant commemorative event held at the *mazar*. In Sufism, the death of a Sufi teacher is understood as a union of the deceased teacher with the divine and as such, *'urs*, literally meaning "wedding" in Arabic, signifies the union of a saint with God at the moment of the saint's physical demise. Hence, the death anniversary is an event to be celebrated, not mourned. In regions like India and Egypt, for example, the *'urs* is a festive and holy occasion that is celebrated at the tomb or a shrine of a Sufi saint. Bawa's *'urs* takes place at the *mazar* on the anniversary of the day of his death, according to the Islamic calendar, and also on December 8 of the Julian calendar. Bawa's *'urs* according to the Islamic calendar follows the culmination of the twelve days of *mawlid* for al-Jilani and it is one of the larger gatherings that take place at the *mazar* as tents are hoisted beside the entrance to accommodate the large crowd of members who drive down from Philadelphia, Boston, and Toronto. This is one of the few times when the *mazar* becomes separated by gender. Women occupy one half of the *mazar* and males the other half. Qur'anic passages, particularly *Surah Ya Sin*, are recited for Bawa while the *salawat* is recited in Arabic for Prophet Muhammad, al-Jilani, and Bawa. The commemoration ritual culminates in the singing of "*Engal* Bawa," a Tamil song in honor of Bawa. This practice of following qur'anic recitations with the singing of the *salawat* and "*Engal* Bawa" is common on special holy days at the Fellowship.

During the years of my research, I participated in two 'urs celebrations at the Fellowship. The first time I experienced Bawa's 'urs was in February 2014, during a severe snowstorm that left trails of icy roads, broken trees, and power outages through much of Philadelphia and its surrounding area. Due to the unexpected severity of the weather, the 'urs was held at the Fellowship in Philadelphia instead of the *mazar*. As the *mawlid* for al-Jilani coincided with the 'urs of Bawa at the *mazar*, the 'urs was scheduled in the morning and the *mawlid* recitation was held in the afternoon. On this particular day, there was an overwhelming South Asian presence and many Pakistani Muslim attendees traveled to Philadelphia from New York. The 'urs for Bawa commenced at 10:00 a.m. All the men were gathered in the classroom where they led the readings. All the women assembled in Bawa's room and sat encircling his bed; the room was packed. Over forty people were present to hear the recitation. The climactic moment of this liturgy took place as everyone stood up and sang *"Engal Bawa"* in Tamil to honor Bawa, which is part of the daily *poosai* at the *ashram* and Mankumban.[36] The recitations took place in the classroom and were also displayed on the large screen in the meeting room that was also full. The recitations were in Arabic and began with the *Surah al-Fatiha*, and then with *Surah Ya Sin*.[37] *Du'as* were also completed and then followed by the recitation of shorter sections from the Qur'an.[38] During the singing, all the women were standing in a circle around Bawa's bed. Some of the females began to cry. These women stood to sing to honor Bawa, understanding that he was present just as the attendees stood for singing of *"Ya Nabi"* during the *mawlid* for Prophet Muhammad.

During Bawa's 'urs, Jonathan Granoff, or Ahamed Muhaiyaddeen (the name given to him by Bawa), a senior European American member of the Fellowship, gave a brief talk about the legacy of Bawa.[39] He explained that all those gathered together should feel honored to have met Bawa in one way or another, explaining that such encounters with Bawa required them to take on the responsibility of continuing Bawa's work. Then Abdur-Razzaq read a chapter from *The Tree That Fell to the West*, on Bawa's life as a farmer and a baker who had also, at some time, cleaned toilets (see Chapter 5).[40] The commemoration concluded with the full *salawat* that, aside from invoking peace upon Prophet Muhammad, also included blessings for al-Jilani and Bawa. At this point, all the women in Bawa's room embraced and repeated *as-salaamu alaykum*, or "peace be upon you." Many of the women also took a moment to stop at Bawa's bed and bow down to kiss it in devotion. The event concluded with the sharing of food and company in the meeting hall.

During this particular '*urs*, one particular group of visitors stood out to Fellowship members because of their attire. There were two men in this group. One dressed in a long and shiny green *kurta* (long shirt) with bright green *kufi* and pants with bells on his ankles that shook with every step. He had also donned nearly ten *tasbih*s (rosary beads) around his neck. The females in the group wore *shalweer kameez* (consists of pants with long shirt) and had loosely veiled their hair. The other gentleman was dressed in a long white *kurta*, pants, and white *kufi* and served food that his group had brought to distribute among the Fellowship. The man in white was Ahmed and he had cooked the chickpea curry, rice, *naan* (bread), and potato curry. Since it was a Saturday, the house was full of Fellowship members and young people who were coming from the youths' and children's meeting.

Those in attendance were relaxed and chatting. I sat with some Fellowship members and shared my enthusiasm for the diverse crowd present that day. As we chatted, one Fellowship member (a woman) pointed to the men in the green and white outfits (Ahmed and his companions) and said to me, "I have no idea who those people are, I have never seen them before, and I am not even sure what their connection to this place is." This was an example of dissonance that can occur at large Fellowship gatherings, similar to events such as the *mawlid* discussed earlier. Those who are part of the Fellowship but do not participate in the *mawlid* events or the mosque prayers come to Fellowship events, such as Bawa's '*urs*, and they encounter South Asian Muslims (e.g. Pakistanis) who come to the same event to receive *baraka* (charisma) and partake in an holy day.

This observation was further noted in my field journal when I met another disciple of Bawa who sat awaiting the beginning of the *mawlid* recitations. Isa, a Hispanic American and former Catholic, senior student of Bawa expressed that the idea of coming for a blessing is a very "foreign" concept for him. When he mentioned this, I asked him why it was important for him to come from New York to visit the Fellowship this weekend for this special commemoration. He said as someone who is part of the Fellowship, this is a Fellowship community event, it was an opportunity to connect with his Fellowship companions that led to his travel to Philadelphia from New York. At these moments, diasporic Muslims and Fellowship members encounter one event from two parallel perspectives: one that honors Bawa, a holy person they knew personally and whose legacy is the Fellowship and their community, and another type of attendee who comes for the "blessings"—quite a foreign practice for some Fellowship members—but who may not necessarily have had a "real" connection with Bawa. The concept of *baraka* as blessing plays an imperative role in Sufism, especially as Sufi saints are said to emit this grace in their death. The act of acquiring this *baraka*, due to their proximity to God and Prophet Muhammad, is what motivates performances of pilgrimage to tombs of Sufi saints or spaces that are associated with them. Devotees also seek to access this grace at the wedding anniversary or *'urs* of a Sufi saint. This practice of veneration is not that different from what happens in Jaffna when Hindu students of Bawa participate in the *mawlid* at the *ashram* as a means to access Bawa's *baraka*.

In 2015, Bawa's *'urs* was held at the *mazar* as usual, but this time members from Philadelphia, New York, Boston, and many more cities drove to Coatesville for the event. Another cold winter day in January, the *mazar* was packed and a tent was set up adjacent to the *mazar* for attendees who could not fit in the *mazar*. Everyone sat around the tomb. The space was gendered with males on one side and females on another, but there was no real partition. As with Bawa's *'urs* in 2014, in 2015, the same qur'anic recitations were led by *imam* Abdur-Razzaq while the song "*Engal* Bawa" was sung. Selections were read from Bawa's biography and the commemoration culminated with the singing of the *salawat* and the changing of the *chaddor* or cloth that covers the tomb. After the formal recitations, many attendees spent time in front of the tomb, privately kissing the tomb or venerating it, as I had observed the previous year around Bawa's bed. Thereafter, everyone dispersed to the tent to partake in lunch and to connect with each other. Once again, the *'urs* attracts both Fellowship and non-Fellowship attendees, just like the *mawlid*.

In addition to his death, other milestones of Bawa's life are also honored at the *mazar*. For example, October 11, 2013, was the forty-second anniversary of Bawa's arrival to Philadelphia and members not only participated in discourse meetings and events at the Fellowship House in Philadelphia that day but they also participated in a prayer service at the *mazar* on Sunday, which was attended by members from the Toronto and Boston branches. The Tamil song "*Engal* Bawa" was sung, selections of the Qur'an was recited (*Ya Sin*), and the names of the members buried at the cemetery, starting with the name of Muhammad Raheem Bawa Muhaiyaddeen, were read out. (Many attendees visited the graves of their families and friends after the reading of the names.) This communal and ritual reading aloud of names highlights another facet of the *mazar* and farm property as a cemetery for deceased members of the Fellowship, an event that does not necessarily attract many non-Fellowship members, as the *mawlid* or *'urs* does.

To date there are close to 200 graves at the cemetery. Membership in the Fellowship is a requirement to have a burial in the Fellowship cemetery. Members of the Fellowship (Muslim and non-Muslim) who have died elsewhere, such as in Europe or Canada, request to be buried at the farm/*mazar*,[41] in which case, their body is transported to Philadelphia to be buried in Coatesville. The burials follow proper Islamic standards, as taught by Bawa, and are conducted by members of the Philadelphia or the Coatesville branch. The same standard of Islamic burial is used for all those buried at the Coatesville cemetery. Despite debates regarding religious identities (and resistance by some to identify the Fellowship with Islam), it is rather telling that everyone who is buried in the Fellowship farm is buried according to Islamic customs (e.g. full ablutions, wrapped in a white shroud facing Mecca, and buried by males only). Despite the varieties of religious identities and relationships to Sufism maintained in the Fellowship, each body interred in the Fellowship cemetery is interred according to Islamic customs and thus *as a Muslim*. There is no comparable cemetery or institutionalization of Islamic burial practice in Sri Lanka.

A Memorial Site for Their Teacher: Bawa and the Fellowship Members

When the *mazar* was initially constructed, it was just an addition to the private cemetery for the Fellowship and a memorial for Bawa. It was also a space for members of the Unionville branch. Bawa's disciples across North America, including the Fellowship in Philadelphia, visited their teacher when they were able, to share in private remembrance and prayers. These included members of the Toronto Fellowship as well as members from Riyadh, Saudi Arabia, and those who live in England. Shoaib—a Muslim Fellowship member from Pakistan who works in Saudi Arabia, travels to Toronto, and visits Philadelphia regularly—explained his reasons for visiting Bawa's *mazar*, both in Sri Lanka and Philadelphia:

> It is an important question, a lot of people ask that, why do you go to a *mazar* okay? . . . If God is everywhere, why do you have to go anywhere? That's true, but as I said, we have not yet reached that ourselves, have not reached that level like the prophets, like Muhammad, like Jesus, like Moses, like Abraham was, who themselves changed into light form and God took them in; we are still on the journey, we still have to realize ourselves, we are aware we have not realized, okay. Until you realize yourself, you need these things, in life to keep you straight . . . It is the love and devotion to Bawa . . . that we think it is important

to go and reaffirm our commitment to him . . . It's not that if you don't go he is going to abandon us. No, he won't. Bawa is looking after you even when you don't know him.[42]

Shoaib relays that it is the "love and devotion to Bawa" that prompts him to travel internationally to visit Bawa's shrine, not only in Coatesville but also Mankumban. When I asked Shoaib about the experience of visiting the *mazar* in Coatesville and Mankumban, he explained what the process entailed for him personally:

> So, when you go in front of a divine presence, and to me Bawa Muhaiyaddeen and so is Mother Mary. They are part of God. They are part of the divine light okay, whether they are physically there or not there is not important to me but that place symbolizes them. So, when I am there, just as I would be in Mecca for example, or when I go to Medina where the Prophet is kept right, to me it is as sacred as that, because there is a lot of divine presence . . . and there I see myself not as the world sees me, but as I am. And there I am in front of the divine with all my frailties, so emotionally it is a very—you know—[a] weak state you are in [and . . .] you can't hide anything, you are open; you're like a naked baby, right in front of the ultimate power and then you feel how small you are . . . Yet you have been given the occasion to be there. So, you think of your unworthiness and you think of the great blessings you have been given.[43]

The *mazar* in Pennsylvania is a sacred space that connects numerous places associated with Bawa across Sri Lanka and North America. This connection was evident in my travels throughout Sri Lanka where I found photographs of Bawa's *mazar* at his *ashram* in Jaffna, the makeshift hut that served as a shrine in the war-torn farm in Puliyankulam, and in the Colombo branch, which also serves as the center of the Serendib Sufi Study Circle. In Toronto, a framed photograph of Bawa's *mazar* hangs at the entrance of the door to Bawa's house where weekly discourse meetings, *dhikr*s, and communal gatherings take place. The connections to the *mazar* of Bawa are not only maintained through material culture, such as photographs, however. For Nur Sharon Marcus, an executive member of the Toronto Fellowship branch, there is a tangible connection between the *mazar* in Coatesville and the shrine in Mankumban established by the water found at both sites:

> The *mazar* in Mankumban was intended to be his burial place and that is now said to be the burial place of Mary, of Maryam, and Bawa has confirmed that she is there . . . The other thing was the well; now, you've been there, so you've tasted the water from that well. Bawa often uses the word *nalla tannir* [good water] as a place name, sweet water is what we would translate that in English and sweet

water is a place name in some places in North America. I have to say that the
water at the well . . . at his *mazar*, in Fallowfield Township [Coatesville], which
is forty miles west of Philly, the water in that well is extraordinary and pure
and delicious. The water at the well in Mankumban was the sweetest, the most
extraordinary taste that I have ever tasted not just for water but for any liquid
form of anything. Bawa has said there is a very subtle underground connection
between the Zamzam well in Saudi and the well in Mankumban. Well, I've tasted
the Zamzam water from Saudi and it has always come in plastic which maybe
has changed the taste somewhat, but I have never tasted anything to compare
with that exquisite water from that huge . . . well at Mankumban.[44]

In Marcus's comments, she draws connections between the three shrine complexes via water: the *mazar*, Mankumban, and the Zamzam in Mecca; and the
experience from drinking the water at these locations confirms, for Marcus, the
"extraordinary" connection between all three shrines even though the distance
between them spans three separate continents. This shared experience of taste
is ultimately a metaphysical experience and, like Shoaib, connects to the established sacred site of Zamzam, a connection that was evoked by the Matron at the
ashram and Mankumban as well (see Chapter 2). These metaphysical connections to Zamzam and Mecca (via the *mazar* and Mankumban), as well as Bawa's
teachings inspired many disciples of Bawa to perform *hajj* or the *umra* (shorter
version of the *hajj*) after Bawa's death.

For members of the Fellowship, such as for Shoaib and Marcus, the *mazar*
in Coatesville has varying significances for them individually. For Shoaib and
Marcus, the *mazar* and Mankumban are important nodes in a larger network of
the Fellowship, the complete linkage of which is only notable when these sancti-
fied and affiliated spaces are seen as portals to God, as explained by Shoaib above.
It is also clear that the shrine in Coatesville serves many purposes: it is a node
that connects to Mankumban and Mecca, while being an important space where
members of the Fellowship hold weekly ritual performances of *dhikr*, wisdom
teachings, and celebrations for milestones in Bawa's life. It is also a resting place
for the deceased members of the Fellowship. Upon entering this space, Bawa's
devotees experience the network of activities and relations through which Bawa
is remembered. These networks of activities and recollections in turn constitute
Bawa's space in Coatesville sacred. The *mazar* creates pathways to the divine
through a recollection of unity that extends from Philadelphia to Mankumban,
and Mecca. These perceived sacred networks by students of Bawa, however, only
capture one purpose of the *mazar*; another perspective that needs attention is
the utilization of the *mazar* by new visitors.

The "Picnic *Mazar*": Pilgrims to the *Mazar* of Bawa-ji

Pilgrims have added a new dimension to the Fellowship, which has further transformed the space and institution as a whole; the scale of change is captured by Finnegan's brief mention of the "five or six hundred Gujarati Muslims from New York, New Jersey, Boston, Connecticut, and Canada [who] come to the farm" regularly.[45] In order to understand this transformation of the Coatesville farm from a private to public religious space, it is helpful to engage with the voices and experiences of new pilgrims and visitors to this site.

When I was present at the *mazar* for the Easter weekend of April 2014, there were pilgrims who were visiting in large groups of families and friends. During this busy long weekend, I met Iranian women from Washington, DC, and Punjabi-speaking Pakistani women from New Jersey and New York State. Most visitors brought food such as rice, curries, Indian sweets, and donuts (i.e. Dunkin Donuts) while being mindful of the no-meat rule practiced by the Fellowship and taught by Bawa. For those visiting for the first time, especially those who came with more regular visitors, the no-meat rule was a point of bewilderment as vegetarianism is not required by Islamic law. Once, I found myself sitting with a member of the Fellowship from the Boston branch, an Indian Muslim, who brought his mother from England to the *mazar*. It was her first visit and she was confused about the no-meat rule on the property. Her son patiently tried to explain to his mother that the *shaykh* did not eat meat but his mother still looked unconvinced of the practice by the end of the conversation.

Visitors usually place their food on the designated table in the welcome center and socialize (and eat) with their companions inside or outside the center, depending on the space that is available and the weather. Some visiting families also bring their children who run around the property (sometimes very loudly), play on the playground, or freely walk through the garden and fields. Most of the visiting pilgrims also bring empty water jugs and bottles to fill with water from the pump (well). They use the water on the property for drinking or ablutions.

Once inside the *mazar*, the regular practice is to sit in silent meditation but activities that unfold at the shrine vary by the pilgrim, particularly if they attend in a group. For instance, during one visit, I observed the following activity inside the *mazar* and recorded it in my field journal:

> A group of Pakistani men, two older men and four young boys have come in. They went and sat in front of the tomb. One had two plastic bags with two sweet boxes inside them. He put it right against the edge of the tomb, making sure the bag was touching the tomb. And they all sat with their hands held out

open in prayer. He began with "*A'udhu billahi min ash-shaytaan ar-rajeem*" [I seek Allah's protection from the accursed Satan] he repeated it twice. He also took photographs of the tomb and of his company praying. Two other younger men also came and they walked around, looked at the pamphlets on the bookshelf, prayed and left. Another young man also came and he prayed. I have seen him around before and I saw him on Monday talking to one of the Fellowship members, asking how to join the Fellowship and what he needed to do. After the Pakistani man finished his prayers, he asked his young boys to get up and touch the tomb and he took photographs of them. He took several photographs and videos on his iPhone. Then he opened the box of sweets and he offered them to everyone in the *mazar*; he offered them first to the young boys, who were walking out at the time. One of the boys said that he did not want one, and the other boy said, "No, you can't say no, you must take one" and he finally took one. I was sitting against the wall and the man walked over to me offered me *salaams* and said "please, sister, take" and I took one. They were *ladoos* (yellow sweet sugar balls) and a cashew-sweet, both traditional Indian sweets. I stayed in the *mazar* for a bit longer and observed as each individual who came in, mainly pilgrims, performed his or her own personal meditation and prayer. Once I was outside, I scanned the areas around the *mazar* and many pilgrims were having picnics outside the *mazar*, near the welcome center, the garden area, and the benches.

The majority of the visitors on this particular day were South Asian Muslims, mainly Bengali, Pakistani, Gujarati, and Punjabi Muslims. And throughout my several years of research at the *mazar*, I found that this ethnic and cultural makeup of the pilgrims remained consistent. They performed individual acts of veneration at the tomb of Bawa by fully prostrating themselves to the tomb or by sitting in silent meditation, often with prayer beads in their hands. On some occasions, like the one documented above, visitors took pictures of themselves (selfies) at the *mazar* or filmed the interior of the space. These images have ended up on social media forums, like Facebook, which has further increased the popularity of the *mazar* and has led to more pilgrims visiting. Social media accounts, and even group accounts on Facebook ("Bawa Muhaiyaddeen Fellowship") and Instagram, has increased Bawa and the Fellowship's online presence. Visitors "check-in" via their smartphones while visiting the *mazar*. At the time of writing this (spring 2017), Facebook indicated that over 600 people checked in (their status between the period of May 2015–July 2017) while at the *mazar*, a couple of dozen posted photographs were tagged on Instagram. A few of the status updates on Facebook included the following: "It's so peaceful, and healing with loving and compassionate hearted Staff, members, brotherhood and sisterhood! Every time I visit Sheikh Bawa Mazar my heart purifies, and fills with God qualities! I just love it. Bless [*sic*] be upon him!"[46] Another visitor posted: "It is so nice and peace [*sic*] here. It is really great to have a mazar in U.S.A. [*sic*]."[47] Most pictures on Facebook and Instagram are taken with the tomb of Bawa, sometimes praying (palms open). Some take selfies while others take photographs of their family standing in front of the *mazar*. Additionally, a prominent practice among South Asian visitors is to offer sweets to Bawa, which are eventually distributed or left at the welcome center. This offering of food to Bawa is parallel to the practice seen at Mankumban during weekly *poosai* where all food was offered first to the tomb and then distributed to those present.

Women's dress code also varied depending on their cultural origins. Most of the women wore *chaddor*s (full-length open cloak) or other traditional South Asian outfits, such as the *shalweer kameez*. Some also wore casual clothing (e.g. jeans) with loosely veiled headscarves. Men wore *kufis* and jeans. Generally, visitors established their own ritual protocol at the *mazar*. Fellowship caretakers post signs for specific protocols at the entrance to the *mazar* and around the property but there is only a presumption of accountability as, despite these signs, there is no one supervising or tending to the pilgrims on a daily basis, especially inside the *mazar*, unless a group visitation has been organized in advance. Women are a regular presence at the *mazar* and no limits are placed on their access to the space unless they are on their menses. This protocol is posted on the *mazar* website and the bulletin board outside the *mazar*, and is practiced in all of Bawa's spaces from Jaffna (e.g. *ashram* and Mankumban) to Philadelphia (i.e. *masjid*). Despite this accessibility, there are often instances where females do not enter the *mazar* and pray outside instead. There may be many reasons that these women may not enter. They may be trying to be mindful of purity regulations because they are on their menses, or they may be visiting from regions where it is not customary for women to enter the *mazars*. Other women enter the *mazar* with ease and do so regularly. In all these examples, pilgrims enacted the rituals and practices known to them from their own cultural and regional context of Islam, a reality that members of the Fellowship continue not to be aware of, but caretakers of the shrine have since learned.

Since pilgrims travel long distances to visit, and travel in large groups, once the pilgrims arrive at the *mazar*, they spend the day and often picnic. This idea of the *mazar* and the farm as a "picnic *mazar*" is a practice that some members of the Fellowship find difficult to accommodate. Picnics at the *mazar* are interpreted by Fellowship shrine-keepers as improper etiquette. Noise levels have been of concern, for instance, as children run around and pilgrims socialize outside the *mazar*, especially in the summertime. These practices contrast with the objectives of the Fellowship caretakers who wish to keep the space quiet, as a place of meditation. For the most part, visitors maintain the practice of silent meditation inside the *mazar* but Fellowship members relayed many incidences in which music or singing took place inside the *mazar*. Kabir, one of caretakers of the farm and *mazar*, recalled a day when he heard singing coming from the *mazar*. Displeased with the noise, he rushed over to the *mazar* to remind the visitors that the space was meant for quiet meditation. Once he arrived inside the *mazar*, he found the visiting group in the middle of singing the *salawat* to the Prophet Muhammad and he was unable to follow through on his initial intention of asking them to stop; instead, he joined them in singing the *salawat*.[48]

The *mazar* is opened from sunrise to sunset each day. At the end of each day, after the visitors to the *mazar* leave, Fellowship volunteers clean up the kitchen and social space. For the caretakers of the *mazar*, the arrival of the new pilgrims and visitors was an unexpected development and one that the Fellowship did not imagine when the *mazar* was being constructed. Kabir described his initial surprise when pilgrims started arriving at the *mazar*:

> *KABIR:* We never knew what it was like, of course, to maintain and take
> care of a *mazar*. We didn't know what was involved in it, other than
> Ajwad, Dr. Markar, and Dr. G [three Tamil and senior disciples of
> Bawa] telling us certain things and parameters and things to do. So,
> we followed that but . . . we didn't realize until people started coming
> because there was hardly anybody out here in the beginning. It was
> very, very quiet. And then very slowly, people started to show up—you
> know . . . And come and we learned—you know—the duty now. There's
> a new duty we have.
>
> *SHOBHANA:* Which is what?
>
> *KABIR:* Which is to protect it; to assure that people can come,
> comfortably, and have something to eat, a cup of tea, a place to get out
> of the cold. We needed to build bathrooms and ablution rooms. Because
> it was very simple in the beginning you know. It was just a little well
> over there and that was it. There were no buildings or anything . . .
> I mean it's been twenty-eight years so we're still growing slowly.[49]

When Bawa's *mazar* was first built, it was a private property with a community cemetery and a small agricultural project. With the arrival of new visitors and pilgrims to Bawa's tomb, a new responsibility of care and hospitality emerged for members of the Fellowship, especially for those who reside near the farm.

For Kabir, this responsibility, or "duty," is now a service to those who visit, and includes the upkeep of the property, maintenance of facilities, and providing of food and shelter to those who travel from afar to visit Bawa. This new responsibility of sharing the *mazar* comes with negotiations for Fellowship members. Observations of Bawa's immediate disciples taking on the role of shrine-keepers have been made at both shrines (in Coatesville and Mankumban), and this further complicates easy categories between visitors, pilgrims, devotees, and immediate disciples in the broader transnational movement, especially across racial, cultural, and religious binaries. Some of these shifts in roles have become evident in the shrine practices that are unfolding in the American landscape in general and for Bawa's shrine in particular, as indicated by changes in the protocol established by shrine caretakers, either through their presence or via the signs posted throughout the shrine.

Kabir and his wife recently traveled through South Asia visiting *dargah*s and *mazar*s, such as Moinuddin Chishti's *dargah* (d. 1236) in Ajmer, India, to study shrine practices and traditions, and even met with caretakers of Sufi shrines during their journey to better understand their role in America. It was only after their visit, and my encounter with him soon thereafter, that Kabir genuinely relayed to me, "I get it now," referring to his realization of why pilgrims were visiting this shrine in Pennsylvania. Kabir and his wife had comprehended the *mazar*'s spiritual capital in the landscape of South Asian Islam and Sufism and the significance of its accessibility for diasporic Muslims in America. Even though the caretakers of Bawa's *mazar* are slowly understanding the culture of *mazar*s in regions, such as South Asia, they still have made conscious decisions to deviate from some of the South Asian *mazar* practices, and one of the most prominent examples of this is in the maintenance of silence.

Such comparisons of the protocol of *mazar*s in South Asian context (where most of the pilgrims come from) and Bawa's *mazar* in Coatesville signals to a point of departure for the American *mazar* as this prescribed silence is actually quite an anomaly from Old World Islam. While speaking to a Pakistani female residing in Philadelphia near the Fellowship community, I asked her about her experience at the *mazar*. She explained that her initial visit felt odd due to the quiet and order at the *mazar*. In her experience, *mazar*s in South Asia or the Middle East were loud places and involved a lot of pushing crowds; they are simply not as quiet as Bawa's *mazar*. This difference was something to which she had to adjust. For pilgrims who mainly hail from South Asian Islamic backgrounds, *mazar*s are known to be culturally and ritually fluid and dynamic sacred spaces. This experience influences individual practices and ritual observances enacted by them at the *mazar*. This is a reality that Fellowship members are now learning. The silence, order, and lack of ritual accouterments (i.e. incense and perfume) are some of the characteristics of Bawa's *mazar* that differ from *mazars* across Muslim societies. These practices are even different from Mankumban in Jaffna, where incense and camphor powder dominate ritual activities of circumambulations.

During the same weekend in April 2014, I was sitting outside the *mazar* with five members of the Fellowship, listening to stories of Bawa and their travels with him to Sri Lanka. Sitting at the table next to us was an older Pakistani man. We asked him to join us, but he explained that his English was "no good" and preferred not to. A few minutes later, a few younger men in the same party of this elder man returned. The older man then interrupted us politely and asked if we could explain Bawa-ji, *ji* being an honorific many South Asian pilgrims use when referring to Bawa, to the younger men. So, both groups formed a large circle and the disciples of Bawa took the opening to share teachings and experiences of Bawa with the pilgrims who were visiting on this Sunday. I took the opportunity to ask this group of Pakistani Americans how they had heard about the *mazar*. One man explained that he had seen it on the internet and could not believe that there was a *mazar* in America; so, they drove down from Brooklyn, New York, just to see if it was true. He explained that in Pakistan, *mazars* are everywhere and so when he walked into Bawa's *mazar* he nostalgically "felt [he] was back home." The young man sitting beside him added that *mazars* "back home" were dedicated to saints only known by their great ancestors so "to be sitting here in America with disciples who sat with Bawa-ji is a great blessing [for them]."

Pilgrims travel to the *mazar* both to access blessings through Bawa's tomb and to connect with Bawa's direct disciples as a means of accessing Bawa's blessings. This practice is qualified in Kelly Pemberton's study of shrines in India and the custom of *suhbat*, or the practice of a disciple keeping "company" with his master; it also translates to keeping "company" with "fellow disciples" of the master.[50] At the *mazar* of Bawa, this tradition manifests in acts of reverence toward Bawa's direct disciples through handshakes, hugs, bowing, and also by taking the disciple's hand to one's forehead. These gestures are usually gendered, especially if they involve physical conduct, and usually occur between men. That said, American disciples are at times taken aback by such levels of affection and respect from pilgrims. Immigrant pilgrims seeking the grace of a Sufi saint interact with his direct disciples not only because they share the space but because some visitors believe that the opportunity to meet and greet a direct disciple of Bawa-ji is a way to access Bawa's grace.

Additionally, stories of healing, or miracles (*karamat*) attributed to Bawa are also particularly common at Bawa's *mazar*. For instance, a couple who were unable to conceive a child, went to the *mazar* and requested this intention to be fulfilled through prayer. After making pilgrimage to the *mazar* and praying there, they relayed to me they received a child through Bawa's grace.

The *mazar* has also become a site where large groups of pilgrims gather to celebrate varying *'urs* festivals. Fakir Muhammad and his family began visiting the *mazar* in 1998 and each subsequent year his networks expanded and his group grew. As the event's popularity grew, Fakir Muhammad began organizing a yearly gathering of Gujarati Muslims at the *mazar* in collaboration with members of the Fellowship.[51] Gujarati Muslims from the Eastern Seaboard had been gathering annually for their own *'urs* celebrations since the early 2000s but the festival was canceled in 2013. When I inquired with senior members as to why the event was canceled, one member explained that the growing presence of pilgrims visiting the shrine but not invested in Bawa's teachings raised concerns for some Fellowship members. Fellowship members want visitors to be interested in Bawa rather than the rituals or the act of receiving blessings and graces. Another reason for canceling the Gujarati festival that year, according to some other members, was due to concerns over the bomb attacks at the Boston Marathon in April 2013.[52] Leaders at the Fellowship were worried that such a large celebration of Muslim immigrants in a small town in Pennsylvania might cause alarm among the neighbors.

As exemplified by Fakir's networking, those who gather at the *mazar* increasingly do so with their own established networks. They are not necessarily institutionally tied to the Fellowship, but this does not mean that these groups are not "connected" to Bawa, as some members of the Fellowship have begun to argue. These pilgrims have created their own affiliations with Bawa and his *mazar*. Since it is a public religious space, it is nearly impossible to keep track of who visits on a daily basis, the Coatesville grounds now host numerous sub-branches and communities that are linked to the *mazar*.

Members of the Fellowship branches, both across North America and globally, play a critical role in how they network with local Sufi communities. These connections with other Sufi orders lead to sharing both Bawa and his spaces, most especially the *mazar*. For instance, the Canadian branch of the Azeemia Spiritual and Healing Center Canada is located in Mississauga, a city in the Greater Toronto Region and is led by Khwaja Shamsuddin Azeemi.[53] This center organizes an annual event known as Adam's Day, or "Unity in Diversity," which also celebrates the anniversary of the order's patron Qalandar Baba Auliya

(d. 1979), who founded the *silsila-e-azeemia* in Karachi, Pakistan. The community has international centers across Europe, the United Kingdom, Thailand, United Arab Emirates, the United States, and Canada. This community also extends invitation to events such as Adam's Day to other spiritual communities including known Sufi groups in the region. It is through such an event that they met members of the Toronto branch of the Fellowship. Informal meetings between the Fellowship members in Toronto and the Azeemia Sufi Order resulted in a formal request by the Azeemia Sufi Order to organize a group visit of sixty to seventy guests to Bawa's *mazar*. The members of the Toronto branch and the *mazar* caretakers facilitated the organization of this trip. About twenty members from Toronto participated, while the majority of the guests traveled to the *mazar* from the tristate area, the US east coast, and even from further south in America. An email was sent out to members of the Fellowship requesting anyone who was available to help host the visitors to the *mazar* to do so. The program for the visit consisted of an arrival time of 10:30 a.m. followed by the changing of the *chaddor* on Bawa's grave, the recitation of *dhikr*, lunch, and then the completion of the visit with *zuhr* (noon) prayers in the prayer pavilion across from the *mazar*.

Members from other Sufi communities also regularly visit Bawa's *mazar*, such as the members of the Threshold Society (a Mevlevi Sufi Order led by Kabir and Camille Helminski who are based in Kentucky) or members of the Chishti Order from Ajmer. Fethullah Gulen, the Turkish preacher and founder of the Gulen movement who is based in Pennsylvania, has also visited the *mazar* of Bawa. Students of North American Sufi groups are also sent by their respective *shaykh*s to the *mazar* of Bawa for their initial spiritual retreats (*khalwah*). This act of retreating or withdrawing from the physical world by isolating oneself in a sacred space, limiting sleep and food, and reciting special prayers is a central practice in one's spiritual discipline in Sufism as prescribed by Sufi teachers. In many ways, the aim of visiting the tomb is a shared experience as a member of the Fellowship, as a member of another Sufi community, or as an individual seeker. Retreating to the *mazar*, or making a pilgrimage there, results in internal spiritual reorientation that many of the disciples of Bawa seek especially if they are members in branches outside of Philadelphia.

In his study of movement across the Indian Ocean, Engseng Ho explains that graves "lie within circuits of movements . . . People move for many reasons; their itineraries are numerous and so are the durations of travel."[54] And thus "this initial motion begins a dynamic of signification that launches the dead and silent person within the earth into discourse."[55] This "semiotic complex" not only elicits a relationship with the "dead" (e.g. Bawa), but also between those who gather around the dead. Though the "dead" remain silent, it is the living who bring their diverse voices to the dead and create new life: "We cannot understand the grave, the destination, without paying attention to the journey behind it."[56] Although the reasons and purpose of the journey and the resulting movements may differ, as suggested by Ho, the emphasis remains the tomb.[57] The legacy of the dead and their connection to a source (e.g. God) transcends the limitations of the materiality of the sacred space and connects all those who arrive at the *mazar* (Figure 3.2).

The members of the Fellowship, some of whom are not Muslim and some, like Kabir, who do identify as Muslim, are now the shrine-keepers of a *mazar*. They have accepted the responsibility of hosting the pilgrims and groups (even college students), maintaining the property, and sharing the teachings and stories of Bawa to those who are interested. The *mazar* remains a meaningful space for Fellowship members. It is a site wherein ritual activity unfolds, including farming, and it serves many including those in the Fellowship and the broader Muslim and Sufi communities in North America and beyond. The *mazar*, an

Figure 3.2 A member of the Toronto branch visiting the *mazar* of Bawa Muhaiyaddeen in Coatesville, Pennsylvania.

American shrine of a transnational movement, is now a space which immigrant Muslims freely utilize.

The composite experiences at the shrine in Coatesville returns us to Eade and Sallnow's theorization of the competing meanings projected to sites of pilgrimages, as found at Mankumban (Chapter 2). In America, though, there is a distinct layer, one that was not evident in Jaffna; that is one of *memory* and *homeland*. Studies on pilgrimage practices to Catholic shrines in North America suggest that for those from immigrant backgrounds in host countries, such as America and Canada, shrines (such as Catholic shrines) offer a space in which memories of the religious practices from their natal homelands (in our case of Old World Islam) can be recreated according to their own cosmology and memory, both in their understanding of the saint's body (in this case Bawa) but also in terms of the general meaning of a shrine.[58] The familiarity of this space, as a space that is normative across Muslim cultures and societies, deems it as a heterotopia although its function has transformed from a seemingly private site of memorial to a public space of pilgrimage in the American milieu. It is the American immigrant's experience that adds a new tier to this unique community. Still, there remains an essential continuity from Mankumban to Bawa's *mazar*, and this is perhaps best captured by Annemarie Schimmel's study of the Mughals. During a time of dispute over religious taxes (*jizya*) between Hindu and Muslim "religious dignitaries," both parties agreed to meet at a holy shrine to settle their dispute, which led Schimmel to conclude that the "the Sufi shrine unifies, the Mosque divides."[59] Within the Fellowship's history, the latter is quite evident. The mosque, for varying reasons, divided students of Bawa within the Fellowship and continues to do so, but the *mazar* has united not only the Fellowship members, but new pilgrims who arrive at its threshold.

Future Developments at the *Mazar* and Farm

When the Coatesville property was purchased, there was a proposal to build the *masjid* on site rather than in Philadelphia. Kabir informed me, in an interview in April 2014, that this project, originating from Bawa, is under way:

> *KABIR:* We're in front of the local government now. We're about sixty-five percent done and . . . it's an institutional zoning [issue]. So, it's an institutional project, which allows us to do both residential and

institutional. So, we have a mosque planned, and we're actually sitting in the mosque right now. Yeah it would go right here [*signaling to the space we are sitting in during the interview*]. So, there's a mosque planned and there's a Fellowship house. There's a school, which could be a retirement facility. It could be anything in the future. And then that garage, we're going to build a new garage down over the hill and that's going to become a library. Archival work and people can go and research. It will be like a small campus. You know, we're trying to keep it simple.

SHOBHANA: What was the idea behind the mosque? Who wanted to have the mosque or was that something Bawa always wanted to have?

KABIR: Oh no, [Bawa] said we'd have to have a mosque here. When we had the cemetery cause that's why we bought the land, [it] was for a cemetery when one of our members died and we realized . . . we needed a good way to bury people. So, to do it properly . . . that's why we were looking for land . . . specifically for the cemetery. But then he [Bawa] said we could farm it if we wanted to, if there was enough land we could farm it. And then he said there will [*sic*] have to be a mosque there. And we have tapes of him saying all of this. We needed to keep all of that together to establish that he did want it done. So, you know, with the mosque comes a kitchen, a place for people to study, a little school and everything . . . So, he was aware of what we were doing. And we actually, we thought there was going to be a mosque built out here before the one in Philly . . . You probably heard that story.

SHOBHANA: Yes, I did. They were initially planning it but I guess the distance was a problem, especially to drive out here?

KABIR: Yeah. Well, this is the way Bawa goes about things. We really thought it was going to be here. We cleared all of the land and then I remember he brought me in and he said, "so, you know we have a little design and everything but *thambi* [younger brother], can I ask you a question?" And he goes, "who is going to pray there?" And I said "well there's some people, we have people out there." And he goes "not too many people though, right?" And I said "no, not too many people." And he said "now tell me if we build that, the only beings that I can see that might pray there all the time would be the birds and the squirrels." He said, "Let's build it in here [*points to the heart*]." And it just went like that. Everything changed. But he was so sweet the way he did it.[60]

Since our initial interview, the new plans have been vetted by the local zoning committees and were finally approved in April 2017. The proposed plan is to tear down the current welcome center and rebuild a larger complex which will include a *masjid*, school, library, industrial kitchen, and dining area. Around the perimeter new residential places (homes) will be erected for Fellowship members, all of which have already been purchased by members of the Fellowship. Historically, Sufi communities have built these complexes, which were also a fundamental component of the development and proliferation of Islam across different regions and cultures. Yet, this proposal signals once again to the ongoing contestations within Bawa's transnational communities as to the nature of Bawa's teachings and its relationship with Islam. Fellowship members who align with more universal tendencies see the proposed plans for the building of the *masjid* as another step in the Islamization of the Fellowship at large. The arrival of Muslim immigrants has already paved the path for this trend, especially with the presence of non-Fellowship Muslims during the *mawlid* and Ramadan practices at the Fellowship to their presence at the *mazar*. Yet the relationship of Bawa to Islam and Sufism is a question that emerged with the construction of the *masjid* during Bawa's lifetime. But, as Kabir indicated in his comments to me above, all the plans for the *mazar* property can be found in recorded tapes of Bawa.[61]

For the members of the Fellowship with more universal understanding of Islam, the building of a *masjid* by the Fellowship is not a necessity and it signals to further potential ruptures that may parallel the schism that unfolded during the process of building of the mosque in Philadelphia. For members who practice *salat*, the space would be welcome because without it they practice *salat* either in the prayer pavilion or in the *mazar*. Fellowship visitors, especially women, also complete *salat* outside in open spaces if the weather permits and nooks inside the welcome center beside food tables. These developments will be critical to follow in the years to come, as it will further transform not only the space but also the community.

As internal pressures continue to unfold, outwardly the sociopolitical climate of Islamophobia in America also has affected the plans to build the proposed mosque. The reason that the zoning approvals took over two decades was because members of the local zoning committee, many who are Christian, stalled much of the process for the acquisition of building permits. The growing number of pilgrims, many who arrive by the busload, has gained attention in the rather small farming community of rural Pennsylvania. Mounting Islamophobia in America and the sensationalizing of Islam in the media has created uneasiness among the largely Christian American neighbors of the *mazar*, which has become even further heightened since the inauguration of President Donald

Trump (2017) and his policies on Islam and Muslims, such as the restricted entry of individuals from Muslim majority nations to the United States. Hearing about the zoning issues, a Jewish legal firm in Philadelphia offered support on the basis of religious discrimination, but members of the Fellowship declined as they did not want any media attention.

The resistance on the part of some members of the East Fallowfield County and the support of Jewish groups in Philadelphia adds to the complex religious history of Pennsylvania, one which hails stories of the Religious Society of Friends (Quakers) and William Penn (d. 1718), who fostered a colony that included various religious minorities, such as the Amish, Mennonites, Moravians, Catholics, Jews, and even African slaves in "Peaceful Kingdom" with the indigenous Americans. Yet, Pennsylvania farm country is also politically conservative, as was indicated by the Republican majority in the state in the 2017 presidential election. This broader political climate and religious landscape (especially of religious farming communities) is the context in which Bawa's *mazar* and farm is embedded. Despite most of the members of the Unionville branch being European Americans (white) from Jewish and Christian heritages, their relationship with Islam, either through conversion, or by association to the Fellowship, has resulted in varying responses (both positive and negative) from the immediate community, which was seen in the prolonged case of the zoning bylaw meetings and hearings for permits for the building of the *masjid*.

Despite the uncertain political climate in America, the *mazar* continues to attract Muslim pilgrims. It is safe to predict, based on the growth patterns in the past decade alone, that the *mazar* will continue to grow as more visitors flock to its threshold and it continues to receive international acclaim.[62] As these negotiations and accommodations between visitors and members unfold at the *mazar*, the practice of *ziyara* is now unmistakably a notable component of Sufi piety in the Islamic landscape of America. Ho writes that "with burial, the dead bring a place to life, as it were," and it is indeed evident that the grave of Bawa has enlivened Sufism in America.[63]

In highlighting how Sufism is lived, it is apparent that labels such as "hybrid" or "immigrant" or even American are not productive in capturing the complex lived reality unfolding within the spaces of the Fellowship. The embodied practices at the Fellowship in Philadelphia and the *mazar* indicates that other ways of thinking about Sufism in America is necessary. One that captures the ever-dynamic intersections and interactions of immigrant, diaspora, and second- and third-generation Muslim American pilgrims from South Asia to the Middle East and beyond. Furthermore, these identities and new networks converge at the heterotopia of the *mazar*, a space that is shared across Muslim cultures and societies. It is this gathering and sharing at the tomb of Bawa that is indicative of the vibrant nature of Sufism in America and one, continuing from Jaffna to Pennsylvania, that is reflective of the globalization of Sufism in the contemporary era.

Conclusion

The Fellowship in Philadelphia was initially Bawa's place of residence but it has now developed into numerous subspaces. With Bawa's death, the Fellowship remains the central site of ritual and communal activities for its members. These activities include daily ritual prayers at the *masjid* or weekly meetings in the Fellowship Hall and Bawa's room. The ritual of communal veneration of Bawa's bed through the use of religious accouterments, which is central to the religious lives of Bawa's followers in Jaffna, is not as present in Philadelphia, though communal rituals and individual veneration do unfold around Bawa's bed in Philadelphia. Friday *jum'a* or Sunday discourse meetings are usually attended by Fellowship and non-Fellowship members, as they provide a moment to share a meal and recollect with members of the community. The Fellowship headquarters in Philadelphia hosts rituals, such as the *'urs*, *mawlid*, and public meetings that demonstrate a similar showing of religious diversity (Muslim and non-Muslim) as found in Jaffna.

Additionally, rituals initially instituted in Jaffna, like the *mawlid* and orientation toward food and service, are still practiced in both Jaffna and Pennsylvania. Just as Hindus and Muslims shared spaces and rituals at the *ashram*, the same comingling of different religious congregations is evident at the Fellowship in Philadelphia among Muslims and non-Muslims (Christians and Jews). In tracing devotion to Bawa from Jaffna to Pennsylvania, the recitation of the *tasliya*, or the blessing upon the Prophet Muhammad, is an example of another meaningful form of piety prominent among Sufi communities, while devotion to Bawa forms the central activity in all his spaces.

This chapter also situated the *mazar* of Bawa in Coatesville and two predominant, and interwoven, narratives were provided in the discussion of the *mazar*. The first was that of the members of the Fellowship who utilize this space for a range of activities. These are inclusive of community commemorations (e.g. Bawa's death anniversary and meetings), burial of members in the cemetery, and farming projects, which are all completed by members who reside near the large complex that includes the *mazar*, and volunteer their time as service to Bawa. For many of the Fellowship members, the *mazar* in Coatesville is connected to Mankumban (the shrine to Maryam in Jaffna). It is also a central communal space of gathering, and one that was solidified with Bawa's burial on this property and the subsequent building of a shrine dedicated to him. Members of the Fellowship who reside in the United States, Canada, and elsewhere (i.e. England and Saudi Arabia) visit the *mazar* to maintain connections with Bawa but also view the *mazar* as part of a larger network of places that includes his spaces in Sri Lanka, as well as other Islamic holy sites such as Mecca. The members of the Fellowship, especially those who live in immediate proximity to the *mazar*, have also been transformed into the custodians of the *mazar* and hosts to visiting pilgrims.

In the past two decades, a new cohort of visitors of immigrant Muslims have started arriving at Bawa's *mazar*, and it is their stories that make up the second narrative referenced above. These visitors from across the United States and Canada, who originate from predominantly Muslim majority nations, have found the *mazar* to be a site that reminds them of their natal lands, wherein memory defines the experience of this space, as much as faith and accessing *baraka*. The thought of a burial tomb for a Muslim saint in the United States is almost too good to be true, and so, as many of the visitors informed me, they come to the *mazar* to see if it is actually real. These pilgrims then share the news of the *mazar* among their families and friends by word-of-mouth, or online by posting of photographs on social media (e.g. Facebook), and via other media such as local or community newspapers. And in so doing, they have spread the message that there is indeed a Sufi saint buried in Pennsylvania and that his *baraka* is ever-present.

In this way, Bawa not only established headquarters in Philadelphia, where regular communal activities take place and Islamic prayers are kept, but his resting place in the United States has helped to solidify him as a Sufi saint and *shaykh*; and so, the Tamil Sufi from Sri Lanka has become the Pennsylvania Sufi of the United States. The varying circuits and movements that take place between the *mazar* and Mankumban is a unique facet of this community and one that further affirms the transnational network of affiliations cultivated by Bawa and his disciples. Bawa's disciples, from Jaffna to Pennsylvania, are living and negotiating individual and distinctive interpretations of Bawa's teachings. Still at the heart of all the rituals and actions, is focused devotion to Bawa. Be it Sufism, Islam, Hinduism, or universal spirituality—from Jaffna to Pennsylvania—Bawa and his teachings are central to how disciples articulate their identity and how they live and perform their belief. With Bawa's formative spaces in the South Asian and North American landscapes laid out in this chapter, the last two chapters shifts to consider the myths and symbols entombed in the shrines of Mankumban (Maryam) and the *mazar* (Bawa).

4

Women's Experiences in Bawa's Spaces

Introduction

Contemporary studies of Sufi women across varying regions have been invested in documenting the complex ways in which Sufi women maintain and create leadership roles, most often as they unfold within negotiated spaces and relationships.[1] Catharina Raudvere's study of Sufi women in Turkey is one such example. In her study, Raudvere called for a shift of scholarly attention away from conventional Islamic spaces, such as the mosque or even the Sufi lodge, when seeking to understand female Sufi presence and activity.[2] She explained that "neither identity nor ritual practices are fixed to particular places"; rather, "new spaces are carved out" by Sufi women whose performance of a religious identity is dominated by familial, political, economic, and social obligations.[3] This paradigm shift does not necessarily speak to gender roles as fully egalitarian or restrictive. Rather it conveys the reality of how women have been viewed in most religious traditions, especially in Sufism, as occupying liminal spaces. In her own study, Raudvere initially began working with "formal Sufi groups" but she found that she needed to move toward "informal group of women with only peripheral connections to the traditional established orders."[4] Raudvere's argument implies a clear distinction between center and periphery, conventional (mosque and Sufi) and nonconventional spaces (domestic) in the presence of women in Sufi life; these binaries of spaces and experiences, however, are not always the reality of Sufi women's movements. Theirs is a complex reality as they constantly negotiate their gendered positionality across metaphysical and physiological and private and public domains, official and unofficial spaces, and in relation to male and female Sufi teachers. If one does not begin by accepting women's liminality and negotiated states of being as the foundational point to engage with gender and Sufism in America, then one has negated a very fundamental reality of being a woman in Sufi orders and movements.[5]

This chapter explores the varying intersections of women's roles, presences, and authority as they manifest in the transnational movements of the Bawa

Muhaiyaddeen Fellowship and the Serendib Sufi Study Circle. I contend that the place of women in Bawa's communities cannot be neatly categorized, nor treated as far more novel (i.e. liberal) in the American context, especially in light of the Sri Lankan milieu. What is apparent in the descriptions of the spatial and ritual practices, as documented in the previous chapters and discussed further below, are the degrees to which women maintain negotiated positions in Bawa's movement. Bawa's own directives for his transnational female students evade easy categorizations. For instance, in Jaffna, Bawa appointed women as active leaders (i.e. the Matron) and he dedicated a mosque to Maryam (Mankumban), while in Philadelphia, he encouraged women to lead and teach the *salat*, but he did not institutionalize female prayer leaders after the construction of the mosque. The watershed event that complicated the presence of women in the Fellowship in America was when a *masjid* was added, which seemingly moved the community toward an Islamic orthodoxy. In so doing, the *masjid* introduced questions about Islamic legitimacy.

However, in its addition to the broader Fellowship spatial composition, the shrine of Bawa in Coatesville *countered* the mosque, particularly in terms of its spatial accessibility, both religiously and culturally, while also being accessible to females. Neither the shrine nor the mosque, as has been noted thus far, were distinct developments in Bawa's American Fellowship, rather they were transformations and transmissions of the seminal sites constructed by Bawa in Sri Lanka. Both these sacred sites changed over time in their own milieus. For instance, where Mankumban was initially a mosque, it transformed into a mosque-shrine complex through the direction of Bawa's senior students in Jaffna, whereas the mosque and the shrine in the Fellowship are maintained as two separate sites. In both instances, the construction of the mosques (God's house) were directed by Bawa, while the shrines were added by Bawa's students. Significantly then, it is in and around these spaces (e.g. mosques and shrines) that the contestations over the presence of women, especially in terms of their accessibility and authority in relation to Bawa, Sufism, Islam, Hinduism, and spirituality, are most palpable. The contours of spatial transformations, practices, and accessibility in these spaces, and its relationship with women, illustrate the intricacies of gender not only in the Fellowship in America, but of lived Sufism writ large. As such, an examination of women's experiences in Bawa's communities raise two significant and interrelated questions—is the Fellowship liberalizing gender norms in the American context or is the movement becoming more Islamically orthodox and thus, limiting female access and presence?

This chapter, then, considers the complex lived and metaphysical realities of feminine presence and authority in Bawa's communities. In Bawa's transnational movements, where the sole spiritual and formal authority of the community remains a male *shaykh* and saint, there is evidence of vibrant and varying intersections of female presences in relation to spaces (not fixed), one that is only realized when the personal and spatial relations in an American movement's natal counterpart in Sri Lanka is fully mapped. I argue that the role of women in Bawa's transnational movement cannot be framed simply as far more liberal (or egalitarian) in America, as some would presume in their engagement with discourses of Sufism in America, but is rather deeply embedded with questions of Islamic orthodoxy. Engagement with women in Sufism in America is not limited solely to their sex or gender, rather it is predicated upon variables that implicate their performance of a Sufi or spiritual identity. The factors that shape the roles of women include metaphysical ideals (e.g. creative feminine or Maryam), spatiality, notions of legitimacy and authenticity (e.g. Islamic orthodoxy), the directives of the *shaykh*, Bawa, and of course women's own wills and desires. The transnational experiences and practices of women in Bawa's movement capture the ways in which contemporary Sufism unfolds spatially in and around mosques and shrines. Gender norms in Bawa's movement is another illustration of the convergences of religious, social, and cultural factors that shape the transmission of Sufism in the global West.

The Feminine Archetype: Bawa's Teachings on the Figure of Maryam

On April 16, 1976, in Toronto, Canada, during a discourse, Bawa provided details of Jesus' conception through Maryam. After relaying the narrative of the archangel Jibril (Gabriel) blowing the "holy spirit," or breath of God, into Maryam to conceive Jesus (the spirit of God), Bawa asks those in the audience, "Who is Maryam?"[6] In his reply, Bawa distinguishes between the "form" known as Maryam, who was the mother of Jesus according to the narratives found in Christianity and Islam, with the essence of what Maryam represents. He explains that Maryam was the "strength of God, . . . the duty of God, . . . the love of God."[7] She was the one who "surrendered" and because of her complete submission to the will of God, she is a "symbol" or "sign" of God.[8] Bawa explains that this understanding of Maryam can be grasped through "wisdom" that allows the seeker to distinguish it from its "form."[9]

It has been difficult to assess the elusive nature of the relationship between Maryam and Bawa. In the narratives that I heard from Bawa's disciples, primarily in Sri Lanka, there is a sense that there was a real encounter between Maryam and Bawa in a historical and metaphysical sense. The essence, that is, Bawa (e.g. the *qutb*; see Chapter 5), met and offered refuge to Maryam during a time of need. At the same time, Maryam had a deeply metaphysical significance for Bawa, which manifested in the dedication of a mosque to her, which then was transformed into a shrine by Bawa's senior students in Jaffna. In Philadelphia, most are apprehensive to speak about Mankumban and its relationship to Maryam. For some of my interlocutors, this idea was "too far-fetched" and too heretical for a community with Islamic orientations. In all Fellowship publications, there are hardly any references to Maryam beyond her historical reality as the mother of Jesus. Others contended that this was one of Bawa's most mystical teachings and could not be easily understood by everyone, and hence it was kept obscure.

In the discourse of Bawa on Mankumban and the Philadelphia *masjid* entitled by Bawa's students as "Bawa's Vision of Mankumban and Philadelphia Mosque," there is no mention of Maryam.[10] In this discourse, Bawa parallels Mankumban and the Fellowship *masjid* as symbols of paradise. By extension, if Mankumban and the *masjid* in Philadelphia are both "God's House" and are representative of heaven, then arguably, Maryam's memorialization in Mankumban is emblematic. She is a vessel that guards the threshold to the ultimate sphere of divinity. According to Bawa's understanding of Maryam, she is the "strength, . . . duty, [. . . and] love of God"; she signifies the exemplary state of a human being and, just as the Prophet Muhammad is viewed as a light that existed before Creation, Maryam exists as a similar light in reality for Bawa. Both are principles of *al-insan al-kamil* (perfected human being) and states of being that Bawa challenged all his disciples to strive for regardless of religious affiliations (see Chapter 5). The idea of Maryam as a historical and perfected personage that brought forth the divine soul (Jesus) is in line with the metaphysical understandings of Maryam as expressed by other Sufi personalities.

In Islam, and its esoteric traditions, Maryam is understood to be the vessel that contained the Word of God (*kalimat Allah*) or Jesus ('Isa) and also the example of a life of complete "surrender" or servitude to the will of God. In the Qur'an, Maryam—the mother of 'Isa (Jesus)—is the only female that is mentioned by name.[11] These references to Maryam in the Qur'an have resulted in a rich tradition of qur'anic exegesis (*tasfir*). Many scholars and theologians have debated Maryam's role as a prophet in line with other prophetic figures of the Abrahamic traditions.

In his qur'anic commentary, the jurist and Shi'a *imam* Ja'far al-Sadiq (d. 765) expounds that Maryam's role is significant for her absolute servanthood.[12] Her womb was the sacred vessel that brought forth the "divine-logos" or the "*nabi-kalimah*" (prophet-logos). Ja'far also comprehends her role as a prophet.[13] Her status as prophet is necessary to his "interfaced-hierarchy" that was developed as part of God's "divine display" of Light which "erupts in a powerfully whirling vortex: Mary, Muhammad, Abraham, Moses, Joseph, all '*muhammad*' [praised] perfect '*ubudiyah* [servitude], reascending to *rububiyah* [lordship] whence they poured down."[14] Accordingly, in this exegetical tradition, Maryam is a prophet, in the company of Muhammad, Abraham, and Moses. Similar exegeses are offered by other jurists, such as the Andalusian Ibn Hazm (d. 1064) who claimed that Maryam, along with Moses's mother and Asiyah (the wife of the Pharaoh), were all prophets.[15] Maryam is viewed as a paradigmatic example of servitude that was solidified even prior to her physical birth as Maryam's mother, Hanna, consecrated Maryam to God while she was in the womb. Many traditions emerged in Islam that portrayed Maryam as the soul in complete submission to God, hence she has also been given the status of a saint.

Although theological debates of the exact prophetic (or nonprophetic) nature of Maryam persist in Islamic mystical traditions, the figure of Maryam is distinctively steeped within a cosmological and metaphysical discourse. She is an exemplar of the *feminine ideal*, an archetype that led 'Attar of Nishapur (d. 1220), the Persian poet and biographer, to write:

> The holy prophets have laid it down that "God does not look upon your outward forms." It is not the outward form that matters, but the inner purpose of the heart, as the Prophet said, "the people are assembled [on the Day of Judgment] according to the purposes of their hearts" . . . So also 'Abbas of Tus said that when on the Day of Resurrection, the summons goes forth, "O men, the first person to set foot in the class of men [e.g. those who are to enter Paradise] will be Maryam, upon whom be peace."[16]

'Attar evokes a traditional idea that on the Day of Judgement, Maryam will be the first among people to "enter Paradise." This belief has historically influenced Sufi women's piety, as Maryam exemplified and affirmed that it was indeed possible to be a woman on the Sufi path. Many women in classical periods aspired to the ideal state of Maryam or were associated with Maryam; in one instance, Rabi'a al-'Adawiyya (d. 801), widely recognized as the first female Muslim mystic, has been called the "one accepted by men as a second spotless Mary."[17] This state of Maryam is captured seminally in the work of the Andalusian Sufi mystic and philosopher Muhyiddin Ibn al-'Arabi (d. 1240).

For Ibn al-'Arabi, as Henry Corbin writes, Maryam is "the feminine [who is] invested with the active creative function in the image of the divine Sophia."[18] Ibn al-'Arabi presents the "celestial woman as a feature of the divine" who stands above the male.[19] To contemplate Eve, "the perfect image of God embodied," was for the mystic to contemplate the divine.[20] Figures like Fatima (the daughter of the Prophet Muhammad) and Maryam became real and symbolic examples in theological and literary traditions (e.g. the works of Jalaludin Rumi) of this ideal "celestial woman."[21] This *sophia* (wisdom) is necessary to participate in the "dialectic of love" and so Sophia (Maryam) becomes "theophany par excellence" resulting in her manifestation of the divine qualities of "Beauty" and "Compassion."[22] Corbin continues,

> That is why feminine being is the Creator of the most perfect thing that can be, for through it is completed the design of Creation, namely, to invest the respondent, the *fedele d'amore*, with a divine Name in a human being who becomes its vehicle. That is why the relation of Eve to Adam represented in exoteric exegeses could not satisfy the theophanic function of feminine being: it was necessary that feminine being should accede to the rank assigned by the quaternity [group of four], in which Maryam takes the rank of creative Sophia.[23]

Thus, where Eve and Adam represented "exoteric exegeses," according to interpretations by Ibn al-'Arabi, Muhammad and Maryam complete the quaternity of the primordial and eternal cosmic plan. For Ibn al-'Arabi, the "spiritual woman" epitomizes the ultimate example of union with the divine.

For the Persian poet and mystic Ruzbihan Baqli (d. 1209), Maryam's significance emerges from her representation as the "meeting of the human and the divine: divine disclosure (*tajalli*) and clothing (*libas*),"[24] which meant that for some Sufis, Maryam's life was also paralleled to Khidr, the perennial mystic. In the qur'anic story alluding to Khidr and his episode with Prophet Moses (Musa) (18:60-82), Khidr has access to knowledge that Moses, a messenger and prophet of Allah, did not.[25] In paralleling Maryam to Khidr, Maryam is no longer simply the mother of 'Isa but a model of chastity, purity, and an exemplar of absolute servitude to God, just like Khidr. According to these esoteric thinkers, the entirety of her role can only be seen when contextualized within a larger cosmic plan. Maryam's perfected status (*kamil*) is dependent on her being the fulfillment of the necessary creative feminine that God needs to complete Creation.

It is these metaphysical interpretations of the cosmic Maryam that popularized visitations to her tombs or associated sites, by Christians and Muslims alike.[26] Churches dedicated to the Virgin Mary are sometimes shared spaces between Christian and Muslim followers, as evident at the shrine to Maryam in Ephesus, Turkey. Aliah Schleifer writes:

> From the perspective of the classical Muslim scholars, Mary, in the Qur'an and Sunna, is a symbol that brings together all revelation. As a descendent of the great Israelite prophets, the bearer of the word, the mother of Jesus, and as traditional Sunni Islam's chosen women of all the worlds, Mary is symbolic of the Qur'anic message that revelation has not been confined to one particular people. This symbolism is embodied in the placement of part of 3:37 above many a prayer-niche (*mihrab*), including that of the Juyushi Mosque, one of the oldest Fatimid mosques in Cairo.[27]

For instance, Catholic devotion to the Virgin Mary is prominent in Sri Lanka and there is even a Catholic shrine to the Virgin Mary near Mankumban. It is perhaps the latter shared traditions of Mary/Maryam across Christian and Islamic traditions and her metaphysical role in the cosmic plan as conveyed in some Sufi interpretational traditions that appealed to Bawa.

As relayed in Chapter 2's discussion of Mankumban's significance, senior students of Bawa expressed that Maryam lived (or was present) at this location historically, hence Bawa constructed the mosque (or God's House) for her. Still, despite the indefinable nature of Bawa's relationship to Maryam, it is believed that Maryam's presence (the creative feminine) is memorialized at Mankumban. Mankumban's dedication to Maryam is notable in Bawa's transnational movement. Maryam is a substantial cosmological principle in Sufism. For Bawa's disciples, her commemoration at Mankumban is a central part of his teaching. Although his *ashram* was his place of residence, Mankumban is the first known institution that Bawa ever built and he sought out this particular property specifically because of its connection to Maryam. Its construction began with Tamils who helped lay its foundation and it was completed with the assistance of American disciples who arrived in Jaffna. Numerous disciples, both from Sri Lanka and North America, have spoken of mystical experiences with Maryam (highlighted in Chapter 2). Maryam's mosque-shrine in Jaffna not only encapsulates metaphysical ideals, it also signals to the crossroads of feminine devotional activities and authority in Jaffna for Bawa's followers.

The Matron and Women's Devotion in Jaffna

The figure of authority at the *ashram* is the Matron. When Bawa was alive, he appointed a "matron" as the caretaker of his residence and the caretakers of this *ashram* have solely been females since then. This particular role of female authority may stem from a cultural and social idea that females more naturally perform the role of nurturing and caring for visitors in an *ashram* or hospice.[28] Since Bawa did not have a wife or children, it was possible that this task of caretaking necessitated the position of a matron at the *ashram* to take over the leadership of this "female task." The Matron maintains the *ashram* and is the treasurer of the Jaffna branch. She leads daily prayers at the *ashram* and Mankumban, as described in detail in Chapter 2. She has even stood up as an authority before the community during *jumʿa* (Friday congregational prayers) and *poosai* in Mankumban. Since those who are present for *jumʿa* on Friday do not participate in *salat* with the *imam*, for this group, it is the Matron who leads the community in prayer as they sit and face the tomb of Maryam. In her role at the *ashram*, the Matron greets North American visitors; she also tends to the upkeep of Bawa's room in the shrine, leads the meal preparation at both the *ashram* and Mankumban, in addition to leading daily prayers at the *ashram*, which includes the singing of "*Engal* Bawa" (Our Bawa) and *salawat* to the Prophet Muhammad. The Matron's authority in Jaffna also extends to Mankumban.

Mankumban serves many purposes. It is the site of daily and weekly performance of Islamic prayers because there was an *imam* in residence. Local Hindus also join in prayer, not for *salat*, but for their own prayers that consist of the singing of the *salawat* to the Prophet Muhammad and "*Engal* Bawa." It is a site where Hindus also celebrate deities such as Murukan by lighting and decorating the shrine with small clay oil lamps for varying festivals throughout the year. However, the embodied practices of devotion to Maryam—regardless of whether she is understood to be literally entombed here or just honoured—calls attention to a critical detail: in Bawa's Jaffna sites, though male leadership and presence is notable, such as that of the *imam* who is active in ritual performance, the shrine to Maryam forms the axis of devotional activity. Mankumban in Jaffna gives some access into understanding Bawa's metaphysics, as well as his relationship with the timeless idea of Maryam in Sufism, not readily apparent among his American sites.

Mankumban is also a pilgrimage site, which hosts individuals and groups of international pilgrims who arrive to honor both Maryam and Bawa. Pilgrims, who are members of the Fellowship or the Circle, upon their arrival at Mankumban perform personal acts of devotion and veneration at the tomb. Mankumban, both as a *masjid* and shrine, is open to females and males. Although females are not permitted access to *masjid*s in Sri Lanka, women freely enter Mankumban without much restriction in movement and even attire (see Chapter 2). Some Muslim women wore long black *abaya*s (cloak) but they were only loosely veiled, while some Hindu women were loosely covered, or uncovered. (By contrast, in the *masjid* in Philadelphia—where the position of women is designated by a separate entrance and their placement at the back of the mosque—women are also required to uphold strict definitions of modesty including covering their hair and much of the body with loose-fitting attire.) Contrasting the *ashram* and Mankumban in Jaffna to the *masjid* in Philadelphia, I saw very different conceptions of modesty and access to space, particularly as it pertained to women. Gender separation is only maintained during Friday prayers, where men and women sit side-by-side at Mankumban, while during *langar* at Mankumban, the meals are first served to all the men in the hall adjacent to Mankumban and then the women are served as everyone sits on the floor to eat. As suggested in Chapter 2, this is likely due to local patriarchal cultural and social norms of serving males first, rather than a product of a religious injunction by Bawa, especially since this particular food distribution practice commenced after Bawa's death and after the war. Mankumban is accessible to males and females equally, without much restriction, except at the time of women's menses.

In Jaffna, one of Bawa's Sri Lankan nodes, one notes the memorialization of the creative feminine at Mankumban, the authority of the Matron at the *ashram*, and the accessibility offered at Mankumban and the *ashram* for the performance of communal and individual ritual activities for female members of the Serendib Sufi Study Circle. Women actively lead service activities (e.g. cooking) both at the *ashram* and Mankumban, as was the case when Bawa was alive. Moreover, female foreign pilgrims who arrived at the threshold of Mankumban also received full access to the mosque-shrine complex. Thus, for my interlocutors in Jaffna, the active presence of women at the *ashram* or the memorialization of Maryam at Mankumban was not treated as exemplary, but rather seen as the normative feature of Bawa's communities in the Jaffna sites, as a result of Bawa's directives. Markedly, Bawa subverted the gender norms commonly sustained in sacred spaces in the region, as Hindu and Muslim women in Jaffna and in Sri Lanka have restricted access to some temples and most mosques respectively. Bawa did not instill similar regional gender norms in his own spaces, but rather set a precedent of allowing equal access to spaces to females and males, while enshrining Maryam's memory at Mankumban.

This approachability offered by the mosque-shrine complex is indicative of shrine experiences in South Asia more broadly. For instance, in Carla Bellamy's study, the fluid structure of the *dargah* in South Asia served as a basis for female activity. Additionally, these female adherents identified beyond Islam or Sufism. She posits that "Muslim saint shrine culture encompasses forms of religiosity, economy, legitimacy and authority that are particular to South Asian culture as it exists in a subcontinental context rather than particular to exclusively Hindu, Muslim, Sikh or Christian institutions."[29] As a result of these specific cultural-religious contexts of pluralistic shrine cultures in South Asia, she understands *dargah*s as "microcosmic public spaces" wherein fluid identities and communities are created among pilgrims and devotees who often go against the norms of socially constructed ideals.[30] The accessibility offered by the Sufi shrine in various Muslim majority cultures, such as South Asia as posited by Bellamy, has now been transmitted to America, as evidenced at the *mazar* of Bawa in Coatesville. It should be added that not all Sufi shrines in South Asia permit women to enter, such as the case with the inner sanctum of Nizam al-Din Awliya in New Delhi, India. Admittedly, the members of the Fellowship did not construct the *mazar* intentionally nor was it an instruction of Bawa's, but rather it was accidental. In building a memorial for their teacher, they did not realize what the consequence of such a building was for many Muslims around the world, for whom it provides a sacred capital unlike a mosque. Bawa's shrine is approachable in the eyes of the pilgrims who travel to it in Pennsylvania, because of the charismatic presence of the saint entombed therein (i.e. Bawa).

The movement around the shrines in Jaffna and Pennsylvania represents one spatial reality of accessibility offered to women. Where Mankumban was a mosque first and then a shrine, and now is a mosque-shrine, the historical trajectory of spatial developments took a different path in Pennsylvania. The *mazar* was not the first site of consequence in Bawa's American context but rather the last. However, it was the *masjid* and its development that adds further complexities to the role of women in the transnational movements of Bawa, particularly in terms of spatial accessibility.

"Where Will the Women Stand for Prayers?": Gender, Islamic Orthodoxy, and the Bawa Muhaiyaddeen *Masjid*

Born Jewish, Maryam Kabeer Faye converted to Islam and adopted Sufism well before she met Bawa.[31] And as a student of Bawa, she was part of the group of

American students who accompanied him to Colombo during his final visit to Sri Lanka. During her stay in Colombo with other American and Sri Lankan students, Maryam Kabeer asked Bawa for permission to complete *salat* (daily ritual prayers). By this period in 1980, *salat* was not a communal activity in the Serendib Sufi Study Circle in Colombo or the Bawa Muhaiyaddeen Fellowship in Philadelphia for that matter. According to Maryam Kabeer, Bawa said she should complete her prayers and some of the female American disciples of Bawa that were present were intrigued by Maryam Kabeer completing *salat* and asked Bawa if they should also complete the prayers. Bawa said they could. At the request of these interested students, Maryam Kabeer taught them the prayers and led the prayers herself.

> So I arrived in Sri Lanka, and . . . I heard the call to prayer. And . . . I was sitting in Bawa's presence, and I didn't say anything. And then he said [to me as . . .] I'm asking him internally should I not pray? And he said, "Yes, of course you should pray." And he said "you just go and do your prayers and the people will follow you." And that's what happened, that's how it manifested. I don't know if you heard that? It's just 'cause he [Bawa] said so. He said that to do it, and so I was standing and leading . . . just doing the prayers and the people were there. [Ahamed] Kabeer[32] was somewhere doing the prayers, and I noticed that. So eventually I got my period, I went to Bawa's room; I said, "can Kabeer lead the prayers now" . . . And . . . so he started leading the prayers. And then we both did, and then Bawa told me to teach [those interested . . .], how to do the prayers . . . And then the men started leading the prayers, so then at that point I had no reason to lead the prayers but I still continued to teach.[33]

Maryam Kabeer indicates that the request to pray was an internal one (or silent), but the response from Bawa was both internal and external (e.g. silent and aloud). Bawa told her she could complete her prayers, but responding to interest from some of Bawa's students, he also let her teach the others. Maryam Kabeer was the first *imamah* (female prayer leader) of this mixed-gender group and only stopped leading the prayers when she was menstruating, at which point her then-husband took over as prayer leader.

Anne, a European American disciple of Bawa initially from a Jewish Christian heritage from Philadelphia, was in Colombo at the time of these changes as well. During our interview, she added how she was also one of the women who, like Maryam Kabeer, led not only the prayers but also the call to prayers (*adhan*):

> It was the women, not the men [who led the prayers]. There were four or five women who really wanted to do these prayers. So we had no *imam*, we had

nobody to give the call to prayer; we had nobody to lead the prayers so I said to Bawa "who shall do this?" It's just these women who are interested in doing this. He said "You be *imam*, you give the call to prayer." These are all women. "But Bawa" I said, "someone might hear us from outside, this is a Muslim area." Bawa said "don't' worry God will protect you, you just go do it." So the women are doing the call to prayer, the women are the *imam*s, I think I did it, Maryam [Kabeer] . . . was *imam* for some of the *waqt*s ['times'] . . .. and so some of us would do the call [to prayer], some of us would [lead prayers] and before I left the men got interested and then once the men got interested you know it's embarrassing [to] do the *rakat*s [cycles of prayer] and the men are behind you. I mean like this is getting like crazy so he [Bawa] finally said now it's time . . . enough of them know it, they can take over doing that [leading prayers] and you must step aside. And that was fine with me; it was a big relief to step aside. But that's how it started. It started in Sri Lanka. Then when we came back we had no mosque. I think they cleared out some rows of chairs in the front of the Fellowship so there would be a little space there for people to do it there. Then when he came back is when we built the mosque.[34]

Bawa had his female students lead *salat* and perform the *adhan* in Colombo for the first time. These European American women from Jewish and Christian backgrounds not only took the initiative to lead the prayers, but also willingly stepped aside when the men became active in this new practice, feeling that it was not appropriate for women to lead. Moreover, Bawa did not lead the prayers himself. Here again is another instance in which the *shaykh*'s directive set the course for communal practice that in turn affected gendered roles. Despite Anne's concern in leading prayers in the SSSC house in a Muslim neighborhood in Colombo, out of fear of potential backlash from outsiders, Bawa authorized the females to lead and teach each other and the men. Still, notwithstanding the female disciple's willingness to take on this practice and teach each other, as Bawa guided them, the central concern that emerged when these students returned to Philadelphia was the ever-growing affiliation of the Fellowship to Islam. For the women in particular, this concern was primarily to do with the negative treatment of Muslim women they associated with Islam and in Muslim majority societies. For non-Muslims in America contemplating conversion to Islam, the issue of gender roles is of foremost concern, especially in light of feminism and womanist rights they associated with American culture.[35] Williams, a senior African American Muslim member of the Fellowship, shared this concern with me:

And I consider myself a feminist. I had become a feminist during the civil rights movement and you may know that, what's called, second wave feminism grew out of the civil rights movement. And many of the women who became the leaders of—and these were primarily white women—of the feminist movement had been in the civil rights movement, and I had gone to one of the early meetings of that group that said we need to work on getting rights for women . . . So, I certainly identified as a feminist, and any religion that said women were not equal to men was a no-no for me you know . . . [*Laughs.*] It was like I was concerned but I was not going to go against something. Once I thought this is what Bawa wants us to do, even though I had questions as to why would we, if we're going beyond religion, why do I need to leave Christianity, which I had already done, since that's what I had been brought up in . . . and go into another religion . . . But nonetheless, I certainly helped with the building of the mosque. You know it was a giant project and, while there were professionals brought in to do a lot of the work, we did a lot of it you know, and we're happy to do it because this was Bawa's project, this was what he wanted us to do.[36]

When Williams felt torn between her civil rights and feminist positions and the emergence of the mosque, she kept focused on Bawa and his guidance on these matters. Just as some women in the Fellowship were concerned with the role of women in Islam, others were teaching members of the Fellowship how to complete *salat*. There also emerged another concern for outsiders, and this had to do with women, again.

During the time of the construction of the *masjid*, women's active leadership roles in the Fellowship garnered negative attention from some Muslim visitors. Williams explained further:

But at one point we were seen, as one of the criticisms was that the women are up speaking and this of course was not in the mosque . . . But in the Fellowship itself women lead the meetings . . . So, for some Muslim men, and maybe women too, this was totally inappropriate . . . I do know that some of us, when Bawa was with us and when the mosque was built, the whole issue of where would the women stand for prayer and questions about whether there was going [to] be a wall built; and a number of us women were very upset about the fact that women had to stand behind men.[37]

Williams emphasized the paradoxical concerns that began to emerge in relation to the role of women within the Fellowship and one of its subspaces, the mosque, both for those within the Fellowship and those outside who were trying to ascertain whether the Fellowship was an authentic Islamic community. And they did so by gauging the role of women. Females were active in the Fellowship, which then also became a point of critique. They were leading meetings and when it came to the construction of the *masjid*, some were at the forefront of that construction project. It was precisely the active roles of women, who spoke and led meetings in the Fellowship (not in the mosque) both before and after the construction of the mosque, that created further criticism for the community from outsiders. These non-Fellowship members were Muslims who cited female presence and leadership as evidence of illegitimacy of the Fellowship as an Islamic community.

The addition of the mosque created anxiety for the Fellowship disciples not only because of its promotion of a particular religious identity (e.g. Islam) but also because it introduced new gender boundaries and practices. The new gender practices, including separate entrances for males and females or sections for sitting, commenced with the construction of the mosque and did not reflect the relaxed gender dynamics the American disciples had already experienced with Bawa (see below). Still, Bawa authorized every minute detail in the construction of the *masjid* and ensured that subsequent rituals that took place within the *masjid* were in complete accordance with Islamic legal norms. This was done to ensure that Muslims viewed the *masjid* as Islamically legitimate, as the concern of illegitimacy was already growing due to the active presence of females in the Fellowship. This impacted female disciples and their presence and roles in the mosque a great deal and proved to be an uncertain moment for some of the American female disciples of Bawa. Williams explains:

And once Bawa said, "well, let's have a curtain you know, a sheer curtain," so that's how the curtain, the sheer curtain, came as a result of some women saying "this is not fair. This is not the way we've been with you. You know we had total access, no separation of men and women and all of that." And then, of course, Bawa said, "we will never be accepted in the Muslim community as a real mosque if we don't have a separation between men and women, and if the women are not in the back." 'Cause the whole issue was raised, well what about on the side? . . . But the way the structure [is constructed] with the women's entrance and the stairs, you know that go[es] up in the mosque feeds into one side or the other. And I know that when there's—like—the *Eid*s and stuff like that, sometimes . . . the men take up much more of the floor space . . . And some of us women grumble about that . . . 'cause they keep moving the curtain back and making our space smaller saying, "well, the women can go downstairs . . . and pray down there." And we're saying "well, the men can go downstairs" and then men can go outside if the weather permits. So, there is sometimes that little animosity about us women feeling that [they're] trying to push us back or out, if there's so many men and you need the space . . . So, . . . there [are] some members of the Fellowship who were close to Bawa loved him dearly, [but] they never accepted the mosque . . . I mean they just couldn't do it and they still don't do it. So, you do have that, you still have a split there.[38]

The actual position of the women within the *masjid* was a looming concern for some senior female members of the Fellowship, like Williams. The idea of being relegated behind men or erecting a partition to ensure segregation of the sexes was not positively received. Female members were the prayer leaders (*imamah*) before males assumed this leadership position. Females were the first American disciples to start performing *salat* (Islamic prayers) in Sri Lanka. Even the adoption of the *salat* at an institutional level was crystallized by the support of the very female members who then felt dislocated from that very space and practice that they helped institute, because as Williams relayed, Bawa felt that legitimacy as an Islamic community was dependent on positioning women to certain spaces, at least in the mosque. The actual construction of the *masjid* in Pennsylvania, as Williams explained above, culminated in questions of where women would stand during prayers. In conveying her experience of this critical time in the Fellowship's institutional history, Maryam Kabeer had a far more metaphysical interpretation of the *masjid*, particularly as it relates to the accessibility it offered to women:

> And that's a particularly clean and clear *masjid*. One reason is women have the beautiful place, we're not closed off we're not . . . removed. We have almost the best place in the sense of the dome and everything and it's a very clean and clear place for me. It's just like, it's nothing but a place of prayer so, literally, that's what it is. It's a place of light, a place of prayer, purification.[39]

Where Williams relates to the uneasiness she felt because she had to pray behind the males of the congregation, Maryam Kabeer expresses a contrasting perspective. Maryam Kabeer views the section that women pray in at the *masjid* as far more sacred than the space occupied by men. Women sit in a space that is directly below the hallmark feature of the mosque, the stained-glass dome with the *asma' ul-husna* (beautiful names [of God]). Maryam Kabeer's justifications are intriguing because of the official leadership role she has beyond the Fellowship. She is a female *shaykha*, formerly initiated into the Mustafawiyya Order, a Senegalese Sufi order with chapters in America, after Bawa's death. Maryam Kabeer is adamant that even though Bawa's intentions may have been partly to challenge gender norms, in the boarder context she did not see it as an act of defiance against Islamic gender rules:

> But that's how Bawa did it, and I'm sure he did it to blow . . . this status quo . . . But in the meantime, we didn't keep doing that, like what happened with . . .

Amina Wadud,[40] is not something that I would do. And I have spoken at count-
less Muslim conferences and especially Sufi conferences and we never had any
tension with anybody. I mean . . . if you go to the right organization . . ., if you're
guided to the right group . . . the fact that I'm a woman doesn't limit me at all
as a person who can share knowledge and wisdom and light . . . And the love
of Allah. But I would not be an *imam* in front of men anymore, I'm just saying
that . . . I think in the old days, when I was in Jerusalem, a young guy came and
I was just doing my prayers and he prayed behind me. This is kind of very informal [leadership . . .]. Only in the context of Bawa did this even happen formally
but who knows for what reason that that happend . . . But furthermore, none of
the men were standing up and doing it. And I don't even think many of them
knew it and we don't know why Bawa waited until this point . . . to introduce
it . . . Nor is it our problem or our question . . . He knows best; we don't know.
So, . . . I did what God told me and I did what he [Bawa] told me and then I knew
that I didn't have to do that.[41]

Maryam Kabeer did not see leading prayers in Colombo at a time when males
and females gathered to be with Bawa as subversive. She asserts that her act was
in no way comparable to the actions of Amina Wadud, who led mix-gendered
congregation in *salat* at Saint John the Divine in Manhattan in 2005. For her,
the purpose of that moment, and her momentary role in Colombo as a prayer
leader, was beyond her comprehension and only known to God and Bawa. In
addition, she further stressed that she would not lead in such a capacity again.
Maryam Kabeer identifies as a Sufi *shaykha* with authority to teach. She attends
Sufi, Islamic, and religious conferences and speaks from a position of authority
that she has been initiated into by her male *shaykh*, and yet she feels that leading a mix-gendered congregation in *salat* is not within her means to perform
ever again.

     During Bawa's tenure in Philadelphia, females were the only disciples who
maintained close proximity to Bawa regularly. His closest disciples were females.
They served as translators, took care of his food, and some groups of female disciples were even known as the "room girls." This accessibility was viewed as a great
honor, as Bawa could erupt into a discourse or song at any moment (even during the middle of the night). This privilege was treated as giving the disciple an
ability to readily access his *baraka*. To access this privilege, the "room girls" slept
on any available floor space in Bawa's room, whereas male disciples slept downstairs on the floor of the meeting room.[42] Of course, this level of convenience to
female students by a male spiritual teacher can be construed as erotic, as was
the case with some spiritual teachers in America during the same period, but

there are no reports of illicit relationships between Bawa and his female, or for that matter, male, students nor were any reported to me during my field research.

Female disciples maintained active roles in other aspects of the Fellowship as well: they were, and still are, involved in the publication of books; they are members of the executive committees and subcommittees where they hold varying executive positions, such as the executive secretary; they have translated and edited Bawa's discourses; and women have even led discourse meetings in the past and still do so today. When it comes to the positionality of women in the Fellowship, there are spatial boundaries that define women's roles and activities and at times contradict one another. One of the defining factors that implicated women's presence in the Fellowship in Philadelphia is the mosque, if they choose to engage this space. Upkeep of particular practices of Islamic *adab* implicates women's outer appearance more than men in the Fellowship, especially if they are converts to Islam. This tendency is captured by Marcia Hermansen, who observed that "to the degree that *sharia*-based ritual is incorporated, gender distinctions become visibly operative in the functioning of American Sufi movements."[43] Hermansen explained that "female participants in Western Sufi movements may feel the need to negotiate their understandings of gender roles so as to reflect both traditional authenticity and a contemporary sense of gender justice."[44] If "traditional authenticity" requires particular religious clothing and gender separation, then this may mean that following these gender norms is a means to affirm their newly accepted Islamic identity for female converts, who participate in American Sufi communities. A pattern that is evident in the Fellowship among female European and African American members who converted to Islam.

Many of my female interlocutors who struggled with engaging with the mosque informed me of the degree to which their attire (or interpretation of modesty) has been critiqued by fellow female Fellowship members who engage the mosque regularly. Female members of the Fellowship who converted to Islam have adopted more permanent attire of head coverings and loose clothing (i.e. beyond the mosque). As Hermansen explains, such transformations in clothing practices are a marker of their new religious identity and their legitimacy as Muslims, according to their interpretation of Bawa's teachings. Those who adopt these modes of "traditional" clothing, are easily marked as the Muslim members of the Fellowship.

One of the first instances when I went to the mosque for prayers, I distinctly remember a female European American convert to Islam, who stopped me and was adamant that I was not dressed modestly enough to enter the mosque.

Despite my hair being covered and my wearing, of what I thought was, modest clothing, she offered me extra clothing that she had before she permitted me to enter the mosque. Similar sentiments were shared by my other female interlocutors who are members of the Fellowship, especially during moments when they tried experimenting with *salat* at the mosque. As a result of such negative experiences, they felt disheartened by the actions of other female Fellowship members in the mosque, who attempted to fix their *hijab* or their clothing—which soured their encounter of this space, and they often felt anxious to return again. These complexities of practices and its accordance with Bawa's teachings was highlighted in an interview with a second-generation member of the Fellowship, who is Canadian (white) and identifies as a Muslim. In recollecting a story of one of the members of the Fellowship, he stressed how Bawa himself varied in his approaches to modesty in his own community, especially in an effort to focus on inner cultivation (or esoteric approaches). He recounted an incident he had heard about a female Fellowship member:

> She went to the mosque once and she felt super weird because someone came behind her, a woman, and put a shawl on her head. She's like the fact that someone would think like that's their right to do that, like I'm in prayer, how can you interrupt another person's prayers. Like that's rough. But she said she remembered working in the garden and [. . . how] Bawa would be talking to her and she'd be wearing what someone might say immodest clothing, right. She'd be working in the garden; she's really sweaty, in shorts, t-shirt. Bawa never saw any of that. And that's sort of the perspective too. And I remember I have another friend and one time they were in Philly and there's these prostitutes on the street and the person's like "oh, look at those prostitutes like disgusting, how could they wear that?" And Bawa turned to the guy and said "I didn't see anything. What were you looking at?" So it's like he turns it around completely, right?[45]

As often is the case, disciples of Bawa do signal to different teachings and events to support the varying inward and outward practices that need to be adopted at the Fellowship. Even when it comes to women's presence, authority, role, and attire, members of the Fellowship point to directives given by Bawa as the reason behind their decisions and their practice. In the American context, it is the leaders of the community who set the trajectory of gender practices, a trend that is captured in William Rory Dickson's study as well.[46] Similar importance of the role of the *shaykh* in directing the types of authority and presence women maintain in Sufi movements has been captured by Rosemary Corbett's analysis on Muzaffer

Ozak's community in New York, as well as Julianne Hazen in her study of the Alami Tariqa in Waterport, New York.

For instance, Hazen found that gender norms were negotiated between the natal cultures of the *shaykh* and the American culture into which they were transplanted.[47] In the Alami Tariqa, compromises were made as traditions, from the Sufi *shaykh*'s land of origin (i.e. the Balkans), intersected with the norms of the new host country, in Waterport, New York. Additionally, however, Hazen found that the dynamics of an individual disciple's "ethnic background" within the American Sufi community also played a critical role in these compromises. According to Hazen, these were the critical factors that impacted the roles of gender, both in the spiritual development of *murid*s and also in the everyday activities (i.e. rituals, dress, etc.) of the *murid*s. Within the Alami Tariqa, though, conversion to Islam is necessary to participate fully in the community and, as such, this creates distinctive gender norms not evident in communities that do not require conversion to Islam, like the Fellowship.

Still, Bawa's respective locations in Jaffna and Pennsylvania have fostered differing gender roles and practices, signaling to the ways in which Bawa's own engagement with women's role in his communities transformed through his teachings and spaces as they were transmitted. For instance, the debates of female attire at the Fellowship signal to a marked departure in terms of practices in Jaffna. Though the Matron wore a *hijab* and a sari (traditional wrap of women in Sri Lanka, especially Tamil women), in my time with her, she never insisted that I or any visitor to the *ashram* or Mankumban wear particular clothing. Women in Jaffna, as I described in Chapter 2, dressed according to their own cultural and religious practice, and instilled their own practices. Clothing and attire is a way in which women have negotiated their Islamic identity in Sufi communities in America, more so than in Sri Lanka. In Philadelphia, the mosque is not a hybrid space (as Mankumban is). Its development and its role in the Fellowship has led to Islamic practices that have affected women more than men.

At the Fellowship, Bawa established concurrent spaces within which to negotiate these gender norms: women had access to the *masjid*, but not as leaders, and their presence is maintained though it is through a separate entrance and separate space, that is, a lace curtain that partitions the mosque with men at the front and women behind them. For Muslim women who are not members of the Fellowship, the accessibility provided by Bawa's mosque is incomparable to that of other mosques they would have attended, either in their natal context or in

America, where they are at times not permitted to enter and/or they have been relegated to the basement or a separate room entirely.

Beyond the mosque, the Fellowship house is fully accessible to women (both members and non-members, Muslims, and non-Muslims). Female members of the Fellowship have formative roles as leaders of the spaces and the institution at large. The role of women in the Fellowship, however, is not only defined by members of the Fellowship, but also immigrant Muslim visitors, such as those who attend the *mawlid*.

Piety and Gender at the Fellowship: *Mawlid al-Nabi*

Women's accessibility is spatially dependent, but also ritually contingent, as evident in Mankumban and the *ashram*. In Philadelphia, during public Muslim practices, such as the *mawlid* or congregational prayers at the mosque, female leadership roles are not as prominent, and separation of males and females lead to gendered spaces, such as Bawa's room which is used by women only. Though women were a regular presence in the *masjid* and attended Ramadan and *mawlid* celebrations, they did not lead these events formally in the American spaces belonging to Bawa. Conversely, this lack of authority does not mean that participation in this sacred ritual was not without meaning.[48]

During *mawlid*s at the Fellowship, women did not lead recitations and gendered spaces were enacted, at least in Bawa's room and the classroom, while those who wish to gather collectively without any gender separation can gather in the meeting hall. And yet, the *mawlid* drew a vibrant number of immigrant Muslims from the greater Philadelphia region and beyond, most of whom were women. During the heights of *mawlid* celebrations (for the Prophet Muhammad or for 'Abdul Qadir al-Jilani), women congregated in Bawa's room, which was filled with ethnic and cultural diversity, be it African American and European American converts to Islam; or diasporic Muslims or American-Muslims (i.e. Pakistani, Syrian, East African Indian, and more). The separation by sex may be seen as a reversal of gender egalitarian practices normally experienced by women of the Fellowship from an American disciple's perspective, but for women from Muslim-majority regions (Old World Islam)—such as those from South Asia, North or East Africa, and the Middle East—*mawlid*s are rituals that they may have only previously experienced from a domestic space and their participation is impactful. This experience and interpretational memory of the *mawlid* became clear to me when an East African Indian Muslim member of the Fellowship informed me that the recitation reminded her of the stories that her mother and aunts used to share with each other when she was a child; stories that male members of her family criticized the women for sharing. Not only did she feel the immensity of the *baraka* of the *mawlid*, which she had just experienced for the first time at the Fellowship, but she also associated it with the nostalgic experience (e.g. memory) from her childhood with her mother and aunts from East Africa and India.

The commemoration of *mawlid*s has historically been affiliated with women. For instance, Marion Katz has shown that the *mawlid* was associated with women's "domestic" realm. The female presence in the commemoration of this particular ritual was an issue in "anti-*mawlid* polemics" as early as the fourteenth century:

> The *mawlid* celebration sidestepped issues of ritual purity and mosque access, provided a religiously meaningful framework for women's sociability, and could be incorporated into the life-cycle occasions (such as marriage, childbirth, and death) that punctuated women's lives. The performance of *mawlid*s could be harnessed to the personal and familial concerns (marriage, fertility, and the health of family members) that were often most vital to women. Nevertheless, the *mawlid*'s tenuous religious legitimacy might simultaneously devalue and marginalize the religious efforts of the women who cultivated it.[49]

According to Katz, *mawlid*s provided a gendered experience intertwined within domestic spaces, relationships, and life cycles. And yet, it was precisely the participation and proliferation of the *mawlid*s by women that garnered this ritual negative attention for women and some traditions of Sufism. Some Muslim theological and legal scholars felt that the *mawlid*s were not part of the *Sunna* and consequently deemed it *bid'a* (heretical innovation); hence, it has been readily and pejoratively labeled as "popular Islam."[50] Suggesting again, similar to the debates surrounding women at the mosque, that women's participation in the *mawlid*s (e.g. rituals) have led to questions of its Islamic legitimacy.

Rituals, and their embodiment in spaces in the Fellowship and the Circle are multidimensional in their reception and resonance for participants. Whereas in the previous chapters, I conveyed how parallel congregations are formed during rituals in Bawa's spaces and may be defined by religious, and at times cultural, factors, the reality is that parallelisms also unfold among women themselves due to religious and cultural factors. For this chapter's purpose in problematizing women's presence in the Fellowship and the Circle, this insight is critical, as it prevents easy taxonomies for women's roles and presence in Bawa's movement. In this example of parallel congregations, at least two differing perspectives are illustrated as it relates to women and the *mawlid* in the Fellowship. First, *mawlid*s are historically associated with women's participation in countries like Egypt in Old World Islam. Second, from an American experience of gender norms, the *mawlid* seems to perpetuate gender inequality in religious practice, as genders are separated (unless one chooses to participate in the meeting hall) and males are the only ones able to lead the recitations of this particular Islamic practice. Still, the experiences of both non-Fellowship Muslim and Fellowship (Muslim and non-Muslim) women in Bawa's spaces in Philadelphia cannot be homogenized. Rather—by valuing the plurality of voices, experiences, and perspectives in a single event—our analysis of Sufism and gender in America can only become more complex and closer to reality. Admittedly, gender is a process (and one that is notable within the Fellowship and Circle specifically), it is negotiated, and it sits on the crossroad of various factors, especially spatially and ritually. When unpacking these intersections, one notes webs—not binaries of gender inclusion or exclusion—simultaneously existing in negotiation with each other as enacted by Bawa's teachings and his interpretation of Islam and Sufism, in the Fellowship and the Circle. As much else in Bawa's movement, the spectrum of the complex and varying roles of women and the feminine reflects the realities of how women have experienced and embodied Sufism historically.

From Metaphysical to Biological
Women in the Study of Sufism

Bawa's transnational movement encompasses the broader complex spectrum of women in Sufism. The memorialization of Maryam at Mankumban as well as the complex and negotiated realities of the Fellowship women's experiences provide avenues for understanding how Sufism has unfolded in historical contexts. For instance, the veneration of the celestial woman (or ideal feminine, such as Maryam) is complicated by the fact that the "perfect woman as Sophia or the creative feminine" is not equal to the social female human being.[51] In the writings of early Sufis in hagiographical and poetical literature one sees the "role of the physical woman as human being . . . minimized so that she becomes an accessory to the course of events in mystic life" while concurrently encountering the veneration of the "celestial woman as the ideal, the creative feminine."[52]

Thus, one of the challenges of studying gender and Sufism (or any religious tradition) is locating female voices amid a tradition that has been primarily penned by male teachers, scholars, and writers. On the one hand, the feminine ideal—both as a creative and theophanic principle—has been central to many Sufi thinkers' theologies because it has been interpreted as a necessity in cosmological creation, one that is readily evident with Bawa's memorialization of Maryam at Mankumban.[53] Nevertheless, this elevation of the ideal feminine in cosmology did not readily translate to women, as earthly and biological entities. These two simultaneous processes of relating to woman—the social role of females and cosmic feminine—resulted in dual methodologies in the study and representation of women and the feminine in Sufism.[54] It is due to this double standard of women's role in Sufism that Arezou Azad frames the historical presence of Sufi women on the path through the state of "reverse genderizations" or "being a man."[55] This approach of "reverse genderizations" is also proposed by Jamal Elias in his studies of women in Sufism wherein he notices that women who reached a state of perfection were often said to have achieved the status of a man, such as the Indian saint Farid al-Din Ganj-i Shakar (d. 1266) who spoke of "pious woman" as "a man sent in the form of a woman."[56] Sufi identities of men were not marked by their "maleness" as a biological and social category while "for a woman, however, the story is rarely told without reference to the dynamics of gender."[57] Exceptional Sufi women were often treated as "truly men" because they transcended their "women-ness" through the rigors of mystical devotion.[58] Despite these varying social factors that have impeded access to voices of female Sufis in historical contexts, Laury Silvers recognizes that "pious, mystic, and Sufi women were engaged socially with one another. They visited each other at home, met at gatherings, travelled to spend time with each other, passed along accounts of each other's knowledge or practices, worshipped with one another, and caught up with each other's news."[59] These opportunities for female participation, even in informal and private domains, have been documented in early Sufism.[60] It is between these two tiers of femininity, one in the physical biological and social form and the other in the spiritual and metaphysical form, that the male Sufi is embedded.[61] Although the male as human being may be hierarchically below the "ideal woman" he is, nevertheless, above the female human being.[62] Woman is a mirror who reflects man's contemplation of the divine. This complex hierarchical relationship between God, the ideal woman, man as Adam, and woman as Eve—as embodied within societal gender norms—is crucial to grasping the representation of Sufi women both historically and in modern times.

These frameworks of classical and historical contexts of Sufi women need to be employed in the study of contemporary Sufism, especially in America, as they highlight the varying intersections within which women's identities and spheres of activities traverse. The presence and engagement of Sufi women is dependent on negotiating religious, social, economic, familial, and cultural norms, which affect women more, as is evident in the South Asian sphere, for instance. The same is true of Sufi women's role in America, as has been discussed in this chapter. It is upon the convergence of various identities that Sufi women forge a path in personal expressions of piety and religiosity, which must be navigated in both the public and private domains but also in various spaces such as the mosque and the shrine, but they are not clearly demarcated, as when it comes to women, questions of religious legitimacy, particularly as it pertains to an *Islamic* ideal, also follow.[63]

Gender and gendered spaces are fluid and dynamic. Moments of gender separation and nonseparation, and moments of female leadership, and lack thereof, call attention to a continual process of gendering in the Fellowship that is not static but organic and constantly fluctuating. Importantly, it is a process with origins predating Bawa's arrival in Philadelphia. In Jaffna, the presence of female devotees and female-led activities in the *ashram* requires a critical reassessment of the assertion that one of the facets of Sufism in America is its adaptation to gender norms of the West. It appears with the Fellowship that this is not necessarily the case. It is possible that this gendering of spaces, especially during Islamic rituals (*mawlid*s and *salat*), is closely tied to the broader trend of Islamization that has been evident among some spaces in the Fellowship, such as the mosque. This trend is deeply tied to authenticating the Fellowship's connection to Islam, which was put forth by Bawa during the construction of the *masjid*. Yet, in Jaffna, where the predominant following are Hindu students of Bawa, Mankumban's relationship to Maryam is openly accepted, and women, such as the Matron, who identifies as a Muslim, are prominent leaders in ritual and spatial activity.

Yet in the modern American phase of Bawa's community, Maryam does not hold a similar platform. Though Maryam's focus among Bawa's Hindu students likely has led to marginalizing her presence among the American communities of Bawa, this shift in theological and philosophical positioning captures Shahab Ahmed's conclusions about the making of *modern Muslims*:

> This *re-calibration of the human relationship with reality* has led modern Muslims to the intellectual, practical, and social *depreciation and invalidation of the authority*

and Truth-value of the practices and discourses of the Pre-Text—philosophy and Sufism—and the concomitant *appreciation and validation of the authority and Truth-value of the practices and discourses of the Text*—law and creed.[64]

As this shift from "Pre-text" to "Text" unfolds, roles and narratives, such as women, namely, Maryam in this example, is "depreciated" as contradicting the "law and creed," when in fact historically seminal figures, such as Ibn al-'Arabi and Bawa, framed their truth within this "Pre-text." In the case of the Fellowship, if one chooses to view it as a modern American Sufi movement, such selective fissures from Sri Lanka, then showcases the trajectories in which even Bawa's communities have validated certain rituals and spaces in the American milieu, while depreciating others, at the behest of a constructed Islamic orthodoxy. Since spaces such as Mankumban are texts in which narratives of Maryam and Bawa are read, the treatment of these multitextual space (and the subsequent appreciation or depreciation) results in selective validation or invalidation of "human and historical Islam," in the name of authenticity and legitimacy, a process which makes the Bawa's American community far more Islamically based on law and creed, while its Sri Lankan community is based on cultural pre-text and rituals, both, however, are part of Bawa's ministry and of Islamic and Sufi history.[65] One of the central variables used to demarcate the authenticity of Sufism and Islam is the role of women. This presents the problematic potential for the double marginalization of Sufi women who must not only present their Sufi identity well, but also affirm their presence in Islam as women who practice both an authentic and "liberal Islam."[66] Such tendencies have been highlighted in historical studies of women in Sufism discussed further above and in contemporary examples from Turkey, Egypt, Senegal, and India; but these nuances have yet to be unraveled in America.

Thus, women's presence in Sufi communities in America are not "modern" (e.g. liberal and progressive) because of the standards of *American gender norms*, such a reading of Sufi women in America reduces the complexity of the lived reality and also purges the historical and cultural factors of the role of women in Sufism and Islam. In the case of the Fellowship, women have reacted differently to their responsibilities, rights, and statuses. Understanding that the presence of women is both space- and ritual-dependent, in addition to the authority of the *shaykh* (e.g. Bawa), in Philadelphia is critical for the advancement of Sufi studies in America, and applying this framework to Bawa's sites in Jaffna opens up the broader context in which women persevere in shrines and mosques, despite their negotiated presence.

Conclusion

From the formative era to its continual development and transformation in modern global contexts, women's involvement has been a barometer with which to measure the *inauthenticity* or *authenticity* of Sufism and Islam. Women's presence within shrine cultures and subsequent spaces associated with Sufi *shaykh*s has troubled those who have viewed women as figures meant to remain in private domains. These same developments are taking place within the American context but there is a particular nuance to the question of gender and Sufism in America. Within the American milieu, all Sufi communities are plagued with the question of authenticity, but Sufi communities have contended to varying degrees with American notions of "gender justice."[67] Women and Sufism in America are read against American cultural and social norms while also attempting to perform authenticity in terms of Islamic practice, especially as it concerns the segregation of the sexes. Thus in the contemporary West, their presence is used to gauge the levels of liberal orientations of an American Sufi movement. The female Muslim immigrant presence adds further complexity to the web of gender embodiment in sacred spaces during rituals in America.

In the Fellowship in Philadelphia, all of Bawa's students are actively involved in the Fellowship house, regardless of gender. In Jaffna, there are more women present. Still, in both instances, women devote their time to helping with the institution and interpret all activity as service to Bawa. From Jaffna to Philadelphia, even though service performed is gendered, the idea of service in general is not. And although the *imam*s in both *masjid*s were males, the Matron occupies the only formal female leadership position. The equivalent of this role does not exist in the Fellowship in Philadelphia. Male and female ancillary leaders have emerged in Philadelphia and in branches across North America (e.g. in Toronto). They sit on various committees and take part in leading their branches. The only figure that could stand out as a figure of formal female authority in Philadelphia is Maryam Kabeer who is now a female Sufi teacher (*shaykha*) in her own right, but members of the Fellowship do not identify her as a leader because she was initiated into another Sufi order. When Maryam Kabeer attends the Fellowship, she attends as a student. In this regard, no one has the same capacity of authority and presence as the Matron of the *ashram*. That said, the Matron at the *ashram* is treated with respect in deference to her devotion to Bawa but she is not an official spiritual leader and she is still seen as a disciple of Bawa.

The Fellowship and its construction of the *masjid* led to a process of *Islamization*, resulting in gender specific conduct (e.g. veiling, gendering of spaces, etc.). Prior to the construction of the *masjid*, women were active players in Bawa's life and they continue to be active at present. Taken together, both these tendencies of gender norms coexist with each other in their respective subspaces. Collectively, these gender norms constitute the experiences of women in the Fellowship and the Circle. So, although women may not be leaders in the *masjid*, they have leadership roles in the Fellowship; they are leaders during Sunday morning discourse meetings, and they are active participants in Islamic and Fellowship activities. But this presence of female leadership in the Fellowship on Sunday morning is not unique to America. Philadelphia served as a useful site of comparison to Jaffna as it signaled how spaces are gendered, usually at the detriment of women during rituals, such as the *mawlid*. The experiences by female participants in rituals in Philadelphia cannot be simply understood as women being excluded or included, but rather the positionality of women during rituals, such as the *mawlid*, depends on who is experiencing a ritual and how (e.g. racial, cultural, and religious identities) they define this experience.

What is far more telling, however, is that in the American Fellowship, the mosque is viewed as a far more Islamic space, than the shrine. It is herein where women are introduced as a problematic to the Fellowship, one which Bawa himself tried to negotiate, and even subverted at Mankumban. In light of these findings, what is apparent is that the complex and imperfect distinctions which refer to women as "Islamic" need to be interrogated. The memorialization of a shrine to Maryam is a distinguishing space, as it represents a timeless Islamic figure and principle in Sufism that is revered as the height of femininity. Maryam, however, is not the only metaphysical ideal in the networks of Bawa. The next chapter turns to the seminal figure who unifies the transnational movement, Bawa, and the varying epithets given to him that situates him as a cosmic principle. Both timeless cosmic ideals, the creative feminine and the perfected being, are essential features of Sufi cosmology and deeply interwoven, and without this, the core of Bawa's ministry, teachings, rituals, and spaces cannot be understood.

5

Swami to *Qutb*: Bawa as *al-Insan al-Kamil*

Introduction

With the physical passing of Bawa, members of the Bawa Muhaiyaddeen Fellowship and the Serendib Sufi Study Circle continue to view Bawa as their *shaykh* (master). Bawa appointed no successor prior to his death. Students of Bawa are passionately resilient to anyone who attempts to claim any leadership away from Bawa. This is reflected in the many debates that have arisen after Bawa's death over visits from Sufi teachers from Turkey or Senegal and Islamic teachers who have subtly attempted to obtain leadership, all without success. Some members have moved to other Sufi communities as they felt that a living *shaykh* was a necessity in their personal paths. But for those who have remained and for new members and pilgrims, they identify Bawa through varying epithets given to him, both by himself but also by his followers. In this chapter, I contend that the varying honorifics ascribed to Bawa have now transformed Bawa into a timeless figure in his death.

This chapter will focus on Bawa as the human authority central to both the Fellowship and the Circle, but it will not attempt to provide a biographical account. Instead, this final chapter examines the different honorifics or epithets given to Bawa by his disciples, both in his life and now in his death to provide insight into the various and distinct cultural and religious milieus that Bawa was embedded within. I engage with the titles and honorifics invoked by his followers including guru, *swami*, father, *shaykh*, and *qutb* in order to comprehend the traditions within which Bawa was located to further elucidate the religious diversity found among Bawa's followers and the relationships they formed with Bawa's spaces and the ritual and devotive activities that unfold therein. In most Sufi orders, teachings become transportable through a *shaykh*-disciple relationship. Here, in the Fellowship and Circle, however, the *shaykh* is not physically present anymore, nor did he authorize anyone to continue his teaching or succeed him. The institutionalization of his teachings and its dissemination has transformed him into a figure who transcends time. He is always present and thus the way to connect with him is through the places he touched and formed. In order to fully comprehend the significance of the centrality of the spaces that I meticulously engaged with in the previous chapters, it is vital to recognize the posthumous role that Bawa continues to play in his transnational community.

Narratives of Bawa: From Early Scholarship to His Disciples

Muhammad Raheem Bawa Muhaiyaddeen began his ministries in northern Sri Lanka in the midst of political and ethnic unrest. He moved to Philadelphia to establish a new community in 1971. He was a farmer, a cook, a healer, a painter, and a philosopher but fundamentally he was a charismatic teacher. His teachings were not limited to a religion, caste, or ethnic community. He kept company with anyone who welcomed him and wished to hear his words. While this did not stop the many bystanders, followers, devotees, and critics from attempting to define or *other* him, Bawa evaded such religious definitions:

> My appearance to the people who see me depends on how the various groups of them choose to view me . . . The Muslims say that I am a Tamil *swami*. The Tamils [Hindus] say that I am a Muslim swami . . . The Christians say that I am a Tamil *swami* . . . In this manner, each such group to whom I go keep on ascribing names to me . . . If there are any more such names, I am happy to have them.[1]

Bawa himself points to the reality of his ministry, as illustrated in these chapters thus far, as inclusive and diverse. And his ability to attract a heterogeneous audience inevitably resulted in the many and varied interpretations of Bawa's personae, particularly in terms of his religious affiliation and authority. Thus far in this study these have included Hindus in Jaffna and Muslims in Colombo, while the Fellowship in Philadelphia is composed of a broad range of members from Muslim Sufis, converts to Islam, universally inclined Sufis, Jewish Sufis, and Catholic Sufis (each individually marrying their inherited religious identities with Bawa's Sufism). In the past two decades, a more prominent faction of immigrant Muslims from various countries like Pakistan, Iran, and Syria now form another significant group in the North American context. Together, this creates a convergence of approaches from various spiritual and religious perspectives of the spaces they occupy both in the Circle and the Fellowship, and the rituals they perform. However, I regularly found throughout my fieldwork that regardless of religious, cultural, and ethnic identities, all the followers, pilgrims, and students from Jaffna and Philadelphia uniformly agreed upon Bawa as the key reason for participating in various rituals and devotion. Upon asking my participants of their understanding of Bawa, I soon discovered that though they accepted Bawa as the central authority and leader of the community, the members, students, and pilgrims' perception of Bawa's authority, metaphysical state, and personae held some unique nuances that complemented the broader understanding of Bawa and thus his transnational movement.

Origin Myths of Bawa

In an early anthology of Bawa's teachings entitled *Guru Mani* (*Teacher's Jewel*), compiled by senior disciples in Sri Lanka, the authors of the text suggest that Bawa arrived in Sri Lanka in 1889 from South India.[2] If this is true, at the time of his death Bawa would have been well over 100 years old.[3] Of course, this is difficult to confirm as Bawa did not relay detailed personal information about himself, especially his age. Furthermore, the vague details of Bawa's early years (i.e. information about his birth, family, or spiritual training), before his sighting at Kataragama, adds to the mystique of his mystical personality, a popular trope found in narratives of holy figures in Sufism specifically as well as in religious traditions in general.

The discourses that address his personal life were collected over time and published in the book entitled *The Tree That Fell to the West: Autobiography of a Sufi.*[4] This is a compilation of different discourses that were given in Tamil, translated into English, and then edited into a book by the Fellowship Press. This text now serves as the sacred biography of Bawa for the Fellowship. In it, Bawa explains that there was once a powerful king who was childless. In the hope of gaining mercy from God, the king promised to perform rituals for twelve years so that God would grant him a child. He built temples, churches, and mosques and performed prayers in each sacred space. In the twelfth year of service the king went to the festival at Murukan temple and on the eve of the festival, the king had a "vision" that directed him to find a baby on the steps of the temple.[5]

On the day of the festival, the king and his driver were walking to the temple when they found a hideous and sickly baby on the steps. The king was disgusted and walked past the baby but the driver was sympathetic and picked him up. The king reprimanded the driver and threatened him to leave the baby or risk punishment but the driver refused. Fired from his position, the driver walked back to his humble home, wife, and two children; but he found that the further he walked, the more the baby began to regain life, beauty, and health. Time passed and the king summoned his driver to return to his job. When the driver appeared at the king's abode, he had brought with him the baby from the temple and the king fell in love "with the light radiating" from the baby's face.[6] The king asked for the child but the driver did not want to give him up but agreeing to share the responsibility of the baby, the driver and his family moved into the king's palace with the child.

Eventually, as the story goes, the baby grew up and, due to his wealth, many tried to kill him and so his father hid him away in the jungles with a *shaykh*.[7] This baby is reputedly Bawa. According to one of his discourses, Bawa gave up his "kingdom . . . to the poor" and stayed with the *shaykh* until he was 18 years old, when he left to wander the world in search of God.[8] Bawa claimed that his search for the Divine led him to "India, Egypt, Iran, Jerusalem[,] and China," during which time he "went into the four religions" of Zoroastrianism, Hinduism, Christianity, and Islam. Within them all, he tried very hard to be with God, yet despite all his efforts to find the truth, he could not find Him:

> The God whom I had within my wisdom was not found there . . . I became crazy, crazy to see my Father. So again, I left and this time I went into the jungle and stayed in the caves. I searched for Him in many, many places. I met the creations called *jinn*s [spirits] and the creation called fairies. They came to me in numbers and I roamed about them . . . Still I did not find God. I did learn some of their tricks from them, but that was not God, and so I left them to search further. I went through indescribable difficulties and countless dangers and troubles, until I came to a point where I had to understand who my Father was.[9]

Upon leaving the life of luxury and wealth, Bawa explained that he cleaned toilets, learned how to bake, and toiled on farms for a living.[10] These various experiences of Bawa's early origin story has left Frank Korom apprehensive about using these narratives as historically legitimate. He writes they are "cobbled together by sympathetic editors from thousands of hours of tape recordings, [and] reads more like a transcendental dialogue with God, unhindered by the fetters of time and space, than an historical account of [Bawa's] life."[11] As I explained in Chapter 1, and repeated above, I am not interested in verifying these origins stories, primarily because the more I probed into these written and oral narratives, especially among his early Tamil disciples in Jaffna, the more mythological they became. So, leaving aside any attempts to determine the legitimacy of Bawa's historical narrative, it is far more productive for our purposes to engage with the varying significances given to Bawa by his devoted students, because according to them, Bawa is the only authority in the Circle and Fellowship.

A consistent trend that I encountered throughout my research on Bawa is that he resisted representing any real familial ties or a formal spiritual geneal-ogy of his training. Familial and spiritual lineage was not the necessary marker for accessing truth for Bawa, instead he modeled how everyone has the capacity to access the same truths he found, by sincerely asking questions and seeking the answers. This approach surely resonated with his American followers. Many of his senior followers were doing precisely that, asking questions and seeking answers to the meaning of their life.

Framing the Personae of Bawa

In his doctoral dissertation, the earliest study to be completed on the American Fellowship and Bawa, Mohamed Mauroof situates the "phenomenon of Bawa Muhaiyaddeen" as both "paradoxical and contradictory."[12] Mauroof framed Bawa as a "living human religious symbol with many modalities of meaning for his adherents."[13] Among the different modes or attributes that Bawa signi-fied for his disciples, Mauroof specifically explored "Bawa" and "Muhaiyaddeen" based on his own personal experience and presented a "mythological theory" of Bawa, that is, of his nebulous origins story, as well as the "liturgical Bawa," that is, one who also performed miracles and cultivated a community.[14] According to Mauroof, Bawa used storytelling and ritual actions to construct his personae, that is, when he asserted his role as a teacher lecturing about the importance of *dhikr* and *mawlid*, but also in singing, and relaying narratives from Islamic and Hindu traditions.[15]

Korom takes a far more historical and sociological approach in his analysis of Bawa.[16] He divides Bawa's life into the "three staged 'comings'" and correlates each stage of Bawa's life with stages of "institutionalization" of the Fellowship. Korom defines the first stage in Bawa's life by his arrival in northern Sri Lanka when he was perceived as a "Hindu guru or Sufi sheikh," during which phase he cultivated land, healed people, and settled disputes among the locals.[17] The sec-ond stage is defined by his ministry "to the elite of Colombo" who were mostly Muslims oriented toward philosophical, theosophical, and mystical tendencies. And the third stage began when his ministry moved to the United States where, Korom argues, Bawa asserted himself as the "typical perennial mystic," like the many other gurus who were also appealing to a new American audience in broad universal terms.[18]

My framework has been influenced by both of these scholars. Where I differ from Mauroof and Korom is in my attempt to further nuance Bawa in a philosophical and metaphysical perspective using what I have gleaned from his disciples and his discourses. It is for this reason that I prefer the method utilized by Mauroof when he writes about the "modalities" of Bawa. Mauroof referred to the liturgical Bawa (i.e. religious leader), though I prefer to use the label of a "timeless" Bawa, because the key to understanding the semiotics of Bawa's authority is to realize that Bawa is not bound by a linear temporality for his followers. Rather more than the historical figure of Bawa, it is the varying metaphysical significations that have given his life and legacy—they have been materialized in his numerous spaces—vitality. I have gleaned this framework from Annemarie Schimmel's approach to the life and legacy of the Prophet Muhammad. Schimmel concluded that after Prophet Muhammad's passing, more than the historical person, it was the narratives that formed about him as the timeless Muhammad that command much of the devotion and pieties among his mystically inclined and pious followers.[19] As such, with the physical passing of Bawa, more than the historical person, it is the individually perceived and mystically venerated Bawa that forms the center of his communities and determines how his followers relate to his spaces, which were discussed in the previous chapters.

As historical details remain scant on Bawa's early life, his self-ascribed names, along with titles given to him by his disciples, serve as valuable sources for understanding how his followers perceived him. In examining some of these names, either self-ascribed by Bawa or given to Bawa by his followers, one begins to see the various narrative constructs of Bawa's personae, metaphysical state, and essence, which then orients the relationships students form with Bawa. Understanding the names then helps illustrate the types of relationships that are formed with Bawa and thus the spaces he is affiliated with, such as the *mazar* in Coatesville. Among Bawa's Sri Lankan and American contexts, there is reference to Bawa as a *qutb*—axial pole or axis of the universe—the highest station given to a Sufi saint. In Sufism, *qutb* can be understood as the "Pole of a Spiritual Hierarchy" or it can refer to the saint of an era (i.e. the "Pole of a Period").[20] Among his Jaffna contingency, Bawa has been called Lord Muhaiyaddeen and *Qutb* Muhaiyaddeen, as well as the Hindu deity Murukan. Similarly, Bawa's Muslim students in Colombo have suggested an affinity to Abdul Qadir al-Jilani.

Bawa's disciples explained that Bawa's essence (or real self) was not limited to the physical form they had seen. Rather, as a universal cosmological principle, the essence of Bawa (or the *Awwal Qutb*, the first axial pole) was described as transcending linear time and space. Bawa's disciples use his discourses to substantiate this belief. These include discourses wherein Bawa explains how he taught the Prophet Adam to toil the lands after Adam's exile from paradise to Serendib (Sri Lanka) while he relayed his time meditating in the caves of Dafter Jailani in central Sri Lanka, and his encounter with the perennial mystic and guide Khidr.[21] These connections to Hindu, Muslim, and Sufi personages continued and followed Bawa into America and solidified him as a Sufi *shaykh*.

By giving him the title of *qutb*, Bawa's followers acknowledge Bawa as having reached the ultimate state of spiritual realization and becoming *al-insan al-kamil*.[22] This state of perfection is paradigmatic of the Prophet Muhammad and was later attributed to the companions of the prophet, and then the saints, *imam*s (in Shi'a thought) and Sufi *shaykh*s. This theological concept contributes to a significant historical legacy in Sufi cosmology, which in turn has defined much of the practices that unfold at Sufi shrines that memorialize these perfected human beings, such as Maryam in Mankumban (discussed in Chapter 4) and Bawa at the *mazar*. This ideal of *al-insan al-kamil* is not only a state of being that the members of Bawa's communities see in Bawa, but it is an ideal formed from Bawa's primary teachings which asserts that anyone can work to reach this potential spiritual state. It is at this intersection of the various interpretations of Bawa as a person (temporal) and Bawa as a metaphysical figure (transtemporal) that one begins to grasp the narrative construction and signification of the essence of Bawa, according to his followers and students. The varying titles given to Bawa by his disciples are based on a common acceptance that he is a perfected human being (*al-insan al-kamil*), a fact acknowledged both in Sri Lanka and North America.

From *Swami* to *Qutb*: The Making of Muhammad Raheem Bawa Muhaiyaddeen

Guru Bawa

Bawa's students and the local community in Jaffna still refer to Bawa as guru or *swami* (lord or priest). In the context of South and East Asian culture and religion, the idea of a guru has both a particular and broad significance. For instance, gurus are seminal in Hinduism in South Asia: the French Sanskritist Louis Renou explained that "the dynamic, sacred centre of Hinduism is . . . the enlightened guru, whose charismatic leadership creates the institution for philosophical, religious, and social change."[23] In their edited volume on the topic, scholars Jacob Copeman and Aya Ikegame point out that one of the critical aspects of the guru is that "the guru was *always* a social form of peculiar suggestibility; a veritable 'vector between domains.'"[24] The title of guru, in traditions such as Hinduism or Sikhism, was ascribed to human beings who maintained positions of liminality. As noted by Renou, the guru's role as a spiritual authority is often closely tied to his/her charismatic personality, which in turn maintains and endorses his/her flexibility in adherence to practice, ritual, and traditions. This charisma may allow for versatility, which enables a guru to cater to different audiences and even, at times, defy social and religious norms. In many regards, the occupation of liminal spheres and charismatic authority were often the linchpin for the success of gurus, as they could then redefine traditional social and religious norms because they functioned outside the conventional traditions. Furthermore, due to their charismatic authority and access to the divine, gurus were sometimes deified.[25] The use of a predominantly Hindu epithet for a Sufi teacher is not problematic as Hindu followers of Muslim teachers were and are common in South Asia. Sufi teachers are known to have Hindu and even Sikh devotees. They also participate in practices, such as visitation to *mazar*s, which are common across different religious denominations in South Asia.[26] These interreligious movements are notable among Bawa's communities and spaces in Jaffna, as seen in Chapter 2.

The members in Jaffna, especially those who I met in the *ashram* and Mankumban, accepted Bawa as a Muslim teacher and even though they religiously identified as a Hindu, they did not think that it was necessary to alter their religious identity in order to be a follower of Bawa. Priya Thambi is a prominent example. He is a dedicated student of Bawa, the president of the Jaffna branch of the Circle, the leader of the reconstruction of Bawa's farm at Puliyankulam, and a Hindu. Originally Hindu, the Matron of the *ashram* now wears the *hijab*, and along with Priya Thambi, leads rituals at the *ashram* and Mankumban, but she relayed to me that Bawa did not expect his disciples to convert to Islam. Priya Thambi's perception of the personae and metaphysical legacy of Bawa is interlaced with both a Hindu and Sufi cosmology.

Priya Thambi believes that while prophets bring the message of God, the *qutb* "synthesizes" this message; and accordingly, that is exactly what Bawa did. Being a Hindu devotee of Bawa, Priya Thambi's interpretation of Bawa is steeped in both Hinduism and Sufism, a reality that is not contradictory for him. In fact, in a newly refurbished center at Puliyankulam, there was a painting of the Sufi Moinuddin Chishti (d. 1236), the famous saint of the Chishti order of Sufism in Ajmer, India, on the wall along with photographs and pictures of Bawa and the *masjid* in Philadelphia. There was also a framed photograph of the sacred Mount Kailasa, the mountain venerated as the abode of Lord Shiva, and adjacent Lake Manasarovar, which is located in Tibet. This particular example illustrates how Bawa's Sri Lankan disciples embed Bawa within Hindu sacred cosmology, deities, and sacred geography.

Among the Hindus in Jaffna, Bawa was described to be like a "god" (*kada-vul*) or a *swami* (lord). They explained to me that they were devoted to him because of his proximity to god that, in turn, created god-like qualities in him. This proximity, or even like-ness of god, was formed in his early ministry in Jaffna. During this period, many of the Hindu devotees found affinity between the deity Murukan and Bawa. This belief of Bawa as a reincarnation of Murukan was drawn from narratives relayed by Bawa, such as his origins story where Bawa was found as a baby at the temple of Murukan by a king, relayed above.[27] Kataragama is a mountain revered by Hindus as an *axis mundi* because it was where Lord Murukan, or Skanda as he is known in Sanskrit, lived when he came to Sri Lanka.[28] Though temples dedicated to Shiva (god of destruction) are common in Sri Lanka, Tamil Hinduism in Sri Lanka traditionally venerates Murukan and his heroism, as seen in pilgrimages completed in honor of him to Kataragama, a site shared by Hindus, Muslims, Buddhists, and Veddas (the indigenous community of Sri Lanka). The correlation between Bawa and Hindu traditions, specifically to Lord Murukan (a popular Tamil Hindu deity), is a convention distinct among Bawa's Tamil devotees in Jaffna.

Conversely, correlations between Bawa and Murukan create a blurring of boundaries that lead one to ask was Bawa God or god-like in the eyes of the Hindus in Jaffna? In 1971, Mauroof documented one such example of this fluidity of Bawa's identities that he observed during a *mawlid* celebration at the *ashram* wherein Bawa

would sit still, almost trance-like, and his body, especially his face seemed to undergo unique transformation. The face would be perfectly still and a glow seemed to emanate from it. Those among the crowd who did not participate in the singing, as performers or as listeners, would be seated facing Bawa basking in the flow of his communion. It is important to note that the singers, although they were singing verses in praise of Kutb [*Qutb* or axial pole] Muhaiyaddeen, and although they might identify Bawa seated with them as the original Bawa or

Kutb [*Qutb*] Muhaiyaddeen, did not seem to address their chants to the figure seated across them.[29]

During the same occasion Mauroof described how

> some young children had boldly written a statement proclaiming that Bawa is God in a light-fixture made to be used as part of the decorations for the feast. That was the nature of their devotion to Bawa. The parents of the children who were also present at the feast did not seem to mind the enthusiasm of the children. However, when the time came to hang the light fixture on the roof of the *ashram* [italics added] as part of the decorations, several of the persons [present] protested, and the fixture was never hung up.[30]

As demonstrated in the above incident, perceptions of Bawa, and the resulting acts of devotion that come from them, are very fluid in northern Sri Lanka. This was also evident in my observation of the rituals in the *ashram* and at Mankumban (Chapter 2), especially during the commemoration of Hindu festival of light to Lord Murukan and the lighting of clay oil lamps at Mankumban. These ritual moments highlight some Hindu follower's perception that Bawa is god.

The title *bawa* is a common label for Sufi mendicants and *fakir*s (wandering ascetics) across Sri Lanka. For instance, these *bawa*s, or wandering ascetics, were and are central to the ritual celebration of the *mawlid* for the Prophet Muhammad and al-Jilani in Sri Lanka. The *bawa*s served as ritual leaders during the *mawlid*, either through leading of singing or performances of self-mortification, with displays of ecstasy, associated with the Rifa'i, a prominent Sufi order. They were the key performers and leaders in ceremonies, music, and rituals during Sufi celebrations at shrines, where they also serve as shrine keepers. In short, they were a regular feature of Sufi traditions in the Islamic landscape, not only in Sri Lanka, but in South India.

Additionally, Bawa's association with the ultimate *baba*/*bawa*/father Adam, the first father of mankind and his casting to Serendib, is necessary to understand Bawa's lineage. Bawa's connection to Adam's Peak and the Prophet Adam (Baba Adam), Dafter Jailani (Abdul Qadir al-Jilani), and Kataragama (associated with Khidr and Murukan) steeps him in a very unique and sacred geography associated with both Islam and Sufism in Sri Lanka. Notably, these are also foundational sites of shared sacred narratives and pilgrimages for Tamil Hindus, as well some Christians and Buddhists in Sri Lanka. In the Sri Lankan context, both "guru" and "*bawa*" connect Bawa to two predominant Tamil religious traditions, Hinduism and Sufism, whereas in the Philadelphia context, Bawa would make "*bawa*" a unique and distinct concept in the American milieu.

During the 1970s, when Bawa arrived in Philadelphia, it was an era of counterculture, and gurus were a regular feature of the American spiritual landscape. These gurus from South Asia and Asia presented various versions of Hinduism, Buddhism, Sufism, and mystical Eastern traditions across the United States. Most of the early members of the Fellowship came from this culture of seeking during the 1960s and 1970s and they were steeped in the spiritual movements of the time. They read memoirs and books of gurus, such as *Autobiography of a Yogi*[31] by Paramahansa Yogananda (d. 1952) or *The Sufis*[32] by Idries Shah (d. 1996).

In the early years of Bawa's time in Philadelphia, the title of "guru" was removed from both his public name and the institutional name of the Fellowship. This decision was made to distance Bawa from the negative connotation of "guru" that had begun to proliferate in America during this time, as some spiritual leaders across the United States were taking advantage of their disciples.[33] During this period, scandals of sexual indiscretion and abuses of power were commonly reported. Bawa did not want this association to blight his character nor the reputation of the Fellowship but members did, and still do, use the name "Guru Bawa" privately within the community. Publicly however, "Guru Bawa" turned into just "Bawa" and it remains a common referent of Bawa to this day.

Another element of Bawa's American appeal was his personal relationship with his American students, one that was based on an expression of "love" to his students, rather than the reverence that was directed at him by his students in his Sri Lankan context. For instance, Mauroof observed that the Sri Lankan devotees maintained a more distanced devotional approach to Bawa compared to the way that American disciples interacted with Bawa.[34] It was this formidable relationship that solidified Bawa as a symbolic, and at times real, father figure and patriarch among his American disciples.

Bawa, the Father

"Bawa," synonymous with father (i.e. *baba*), was a title that was commonly used among his Colombo contingent and became formalized among his American followers. Khair ul-Nissa, a member of the Fellowship in Philadelphia who met Bawa when he first arrived in America, explained her personal understanding of Bawa as "the father" during our interview:

> Who is Bawa? *Bismillah ar-rahman ar-rahim* [In the name of Allah, the most Compassionate, most Merciful]. What came to my mind is, like, he's my primal father. I feel that I knew Bawa before ... I had seen him before and it was all

comfortable and familiar to me. And some people see Bawa as a brother according to their exalted state. For me, I feel like a moth in a flame to him. That he is
a father who taught me and is teaching me the true path of God and the light of
God and to be like him; to intend to be like him. I feel like that story when the
wasp was flying around and telling the insect, "be like me. Be like me."[35]

"Bawa as father" is both symbolic and literal for some disciples. Bawa, the father,
is also cosmologically oriented as the "primal father" and defined as a *shaykh*
who taught his students how to reach an "exalted state." According to his disciples, Bawa taught about this "exalted state" and modeled it as well. For members like Khair ul-Nissa, Bawa was the ultimate teacher in the master-disciple
(*murshid-murid*) relationship. This dynamic often resulted in identifying the
Fellowship as Bawa's "funny family" wherein Bawa was the father figure and his
disciples were his children. He became both the real father and mother, or parent, in that he tended to his children's needs, cooked for them, and healed many
of them both spiritually and physically. In these acts of caretaking members,
such as Khair ul-Nissa, understood Bawa as both a parental figure and a true
representative of the one true father/mother: God.

Another student of Bawa, Hussein described an experience during his pilgrimage to Jaffna to see Bawa's *ashram*.[36] In response to my query about how he
imagined Bawa, he explained, "Bawa is my Father, my Master, and my Shaykh.
The Emerald jewel of my Heart and the Emerald light of my Eyes. He who pulled
me out of the Fire, wrote upon my hands, and took me under his protection."[37]
Bawa's role as the father begins to illustrate his larger sacred role as a *shaykh*,
teacher, and protector for his students who, like Hussein, invoke Bawa during
prayers. Similar to Hussein, for Khair ul-Nissa, Bawa is more than an earthly
father; he is an ever-present father and entity that remains spiritually present to
his "children."

Rick Boardman is a senior student of Bawa from Philadelphia. He joined the
Fellowship via his involvement in nonviolence and antidraft movements, especially with the Religious Society of Friends (Quakers) in Philadelphia, that he
was part of during the countercultural era. Boardman explained that being in
the presence of such a guru and "father" was, itself, a process of enlightenment:

> You asked what it was like being in Bawa's presence: [it was] *darshan* [divine
> sight, discussed further below], the concept of *darshan*, sitting in the presence of
> the master. What do you experience? You experience bliss. Why do you experi-
> ence bliss? Because there's an energy field . . . that's coming through the master
> but floats all boats. What am I talking about there? I'm talking about the impact

of his consciousness on my consciousness. Not touching each other, not doing anything, not common prayer, not anything. Being in his presence elevates my sense of being, gives me peace, feels familiar, feels safe, feels hopeful; [it] is experienced sometimes as great power and sometimes simply as great safety. Reassurance. He's a father, right? He's a loving father. He's my father. And he talks about God that way himself. "Allah is my father," says the Muslim *shaykh*. And we all know that Islam doesn't believe in that kind of relationship between man and God.[38]

It was the intimacy and accessibility to Bawa's presence, which Boardman parallels to the act of *darshan*, the Hindu concept of receiving grace from the sight of a deity. This experience of *darshan* profoundly influenced his spiritual development. The same practice of *darshan* was held by Bawa's Tamil Hindu followers in Jaffna. Though Khair ul-Nissa and Hussein do not evoke the principle of *darshan*, they, along with Boardman, view their relationship with Bawa as embodying the ultimate dynamic of the relationship between humanity and the one Father (i.e. God or Allah). But such an intimate relationship between God and humanity is not the norm in Islam, at least according to Boardman's perception. To further this understanding of Bawa as *guru*, *swami*, and *shaykh*, which is dependent on and encompassed by Bawa as the loving father, the following section will examine Bawa as *qutb*, or the axial pole.

Muhaiyaddeen, the *Qutb*

Rahmat Bibi's (a Jewish American member of the Fellowship) perception of Bawa was, and still is, dependent on Bawa as a father figure and thus her *shaykh*.[39] What is more significant is that for Rahmat Bibi, Bawa the *shaykh* and father figure is intimately predicated on his state as *qutb*, or the axial pole of the universe:

> You know, at the very beginning that was part of what really solidified my connection . . . I didn't know it myself but he saw something worthy in me that I didn't see. I didn't see it but . . . that is what he cultivated, going back to the father and the child and that when you think of a father's love for his child, no matter how much love he has there most likely will be biases. But because Bawa wasn't my biological father, his love exceeded that line and was in a different realm. It was like a father in the way that God is the father. You know, I don't call him God but he is an integral part of that process for me, to get to God. And he's . . . he's not even a he, he's really. . . as the *qutb*, he's actually mingled within the conscience of man and Muhaiyaddeen is the reviver, the reviver of faith. So, within that—like—conscience is that guide, the one that guides from within.

So, you don't have to meet Bawa who came, whatever the reasons he came, but beyond his form and in that form of the *qutb*, that is within every man. It's mingled with the *nur* (light) of the *qutb*. The *nur* is the light and the *qutb* is the guide, the reviver, the explainer.[40]

Without biological ties, Bawa's love "exceeded" the common love between a father and a child and, for Rahmat Bibi, it more truly reflected the love of God. It is this central act of love, and its marriage with the *"nur"* (light), that is the basis of the *qutb* as the "guide, the reviver, the explainer" for Rahmat Bibi. However, the attribute of the "reviver" that Rahmat Bibi bestows upon Bawa is not unique to Bawa.

"Muhyi" is one of the ninety-nine names of Allah, which Bawa translates as "the bestower of life."[41] *Muhyi ud-din* translates as "the reviver of religion," and is also the names of formidable Sufi teachers, such as Ibn al-'Arabi and is the honorific given to al-Jilani. Al-Jilani forms a significant esoteric lineage in Bawa's life. Bawa relayed spending time at al-Jilani's shrine in Sri Lanka, while at other times he is reputed to have suggested that he was al-Jilani, according to his immediate students.[42]

Al-Jilani was from Gilan, south of the Caspian Sea, and was an "ascetic preacher" who gained popularity as a saint within Islam. Schimmel describes him as a "stern, sober representative of contrition and mystical fear" and a prominent Hanbali theologian, who was also known for renewing the Islamic faith, a quality that is evoked in Bawa by both his name and his students, like Rahmat Bibi. Schimmel relays the following narrative of al-Jilani:

> 'Abdul'l-Qadir's fame soon reached incredible heights. He is called *Muhyi ud-din*, "the reviver of religion." A charming legend tells how the pious man helped a weak and destitute person who was lying, completely exhausted, on the road; after he had given him some sustenance and almost revived him, that person revealed himself to 'Abdul'l-Qadir as "the religion of Islam," and hence he gained this honorific title.[43]

Schimmel further relays a tradition from Baluchistan associated with al-Jilani and the *mi'raj*, or the ascension of Prophet Muhammad through the seven heavens. It is commonly understood that archangel Gabriel guided Prophet Muhammad during this celestial journey with a mystical creature, the Buraq. But in another rendition of the *mi'raj* offered by Schimmel, it is al-Jilani who came forward to guide Muhammad when Gabriel was unable to continue the journey to the highest of heavens:

The future founder of the most widespread mystical fraternity in the Islamic world offered the Prophet his neck that he might step on it to alight without discomfort. Out of gratitude, Muhammad granted the future saint a very special rank: when he would appear on earth for some five centuries later his foot would be "on the neck of every saint." Thus 'Abdul Qadir's ['Abdul'l Qadir Jilani] famous claim to precedence, "My foot is on the neck of every saint."[44]

The *tariqa* (Sufi order) attributed to al-Jilani is known as the Qadiriyyah. Traditions of al-Jilani, as the "reviver of religion," resulted in numerous poems devoted to him as the *Ghauth-i a'zam* (the Greatest Help), or the greatest saint.[45] These poems are recited on his death anniversary (*'urs*), which is celebrated on the fourth month of the Islamic calendar among various Sufi communities.[46] This practice is also prevalent among some Muslims in Sri Lanka who hold monthly, and sometimes even weekly, *mawlid*s for al-Jilani at shrines devoted to him and also in their homes. The same tradition of *mawlid* is maintained in the Fellowship and the Circle, a tradition that originated in Jaffna. Rahmat Bibi's labeling of Bawa as the *qutb* concurrently evokes this broader tradition of the "reviver of faith" found within Sufism. Not only is "Muhaiyaddeen" one of Bawa's names, but he is said to possess the quality of one who revives religion (or faith). The latter quality is attributed to Bawa, which further solidifies Bawa's cosmological state as the *qutb*.

Understanding Bawa as *qutb* Muhaiyaddeen may be one interpretation of Bawa's genealogical tree, which he painted, and entitled the *Tree of the Prophets*. Copies of this painting hang in the Fellowship house in Philadelphia, the *ashram* in Jaffna, and the Toronto branch of the Fellowship.[47] In this painting, the main branch that forms the central pillar includes a map of the prophetic descendants beginning from Adam (at the bottom of the pillar) and ending with Muhammad (at the top of the pillar). Vines emerge from the main branch of the prophetic pillar that turn into leaves and inscribed upon these leaves are the names of other prophets, their family members (wives and children), and associated followers. For example, Nuh/Noah and Isa/Jesus and their families are a part of the leaves that emerge out of the main pillar. The names are in Arabic script as well as in English. The circle that contains the name of Adam forms not only the base of the prophetic pillar but it is also the center of an additional lineage, one that branches out to the left and right to include seven circles. The seventh circle, larger and in gold paint, contains the name of Abdul Qadir al-Jilani (Muhaiyaddeen) on both the left and the right, and the six smaller circles between Adam and Muhaiyaddeen, on the left and the right, contains another name of a historical Sufi (first) and then various titles of Muhaiyaddeen:

1. Sayyid ʿAli ibn Usman Hujwiri (eleventh-century Sufi teacher)
2. *Fakir* Muhaiyaddeen (or *faqir*, "poor person," mendicant, or seeker of God)
3. *Darwish* Muhaiyaddeen ("door-seeker," mendicant)
4. *Baba* Shah Muhaiyddeen (father)
5. *Makhdoon* Muhaiyaddeen (*makhdum* or "one who is served"; title for *shaykh* or family affiliation with shrine-keepers)
6. *Khawajah* Muhaiyaddeen ("master"; great teacher)
7. *Sultan* Muhaiyaddeen ("strength"; ruler)
8. *Ghaus* Muhaiyaddeen (or *ghawth* "help"; often synonymous with *qutb*)
9. *Bawa* Muhaiyaddeen (father)
10. *Awliya* Muhaiyaddeen ("friend" of God or saint)
11. *Shaikh* Muhaiyaddeen (or *shaykh*, "elder"; spiritual guide)
12. *Sayyid* Muhaiyaddeen ("sir" but can also be used to refer to a Sufi master or a referent to one who has descended from the Prophet Muhammad)

These names also reappear in the Fellowship's daily *dhikr* recitation, which was passed down to his students in Philadelphia. All of these titles of Muhaiyaddeen are invoked along with the name of Hujwiri (d. circa 1072–77), who is known as Data Ganj Bakhsh (*the master who bestows treasures*). He was a Sunni theologian, preacher, and mystic, who was known for helping to spread Islam and Sufism to South Asia.

During a discourse given on May 18, 1978, at the WBAI Studio during an interview with Lex Hixon, Bawa spoke about the "True Dimensions of *Dhikr*."[48] In this discourse, Bawa stated "God (*Andavan*) must pray to God (*Andavan*) for this is *dhikr*."[49] He went on to say,

> Rising from God, it must unite with God and grow in God and move in and out of God. One is his treasure (Man) and God, so there must be a connection. If *dhikr* comes from another place, it is not true prayer. That is the point about the *dhikr*. The benefit is like the sun that shines everywhere, the ray that shines on all things, that is like God, in *dhikr*, it is the power of God that shines everywhere. That is the power of the *dhikr*, God loving God, Man becomes God.[50]

Hixon asks Bawa, "How is it done?" And Bawa responds with a story wherein he encounters a guru, whom he never names, that taught him about the point of "Man-God, God-Man."[51] Bawa's guru taught him that first one must acquire all of *Devam*'s (God) qualities, his beauty, speech, and light. All of God's qualities needed to be perfected and performed in order to transcend the elements of earth, fire, water, wind, and ether.[52] The realization of these divine qualities and *asma'ul-husna* of Allah, or the ninety-nine names of God, plays a crucial metaphysical role for Bawa, which he imparted through the practice of *dhikr*. Bawa taught that it is by remembering and meditating on the qualities of Allah that one remembers one's true self.[53]

The practice of *dhikr*, or the remembrance of Allah through the recitation of God's names, is an effort to achieve ultimate union.[54] In the beginning of this *dhikr*, the third *kalimah* is recited eleven times along with *Surah al-Fatiha* (the Opening), which is repeated twice. *Surah al-Ikhlas* (the Sincerity) is repeated four times during *dhikr*:

> In the name of God, most Merciful, most Compassionate.
> Say: He is God, the One and Only
> God, the Eternal, Absolute
> He begetteth not, nor is He begotten
> And there is none like unto Him.
> Amin.[55]

This *surah* points to the theological understanding of absolute unity and emanation of creation from one being as it is intrinsic to the Qur'an (112:1-4) and fundamental to Bawa's teachings. Scholar of Islam Michael Sells writes: "The most famous Qur'anic passage of *tawhid* is among the short *suras* of the Qur'an [*Sura al-Ikhlas*]. In this passage, Allah is affirmed as one, as not begetting, and as not begotten, and as *samad*, an enigmatic term in classical Arabic, with connotations of perdurance and indestructibility."[56] *Surah al-Falaq* (the Daybreak, 113)[57] and *Surah an-Nas* (the Mankind, 114)[58] are both declared once at the beginning and at the end of *dhikr*.[59] The following invocation to al-Jilani is repeated eleven times during *dhikr*, while the others are invoked only once: "*Ya Baghdadiy Shaikh Sultan Fakir Muhaiyaddeen 'Abdul-Qadiril-Jilani, radiyallahu' anh*" (O Baghdadi, King of *Shaykh*s Pauper Muhaiyaddeen, slave of the Almighty, 'Abdul-Qadiril-Jilani, may Allah be pleased with him).[60]

The Fellowship is not formally organized as a Sufi *tariqa*, or order, with an institutionalized lineage of teachers and formal initiation of students. This became the institutional model for Sufi orders in the medieval period and thus there has been a tendency to measure the legitimacy of Sufi orders based on this institutional model. But not all Sufi orders institutionalize into a *tariqa* or even follow the classical *tariqa* model of hierarchy. Bawa followed no official lineage nor did he institutionalize one prior to his death, but he did have the name of a Sufi order, the "Qadiriyya," imprinted on the Fellowship *masjid* entrance. This organizational framework is not novel in the history of Sufism. In his study of a contemporary Sufi community in South Asia, Afsar Mohammad uses the term "uninstitutionalized Sufism" to refer to Sufi groups that do not have a particular or traceable Sufi lineage but have "ritual frameworks [that] are instead defined by local devotional networks."[61] Though no formal *tariqa* configuration is found within the Fellowship, Bawa does embed his lineage and personage within the tradition of al-Jilani, especially with his genealogical painting on the prophets and al-Jilani. Upon inquiring about these names, I was informed by members of the Fellowship that these refer to Bawa himself. However, it is possible to view this as a genealogical lineage that Bawa placed himself within. Another possible interpretation of the genealogical map is that Bawa indeed has provided a *silsila* (lineage), and it transmits from al-Jilani to Bawa. These possible interpretations certainly warrant more investigation. Beyond this painting or veneration during the *mawlid*, al-Jilani is also summoned during daily *dhikr*.

Further, in his own discourses, Bawa emphasized al-Jilani as the *Muhyi uddin* or the "reviver of religion." Bawa's student, such as Rahmat Bibi, have also then relayed Bawa with the same quality, Bawa Muhaiyaddeen, the reviver of religion. So then, when reciting *dhikr*, and the name of Muhaiyaddeen is recited, students of Bawa not only invoke al-Jilani, the twelfth-century Sufi teacher, but also Bawa, the twentieth-century teacher, who they personally encountered. Disciples of Bawa ascribe contrasting approaches to what constitutes the *qutb*. Thus far, there was some correlation highlighted both in practice and description (by Rahmat Bibi) of the *qutb* with al-Jilani, whereas for others, the *qutb* is a far more cosmological principle.

The Primal *Qutb*

"Bawa the *qutb*" is not only understood as the *qutb* affiliated with al-Jilani. Another notable trend that I came across during my interviews was the perception that Bawa is the primal *qutb*, the one whose *nur* (light) was formed second only to the Prophet Muhammad in primordial time. Nur Sharon Marcus, a poet and author who has published extensively on her experiences with Bawa, elegantly explained this concept when I asked her,

> I can't use the past tense because he is. If you want to know who Bawa Muhaiyaddeen really is, you have to know that this Muhaiyaddeen has always been and will always be. At the time of creation, when the *nur* separated, that radiant resplendence, that divine plentitude of Allah separated from Allah and was the first thing that spoke; and Allah looked at the *nur* (this is before any creation, this is in the time frame that Bawa calls *anathi*, the time before the primal beginning at that time when the *nur* separated, there was like an agitation in totality which was the existence of everything) the *nur* separated from the rest and Allah looked at the *nur* and said, "who are you?" And the *nur* said, "I am the light which existed within you. I have always existed within you." After that, there was a shadow that separated from the *nur* and that which separated from the *nur* was the *qutb* [. . .], the resonance of the divine wisdom. So, there is the light and wisdom, which have come directly from Allah. We have each of us, within us, that recognition of that perfect note, which is that light and that resonance.[62]

This *nur* that separated from the *nur* of Muhammad was the Muhaiyaddeen, or the *Awwal Qutb* (primal or first axial pole). This idea of Bawa (Muhaiyaddeen) as the *nur* that manifested from the creation of *Nur* Muhammad is a concept that was repeated to me several times when speaking with his different disciples, such as by Shoaib. Shoaib is a Pakistani student who came to the Fellowship after Bawa's physical passing through an encounter with one of Bawa's senior disciples.[63] When I asked him the same question, he expressed the following:

> Bawa is the part of the original *nur,* the light, the original light that emanated from God. The light that emanated from God is what we believe, in mysticism, is the light of Muhammad. Not Muhammad as a person, not [the] prophet, but the light, the light of Muhammad that was the first creation in the world. God was in a state of darkness and the light emerged from it, within that light another light emerged from it. One is light of God and the other is the wisdom of God. The light of God was personified as the last prophet as Muhammad, the wisdom, has been there from day one. Okay, in different forms, even Muhammad has been there in different forms [and] we don't know what these forms are but Bawa is the wisdom. He is the one who taught Adam in Jailani, in Sri Lanka, for twelve years how to till the land, how to—you know—provide shelter for himself, and so he is the wisdom. He has been appearing and reappearing and appearing and reappearing and appearing and reappearing; this was his last manifestation. Now he won't come again—okay—in that form.[64]

In Shoaib's explanation, the Prophet Muhammad is a timeless figure but the timeless Bawa (i.e. the essence) is a "light" that emerged from the timeless Muhammad, both of which are emanations of the one reality, Allah.

In a discourse given on June 26, 1982, Bawa speaks of the "Nine Muhammads" as opposed to a historical Muhammad, the son of Aminah and Abdullah. According to Bawa, the "Nine Muhammads" are cosmological, timeless, and universal states of consciousness. These include the following:

1. *Anathi* Muhammad (Muhammad within Allah or the unmanifested)
2. *Athi* Muhammad (beginning of creation or the manifested)
3. *Awwal* Muhammad (comes into creation, soul comes out)
4. *Hayat* Muhammad (the eternal soul or life)
5. *An'am* [*Anna*] Muhammad (the nourishment that comes as food, as earth, fire, water, air, and ether)
6. *Ahamad* (the beautiful light form in the heart/*qalb*)
7. Muhammad (as beauty of the light of Allah, in his heart and reflected in his face)
8. *Nur* Muhammad (the wisdom, radiates Allah's essence)
9. Allah Muhammad (the light of Allah within Muhammad and the light of Muhammad within Allah)[65]

For Bawa, when one speaks of Muhammad, one must be cognizant of the differing roles and facets that form Muhammad, similar to Bawa's interpretation of Maryam (Chapter 4). The historical person of Prophet Muhammad is solely a manifestation of the cosmological Muhammad.[66] Mauroof clearly explains this aspect of Bawa's teaching when he writes,

> On the one hand, we are given a picture of the prophet that emphasizes the intermediary role of the prophet in a chain of historical events. That picture is consonant with the Biblical and Qur'anic picture of prophets. On the other hand, we have a picture of the prophets and their communities of all times as part of a universal consciousness, over and beyond the space-time orientated consciousness of the world.[67]

Bawa's interpretation of Muhammad is steeped in the principal understanding of the primordial creation of Muhammad as the *Nur* Muhammad, and these are the teachings that both Marcus and Shoaib evoke in their readings of Bawa, because according to their interpretations, "Bawa the *qutb*" emanates from the light of the primordial Muhammad. These metaphysical correlations are essential in solidifying Bawa as *al-insan al-kamil* (perfected human being) as it is the

Prophet Muhammad who is the paragon of this state in Islam. This is discussed further below.

As the archetypical human being for Bawa, the significance of *Nur Muhammad* is as a state of realization and the point of access to wisdom. In the teachings of Bawa, the *nabi* (prophet) represents the manner in which any human being can achieve a state of unity with the divine and become the universal prototype, the perfected human being, *al-insan al-kamil*. Bawa uses these prophetic figures in his teachings to stress that these individuals bonded with Allah because of the beauty of their *qulub* (hearts), a state of beauty that always has been accessible to humanity but that has been lost in the recent age of earthly desires.[68] It is taught that *Nur* Muhammad existed in *arwah* (literally meaning "spirits" as the divine kingdom) as the *satguru*, the divine teacher, for although our source of "awareness" comes from *Nur* Muhammad, our "wisdom" comes from the *Qutb* Muhaiyaddeen; this figure is then manifested and represented by Bawa (the guru, *shaykh*, and *qutb*) to many of his disciples. For his disciples, such as for Marcus, "Bawa the *Muhaiyaddeen*" harkens back to the beginning of cosmological existence, even prior to creation, when the first *nur* (Muhammad) emanated and from which another light (Muhaiyaddeen or wisdom) came forth. The second light which emanated was the *qutb*. The essence of this primordial *qutb* is the essence of Bawa Muhaiyaddeen. This dual prophetic and *qutb* lineage is captured in Bawa's painting of the genealogical map, as well as the rituals of *mawlids* and daily *dhikr*. And his students understand these teachings to mean that the primordial light of Muhaiyaddeen, second only to Muhammad, is the essence of Bawa. For Shoaib, "Bawa as *Qutb* Muhaiyaddeen" is regional and dependent on hagiographical oral traditions of the Prophet Adam and the Baghdadi saint al-Jilani in Sri Lanka, which qualifies it as a legitimate lineage of Bawa, the *qutb*. Both Marcus and Shoaib articulate that the essence of Bawa is primordial and thus not limited to the physical "Bawa" they encountered; his essence exists beyond his physical form. It is also this primordiality of Bawa's essence that has led some to believe that he will return again, albeit not in the same form, but indeed having the same essence (i.e. the *qutb*).

The *Qutb* as Universal Consciousness

For other members of the Fellowship, the *qutb* is understood as a universal state of being as opposed to a cosmological creative principle, a symbol of a mystical lineage, or even an intermediary between Hindu and Sufi way of life. For instance, for Boardman, the *qutb* is not necessarily a cosmological or theological designation, as suggested by Marcus or Shoaib above, but rather the *qutb* is one who has reached a state of complete annihilation of the self, wherein the lower self and ego (i.e. the "I") no longer exists:

> A realized human being is one who has gone through a process of rigorous discipline and self-work and so forth and finally, by the grace of Allah, been permitted to become a channel for that power. The *qutb*—you see—is traditionally the axis of the moral universe. What does that mean? It means that he has emptied himself to the point, the point [*taps on table*] where on earth that power is able to come and be radiated out. Not because of who he is: his body is a body like any other body; his personality was like any other personality. His hunger, disease, old age, and death are ever present and ever evident but he got himself out of the way and became a channel for that [divine] power.[69]

Boardman sees Bawa as a simple human being but distinguishes Bawa as *qutb* based on Bawa's ability to get his lower self, or ego, "out of the way." His understanding of Bawa as the *qutb* is similar to that of Mauroof who stated that the "Bawa[,] in his teachings also[,] presents Muhaiyaddeen as being synonymous with a kind of knowledge potentially present within the human self, i.e. as a human psychic characteristic" or "consciousness."[70] This consciousness or state of being is what ascends through the seven states in the spiritual journey, of which the sixth state represents the state of the *qutb* (these states are discussed below).[71] The "psychological" *qutb* (as consciousness) is one and the same as the "mythological Muhaiyaddeen" referred to by Bawa's disciples such as Marcus or Shoaib. They both are referents to the mystical states of Bawa and also the state that Bawa taught his disciples to aspire to.[72] It is here that one sees the convergence of different but complementary conceptualizations of the *qutb* as constructed by the various members of the Fellowship, with different religious leanings. These understandings of the *qutb* include the *qutb* as "reviver" of faith and as the light that emanated from the first light (*Nur Muhammad*); both metaphysical states are accessible to everyone, because it is a "universal consciousness."[73]

A similar sentiment of the universal consciousness espoused by the state of the *qutb* is suggested by Musa Muhaiyaddeen, who came to Bawa as a Jewish American, and is one of the current presidents of the Bawa Muhaiyaddeen Fellowship in Philadelphia.[74] During an interview, he explained:

> Consciousness doesn't necessary have a name but we have given it names. The consciousness... that came at around the year zero was labeled Jesus. The consciousness that came around the year 642, or something like that, was labeled

Muhammad. But the consciousness that was Jesus may have also been the consciousness that was called Bawa. The consciousness that was as Muhammad may have been labeled Bawa, the consciousness that was 'Abdul Qadir al-Jilani may have been labeled Bawa. I don't know nor want to conjecture. For some, to label Bawa as having Muhammad in consciousness would be blasphemous. For some, to label Bawa as having Jesus [in] consciousness would be blasphemous and *shirk,* which means innovation or outside the belief system of the religion. So, it is difficult to talk about things with words which are beyond words because it is a form of game playing that occupies this world.[75]

For Musa Muhaiyaddeen, a universal consciousness is based on a connection with the prophetic figures of the Abrahamic traditions. And although he carefully navigates the difficulty of linking the *qutb* consciousness with prophetic states, as this verges on what he understands as blasphemy, he still alludes to the continuous tradition of the prophetic figures as an unbroken consciousness, one that is maintained by Bawa as the *qutb*. From what has been charted thus far, as a spiritual leader, Bawa was culturally and religiously situated as a guru, Sufi *shaykh*, and ultimately a cosmological being (*qutb*) who was metaphysically and historically oriented, and also existed within a particular geographically situated sacred lineage in Sri Lanka. For some of the Fellowship members, the *qutb* is a state of formlessness and a universal consciousness. According to Bawa's disciples, this versatility of states of being is in essence dependent on Bawa modeling what it is to be the perfected human being, or *al-insan al-kamil.*

Bawa as *al-Insan al-Kamil*

Massoud is a Shi'a Muslim from Iran who immigrated to Toronto in early 1990s. He is currently one of the executive members of the Toronto branch of the Fellowship. As a young teenager, he became affiliated with the Jerrahi Sufi Community in the west end of Toronto, where he met Wilhelm Poolman (d. 2009), who remained the central leader of the Toronto branch until his passing. It was through Poolman that Massoud learned about Bawa and his Fellowship. When I asked him who Bawa was, he explained:

[Bawa is] an example . . . of the ultimate state of a human being, of who you can be, of a man, of a human being to be, that is who Bawa is in physical form. Now his station, or who he was, is something known only to God. We call him a *qutb*, we call him a *shaykh*. We have given him titles and he has never said anything. He calls himself an ant-man; you have heard him say that. And I think to me,

> Bawa is . . . his being is the ultimate state that a man can attain in a lifetime. Beyond that—like I said—it's . . . I don't know. It is not my area [*laughs*].[76]

As Massoud observed, Bawa often did not give himself titles. Most commonly, he referred to himself simply as the "ant-man."[77] Still, it is the ultimate state of being, emblematic of the ideal state that any human being can achieve, that Bawa represents for Massoud. It is for this reason that interpretations of Bawa as the guru, the *shaykh*, and the *qutb* are all encapsulated in the understanding that he is the perfected human being, or an *al-insan al-kamil*.

When visitors asked Bawa who he was, Bawa would reply, "find out who you are." During my interviews with members of the Fellowship, I would conclude our conversations with the question, "Who are you?" In their responses, I received what could be interpreted, in totality, as a culmination of Bawa's teachings. And no single disciple illustrated this response more expressively than Captain, a European American female member of the Fellowship from a Jewish Christian background. Captain met Bawa during his visit to Toronto when he was giving a talk at the University of Toronto. At the time, she was involved in a yoga group but she eventually gave up this practice and moved to Philadelphia to be with Bawa; she even visited him in Sri Lanka. Since the beginning of her time at the Fellowship, she has been involved in the transcription and publication of Bawa's discourses at the Fellowship, work that she still continues in service to Bawa and the Fellowship. At the conclusion of our interview when I asked her "Who are you?" She replied:

> Um . . . well, "who am I" is the question. Who am I? Why am I here? Where am I going? I mean those are the questions because—you know—I think I'm a light of God, I do. And I think Bawa helped turn on the switch to make that light shine. You know, I think I was basically who I was when I met him. I was thirty something [years old] when I met him so I was already formed. I had a sense of humor. I have a kind nature. But I think that he made me strive to have more understanding of the human condition, not be so judgmental, not shut people off, more accepting but I still don't know who I am. I mean, I can't claim to know who I am. I always have this little thing that I do: you know how they refer to God as *Hu* [He]? Allah Hu? *Hu* am I? I am *Hu*.[78]

For Captain, it is the *kamil shaykh*, the perfected *shaykh* Bawa who reached this state and was able to guide his disciples through the journey of return to their primordial origins, when the souls where united with Allah. Without a *shaykh*, the remembrance of this primordial and essential origin of the individual is not possible. As a result, Bawa is perceived by his disciples to be the perfected human being, *al-insan al-kamil*. For his disciples, it is a teaching that challenges them all to return to their origins and the birthright of *al-insan al-kamil*.

According to Bawa, human beings are made up of two sections, the *zahir* (outer) and the *batin* (inner). The outside form, or body, is often referred to as the shirt and represents the damaging qualities of arrogance, karma, and *maya* (illusions) that must be overcome. The shirt contains "four fangs" with "seven kinds of poisons," or *shaktis* (energies), that can be signified by the five elements of earth, water, air, ether, and fire, which are associated with arrogance, karma, *maya*, and Satan. These five elements are also part of what Bawa refers to as the nine precious stones: earth, fire, water, air, ether, mind, desire, wisdom, and the soul. Bawa elaborates that, of these nine precious stones, "wisdom is the gem, the soul is the light, and the rest are the body."[79] It is for this reason that Bawa compares human beings to animals, referencing the five elements of creation that are common and shared between them.[80] This shared nature to the "beasts" prompts the individual to question, "What is the difference between man and animal?" To this Bawa responds that the central point of difference that elevates human beings above the animals is wisdom (*arivu*) "to be able to differentiate, which is night, which is day, which is light . . . which is hell, what is heaven, which is true and false, which is tasty, and not tasty, to know this is the wisdom man has. Where was I before, where am I now? What is this body made of?"[81] Therefore, the body, and the qualities associated with it, are elements that must be transcended so that one may "return to [his or her] original state of beauty."[82]

Bawa taught that the goal of the human being is to search within oneself because it is only by returning to one's primordial state in which all illusions, or *nafs* (lower or base desires), are destroyed that one can perform the duty set by Allah.[83] The self consists of seven qualities of the body—falsehood, murder, theft, sex, intoxicants, miserliness, and envy—and seven qualities of the mind—egoism, attachment, anger, lust, *maya*, karma, and arrogance.[84] It is upon transcending these negative qualities of the body and mind that the *insan* (human) becomes *al-insan al-kamil* (perfected human being).

In order to achieve this state of *al-insan al-kamil*, one must go through a process of analysis, filtering, separation, and refiltering. Bawa also refers to these steps as a "beautifying" process wherein one beautifies one's inner self by merging with Allah.[85] He adds that one must analyze the worlds that exist within the body, the beasts that exist within the body, various animal qualities such as arrogance and desire, separate them from the elements (earth, water, air, ether, and fire), and filter them from illusion.[86] The purpose of this process of analysis and filtration is to determine these qualities' various uses after which "man can use these as instruments throughout the universe."[87] The last process of refiltering, or wiping clean the mirror of the soul, constitutes "man's most important duty" (*dharma*) and requires man to "filter and re-filter himself so that he may discover himself."[88] When the steps of research and analysis are complete, the self within oneself climbs through seven layers of wisdom (*arivu*), in the following ascending order:

1. Perception (*unarvu*)
2. Awareness (*unarchi*)
3. Intellect (*puthi*)
4. Assessment (*mathi*)
5. Wisdom (*arivu*) (sometimes associated with the state of Khidr)
6. Divine Analytic Wisdom (*Pahuth-Arivu*) (sometimes associated with the state of Jesus/Isa or *Qutb* Muhaiyaddeen)
7. Divine Luminous Wisdom (*Per-Arivu*) (state of Nur Muhammad)[89]

Through this analysis, the aspirant realizes that human beings and animals share the first three levels of consciousness: that is, both humans and animals have perception, awareness, and intellect; they eat, defecate, and sleep but they do not know the difference between right and wrong.[90] In this regard, human beings are "created in the ocean of *maya*," which is not a proper building block. It is only when "wisdom is realized, can man be called man, otherwise he is a beast."[91]

For Bawa, the perfect human being embodies the compassion of Allah (*Andavan* or God) to all creation, regardless of religious creed, race, gender, or any other forms of division. The perfect human being represents *islam*, which for Bawa was understood as the embodiment of *anbu* (love in Tamil) or *ishk* (love) of the inner heart where *anbu* is personified in one's actions toward fellow human beings. In Bawa's discourse "Change to *Insan Kamil* [*sic*] the Direct Connection,"[92] he mentions that it was this aspect of the *qalb* (a gnostic heart)[93] that he felt humanity neglected. Bawa understood that in the past, humanity was not concerned with the beautification of outer form nor obsessed with material gain. Instead the human being, the *insan*, beautified his/her *qalb* so that the heart had a strong bond with Allah and remained united with all His qualities. It is this beauty, ideally manifested, that reflects the true Beauty of God (*jamal*). *Al-insan al-kamil*'s honored position, that is, both in God and His creation, is due to the divine reality of *al-insan al-kamil*, a reality that is the ultimate reality itself and dependent on being in the world. When this potential is reached, one becomes the microcosm (world) of the macrocosm (universe).

In classical Sufism (as well as in Islamic mysticism in general), *al-insan al-kamil* is commonly understood as the perfect human being, the servant, or the universal being.[94] In this doctrine, the human being is positioned as the isthmus between God and the cosmos.[95] The human is the mirror that reflects *tawhid* (unity) and the *barzakh* (interface) between God and the world, and *al-insan al-kamil* is the perfect human who preserves the existence of the universe.[96] Prophet Muhammad is emblematic of this state of being. Schimmel writes that "as the *insan kamil*, the Perfect Man, Muhammad is as it were the suture between the divine and the created world; he is, so to speak, the *barzakh*, the isthmus between the necessary and contingent existence."[97]

As mystics, such as Ibn al-'Arabi, have surmised, this worldly contingency is the "manifested principle," the *rasul* (the messenger) is the "manifesting principle," and Allah the "Principle in Itself."[98] The latter is parallel to Bawa's particular outline of the "nine Muhammads" clarified above, as interpretations of Muhammad extend beyond the historical personage to various versions of Muhammad, especially as the universal principle. The latter interpretative tendency is a dominant trend in Sufi traditions.[99] These esoteric interpretations assert that Muhammad was the first creation before time and thus the last prophet to manifest on earth.[100] Bawa also referenced similar traditions in his own cosmology, as I highlighted in the section on the "nine Muhammads," and his teachings on the mystical Muhammad that are still employed by his disciples. It is the mystical presentation of the *qutb*, as a being that is transcendental and eternal, that places this concept within a particular Islamic milieu (especially in the lineage of Abdul Qadir al-Jilani) and within the realm of a universal consciousness.

The concept of *al-insan al-kamil* is central in Islamic theology, particularly in Sufism. It forms the basis for acts of piety and rituals, such as the *mawlid*, that honor holy figures such as the Prophet Muhammad and his saints, such as al-Jilani, who are perfect human beings that transcend time. It is also precisely this perfection and its grace (emitted because of union with the divine) that adherents seek when they approach saintly Sufi teachers, both in life and subsequently in their death, at their *mazars*. Bawa's discourses are immersed within this same tradition of Sufism. Furthermore, his disciples have given Bawa the title of *al-insan al-kamil*. Thus, Bawa has been transformed into a universal state of being and a saint of God. Aside from the legacy that Bawa arguably invokes, Bawa also provided his own interpretations of these varying names.

> Bawa means father, a title given to someone who is a father of wisdom for all mankind. Muhaiyaddeen is a name given to the *Qutb*, the being who brings the

divine explanation, who has perfect wisdom. The name Muhammad Raheem Bawa Muhaiyaddeen is a name of light which was given to the *Qutb*; it is just one of his titles. Muhammad means the primal Light which came as a gift from God to all mankind. Raheem is the name of the being who uncovers the primal light and reveals it. This means that Bawa is the primal father of mankind emanating from the primal light which is then made manifest. Muhaiyaddeen is the name given by Allah to one who has received the pure light of God. He is the one who gives the light of wisdom, the clarity of *iman*, of faith, certitude, and determination to the heart of man. That is the meaning of the names, which are given only to someone who has the qualities of these names. The names must be appropriate for that person, and that person must be a father for all mankind. He must have the capacity to give peace to the hearts of his children, he must guide these children along the right path with the benevolence of the *din* [religion], the path of perfect purity, and he must make them understand the difference between *halal* and *haram*, what is permitted and what is not. When all the names work together in unity, with perfect qualities, the name Muhammad Raheem Bawa Muhaiyaddeen is appropriate for that person.[101]

In this particular explanation, Bawa examines each of his given names. In it he uses Muhammad (primal light), Raheem (compassionate, the one who "uncovers" the light), Bawa (the "primal father"), and Muhaiyaddeen (he who "received" from the light of God). Though one may comprehend these names as culturally, religiously, and linguistically connected to particular milieus (i.e. Islam or Sri Lanka), Bawa implores an esoteric interpretation of his names that elucidates their meanings beyond form. These various names individually resonate with his followers, but they also collectively represent the figure and legacy of Bawa. In the above discourse on his own self-ascribed names, Bawa signals a comprehensive approach to the various appellations utilized by him, and subsequently evoked by his devotees. When Bawa's names, and epithets given to him by his disciples, are viewed holistically, one begins to realize the plurality of inclination within this singular being. This plurality of names and titles are also reflected in his ministry, most especially his spaces, as seen throughout this study.

One of the challenges in examining the timeless Bawa is that the construction of his personaes and their interpretation unveil numerous "Bawas." Both as a disciple of Bawa and an anthropologist, even Mauroof (in his early work) struggled to identify Bawa and fluctuated between perceiving him as a mystic, a prophet, an "object of veneration," or an "Islamic reformer" while trying to account for his Tamil linguistic tradition that supposedly associated Bawa with Saivite or Vaishanvite Hinduism.[102] Some of Bawa's disciples, as discussed above, revered him as a guru, *swami*, *shaykh*, *qutb*, and someone who may be a manifestation of God, both in a Hindu and Sufi context (the latter with respect to a complete self-annihilation [*fana*ʿ] of the ego). According to his students, from Jaffna to Pennsylvania, there was no ego-self in Bawa and he was in a state of complete union with God. In this regard, it is fair to use Mauroof's description of Bawa as "polysemic" because it accurately encapsulates the broad spectrum of his titles, ranging from *swami* to *qutb*. It is precisely this state of nonbeing or perhaps multiple beings (polysemic) that forms the basis, or the common denominator, of Bawa's diverse ways of being.

Bawa and his numerous honorifics signal to the milieus he was embedded within and this is then reflected in his ministries, as we already have encountered in previous chapters. The pluralism espoused by his followers, and subsequent ministries, is a testament to the pluralism of Bawa's own being. This pluralism is a self-constructed representation of Bawa; this is the story of who Bawa is, timeless or otherwise; and this identity impacts the acts of devotion and ritual activity seen at his spaces from Jaffna to Pennsylvania and most especially his authority that is enshrined at his *mazar* in Coatesville, one that has been evident throughout Sufism historically and is now deeply rooted in the global West.

Conclusion

Much is not known about Bawa prior to his emergence from a Sri Lankan jungle, leaving the historical person, beyond his public ministries, an enigmatic story. The little that is known about his personal history is related to his spaces, as explored in Chapters 2 and 3. Due to the scarcity of matter that can be verified, this chapter proposed a different approach to understanding Bawa, one that moved away from a historical analysis and considered him as a timeless entity, which he has become for his disciples. This approach provides a framework to comprehend why and how Bawa remains the central figure of authority at the heart of a contemporary, transnational Sufi community.

Throughout Bawa's ministries, he was known as a healer, farmer, cook, painter, and singer but he was ultimately a teacher who expounded the principal relationship between the divine and its creation, humanity. His diverse devotees not only perceived Bawa to be a father figure (reflective of the definitive father, God) but he was also their *guru*, *swami*, and *shaykh* who had perfected his essence to lead his disciples, on the path of return, to God. They, thus, understood Bawa to be the *qutb*. To further nuance the figure of Bawa, some of the theological and cosmological narratives of his disciples, based either on personal experience or surmised from listening to his numerous discourses, suggest that he was the *Awwal Qutb* (or the Primal *Qutb*) that manifested from *Nur* Muhammad, the paragon of *al-insan al-kamil* (the perfected human being) from the first moments of cosmological activity. The particular theological tradition of *al-insan al-kamil* and the Prophet Muhammad as an exemplar of this perfected state places Bawa's ideas within a larger Sufi milieu. Bawa's ministry was both inclusive and expansive as his perception of himself and his teachings appealed to the diverse members of his Sri Lankan and North American contingencies. Bawa and his ministries were formed specifically in a Tamil Islamic Sufi and Hindu milieu and further refined in America. These settings enabled an approach to God and his agents (i.e. prophets and saints) that transcends religious affiliation. All of the individual titles used in reference to Bawa, along with Bawa's self-ascribed names, explored in this chapter were an attempt to comprehend the trans-temporal interpretations of Bawa and to highlight a broader mystical and cosmological reality of Bawa.

These titles capture states of interface within Islamic, Hindu, and Tamil cultural and religious milieus. In this regard, as Bawa himself articulated, when one considers these names in unity with each other, as opposed to being read in contradiction with each other (i.e. a Hindu or a Muslim), then one is able to transcend definitive categories. It is in the transcendent realms that his disciples are then able to perceive and relate to Bawa. This is the same reality that defined his ministries and his spaces, and subsequent ritual activity and devotion. Yet, this preeminence is dependent on the most fundamental understanding of the true metaphysical essence of Bawa, who to his followers is *al-insan al-kamil*, wherein his state of perfected humanity is related to his status as *qutb, shaykh*, and guru. It is this state of being a perfected human, beyond gender, that then unifies Maryam and Bawa, and Mankumban and the *mazar*, respectively. From Jaffna to Pennsylvania, all the heterotopias mapped in Bawa's transnational network are oriented toward these two prominent metaphysical realities of the creative feminine and the perfected human being, that defy spatiality and temporality.

Conclusion

In June 2016, upon my return to Mankumban, I was greeted by Bagoos, the *imam*. At the time, I did not realize that this was my last encounter with him, as he died a few months later. During this visit, I noticed that in the inner sanctuary, the canopy that covered the memorial tomb for Maryam and Bawa was gone. Surprised, I turned to Bagoos and asked, "What happened?" Bagoos sighed heavily and expressed that (reputedly) some members of the Circle, who were Muslim students of Bawa, snuck into Mankumban recently, and demolished the canopy. They intended to dismantle the tomb itself, but they were stopped by the leaders and members of the community. Apparently, they did not like what was unfolding at the tomb and the Hindu presence it cultivated. They found it contaminating Bawa's teachings, and thus Islam. Though, it would appear that this encounter was only to be a foreshadowing of what was to come a year later. In late 2017, at the time of publication of this book, I was informed that the tomb in Mankumban was fully removed. The decision came from the executive members of the SSSC (who are mainly Muslims), who felt that the tomb itself was not representative of Bawa's teachings. The consequences of this decision, especially for Hindus in Jaffna and for North American pilgrims requires a return to the field for more research. Still, this particular incident at Mankumban between members of the same community with a shared *shaykh* and differing interpretations of his spatial legacy is a potent reminder of the vacillating contours of religious pluralism and practices at Sufi shrines.

Sufi shrines be they in Sri Lanka, Pakistan, Syria, or elsewhere have come under attack in the modern era. The focused destruction of Sufi shrines in the contemporary period in certain Muslim-majority countries by violent opponents of Sufism, such as ISIS, starkly contrasts the treatment of shrines centuries ago.[1] Under Muslim empires, be they the Mughals or the Ottomans, shrines were not only given patronage by rulers, they were also an essential feature of Muslim life and society (i.e. socially, economically, and religiously). Today, Sufi shrines have garnered violent responses. For some in the Muslim world, they exemplify a form of deviancy found in Islam. Shrines, with its penchant for religious plurality, cultural propensity, porous sacrality, and variations of accessibility, was and is proof positive of what was inherently problematic with Sufism.

The criticism that loiters around the physicality of the shrine in Sufism, though, is not merely spatial, but fundamentally theological.

Some aspects of Sufi-Islam (i.e. activities at Sufi shrines and devotions to Sufi saints), from its medieval manifestations to the contemporary era, garnered criticism. Sufi shrines and activities that unfolded in them were viewed by some fractions within Muslim societies, such as the Sunni theologian and jurist Ahmad Ibn Taymiyya (d. 1328) and later his proponent, the Arab leader and theologian Muhammad ibn 'Abd al-Wahhab (d. 1792), and their followers, as examples of the cultural stains and pernicious blemishes on an idealized, homogenized, and textual (Arab) Islam (one that was reputedly purely maintained by the companions (*salaf*) of the Prophet Muhammad in the early generations of Islam's origins).

For Sufi Muslims, however, the shrine provided a means through which to experience God. In Islamic theology, it is held that God contains both transcendent (*tanzih*) and immanent (*tashbih*) attributes. Over time different interpretative legacies emerged with regards to the types of God's qualities that were stressed, which then implicated the ways in which one performed Islam. For instance, Sufis stressed God's immanence (intimacy), while their opponents tended to emphasize God's transcendence (incomparability). According to the latter inclination, which underscored God as an inaccessible being, adherence to Islamic law (based on an exoteric reading of the Qur'an) was the best way to please this powerful being. According to the former, a position held by some Sufis such as Bawa, God was a knowable being (based on an esoteric reading of the Qur'an), and complete union with God was defined through the experiential (such as through love), which at times superseded merely following the letter of the law. These theological traditions resulted in a dynamic spectrum of Islamic and Sufi practices and beliefs which proliferated simultaneously for most of Islamic history and continues to do so today.

Sufism's methodological approach to knowing and experiencing God was mediated by the cosmic and mystical figure of Prophet Muhammad and his heirs, namely, the saints (*awliya* and/or *qutb*) (Chapter 5). These holy figures, such as Sufi saints and *shaykh*s, interpreted the scriptural traditions of Islam and taught them to their disciples and followers. As such, reverence to a saint or holy figure became recognized practice in Sufi Islam, and was further institutionalized at their residences, complexes, and their tombs (shrines), especially as these itinerant figures in Islam traveled beyond the Arabian world and spread Sufism. In disseminating their interpretations of the traditions of the Prophet Muhammad and the Qur'an, they themselves became the heirs of the prophetic legacy and thus another axis of devotional Islam. Nevertheless, some felt that the fundamental monotheism (*tawhid*) of Islam was tarnished due to the reverence given to these figures (i.e. devotion and veneration should only be directed at God and not at another human being, not even Prophet Muhammad). However, some Sufi schools held that it was the same principle of *tawhid*, the fundamental oneness of all creation (a position espoused especially by Ibn al-'Arabi and his notion of *wahdat al-wujud* or "oneness of being") that led to the practices of veneration toward Sufi figures and their spaces. Sufi *shaykh*s and saints were said to have reached a spiritual state wherein only the divine remained and the lower self was fully annihilated (*fana*'). Still shrines and the practices that unfolded in and around them were viewed as novel and culturally based, and thus outside the bounds of what could be constituted as proper Islam.

As a result of these reputedly "innovative" practices in and around Sufis and their shrines, Sufism in practice was pejoratively touted as popular Islam, a view that was further perpetuated by Orientalist scholars, most of whom simultaneously were captivated by Sufi poetry of Hafiz and Rumi. So, whereas Sufism in practice was viewed disdainfully, Sufi theology and philosophy or metaphysical Sufism was generally respected. Therefore, even within the varying facets of Sufism, textual traditions (i.e. theology, law, philosophy, poetry, and at times even metaphysics) were more easily accepted as compatible with scriptural Islam (and so Islam proper), while lived Sufi Islam was treated as less authentic. For instance, scholars of Islam and Muslims tended to evaluate normative Islam through "legal discourse" (*shari'a*) based on a literal exegesis of the Qur'an and consultation of traditions of Prophet Muhammad, and thus in turn treated lived Sufi Islam, such as the enactment of rituals (*mawlids* and *'urs*), as outside the mandates of Islamic norms and orthodoxy.[2] However, for Sufi figures, such as Bawa, these same practices, that is, acts of personal piety and devotion, formed the parameters of Islam proper. As a result, such forms of Sufism were seen as an "alternative and particular Muslim self-construction and self-articulation" and not as the "normative and representative" Islam.[3] The latter is evident in Orientalist scholars' categorization of Sufi Islamic rituals and spaces (i.e. shrine and *shaykh* based) as "popular" or "rural-based" (i.e. superstitious and backward), which they surmised was bound to wane in the modern era. Still, notwithstanding the sustained vitriolic, which sometimes has led to acts of destruction of these spaces by opponents to Sufism, in addition to the general criticism that shrines have garnered in early scholarship on Sufism, *the Sufi shrine has persevered* in the contemporary era.

The purging of Sufi shrines, in some Muslim majority contexts, and its rise in America, in rural Pennsylvania, is rather telling of the trajectory in which Sufism has been historically transmitted, one that has continued into the global West. The resiliency of the Sufi shrine is not indicative simply of the internment or memorialization practices of holy figures in Sufism. This heterotopia, as this study has shown, is the context (and the multidimensional text) upon which myths, symbols, movements, memories, pilgrimages, and devotions, and thus contestations and convergences have formed and re-formed. It is here that the story of Bawa and his two communities, the Serendib Sufi Study Circle and the Bawa Muhaiyaddeen Fellowship, are formidable markers of the modes in which contemporary Sufism and Islam has endured and transformed, yet again, into a new milieu, but in so doing has retained much of the consistent movements, devotions, rituals, and metaphysics that have defined Sufism, both Islamically and universally, across space and time.

Cross-Cutting Themes from Jaffna to Pennsylvania

The Bawa Muhaiyaddeen Fellowship has been variously labeled by scholars and members alike. But a spatial examination of the Bawa Muhaiyaddeen Fellowship (Chapter 3) and its counterpart in Sri Lanka, the Serendib Sufi Study Circle (Chapter 2), has showcased that Bawa's transnational movement evades any neat categorizations. Bawa's communities and the activities that take place therein, especially in and around heterotopias, serve as a valuable window in comprehending the varying tendencies of Sufism, Islam, Hinduism, and spirituality as they unfold in South Asia, America, and the contemporary global context at large.

The origins of Bawa's ministry in Sri Lanka and its transformation and continuity into America is a poignant narrative in the aftermath of a nearly three-decade civil war in Sri Lanka. Bawa's story is not one of war but rather of unity and peace, and it comes out of a legacy of Sufi Islam in Sri Lanka, which was historically cultivated by wandering ascetics, pious pilgrims, and traders who traveled across the Indian Ocean for centuries, as seen in Chapter 1. In journeying from Bawa's place of residence (*ashram*) in Jaffna to his burial tomb (*mazar*) in Coatesville, new pathways were mapped while ancient sacred pilgrimage routes were traversed. Highlighting that even Sufism in America has not developed in a vacuum, but rather builds upon networks that are trans-spatial and trans-temporal in nature. In this particular example, the center of such a network in the Fellowship in Pennsylvania was the *mazar*, a heterotopic node that has transformed through migration and localization, but one that has been (re)translated from the Sri Lankan context.

In the context of America and South Asia, wherein our case study is based, Bawa and his spaces showcase how communities, spaces, identities, and interpretations found within this one movement are actually emblematic of the currents found in Sufism as a whole, particularly when it concerned metaphysical ideals such as the reverence for the timeless figure of Bawa (Chapter 5), while others, such as devotion to Maryam (the creative feminine, Chapter 4), have not been put into practice in America, but is sought out through pilgrimage to Sri Lanka by Bawa's international followers. These inclinations of Sufism that coexist within one community remind scholars that Sufism and Islam as it is lived is not homogenous. Both Bawa and his disciples' stories transcended prescribed borders, geographies (both sacred and secular), and identities, because they dwelt in spaces of in-betweenness. The story of Bawa and the legacy of his disciples across the globe is a story that is American, for it has deep roots in America but it is also Sri Lankan, as it emerges out of Tamil Sufi Islam. In this regard, such legacies are important not only for scholars who theorize about Islam and religions in America and South Asia, but they are much needed reminders to American Muslims and non-Muslims of the manifestations of Islam and its influences on non-Islamic and Islamic spiritualties.

Though many cross-cutting themes emerged between these localities, in concluding this study, I would like to highlight some select themes and ideas, because of their implications for the field of Sufism in America: (1) racial and cultural categories and the use of congregational parallelism as an analytical category, (2) the processes of Islamicization and negotiations of authenticities, and (3) Bawa's directives on the roles of women in his transnational communities.

Beyond Racial and Cultural Categorizations in Congregational Parallelism

As discussed in the Introduction, the theoretical framework of parallel congregations was developed in discussions of Buddhism in America, and was critiqued, as other taxonomies in studies of Buddhism in America, for its overemphasis on racial and cultural categories in the framing of this transplanted religious movement in America (e.g. "Asian Buddhist" and "white Buddhist"). In theorizing about Buddhism in America, too much focus was given to the Americanness or "whiteness" of members in Buddhist communities in the performance of a Buddhist identity. A tendency which was also notable in discourses of Sufism in America, but one which this current study has challenged.

For instance, in Chapter 3, three of Bawa's senior disciples, all from European American Jewish Christian backgrounds, held dissimilar interpretations of Bawa, his teachings, and the Fellowship's religious identity. Two of them framed

Bawa and the Fellowship in the language of Islam, while the last did not associate Bawa or the Fellowship as Islamic. Additionally, take, for example, the women in Colombo who started the *salat* (Chapter 4). Though Bawa intended to construct "God's House" or a mosque in Philadelphia as he had in Jaffna, the impetus for the eventual construction of the mosque was catalyzed by European American (white) women in Colombo. In this case, racialized expectations about the ethnicity of "traditional" Muslims are inverted. Seemingly, then, in the Fellowship, it is incidental that Sufis are white and their whiteness does not mean they are less Islamic, as has been suggested by some scholars in the study of Sufism in America. A focus on whiteness can be analytically revealing in the study of Sufism in America, but it can also serve to obscure other important dynamics, especially when we focus too much attention on it as a category for classification. For example, a focus on a convert (white) and ethnic (immigrant) based frameworks in the study of Sufism in America neglects the African American members and their race- and class-based experiences in the Fellowship. That said, these racial categories do need to be problematized within the context of colonial and imperial receptions of Sufism in the West, as mentioned in the Introduction. This broader historical trajectory of the transmission of Sufism in European and American milieus are needed in any discussion of Sufism in the contemporary global West. They form a part of the broader phenomenon of Sufism in the contemporary global context, which further challenge racialized taxonomies in America historically.

To further this insight of racial and cultural dynamics in this case study, the framework of parallel congregation was valuable, in that at times parallel membership and congregation were not defined purely by ethnic or cultural identities (i.e. "white" and "immigrants") in a space, rather it was implicated by varying religious orientations and interpretations of Bawa and his spaces. What was at times even more disorientating, such as during *maliwd*s and *'urs* celebrations and the experiences of pilgrims to Mankumban and Coatesville, was that the parallel relations between members, students, devotees, pilgrims, and visitors were constantly shifting across both localities. It was here that an in-depth analysis of ritual experiences and spatial participation served to further clarify how parallelisms were negotiated beyond the contours of racial and cultural identities.

Ritual activities such as the *mawlid*, *'urs*, and *langar* of Bawa in Pennsylvania and Jaffna illustrated the ways in which parallel congregations developed in the different centers. These congregations did not remain hermetically sealed from one another. During such rituals, they were fluid, they intersected and interacted at times (i.e. pilgrims interacting with Bawa's senior disciples at the *mazar* seen in Chapter 3). Despite participants' various ethnic and cultural identities, namely, those from American immigrant or diasporic backgrounds as well as the European American and African American converts in the Fellowship, their participation during rituals, though appearing parallel and thus distanced was actually not the case. Their reasons for partaking in the spaces and rituals, were actually closer to each other than one would expect.

For instance, where diasporic Muslims in America participated in *mawlid*s because of a natal memory of the ritual and devotion to Prophet Muhammad or al-Jilani, members of the Fellowship likewise participated in the same ritual activity due to a memory, but not of Prophet Muhammad and al-Jilani but Bawa, their *shaykh*. At the same time, the Fellowship members themselves formed further subgroups among themselves during the same rituals, as some of them were Muslims and non-Muslims, but they, along with everyone else present, maintained a concurrent and nuanced relationship with Bawa and Sufism. The embodied reality of these ritual activities, as well as movements in and around sacred spaces, like the *mazar*, indicated the complexity of lived Sufi Islam and its diverse adherents, be they Hindus, Muslims, Christians, and Jews, and those with spiritual orientations but no religious identities.

Arguably, one of the most significant insights of the transnational movements of Bawa's communities is that the parallel congregations are not unique to the Fellowship in America. They are also found in Jaffna. For example, Mankumban, Maryam and Bawa's shrine, is shared between Hindus and Muslims on a daily basis and by Americans and many others annually (during pilgrimages). During weekly Friday *jum'a*, Hindus wait in the prayer hall to perform veneration at the tomb of Maryam by lighting incense and circumambulating the inner sanctum, but they do not participate in *salat* that was led by the institutionally appointed *imam* (again these parallelism are not ethnically or culturally bound, but more relationally dependent on Bawa and what he signified). Those gathered in the prayer hall, most of whom were Hindus and Muslims (and women) performed their own rituals of veneration, such as the singing of *salawat* to Prophet Muhammad. Most in attendance were devoted to Bawa and Maryam. They partook in the ritual activity with the hope of accessing divine blessings, be it through *darsan* or *baraka*, but the original source of this grace was fundamentally God. It is at this juncture that studies of Sufi communities in America with transnational linkage to localities such as Sri Lanka proved to be analytically useful.

American Sufism and its relationship to "traditional" Islam in the scholarship on this topic is theorized through narrow paradigms of what Sufism should be, especially as it is textually bound or legally defined. However, Sufism in regions such as Sri Lanka (which are reputedly more authentic cultural preserves of Islam, or Old World Islam) reveal that scholar's textually and legally created taxonomies of Sufism in America do not work well in Bawa's Sri Lankan communities. Furthermore, what was found in the Fellowship need not be treated as *alternative* forms of Islam or Sufism; it may indeed be *representative* of *normative* Islam across space and time. As such, not only are the taxonomies and frameworks employed in studies of Sufism in America reductive, but they have stagnated the potential for productive and more representative studies of Sufi communities in America. Closely intertwined with these complex dynamics of race, culture, and religion is another consistent debate found in both localities and that is a debate about Islamic orthodoxy.

Processes of Islamization and Spatial Negotiations

Even though Bawa's movements first started in Jaffna, and spread to Colombo to form the Circle, this movement has not grown in numbers after his death because of a lack of a living teacher. The latter pattern is actually countered in America. Despite this lack of a physical charismatic figure, the Fellowship in America has gained attention beyond its members because of the novelty of the *mazar* in Pennsylvania. This growth in membership and in the number of pilgrims to Pennsylvania has reignited itineraries to Jaffna and to Bawa's other Sri Lankan sites. American Sufism is deeply rooted in the American landscape but has also added to the itineraries of other ancient Sufi shrines in Sri Lanka, such as Adam's Peak and Dafter Jailani. Here, at the locus of two parallel shrines, in different localities linked to a single teacher, one observes how spaces can be disassociated from cultural, religious, and ethnic identities, and yet be recognized and shared across religious traditions (Muslims, Hindus, Christians, and Jews) and cultures (Americans, Sri Lankans, Pakistanis, Gujaratis, Persians, etc.). As these varying movements and itineraries unfolded at the shrines of Bawa transnationally, what remained constant were internal questions of orthodoxy (particularly an Islamic one).

Bawa's *mazar* in Pennsylvania has transformed from a private mausoleum to a public Sufi pilgrimage site in America, particularly for non-Fellowship members. Most of these pilgrims visit without maintaining institutional affiliation to the Fellowship, officially or otherwise. The majority of the pilgrims arriving at Bawa's *mazar* in Coatesville are American Muslims (with generational variances but with linkages to Muslim majority nations). In performing pilgrimages to the shrine of Bawa in Pennsylvania, immigrant American Muslims bring with them practices associated with their own natal lands, such as the use of rose perfume, lighting of incense, and singing of praises to the Prophet Muhammad, very much similar to what was highlighted at Mankumban among local Tamils (Chapter 2). The activities of the pilgrims, though, are being disallowed by caretakers of the shrine in America (Chapter 3). The senior caretakers of the shrine want the *mazar* to be a space for quiet contemplation and are creating their own form of orthodoxy of their American shrine, defined in part by their Americanized Islam. For instance, to curate these practices at the *mazar* and farm, signs are posted around the property indicating what is acceptable behavior (i.e. quiet meditation) and what is not (i.e. incense and singing).

Likewise, in Jaffna, Muslim members of the Circle tried to sway the ritual practices that were unfolding at Mankumban. Both the Matron and Priya Thambi in Jaffna participated and organized what could be labeled as Islamic rituals (*mawlid*, and *'urs*) in addition to the *poosai* and Tamil Hindu practices (e.g. lighting incense). The process of Islamizing Bawa's spaces and teachings were unfolding between Tamil Muslims and Hindus, and has culminated with the removal of the tomb in Mankumban. While in Pennsylvania, the members of the Fellowship who identified with Islam but were also European American converts to Islam were at odds with corresponding Fellowship members who were also European Americans, but who held more universalistic understandings of Bawa's teachings.

At the heart of these dynamics in and around Bawa's spaces and the enactment of varying rituals are movements toward and away from an ideal Islam. These double movements are orientated around questions of authenticity, both of Bawa and his teachings and of Sufism and Islam. In both our localities, contestations for authentic representation of Sufism was centered on the perception of the true essence of Bawa and his teachings. This devotion to these perfected beings (Maryam and Bawa) then resulted in variations of ritual practices and spatial relationships, which has led to the diversity seen in the Circle and the Fellowship. It is the effective enactment of a utopia that is shared through the agreement of the presence of a holy figure (i.e. Bawa) that enables parallel tendencies at the *mazar*. It provided "access" to pilgrims, from Old World Islam, while for members of the Fellowship, it was a means to return to their *shaykh*, father, *qutb*, and guru (Chapter 5), who is entombed in the shrine. This reality is one of the factors that makes Bawa's transnational movement an important case study. Often in Sufi orders, a living *shaykh* sets the trajectory of practices that defines the order's theological, philosophical, contemplative, and ritual orientations. In Bawa's communities, there is no such living figure any longer, rather the spiritual leader remains Bawa. In his physical absence, the teachings provided by Bawa and connections to him are maintained through his spaces and the rituals performed there. Yet, Bawa, his teachings, and spaces are diversely cultivated, shared, and interpreted by his students. These diverse manifestations have included Hindu, Sufi, Islamic, Christian, Jewish, and universal (i.e. Sufism as a perennial spiritual tradition) outlooks. They coexist in the Fellowship and the Circle. Despite attempts by various members of the movement to present a singular framework for Bawa and his teaching, these various interpretations of Sufi Islam (*shari'a* to universal) coexist and function in close proximity to one another.

That said, lived Sufism has generally been treated as wholly inauthentic by opponents to Sufism, but it is notable in our example that the authenticity of Sufism and its relationship to Islam is an *ongoing process* even among those who practice Sufism. Even within the experiences of the Fellowship and the Circle's senior students of Bawa, that is, the first generation of Bawa's immediate students, there are debates and contestations unfolding with regards to the types of authentic practices and spaces that can and should be maintained within the community. They are constantly shifting and being renegotiated based on varying interpretations of what Bawa's discourses really meant. The authentic, then, is not permanently defined, but rather it is continually fluctuating and constantly redefined.

The Presence, Authority, and Role of Women

Finally, questions of Islamic authenticity were debated in relation to women's position within the community but this does not mean that active leadership and participation of women in Sufi communities in America was unique. In the case of the transnational community of Bawa, the presence, authority, and role of women was not simple, but rather shaped by various factors; however, this in no way meant that women lacked agency. Women in Bawa's transnational movement actively negotiated their differential rights, statuses, and responsibilities relative to their relationship with Bawa. Women were active members as Executive Committee members, translators, and editors of Bawa's discourses or as leaders of meetings held in the Fellowship regularly. When it came to the mosque, however, their presence was far more complicated. On the one hand, women in the Fellowship were at the forefront of instituting the practice of *salat*. On the other hand, once the mosque was constructed they were spatially segregated behind men because this was what was seen as proper Islamic practice according to Bawa. Women do not maintain formal leadership authority in the mosque (Chapter 4). Though non-Fellowship Muslim women, especially from Muslim majority countries, found the accessibility offered by the mosque refreshing. The *mazar*'s accessibility, as well as the ability to participate in rituals such as *mawlids* and *'urs*, were critical for non-Fellowship Muslim female visitors.

The Jaffna sites of Bawa's communities showcased further roles of women, which at times markedly contrasted with the American context. For instance, noteworthy examples of female authority were found in the Matron, as well as other women, and their service at the *ashram* and Mankumban. Additionally, the memorialization of Maryam at Mankumban, and the varying ritual activities that unfolded in and around her memorial tomb, and the shrine as a whole, exemplified the complex spectrum of experiences and positionalities of women and the idealized feminine maintained by Bawa and his communities in Jaffna. As such, women's roles in the Fellowship and the Circle cannot be easily categorized, rather they depended on varying factors, such as Bawa's directives, local context, and spatiality, as well as women's wills and desires. For instance, Bawa allowed for full access to male and females in Mankumban, while gender segregation was maintained at the mosque in Philadelphia, which some Fellowship women chose not to engage with, but they remained devoted disciples of Bawa. Fundamentally, then, women's role in Sufi communities in America cannot be viewed as unique or more progressive or egalitarian.

Thus, Bawa's own gender politics and its manifestation within Sufism and Islam shifted. His universalistic teachings of Islam and Sufism ideally negated any focus on divisive categories (gender, race, caste, and religion), but in actualization not even he was able to evade its limitations. Despite his continual challenge to his students to transcend these illusory categories of race, gender, caste, and religion, as they were distractions from a unified and singular framework of God, these varying experiences of women in Bawa's communities and Bawa's own implementation of and departure from certain gender norms is representative of the spectrum of roles, presences, and authoritative experiences of women/females in Sufism and Islam across space and time. On the one hand, the feminine is the highest cosmic ideal (Maryam) and thus women have the most potential for full realization of the divine from a metaphysical exegetical legacy. On the other hand, categorically in terms of social gender norms, Sufi women are frequently relegated to the margins merely for their physiology (despite some tendencies in Sufism which consistently challenged gender norms and maintained gender fluidity).

These varying cross-cutting themes from Jaffna to Pennsylvania counter different scholar's attempts to define the Fellowship categorically, for typologies are intrinsically limiting. The Fellowship contains universalist tendencies as well as *shari'a*-based Sufism. Beyond these religious characterizations, there are far more negotiations unfolding within the Fellowship and the Circle, be it in terms of spaces, rituals, and gender. When we place the Fellowship only in one category, as previous scholarships have attempted to do, we are presented with only a small piece of this diverse and transnational community with varying currents of Islam, Sufism, Hinduism, and spirituality. Highlighting these complexities within one community through networks, connections, movement, and embodiment allows scholars to assess the differing but complementary currents of Sufism and Islam in America and South Asia, as it uniquely coexists within a singular network.

The Future of the Fellowship

Internally Bawa's communities are at a crossroads because of its inherent diversity. With no appointed leader and a range of Sufi outlooks, what will the future of the Fellowship be, especially as a mosque is proposed for the *mazar*/farm in Pennsylvania and the tomb has been removed in Mankumban? Future studies will have to contend with the answer to this question, but I propose that two key factors will influence the direction of the current Fellowship in America. First, the future of the Fellowship in America will depend on the second and third generation, or those born into the Fellowship, and the types of institutional roles that they partake in. Whether or not the second- and third-generation members of the Fellowship choose to engage with the direction of the Fellowship, and how they choose to do so will have a major impact on what the Fellowship will look like in the next decades. Due to the scope of this particular study, I was not able to provide a discussion of intergenerational concerns which I came across in my research. For instance, one of the issues that unfolded during my fieldwork in Philadelphia was the question of Bawa's, and thus the Fellowship's, stance on homosexuality. Debates with regards to sexual ethics impacted the second and third generation the most because some younger members of the Fellowship openly identified as gay and lesbian, while seeking to actively participate in the Fellowship spaces and rituals. As executive leaders and members deliberated how to navigate these concerns and how to respond officially, many young members left the Fellowship altogether feeling that the community was not progressive enough for them and/or did not interpret Bawa's teachings as they would have. Some young members assembled informally beyond the Fellowship. They started to congregate in their own homes and began to study Bawa among themselves. As the Fellowship continues to navigate its moral and ethical stances, both in relation to Bawa and Islam, how these deliberations unfold and who participates in these discussions will define the young community, particularly among those born into the Fellowship.

The second key factor will be the role, involvement, and presence of Muslims from immigrant backgrounds (of different generations) who are a common feature of this community already. For example, Pakistani members from Bawa's Toronto branch have established informal branches in Karachi, Pakistan, suggesting that members are disseminating Bawa's teaching from America back to South Asia (beyond Sri Lanka). The degree to which these two contingencies of the Fellowship interact with each other and work together will define how the Fellowship continues to grow, especially as senior disciples, or the first generation of Bawa's followers pass on.

My projection of the future of the Fellowship in America is informed by my analysis of patterns that I documented among Bawa's spaces in Jaffna. As I qualified in my introduction, my focus was on the Jaffna branch of the Serendib Sufi Study Circle, and not Colombo or Matale spaces. These spaces are institutionally significant, but despite the civil war that wreaked havoc on the Jaffna branch and the Muslim expulsion from Jaffna, it is still the Jaffna branch that is far more active than any of Bawa's other spaces in Sri Lanka and I contend it is because of the shrines found in Jaffna, such as the *ashram*, but most especially Mankumban. During my fieldwork, those at the forefront of ritual activity and devotion at Mankumban were Hindu students of Bawa, most of whom are women. The accessibility given to women at Mankumban results in a prolific female presence, led by the Matron and Priya Thambi, with daily devotion centered on Bawa and Maryam. Now, however, without a tomb to honor Maryam and Bawa, new questions arise with regards to the continued presence of Bawa's Hindu students and pilgrims from the Fellowship in America. It also affirms that the legacy left behind by Bawa is not only his presence in his *ashram* or home in Philadelphia, but ultimately his shrine in Mankumban (with or without a tomb), a pattern which is also unfolding at his *mazar* in Coatesville. In a Sufi community with no living *shaykh*, Bawa's charisma is accessed through his shrines, and it is these spaces that will continue to remain significant in this broader transnational network from Jaffna to Pennsylvania.

Embodied Sufism and Its Implications for the Study of Religions

This case study has showcased that the historical precedent of Sufism and its contemporary reality is one in which there were dialogical encounters between manifestations of Sufism in a non-creedal form of universalism as well as a spiritual ethos that was uniquely Islamic. These internal negotiations, dynamisms, and fluidities of Sufism sometimes are positioned against notions of Islamic authenticity, especially in discussions of American Sufism or the role of women. Although scholars and practitioners contend with questions of authority, legitimacy, and orthodoxy, this inherent plurality has been a reality of Sufism and Islam since its formative period across the Middle East and South Asia, and it should not come as a surprise that it is also deeply rooted in America. As such, studies of Sufism of the global West must engage with these historical and contemporary examples of continuities and discontinuities, such as the complex emergence, development, and proliferation of Sufism from the historical region of Baghdad to eventually a global scale. In framing Sufism through this trajectory of both expansive and subtle continuities and discontinuities, it highlights the fluidity and dynamic formations of Sufism, not only as it manifested through shrines, but also through other mediums and traditions, such as metaphysics, theologies, and philosophies (i.e. text and context). This approach also moves it away from approaching Sufism as a reified and static entity and shifts scholars' efforts away from wanting to define Sufism and Islam through paradigms of authenticity, especially in relation to legal precepts. In the context of Bawa's transnational communities, it was shown that the type of Sufism and Islam that was embodied institutionally and spatially was specifically outlined by Bawa's (*shaykh's*) explanation of Islam (scripturally and/or otherwise).

The study of Sufism in this capacity speaks to the ways in which we approach religious studies as a discipline generally, particularly as it relates to lived religions, such as through spaces and rituals, which ebb and flow. Individuals who practice religion(s) maintain agency and ascribe meaning to their actions that challenge homogenous categories and labels used by scholars. It is the full encounter of the everyday that unearths complexity but that can also be disorientating for scholars of religion. This is what the Religious Studies scholar Robert Orsi summoned in advocating for a "third way" for Religious Studies scholars and students, one that is between "heaven" and "earth," this liminal position of the scholar who goes forth into a field to encounter.[4] These moments of "radically destabilizing possibilities of a genuine encounter" reveal how we perceive the world and how we choose to tell new narratives, or retell forgotten ones.[5] This of course "necessarily entails risk, vulnerability, vertigo; it invites anger and creates distress" but it is this "dialectic" between the self and the other, between new paradigms and ancient ones, between the dead and the living that we were reminded of as we followed in the footsteps of Muhammad Raheem Bawa Muhaiyaddeen from Jaffna to Pennsylvania, and back again.[6]

Notes

Introduction

1 Miriam Cooke and Bruce Lawrence, eds, *Muslim Networks: From Hajj to Hip Hop* (North Carolina: The University of North Carolina, 2005); Engseng Ho, *The Graves of Tarim: Genealogy and Mobility across the Indian Ocean* (Oakland: University of California Press, 2006); Pnina Werbner, *Pilgrims of Love: The Anthropology of a Global Sufi Cult* (Bloomington: Indiana University Press, 2004); Catharina Raudvere and Leif Stenberg, eds, *Sufism Today: Heritage and Tradition in the Global Community* (New York: I.B. Tauris, 2008); Peter Mandeville, *Transnational Muslim Politics: Reimagining the Umma* (Oxon: Routledge, 2001); Ron Geaves, Markus Dressler, and Gritt Klinkhammer, eds, *Sufis in Western Society: Global Networking and Locality* (New York: Routledge, 2009); Zareena Grewal, *Islam Is a Foreign Country: American Muslims and the Global Crisis of Authority* (New York: New York University Press, 2013).

2 Nile Green, *Sufism: A Global History* (West Sussex: Wiley-Blackwell, 2012).

3 Ibid.

4 Jeffrey Einboden, *Islam and Romanticism: Muslim Currents from Goethe to Emerson* (London: Oneworld Publications, 2014); Mehdi Aminrazavi, ed., *Sufism and American Literary Masters* (New York: SUNY Press, 2014).

5 Catherine L. Albanese, *A Republic of Mind and Spirit: A Cultural History of American Metaphysical Religion* (Connecticut: Yale University, 2008); Leigh Eric Schmidt, *Restless Souls: The Making of American Spirituality* (California: University of California Press, 2012).

6 Mark Sedgwick, *Western Sufism: From the Abbasids to the New Age* (Oxford: Oxford University Press, 2017).

7 Geaves et al., *Sufis in Western Society*; Martin Van Bruinessen and Julia Day Howell, eds, *Sufism and the "Modern" in Islam* (London: I.B. Tauris & Co Ltd, 2007); Ron Geaves and Theodore Gabriel, eds, *Sufism in Britain* (London: Bloomsbury Press, 2014). Suha Taji-Farouki, *Beshara and Ibn 'Arabi: A Movement of Sufi Spirituality in the Modern World* (Oxford: Anqa Publishing, 2010); Ron Geaves, *The Sufis of Britain: An Exploration of Muslim Identity* (UK: Cardiff Academic Press, 2000); Milad Milani, "The Cultural Products of Global Sufism," in *Handbook of New*

Religions and Cultural Productions, ed., Carole M. Cusack and Alex Norman (Leiden, Boston: Brill, 2012).

8   M. A. Vàsquez, "Studying Religion in Motion: A Networks Approach," *Method and Theory in the Study of Religion*, 20 (2008): 151–2.

9   Ibid.; Arjun Appardurai, *Modernity at Large: Cultural Dimensions of Globalization* (Minneapolis: University of Minnesota Press, 1996), 42–6.

10 Appardurai, *Modernity at Large*, 46.

11 Rory Dickson, *Living Sufism in North America: Between Tradition and Transformation* (Albany: State University of New York Press, 2015); Julianne Hazen, *Sufism in America: The Alami Tariqa of Waterport, New York* (Lanham, MD: Lexington Books, 2017); Marcia Hermansen, "Global Sufism: 'Theirs' and 'Ours,'" in *Sufis in Western Society*, ed. Geaves et al., 26–45; Marcia Hermansen, "Literary Production of Western Sufi Movements," in *Sufism in the West*, ed. J. Malik and J. Hinnells (New York: Routledge, 2006), 28–48; Rosemary R. Corbett, *Making Moderate Islam: Sufism, Service, and the Ground Zero Mosque Controversy* (Stanford: Stanford University Press, 2016).

12 Albanese, *A Republic of Mind and Spirit*.

13 John D. Yohannan, "Emerson's Translations of Persian Poetry from German Sources," in *American Literature*, 14, no. 4 (1943): 407–20; Franklin D. Lewis, *Rumi: Past and Present, East and West: The Life, Teachings and Poetry of Jalal al-Din Rumi* (Oxford: Oneworld Publications, 2000).

14 Zia Inayat Khan, *A Hybrid Sufi Order at the Crossroads of Modernity: The Sufi Order and Sufi Movement of Pir-o-Murishid Inayat Khan* (PhD thesis, Duke University, 2006); Karin Jironet, *Sufism into the West: Life and Leadership of Hazrat Inayat Khan's Brothers 1927–1967* (Leuven: Peeters, 2009).

15 Dickson, *Living Sufism in North America*; Hazen, *Sufism in America*; Sedgwick, *Western Sufism*.

16 Dickson, *Living Sufism in North America*.

17 Alan Godless, "Sufism, the West, and Modernity," http://islam.uga.edu/sufismwest. html (accessed March 31, 2017); Oluf Schöbeck, "Sufism in the USA: Creolisation, Hybridisation, Syncretisation," in *Sufism Today: Heritage and Tradition in the Global Community*, ed. Catharina Raudvere and Leif Stenberg (London: I.B. Taurus, 2009), 177–88.

18 Gisela Webb, "Tradition and Innovation in Contemporary American Spirituality: The Bawa Muhaiyaddeen Fellowship," in *Muslim Communities in North America*, ed. Yvonne Haddad and Jane Smith (Albany: SUNY, 1994).

19 Ibid.; Schöbeck, "Sufism in the USA"; Frank Korom, "Speaking with Sufis: Dialogue with Whom and about What?," in *Interreligious Dialogue and the Cultural Shaping of Religions*, ed. C. Cornille and S. Corigliana (Oregon: Cascade Books, 2012), 224–49. A similar critique has also been offered of the ways in which Buddhism in America has been classified. For instance, Wakoh Shannon Hickey points out

how the categories of "heritage" and "ethnic" Buddhists in studies of Buddhism in America have highlighted not only the "effects of white racism on the development of American Buddhism community" but also "the effects of unconscious white privilege in scholarly discourse about these communities." Wakoh Shannon Hickey, "Two Buddhisms, Three Buddhisms, and Racism," *Journal of Global Buddhism*, 11 (2010): 1. For more, please see ibid., 1–25.

20 Shahab Ahmed, *What Is Islam? The Importance of Being Islamic* (Princeton: Princeton University Press, 2016).

21 Ibid., 123.

22 Elizabeth Sirriyeh, *Sufis and Anti-Sufis: The Defence, Rethinking and Rejection of Sufism in the Modern World* (Richmond, UK: Curzon Press, 1999).

23 Dickson, *Living Sufism in North America*.

24 Ron Geaves, "The Bawa Muhaiyaddeen Fellowship," in *Encyclopedia of New Religions: New Religious Movements, Sects and Alternative Spiritualities*, ed. Christopher Patridge (Oxford: Lion Publishing, 2004); Eleanor Finnegan, "Hijra and Homegrown Agriculture: Farming among American Muslim Communities" (PhD thesis, University of Florida, 2011); Frank Korom, "Charisma and Community: A Brief History of the Bawa Muhaiyaddeen Fellowship," *The Sri Lanka Journal of Humanities*, 37 (2011): 19–33; Korom, "Speaking with Sufis"; Frank Korom, "Longing and Belonging at a Sufi Saint Shrine Abroad," in *Islam, Sufism and Everyday Politics of Belonging in South Asia*, ed. Deepra Dandekar and Torsten Tschacher (New York: Routledge, 2016); Gisela Webb, "Third-Wave Sufism in America and the Bawa Muhaiyadeen Fellowship," in *Sufism in the West*, ed. Jamal Malik and J. Hinnells (New York: Routledge, 2006), 86–102; Webb, "Tradition and Innovation," 75–108; Gisela Webb, "Negotiating Boundaries: American Sufis," in *The Cambridge Companion to American Islam*, ed. Julianne Hammer and Omid Safi (Cambridge: Cambridge University Press, 2013), 190–207.

25 Mohamed Mauroof, "The Culture and Experience of Luminous and Liminal Komuenesam" (PhD thesis, University of Pennsylvania, 1976), 249.

26 Webb, "Tradition and Innovation," 99.

27 Ibid., 77.

28 Marcia Hermansen, "South Asian Sufism in the United States," in *South Asian Sufis: Devotion, Deviation and Destiny*, ed. Charles Ramsey (New York: Continuum, 2012), 247–68; Marcia Hermansen, "In the Garden of American Sufi Movements: Hybrids and Perennials," in *New Trends and Developments in the World of Islam*, ed. Peter Clark (London: Luzac Oriental Press, 1997).

29 Korom, "Speaking with Sufis," 248.

30 Ibid.

31 Jane I. Smith, *Islam in America* (Columbia: Columbia University Press, 2010), 72.

32 Webb, "Negotiating Boundaries."

33 Ibid., 197.

34 Ibid., 198.

35 Ibid.

36 Ibid.

37 Werbner, *Pilgrims of Love*; Geaves, *The Sufis of Britain*; Geaves and Theodore, *Sufism in Britain*.

38 Pnina Werbner, "Transnationalism and Regional Cults," in *The Cambridge Companion of Sufism*, ed. Llyod Ridgeon (Cambridge: Cambridge University Press, 2015), 283.

39 Historically Sufi spaces developed according to their local and cultural contexts; however these institutions shared similarities in their purpose and function. In Turkish Sufi tradition, for instance, the *tekke* was the name given to the buildings in which Sufi brotherhoods would gather, while *khanqah* is the Persian equivalent of a similar institution. The Arabic *zawiyyah* refers to a Sufi lodge, while *ribat*s were initially understood as a "fortress located at a sensitive point along the Islamic frontier, garrisoned by pious individuals" (Mortel 1998, 29) along the North African coast. Mortel, Richard T., "Ribats in Mecca during the Medieval Period: A Descriptive Study Based on Literary Sources" *Bullentin of the School of Oriental and African Studies*, University of London, 61, no. 1 (1998): 29–50. Over time it came to be understood as a resting place for travelers and those in need. It was also associated with Sufi orders, while being funded by Muslim leaders.

40 Werbner, *Pilgrims of Love*; Scott Kugle, *Sufis and Saint's Bodies: Mysticism, Corporeality, and the Sacred Power in Islam* (North Carolina: University of North Carolina Press, 2007); Ho, *The Graves of Tarim*.

41 Pnina Werbner and Helen Basu, "The Embodiment of Charisma," in *Embodying Charisma: Modernity, Locality and the Performance of Emotion in Sufi Cults*, ed. Pnina Werbner and Helen Basu (London: Routledge, 1998), 3.

42 Kelly Pemberton, "Muslim Women Mystics and Female Spiritual Authority in South Asia Sufism," *Journal of Ritual Studies*, 18 (2004): 2.

43 Kugle, *Sufis and Saint's Bodies*, 47.

44 Werbner and Basu, *Embodying Charisma*; Carla Bellamy, *The Powerful Ephemeral: Everyday Healing in an Ambiguously Islamic Place* (Berkeley: University of California, 2011); Anna Bigelow, *Sharing the Sacred: Practicing Pluralism in Muslim North India* (New York: Oxford University Press, 2010); Joyce Burkhalter Flueckiger, *In Amma's Healing Room: Gender and Vernacular Islam in South Asia* (Bloomington: Indiana University Press, 2006); Peter Gottschalk, *Beyond Hindu and Muslim: Multiple Identity in Narratives from Village India* (New York: Oxford University Press, 2000); Yoginder Sikand, *Sacred Spaces: Exploring Traditions of Shared Faith in India* (New York: Penguin, 2007).

45 Mircea Eliade, *The Sacred and the Profane: The Nature of Religion* (Florida: Harcourt, Inc. 1957), 47, 38.

46 Ibid.

47 Ibid., 45. For Eliade, the sacred becomes an essential feature, unto itself or *sui generis*, which is different from scholars, such as the sociologist Emile Durkheim who argued that society defines the sacred and the profane. I am aware that Eliade has been critiqued for his ahistorical approach to the study of religion. My intention in employing him in this study is for the language he developed, which is useful in my discussion of spaces and rituals. His theoretical frameworks are limited because he did not complete ethnographic analysis of the religions he theorized as they actually manifested in real space and time.

48 Ibid., 50.

49 Ibid., 68.

50 Michel Foucault, "*Des Espace Autres*," in *Architecture/Mouvement/Continuité*, trans. Jay Miskowiec (1967/1984), 22.

51 Ibid., 3.

52 Ibid.

53 Ibid., 4.

54 Ibid.

55 Paul Numrich, *Old Wisdom in the New World: Americanization in Two Immigrant Theravada Buddhist Temples* (Knoxville: University of Tennessee Press/Knoxville), 64. For an important analysis of some of the limitations of this framework, please see Wakoh Shannon Hickey's "Two Buddhisms, Three Buddhisms, and Racism," *Journal of Global Buddhism*, 11 (2010): 1–25.

56 Ibid., 64.

57 Ibid., 65.

58 Ibid.

59 Ronald L. Grimes, "Defining Nascent Ritual," *Journal of American Academy of Religion*, 50, no. 4 (1982): 542.

60 For more discussion on this, see the excellent collection of case studies in Dionigi Albera and Maria Couroucli, eds, *Sharing Sacred Spaces in the Mediterranean: Christians, Muslims, and Jews at Shrines and Sanctuaries* (Bloomington: Indiana University Press, 2012).

61 Cemil Aydin, *The Idea of the Muslim World: A Global Intellectual History* (Boston: Harvard University Press, 2017).

62 Bose Neilesh, *Recasting the Region: Language, Culture, and Islam in Colonial Bengal* (Oxford University Press, 2014); Torsten Tschacher and Deepra Dandekar, eds, *Islam, Sufism and Everyday Politics of Belonging in South Asia* (London: Routledge, 2016).

63 Alexander McKinley and Merin Shobhana Xavier, "The Mysteries of the Universe: The Tamil Muslim Intellectualism of M. C. Sidde Lebbe," *South Asia: Journal of South Asian Studies* (2017): 1–18.

64 Ameer Ali, "Muslims in Harmony and Conflict in Plural Sri Lanka: A Historical Summary from a Religio-economic and Political Perspective," *Journal of Muslim*

Minority Affairs, 43, no. 3 (2014): 227–42; Victor De Munck, "Islamic Orthodoxy and Sufism in Sri Lanka," *Anthropos*, Bd. 100, H. 2 (2005): 401–14: John B. Wright, "Sri Pada: Sacred Pilgrimage Mountain of Sri Lanka," *Focus on Geography*, 50, no. 2 (2007): 1–6.

65 Susan Bayly, *Saints, Goddesses and Kings: Muslims and Christians in South Indian Society* (Cambridge: Cambridge University Press, 1989); Elizabeth Schomburg, "'Reviving Religion': The Qadiri Sufi Order, Popular Devotion to Sufi Saint Muhiyiddin 'Abdul Qadir al-Gilani and Processes of 'Islamicization' in Tamil Nadu and Sri Lanka" (PhD thesis, Harvard University, 2003); Dennis McGilvray and Mirak Raheem, *Muslim Perspectives on the Sri Lankan Conflict* (Washington: East-West Center Washington, 2007). For more on Muslim networks across the Indian Ocean please, see Engseng Ho's *The Graves of Tarim*. Ho's study explores networks across the Indian Ocean that formed the Hadrami Yemeni network, which are further linked to itinerant Islamic traditions that developed in Indonesia (Michael Laffan, *The Makings of Indonesian Islam: Orientalism and the Narration of a Sufi Past* (New Jersey: Princeton University Press, 2011)), Malaysia (Ronit Rocci, *Islam Translated: Literature, Conversion, and the Arabic Cosmopolis of South and Southeast Asia* (Chicago: University of Chicago Press, 2011)), and Singapore (Torsten Tschacher, "The Impact of Being Tamil on Religious Life among Tamil Muslims in Singapore" (PhD thesis, National University of Singapore, 2006)).

66 De Munck, "Islamic Orthodoxy", 404.

67 McGilvray and Raheem, *Muslim Perspectives*, 9.

68 Jonathan Spencer, ed., *Sri Lanka: History and the Roots of Conflicts* (London: Routledge, 1990), 8; McGilvray and Raheem, *Muslim Perspectives*, 9.

69 Amarnath Amarasingam, *Pain, Pride, and Politics. Social Movement Activism and the Sri Lanka Tamil Diaspora in Canada* (Georgia: University of Georgia Press, 2015).

70 For more on the expulsion, please also see *The Quest for Redemption: The Story of the Northern Muslims* (2011), which is a report completed by the Citizen's Commission and published by the Law & Trust Society. Muslims in the Northern Province, such as Jaffna town, historically have made up 5 percent of the overall population of Sri Lanka up until their expulsion in 1990 by the LTTE. When they were expelled by the LTTE in 1990, the displaced Muslims were living in camps in Kalpitiya and Puttalam town.

71 Jonathan Spencer, Jonathan Goodhand, et al., *Checkpoint, Temple, Church and Mosque: A Collaborative Ethnography of War and Peace* (London: PlutoPress, 2015), 7.

72 The most recent Sri Lankan census can be found at: http://www.statistics.gov. lk/page.asp?page=Population%20and%20Housing (accessed August 15, 2014). Tamil identity politics itself was not unified till soon after independence. After independence from the British, debates arose within political parties with regards

to voting eligibility of Indian Tamils, or Estate Tamils, Up-country Tamils or Malaiyaha Tamils, and formed the basis of various citizenry laws that added to ongoing legal definitions of who constituted a Tamil. Among the Tamils, shared linguistic identity ends where ethnic and religious ones begin. For instance, Up-country Tamils are a marginalized block in Sri Lanka. They are mainly descendants of Indian Tamils brought to the island from Tamil Nadu (India) by the British to work on tea plantations and who currently work in tea estates. For more on these ethnic and linguistic histories and the contemporary challenges of the Up-country Tamils, please see Daniel Bass, *Everyday Ethnicity in Sri Lanka: Up-country Tamil Identity Politics* (New York: Routledge, 2013).

73 McGilvray and Raheem, *Muslim Perspectives*, 4.

74 Spencer et al, *Checkpoint, Temple, Church and Mosque*, 7.

75 McGilvray and Raheem, *Muslim Perspectives*, viii.

76 Wright, "Sri Pada"; Ross E. Dunn, *The Adventures of ibn Battuta: A Muslim Traveler of the 14th Century* (Berkeley and Los Angeles: University of California Press, 2012); Carl Ernst, *Refractions of Islam in India: Situating Sufism and Yoga* (London: Sage, 2016).

77 Quoted in Ananda Abeydeera, "Paths of Faith: Following the Blessed Footsteps of Adam to Ceylon," *Diogenes*, no. 159 (1992): 70.

78 Ibid.

79 Quoted in ibid., 87–8; Carl Ernst, "Forgotten Sources on Islam in India," *Refractions of Islam in India*, 30.

80 Dunn, *The Adventures of ibn Battuta*, 242.

81 Ernst, "Forgotten Sources on Islam in India," 28. Amir Khusraw Dhilawi's (d. 1325) *The Eight Paradises* in Persian also engages with Adam's Peak Islamic significance.

82 Dennis McGilvray, "Islamic and Buddhist Impacts on the Shrine at Daftar Jailani," in *Islam, Sufism and Everyday Politics*, ed. Dandekar and Tschacher, 62–76; Schomburg, "Reviving Religion."

83 Sunil Goonasekera, *Walking to Kataragama* (Colombo: International Center for Ethnic Studies, 2007), 62.

84 Khidr is known locally as Hayath Nabi Appa or "Our Father, the Eternal Prophet" or "Hilr Alaihissalam" (Khidr). Many local devotees believe that Khidr remains a perpetual youth, and reappears to devotees in cyclical years, especially at his shrine at Kataragama. Local Muslims venerate Khidr Nabi at Kataragama, a sacred site also dedicated to Murukan (Skanda) among Hindus, but the mountain also contains a mosque and shrine for "the green saint" of qur'anic lore, which has drawn international visitors, such as the recently deceased *Shaykh* Nazim al-Haqqani (d. 2014) and his followers. Asiff Hussein, *Sarandib: An Ethnological Study of Muslims of Sri Lanka* (Nugegoda: Asiff Hussein, 2007), 379; Mauroof, "The Culture and Experience of Luminous," 26.

85   Murukan is the Tamil name for the deity who in Sanskrit is known as Skanda, Subrahmanya, Kumara, or Karttikeya. The name itself in Tamil was translated as "beautiful, fragrant, young or vibrant one" (Fred W. Clothey, *The Journal of American Academy of Religion*, 40, no. 1 (1972), 80). Murukan is a central figure in Tamil Hindu devotion and piety. For an early study of this, please see pages 79–95.

86   Hussein, *Sarandib*, 378. When referring to the group of bawas as examples of wandering Sufis in Sri Lanka, I do not use a capital, unlike when I speak about Bawa Muhaiyaddeen.

87   De Munck, "Islamic Orthodoxy"; Hussein, *Sarandib*; Schomburg, "Reviving Religion."

88   Dennis McGilvray, "A Matrilineal Sufi Shaykh," *Sri Lanka in South Asian History and Culture*, 5, no. 2 (2014): 252.

89   This mountain has acquired other names, such as Shiva's Peak (*Shivanoli Patha Malai* or the peak of the foot of the light of Shiva), *Pico de Adam*, and St. Thomas's Peak (who is said to have brought Christianity to the east). Wright, "Sri Pada."

90   The head-monk (*nayaka thero*) position of the Sri Pada temple is reserved for senior monks of the Sabaragamuwa Chapter of the Malwatte Nikaya, and only monks of the Sabaragamuwa Chapter who have received full higher-ordination ceremonies may vote in the elections for that position. The Siam Nikaya is the overarching order. Within the order are two branches, one is the Malwatta Vihare branch, and a chapter within this is the Sabaragamuwa. For more on this, please see Alexander Mckinley, "Mountain at a Center of the World" (PhD thesis, Duke University, forthcoming).

91   Dunn, *The Adventures of ibn Battuta*, 241–2.

92   For more on this, please also see "Midweek Politics: The Battle for Sacred Ground" (April 10, 2013) in *Colombo Telegraph* by Dharisha Bastians via https://www.colombotelegraph.com/index.php/midweek-politics-the-battle-for-sacred-ground/ (accessed June 12, 2015). For a letter from the current trustee of the shrine, Roshan Absoosally, to the former President Mahinda Rajapakse and photographs of the demolition of the sites, please see "Pictures of the Kuragala Islam Holy Site Demolition" (May 17, 2013) via https://www.colombotelegraph.com/index.php/pictures-of-the-kuragala-islam-holy-site-demolition/ (accessed June 12, 2015).

93   For instance, a miraculous story, and there are many, associated with Soragam Cave at Dafter Jailani is of an 8-year-old child who fell into this deep and dark cave where mendicants were said to have spent years meditating (Bawa was said to have meditated in this cave). When the child was rescued after two days she reportedly said, "*appa vandal pal tanda*" (father came and gave me milk) and became known as the "Lady of the Cave" (Hussein *Sarandib*, 383).

94   McGilvray, "Impacts on the Shrine at Daftar Jailani," 69.

95 The book *Dafther Jailany* (2002) by M. L. M Aboosally includes varying local
    narratives of this mountain-top shrine complex, including lists of names of Sufi
    saints along with colonial visitors. Please see it for more details of these oral
    narratives. Aboosally and his family are the trustees of this shrine complex.
    This text should be interpreted as a primary source that captures hagiographic
    traditions of Dafter Jailani and other shrines in Sri Lanka and not necessarily as
    archeological and historical proofs.

96 McGilvray, "Impacts on the Shrine at Daftar Jailani," 69.

97 Amarnath Amarasingam and Merin Shobhana Xavier, "Caught between Rebels
    and Armies: Competing Nationalisms and Anti-Muslim Violence in Sri Lanka,"
    Islamophobia Studies Journal, 7 (2016): 22–43.

98 I saw this dismantled flagpole when I visited in August 2013.

99 Sirriyeh, *Sufis and Anti-Sufis*.

100 McGilvray and Raheem, *Muslim Perspectives*, 13; De Munck, "Islamic Orthodoxy";
    Haniffa, "Piety as Politics amongst Muslim Women in Contemporary Sri
    Lanka," *Modern Asian Studies*, 42 (2008): 347–75; Bart Klem, "Islam, Politics
    and Violence in Eastern Sri Lanka," *Journal of Asian Studies* 70 (2011): 744;
    Barbara Metcalf, *Islamic Revival in British India: Deoband, 1860–1900* (New
    Jersey: Princeton University Press, 2002); Peter Mandaville, *Global Political Islam*
    (New York: Routledge, 2007).

101 Ameer Ali, "The 1915 Racial Riots in Ceylon (Sri Lanka): A Reappraisal of Its
    Causes," *South Asia: Journal of Asian Asian Studies*, 4, no. 2 (1981): 8.

102 McKinkley and Xavier, "Mysteries of the Universe."

103 Hussein, *Sarandib*, 386.

104 De Munck, "Islamic Orthodoxy," 402.

105 The two main sectarian differences in Islam are Sunni and Shi'a. Sunnis make
    up the majority of Muslims (currently estimated at around 85 percent). They are
    generally defined as those Muslims who accept the religio-political legitimacy
    of Muhammad's closest companions as successors (Abu Bakr, 'Umar, 'Uthman,
    and 'Ali). Under the Umayyad and Abbasid dynasties that followed these, a
    "Sunni consensus" formed around four schools of law (Hanafi, Maliki, Shafi'i,
    and Hanbali), two schools of theology (Ash'ari and Maturidi), with a general
    acceptance of Sufism as the spiritual/inward aspect of Islam. Shi'a Muslims,
    however, understand that it was the "people of the house" or the family of the
    Prophet who were to be the religious leaders after Muhammad's death. As such,
    they understand that the successor to Prophet Muhammad was his son-in-law and
    cousin 'Ali. They are further divided in interpretations over lineage of descendants
    of Muhammad and include Zaydis (followers of Zayd ibn 'Ali ibn al-Husayn and
    found in Yemen), Ismailis (followers of Ja'far al-Sadiq's eldest son Ismail and found
    in South Asia, East Africa, and Central Asia), and IthnaAshari (who believe in

twelve *imams*, and the occultation of the twelfth *Imam* Muhammad al-Mahdi, who will return at the end of time). Shi'a Muslims follow the Jafari School of law. They are predominately located in Iran.

106 The only time any interview content was edited was for flow and diction. These are indicated with square brackets in text (i.e. "…") and thus are my additions.

107 George Marcus, "Ethnography in/of the World System: The Emergence of Multi-Sited Ethnography," *Annual Review of Anthropology*, 24 (1995): 112; Marta Dominguez Diaz, "Shifting Field Sites: An Alternative Approach to Fieldwork in Transnational Sufism," *Fieldwork in Religion* (2011): 64–82.

108 Grewal, *Islam Is a Foreign Country*, 17.

109 Taji-Farouki, *Beshara and Ibn 'Arabi*, 23.

1: Charting Bawa's Spaces from Jaffna to Pennsylvania

1 Kambiz GhaneaBassiri, *History of Islam in America: From the New World to the New World Order* (Cambridge: Cambridge University Press, 2010), 8.

2 Ibid.

3 Ibid.

4 Ibid., 8.

5 Quoted in B. K. Narayan and Rajeev Sawney, eds, *Dialogues of the Sufi Mystic Bawa Muhaiyaddeen* (New Delhi: Vikas Publishing House, 1999), 10.

6 Frank Korom, "Speaking with Sufis: Dialogue with Whom and about What?," in *Interreligious Dialogue and the Cultural Shaping of Religions*, ed. C. Cornille and S. Corigliana (Oregon: Cascade Books, 2012), 226. Korom has dated this moment to 1952.

7 Supplicatory prayers in Islam or *du'as* are completed for personal appeals. It may be added after regular prayers (*salat*). Usually, those who are completing *du'as* kneel and hold their open palms out facing up. *Du'as* attributed to the Prophet Muhammad or other saintly figures are also completed. The use of protective amulets in Islam is found among many Muslim communities and is culturally dependent. One common amulet often found is of the five holy persons associated with the Prophet Muhammad, which includes Fatima (his daughter), 'Ali (his son-in-law and cousin), and his grandsons Hasan and Husayn. These amulets are shaped like a hand with five fingers, to symbolize this holy family.

8 Kabeer's grandfather and uncle used to perform these tasks and thus Kabeer explained to me that Bawa knew Kabeer's ancestral lineage. Interview with author, Bawa's room in the Bawa Muhaiyaddeen Fellowship, Philadelphia, April 16, 2014.

9 I refer to the female custodian of the *ashram* as the "matron" throughout my study. When I asked her about using her real name, she was apprehensive and told me

that the focus of my study should be Bawa and not her. I negotiated this by using the epithet of her title and role she occupies, as opposed to her given name.

10 I have given Priya Thambi a pseudonym.

11 The Satya Sai Baba movement developed around Sathyanarayana Raji who was born in 1926. In 1940, he identified himself as the reincarnation of Shirdi Sai Baba (d. 1918), a holy man from Maharashtra. Sai Baba's tradition has amalgamated elements of Hinduism and Islam. For more, see Jacob Copeman and Aya Ikegame, ed., *The Gurus in South Asia: New Interdisciplinary Perspectives* (London: Routledge, 2012).

12 Dr Ganesan, interview with author, Bawa Muhaiyaddeen Fellowship kitchen, Philadelphia, Pennsylvania, April 23, 2014.

13 Mohamed Mauroof, "The Culture and Experience of Luminous and Liminal Komunesam" (PhD thesis, University of Pennsylvania, 1976), 48.

14 Ibid.

15 The titles "guru" and "swami" are common referents used in South Indian religious traditions to honor deities, but also to denote religious figures and leaders by Tamil Hindus and also Tamil Christians.

16 In late 2017, as this book was going to press, the tomb in Mankumban was removed by the new incoming executive members of the Serendib Sufi Study Circle in Colombo. The predominantely Muslim contingent felt that the tomb was not in keeping with the practices of Bawa or what he intended for Mankumban especially the rituals performed by Hindus I document in Chapter 2.

17 In fact, much of the recipes that remain, such as *kanji* (rice soup) that is cooked during Ramadan, both in Jaffna and Philadelphia, are based on Bawa's recipes. For Bawa's recipes, please see the Fellowship's *The Tasty, Economical Cookbook Volume 1 and 2* (Philadelphia: The Fellowship Press, 1983). Bawa taught Ayurvedic philosophies and herbology based on plants and foods common in Jaffna. He trained many of his disciples spiritually through cooking.

18 For more on Sufism and sustainable agriculture through the teachings of Bawa and the Fellowship, please see Eleanor Daly Finnegan, "Cultivating Faith: The Relationship between Islam and Sustainable Agriculture in Rural Communities of American Muslims," in *Global Food Insecurity: Rethinking Agricultural and Rural Development Paradigm and Policy*, ed. Mohamed Behnassi, Sidney Draggan, and Sanni Yaya (Netherlands: Springer, 2011), 53–62, or her dissertation work, "Hijra and Homegrown Agriculture: Farming among American Muslim Communities" (Florida: University of Florida, 2011).

19 Marion Holmes Katz, *The Birth of Prophet Muhammad* (New York: Routledge, 2007), 1.

20 Ibid., 1, 2.

21 Ibid., 6–7.

22 Ibid.

23 Ibid.

24 There is a vast cosmological tradition within Islam, and especially in Sufism, in which Prophet Muhammad is understood as the first manifestation of the light of Allah. Such interpretations developed from qur'anic passages that refer to God as light (*nur*), such as in *an-Nur* (24:35), and reference Prophet Muhammad as light (33:46, 25:61). For some Sufis, Prophet Muhammad or *Nur* Muhammad became representative of the highest intellect. For more, see Annemarie Schimmel *And Muhammad Is His Messenger* (North Carolina: The University of North Carolina, 1985).

25 Tayka Shu'ayb Alim, *Arabic, Arwi, and Persian in Sarandib and Tamil Nadu: A Study of the Contributions of Sri Lanka and Tamil Nadu to Arabic, Arwi, Persian, and Urdu Languages, Literature, and Education* (Madras and Colombo: Imamual Arus Trust for the Ministry of State Muslim Religious and Cultural Affairs, 1993), 209.

26 N. J. G. Kaptein, *Muhammad's Birthday Festival: Early History in the Central Muslim Lands and Development in the Muslim West until the 10/16th Century* (Leiden: Brill, 1993).

27 "Sal" here is the invocation of the blessing on Muhammad, *salla Allahu alayhi wa-sallam* (peace and praise be upon him).

28 Richard Miller and Ruqaiyyah Lee- Hood, E. R., trans., Bawa Muhaiyaddeen, *The Subhana Maulid: Maulidun-Nabi (Sal.)* (Philadelphia: The Fellowship Press, 1991, 2013), 10, 11, 14.

29 Ibid., 11, 14.

30 Mauroof, "The Culture and Experience of Luminous and Liminal Komunesam," 51.

31 Ibid., 49.

32 Ibid., 51.

33 Chloë Le Pichon, Dwaraka Ganesan, et al., eds, *The Mirror Photographs and Reflections on Life with M. R. Bawa Muhaiyaddeen* (Philadelphia: Chloë Le Pichon, 2010), 8.

34 Fuard Uduman was a successful businessman who started one of the first security guard companies in Sri Lanka. His home in Wattala remained another place for gatherings and also included a bedroom for Bawa, which was treated as a shrine. Uduman and his family eventually came to Philadelphia to be with Bawa and for safety during the growing ethnic conflicts in Sri Lanka, in 1983.

35 Bawa also traveled between with the Macan-Markar family to Peradeniya where Dr. Macan-Markar was posted at the University of Peradeniya (in Kandy, Sri Lanka) as a lecturer.

36 The Serendib Sufi Study Circle Chapter 495, "A Law to Incorporate the Serendib Sufi Study Circle," November 27, 1974.

37 Ibid., XV/318.

38 The senior members of Colombo no longer publish books or edit lectures as they did in the early years. This discontinuation is likely due to the aging or passing away of most of the senior disciples of Bawa in Colombo who completed this early task. In Jaffna, Bawa did have his students begin to transcribe some of his teachings, but the study of his teachings through written work was not a central focus in Jaffna. All of Bawa's works, recorded or written by his disciples, was in Tamil.

39 Sri Lankan Malays are descendants of soldiers, political prisoners, and slaves that were brought over by the Dutch and British during their colonial rule between the seventeenth and nineteenth centuries. Umberto Ansaldo, "Sri Lanka Malay and Its Lankan Adstrates," in *Creoles, Their Substrates and Language Typology*, ed. Claire Lefebvre (Amsterdam: John Benjamins Publishing Co. 2011), 365. Ansaldo has highlighted how the label "Malay" is really a "misnomer" as the British used it as an umbrella term to label people from Java and the islands of Indonesia. The Malay diaspora in Sri Lanka consist about 50,000 people (369). Malay Muslims maintain strong numbers in Sinhala regions, such as the Kandy region where Matale is located. Malay communities can also be found in rural areas such as Hambantota district and villages of Kirinda and Bolana. Malay majority regions also exist in predominately Tamil areas as well. For an analysis of the transformation of linguistic features of Malay to Sri Lankan Malay and Sri Lankan Muslim Tamil, please see Peter Slomanson, "Dravidian Features in the Sri Lankan Malay Verb," in *Creoles, their Substrates, and Language Typology*, edited by Claire Lefebvre (2011), 383–409. Malay Muslims remain another example of the heterogeneity of Islamic heritages found in Sri Lanka.

40 T. K. P. Rahman, "In Loving Memory of Our Beloved Shaikh Muhammad Raheem Bawa Muhaiyaddeen May Allah Be Pleased with Him" (Matale: Serendib Sufi Study Circle, 1990), no pagination.

41 Mauroof's dissertation, which he completed in the Anthropology Department at the University of Pennsylvania, was on Bawa Muhaiyaddeen and the early years of the Fellowship. It is entitled "The Culture and Experience of Luminous and Liminal Komunesam" though he anonymized his case study. It is evident that he wrote on the Fellowship, especially as his methodology section spends much time deliberating the issue of the ethnographer's insider/outsider positionality. Mauroof was teaching at Cheyney University in Pennsylvania, known as the first institute for higher learning for African Americans.

42 The Philadelphia race riot or the "Columbia Avenue Riots" unfolded due to an incident that took place on August 28, 1964, in north Philadelphia, when the city's police responded to a call at the home of an African American couple, over a domestic issue. Rumors immediately surged that the police were assaulting a pregnant black

woman which attracted a crowd and led to attacks on the police. The rioting took place for days, and included looting, hundreds of injuries, and millions of dollars in damage, while the cause of the civil rights and black militancy came to a head.

43 Carolyn Fatima Andrews or "Secretary" as she is commonly known relays some of her experiences in the "Introduction" to *The Tree That Fell to the West* (Philadelphia: The Fellowship Press, 2003), xi–xv.

44 Interview with author, via Skype, May 16, 2014. This name is a pseudonym.

45 Ibid.

46 Mauroof notes that there were twenty-one members who went to visit Bawa at the airport, nine who were regular members of the group that was established for Bawa, and the remaining were companions of the nine (Mauroof, "The Culture and Experience of Luminous and Liminal Komunesam," 71). Mauroof also dates Bawa's arrival to August 11, 1971, while everyone whom I have spoken with has dated his arrival to October 11, 1971. It is possible that Mauroof did this for anonymity for his dissertation, since pseudonyms were used for names and places in his study. He also writes that three interested members were corresponding to Bawa via mail prior to his arrival.

47 Khair ul-Nissa, interview with author, Bawa Muhaiyaddeen Fellowship, Philadelphia, Pennsylvania, April 18, 2014. This is the Arabic name she uses.

48 Ibid.

49 Mauroof, "The Culture and Experience of Luminous and Liminal Komunesam," 70. Mauroof gave pseudonyms to his sites, so it is unclear the exact localities he is referring to. He notes though that even in this early period many were visiting from as far north as Montreal to as far west as San Francisco, Kansas City, and Chicago (ibid.). From early January 1972, many of the visitors were locals from the neighborhood (i.e. African Americans) but "the congregation changed colour" (ibid.).

50 In his dissertation, Mauroof suggests other personal reasons, some due to tensions and "attendant scandal, gossip etc." as the reason that he had to remove himself from this community. His decision to write an analytical account of the community did result in souring relationships, not only with the group members but also with Bawa (ibid., 13–15). I was not able to connect with Mauroof for this project; in fact I am not sure if he is still alive, and so I am unable to confirm these events from his dissertation.

51 Ibid., 71.

52 Ibid.

53 Ibid., 70.

54 The practice of *dhikr*, or the remembrance of Allah through the recitation of Allah's Names, is an effort to achieve ultimate union with God or to annihilate one's ego. Bawa's explanation of the Names of Allah is found in the *Asmā'ul Husnā: The 99 Beautiful Names of Allah* (Philadelphia: The Fellowship Press, 1979). William

Chittick refers to this ability to comprehend the Names of God and the names' corresponding essence (*dhat*) as the "distinguishing feature of man." William Chittick, *Ibn 'Arabi* (Oxford: Oneworld Publications, 2005), 62. To remember the true reality of the existence of the human being is to know that "God cannot be understood apart from the object that it reflects." William Chittick, *Sufism: A Beginner's Guide* (Oxford: Oneworld Publications, 2000), 8.

55 M. R. Bawa Muhaiyaddeen, *Dhikr Instructions Booklet* (Philadelphia: The Fellowship Press, 1974).

56 *Kalima Tyyibah* refers to specific sayings or affirmations repeated by a Muslim, that is, "There is no god but God, and Muhammad is his Messenger." *Kalima Tyyibah*'s literal meaning is the "good word."

57 This *kalimah* was the repetition of *la illaha illa llah*, the first part of the Islamic testament of faith (*shahadah*). Bawa also taught the third *kalimah* (Glory be to Allah and Praise to Allah, and there is no God but Allah, and Allah is the Greatest. And there is no Might or Power except with Allah), which is included in the *dhikr* recitation, while he usually handed out the first *kalimah* (There is no God but Allah).

58 Interview with author, at her home, Philadelphia, Pennsylvania, April 14, 2014.

59 *Salat* or *namaz*, in Persian, is prayer or worship. It is one of the pillars of Islam, or requirements of Muslims. The exact amount varies according to different sectarian communities within Islam, but for most Sunni Muslims it is performed five times through the day. It consists of (1) daybreak (*fajr*), (2) noon (*duhr*), (3) midafternoon (*asr*), (4) sunset (*maghreb*), and (5) evening (*'isha*). The exact times of these prayers depends on geography and time of the year, as it is dependent on the sun's position. These prayers are usually performed individually at home, while the Friday noon prayer (*jum'a*) is performed as a community at the *masjid*.

60 Mauroof, "The Culture and Experience of Luminous and Liminal Komunesam," 71.

61 In the early days, the first translators were native Tamil speakers and included Mauroof, Dr M. Z Markar, Dr Ajwad Macan-Markar, Fuard Uduman, Rajis Ganesan, and Dr Ganesan. Crisi Baye, an American student who keenly studied Tamil to communicate with Bawa without a mediator, was reputedly tapped by Bawa on her head and miraculously was able to comprehend Tamil. She was also a regular translator.

62 Ibid., 262.

63 Ibid., 263.

64 During Bawa's first trip back to Sri Lanka from Philadelphia in June 1972, thirteen American disciples returned with him, while another twenty-eight students visited during the duration of Bawa's stay.

65 Mitchell Gilbert's *One Light: An Owner's Manual for the Human Being* (Philadelphia: One Light Press, 2005) is a memoir of his experiences with Bawa and

his teachings. The book has an introduction by Bawa and also includes some of the radio commentaries, provided by his wife, Sonia Gilbert, who is one of the current executive members of the Fellowship.

66   Hixon interviewed many spiritual and religious personalities from different religious and spiritual traditions and Bawa was a regular guest on this show from 1973 to 1978. Hixon eventually became a student of *shaykh* Muzaffer Ozak (d. 1985), who was another regular guest on his radio show. He became a *shaykh* in the Sufi tradition of the Jerrahis and co-founded the Nur Ashki Jerrahi Sufi Order in New York City, New York.

67   This study is unable to map and detail the development of all of these individual branches. I hope future scholarship can capture these institutional establishments and their history further. Since it was the members of the Boston and Toronto branch that I engaged in addition to Philadelphia, I can provide some initial details of these two branches. The Boston branch was formed when Bawa visited Boston on November 10, 1979, for a one-day visit. During this time, he discoursed and stayed with Dave and Carol McNitt in West Newton and also gave one public talk at Harvard Science Center. It was at the home of the McNitts that he made a small branch that would become the Boston branch. The Toronto branch was officially incorporated on June 28, 1976, again with a visit by Bawa to Toronto, though Bawa visited a year prior to this before the official incorporation of the Toronto branch. Most of the early members of the Toronto branch were involved with Hazrat Inayat Khan's son Vilayat Inayat Khan's (d. 2004) movement in Toronto.

68   Georges Ivanovitch Gurdieff's (d. 1949) search for wisdom brought him to different traditions of Central Asia and Tibet and the creation of way he called the "Fourth Way." He would also incorporate music into his spiritual practices, while his publications of various titles would be popular for those interested in spirituality and Sufism.

69   Swami Muktananda (d. 1982) (Siddha Yoga) was an Indian guru who was part of the broader trend of Hindu-inspired gurus in the United States. He later became known for his charlatanism and abuses of power.

70   Terms such as Judeo-Christian or Abrahamic, which are terms used by faith communities, such as the Fellowship, are problematic, as Aaron W. Hughes shows in his *Abrahamic Religions: On the Uses and Abuses of History* (Oxford: Oxford University Press, 2012). I do not wade into these complex discussions here. Needless to say, I am aware of the discourses around the uses of these various terminologies. As such, I use "Jewish Christian" to highlight that members of the Fellowship came from Jewish Christian religious upbringings.

71   Interview with author, via Skype, May 16, 2014. This name is a pseudonym.

72 GhaneaBassiri, *History of Islam in America*; Su'ad Abdul Khabeer, *Muslim Cool: Race, Religion, and Hip Hop in the United States* (New York: New York University, 2016); Jamillah Karim and Dawn-Marie Gibson, *Women of the Nation: Between Black Protest and Sunni Islam* (New York: New York University Press, 2014); Sherman Jackson, *Islam and the Black American: Looking Toward the Third Resurrection* (Oxford: University Press, 2005); Edward E. Curtis IV, *Islam in Black America: Identity, Liberation, and Difference in African-American Islamic Thought* (Albany: State University of New York Press, 2002).

73 Marcia Hermansen, "South Asian Sufism in the United States," in *South Asian Sufis: Devotion, Deviation and Destiny*, ed. Charles Ramsey (New York: Continuum, 2012); Korom, "The Presence of Absence: Using Stuff in a South Asian Sufi Movement," *AAS Working Papers in Social Anthropology* (2012): 1–19.

74 In the early 1970s, Michael Toomey was studying "Oriental Philosophy" and encountered different spiritual and meditative traditions when he first heard, from his brother, about Bawa. Having become interested in Bawa by reputation, Toomey traveled to Philadelphia on April 11, 1972, to meet Bawa.

75 Michael Toomey, interview with author, at the Farm of Bawa Muhaiyaddeen in Coatesville, Pennsylvania, April 19, 2014.

76 M. R. Bawa Muhaiyaddeen, *Islam and World Peace* (Philadelphia: The Fellowship Press, 1987), 12–19.

77 Premadasa, who later became the prime minister of Sri Lanka (1978–88) and the president (1989–98), pursued Bawa for counsel during his early election campaign. Premadasa sought out many holy sages across Sri Lanka hoping to find someone to help him get elected into the government and finally he heard about Bawa. President of Sri Lanka J. R Jayewardene (d. 1996) and Premadasa both visited Bawa regularly in Colombo at the home of the Macan-Markars. In 1982, during Bawa's final trip, they even shared a moment looking over the article of Bawa in *Time* magazine. Premadasa eventually won the election. He was the president from January 2, 1989, to May 1, 1993, while Jayewardene was prime minister from February 1978 to January 1, 1989. Premadasa was killed in a suicide bomb attack on May 1, 1993, orchestrated by the Liberation Tigers of Tamil Eelam (LTTE).

78 Amina, interview with author, Toronto Fellowship branch, Toronto, Canada, December 21, 2013. This name is a pseudonym.

79 For more, please see the special thematic issue of the *Journal of Islamic Studies* on "Engaged Sufism," edited by Kugle and Shaikh, and *Peace and Conflict Resolution in Islam: Precept and Practice*, ed. Abdul Aziz Said, Nathan C. Funk, et al. (Lanham, MD: University Press of America, 2001).

80 Interview with author, via Skype. Toronto, Canada, May 16, 2014. This name is a pseudonym.

81   Interview with author, the Bawa Muhaiyaddeen Fellowship classroom, in
     Philadelphia, Pennsylvania, April 2, 2014. This name is a pseudonym.
82   Ibid.
83   Ibid.
84   Bawa Muhaiyaddeen discourse, "Talk to Executive Committee: As One Family,
     Look for the Truth. This Is God's House" (May 1, 1984). Translated by Dr Ganesan.
     I have gleaned from Dr Ganesan's translations, but I have made some changes in
     word choices.
85   Ibid.
86   Ibid.
87   Gisela Webb, "Negotiating Boundaries: American Sufis," in *The Cambridge
     Companion to American Islam*, ed. Julianne Hammer and Omid Safi
     (Cambridge: Cambridge University Press, 2013), 201.
88   "Bylaws of the Bawa Muhaiyaddeen Fellowship," 1979, 5.
89   Ibid.
90   "Bylaws of the Bawa Muhaiyaddeen Fellowship," 1973, 6.
91   "Bylaws of the Bawa Muhaiyaddeen Fellowship," Section 2, A, 1979, 6.
92   Similar to the Fellowship bylaws, property and land titles are within the authority
     of the Board of Trustees, while a "special general meeting" can be called and votes
     cast "of at least two-thirds of the members present and voting such meeting to
     make such rules as are not inconsistent with the principles and provisions of this
     Law" (6.1).
93   There are two amendments to the original documents. One was dated March
     19, 1973, with all the same leaders signing except the secretary's signature is that
     of Charles Hurwitz; the document pertains to "Article II: Period of Existence."
     A further amendment to the bylaws, with regards to "Decision-Making," was
     added on August 25, 1979; on the copy that I accessed, the document contained no
     signatures.
94   Leaders of the community relay that there may be a thousand families officially
     registered, with many who are not registered, in Philadelphia alone. Individual
     branches, such as those in Toronto and Boston, also maintain their own registration
     numbers. On a global scale, it is difficult to gauge the movement simply based on
     official membership, which I would estimate to be over two thousand in North
     America. Much of the participation of this community, both in Sri Lanka and in
     America, is community-oriented rather than membership-based; for example, local
     Muslims in Philadelphia may attend Bawa's mosque for Friday prayers, but may not
     be members of the Fellowship community, and vice versa. As such, official numbers
     are not representative of this community.
95   For instance, in the United States alone, there are branches in Boston, MA, Ames
     and Des Moines, IA, Detroit, MI, New York City, NY, Sacramento, CA, Stamford,

CT, and Washington, DC. There are also branches in Toronto (Ontario, Canada), as well as numerous sites in Sri Lanka, including Colombo, Matale, Jaffna, Velanai Island, and Puliyankulam. Informal monthly meetings are also held in Berkeley, CA, Madison, WI, Los Angeles, CA, London, England, and Karachi, Pakistan.

96 M. R. Muhaiyaddeen, *The Tree That Fell to the West* (Philadelphia: The Fellowship Press, 2003), 17.

2: From the *Ashram* to Mankumban: Everyday Practices among Bawa's Sri Lankan Followers

1 For consistency, these lyrics have been reproduced from the transliterated Arabic and English translation used by the Fellowship.

2 For consistency, these lyrics have been reproduced from the transliterated and translated version used by the Fellowship.

3 Annemarie Schimmel, *And Muhammad Is His Messenger* (North Carolina: The University of North Carolina, 1985), 92–104.

4 Quoted in ibid., 92–3.

5 Ibid.

6 Rehman Uzma, "Sacred Spaces, Rituals and Practices: The Mazars of Saiyid Pir Waris Shah and Sha 'Abdu'l Latif Bhitai," in *Sufism Today Heritage and Tradition in the Global Community*, ed. Catharina Raudvere and Leif Stenberg (London and New York: I.B. Tauris, 2009), 137–58.

7 Carla Bellamy, *The Powerful Ephemeral: Everyday Healing in an Ambiguously Islamic Place* (Berkeley: University of California, 2011); Joyce Burkhalter Flueckiger, *In Amma's Healing Room: Gender and Vernacular Islam in South Asia* (Bloomington: Indiana University Press, 2006); Kelly Pemberton, *Women Mystics and Sufi Shrines in India* (Columbia: University of South Carolina Press, 2010).

8 During my fieldwork at Mankumban, a female Muslim member of the Fellowship (from the Toronto branch) and I tried to visit this *masjid-mazar* complex. There was a woman who was sitting outside the main entrance to the building with her children. After offering each other *salaams*, we asked her if we could go inside and she said that we could not. The Fellowship pilgrim explained that we were Muslim, and the woman smiled back and said, "so was she." The reality is that women are not usually allowed inside of most *masjids* in Sri Lanka, including this particular *masjid-mazar* complex. As such, I was unable to explore this mosque-shrine complex further.

9 Ahamed Kabeer later served as the Tamil *imam* of the *masjid* in Philadelphia; see the section "Bawa's Early Ministry" in Chapter 1 for more information.

10 Ahamed Kabeer, interview with author, Bawa's room in the Bawa Muhaiyaddeen Fellowship, Philadelphia, Pennsylvania, April 16, 2014.

11 It is also possible that this is a variation of the name of Abd al-Qadir al-Jilani, but I do not know enough about this particular local history and site to know for certain.

12 He resides in Saudi Arabia and travels regularly to Jaffna, Colombo, Philadelphia, and Toronto. This name is a pseudonym.

13 This name is a pseudonym.

14 This belief that the presence of holy figures resides in the sites associated with them is common across religious traditions. We find this in historical spaces associated with Jesus or Muhammad, as well as in Buddhism. An example is seen among the Shingon Buddhists and their cemetery at Koyasan. For an interesting analysis of Buddha's residual presence and the development of stupas (with varying burial deposits as centers of shrines), please see Gregory Schopen, "Burial 'Ad Sanctos' and the Physical Presence of the Buddha in Early Indian Buddhism: A Study in the Archaeology of Religions," *Religion* 17 (1987): 193–225.

15 Varying traditions describe what happened to Mary after the death of Jesus. The Catholic and Orthodox Christian traditions hold that she ascended into heaven where she rules as the "Queen of Heaven" and serves as an intercessor to all those who faithfully appeal to her. In contrast, most Protestant traditions do not ascribe her much agency as it interferes with the Protestant theological focus on scripture and faith. Catholic and Orthodox traditions ascribe many sacred spaces to her, and a significant one is Ephesus near Izmir in Turkey where Mary is reputedly said to have lived out the rest of her days after Apostle John took her there for safety and refuge. Shrines to Mary are a common feature in Catholic, Orthodox, and Muslim traditions where individuals invoke her intercession. Examples include: Our Lady of Zeiton a Coptic Orthodox Church in Egypt and the Church of the Tomb of the Virgin Mary in the Garden of Gethsemane in Jerusalem. Christians and Muslim regularly visit sites, such as churches, dedicated to Mary. Some Muslim traditions hold that Mary's grave is located at the foot of Mount Olives, near the old city of Jerusalem.

16 Bellamy, *The Powerful Ephemeral.*

17 Interview with author, Bawa's room in the Bawa Muhaiyaddeen Fellowship, Philadelphia, Pennsylvania, April 16, 2014.

18 When I helped prepare food for *jum'a* prayers, I sat in this room with the other female devotees and helped set biscuits on trays or seed pomegranates that would then be placed before the tomb prior to the commencement of *poosai.*

19 *Prasad* can be in the form of food, flowers, or gift packets (at the *ashram* and Mankumban it is usually in the form of food packets) that are given to the deity (or Bawa in this case) during *puja/poosai* and then returned to the worshippers as *prasad*, which then contains the blessings of the deity who has taken the offering. For more on *prasad* and Hindu practices, please see Andrea Pinkey, "Prasada, the Gracious Gift, in Contemporary Classical South Asia," *Journal of the American Academy of Religion* 81, no. 3 (2013): 734–56.

20 Richard Eaton, *The Rise of Islam and the Bengal Frontier 1204–1760* (Berkeley: University of California Press, 1996).

21 Kelly Pemberton, "Muslim Women Mystics and Female Spiritual Authority in South Asia Sufism," *Journal of Ritual Studies*, 18 (2004): 10.

22 Ibid., 9–10. *Shaykh* Nizam ud-din Auliya (d. 1325) was a member of the Chishti Sufi order, one of the main Sufi groups in South Asia. This group stressed love as a way to experience God and centered on rituals of listening to music and poetry.

23 Afsar Mohammad, *The Festival of Pirs: Popular Islam and Shared Devotion in South India* (Oxford: Oxford University Press, 2013), 5, 102. Mohammad discovered that the shared celebration of *Muharram* (the month when the martyrdom of Husayn, the grandson of Prophet Muhammad, is commemorated) by Shi'i communities and Hindu devotees was based on a unique local tradition of the *pir* Kullayappa, a charismatic holy figure shared across different religious communities.

24 Ibid., 7.

25 Dominique-Sila Khan, "Being One and Many Among Others: Muslim Diversity in the Context of South Asian Religious Pluralism," in *Diversity and Pluralism in Islam: Historical and Contemporary Discourses amongst Muslims*, ed. Zulfikar Hirji (London: I.B. Tauris, 2010), 58.

26 Ibid., 60.

27 I have used a pseudonym here for protection.

28 Follow-up interview with member via email, Toronto, Canada, October 17, 2013. This name is a pseudonym.

29 Ibid. Since this was part of an email correspondence, I have kept the spelling and transliterations used by the interviewee.

30 Michel Foucault, "*Des Espace Autres*," in *Architecture/Mouvement/Continuité*, trans. Jay Miskowiec (1967/1984).

31 Ibid.

32 Interview with author, the Fellowship classroom, in Philadelphia, Pennsylvania, April 2, 2014. This name is a pseudonym.

33 Ibid.

34 Follow-up interview with member via email, Toronto, Canada, October 17, 2013. This name is a pseudonym.

35 Kabir is an example of an antinomian figure from South Asia. He was born sometime in the fifteenth century into a family of weavers from Varanasi. All else that is known about Kabir is better relegated to the realm of hagiography. As a testament to his legacy, Kabir has been claimed by Muslims, Sikhs, and Hindus. Linda Hess argues that the diversity of claimant "illustrates the element of absurdity or futility that underlies the career of a great and courageous figure who passes from public contempt to adulation" (Linda Hess, *The Bijak of Kabir* (New York: Oxford University Press, 2002 [1983]), 4). Much of what is known about him has been

passed down through generations via written compilations of his oral poems in which he encourages his listeners to be seekers of truth. Most followers have also experienced Kabir via some of his teachings included in the Sikh sacred text, the *Adi Granth*. See *The Bijak of Kabir* (Oxford: Oxford University Press, 2002) for English translations of some of Kabir's poems. For more on Kabir, please see Charlotte Vaudville's *A Weaver Named Kabir: Selected Verses with a Detailed Biographical and Historical Introduction* (Oxford: Oxford University Press, 1993).

36 John Eade and Michael Sallnow, Jr., eds, *Contesting the Sacred: The Anthropology of Christian Pilgrimage* (London: Routledge, 1991); Victor Turner, *The Ritual Process: Structure and Anti-Structure* (Chicago: Aldine Publishing, 1969).

37 Eade and Sallnow, *Contesting the Sacred*, 15.

38 Hindu followers of Bawa understand him to be a "god-like" figure but many are cautious in openly asserting Bawa as God. This reservation may have been due to their awareness that I was a visitor from Canada.

3: From the *Masjid* to the *Mazar*: Rituals and Spaces in the American Fellowship

1 During a discourse given by Bawa on May 18, 1978, at the WBAI Studio in an interview with Lex Hixon, Bawa spoke about the "True Dimensions of *Dhikr*." In this discourse Bawa stated, "God (*Andavan*) must pray to God (*Andavan*) for this is *dhikr*" (Muhaiyaddeen, May 18, 1978). Bawa continues to say, "Rising from God, it must unite with God and grow in God and move in and out of God. One is his treasure (Man) and God, so there must be a connection. If *dhikr* comes from another place, it is not true prayer. That is the point about the *dhikr*. The benefit is like the sun that shines everywhere, the ray that shines on all things, that is like God, in *dhikr*, it is the power of God that shines everywhere. That is the power of the *dhikr*, God loving God, Man becomes God" (May 18, 1978).

2 The Toronto branch recites *dhikr* on Friday nights, which is followed by dinner.

3 Michael Muhammad Knight describes his attempt to perform *istikharah* at the *mazar* of Bawa in Coatesville, before he is woken up by the groundskeeper of the farm, explaining that it is not a place to be sleeping. For more, see *Blue-Eyed Devil: A Road Odyssey through Islamic America* (Brooklyn: Soft Skull Press, 2006), 86.

4 Books, like *The Resonance of Allah* (Philadelphia: The Fellowship Press, 2001), for example, are often placed on Bawa's bed or nightstand when newly published.

5 For a baby blessing, the newborn baby is laid on the bed of Bawa and members of the family gather around the bed. Then a senior member of the community, such as Ahamed Kabeer, reads from Bawa's discourses and makes a *du'a* for the well-being of the newborn. At the side of this room is also an office in which

administrative duties are performed: these include answering the telephone, completing transcriptions, or typing publications, and so on. Most of the paintings that were completed by Bawa are also in this room, as well as throughout the Fellowship. Also notable is a photograph of Mankumban, the shrine of Bawa and Maryam.

6 Food practices of the Philadelphia Fellowship require more scholarly attention to further capture immigration patterns through food ways.

7 Interview with author, via Skype, May 16, 2014. This is a pseudonym.

8 Paul Numrich, *Old Wisdom in the New World: Americanization in Two Immigrant Theravada Buddhist Temples* (Knoxville: University of Tennessee Press/Knoxville, 1996), 64.

9 Ibid.

10 If he is unable to complete Friday *jum'a* prayers, there are several other leaders, or sub-*imam*s, who lead the prayers, all of whom are devotees of Bawa in some capacity. Sub-*imam*s include a Syrian American Muslim and an African American convert to Islam; the former lives at the Fellowship and also serves as a *muezzin*, or the one who gives the call to prayer.

11 Interview with author, the classroom of the Bawa Muhaiyaddeen Fellowship, April 16, 2014.

12 Ibid.

13 Ibid.

14 Ibid.

15 Ibid.

16 Interview with author, via Skype, May 16, 2014. This name is a pseudonym.

17 In contrast, at Mankumban there is a unique manifestation of diversity at *jum'a* prayers that differs in structure from what is called *jum'a* prayers at Philadelphia where *imam* Abdur-Razzaq leads in the *masjid*.

18 Interview with author, Bawa Muhaiyaddeen Fellowship, April 8, 2014. This name is a pseudonym.

19 Ibid.

20 The *mawlid*, especially in honor of Prophet Muhammad's birthday, is a central act of veneration and piety among various Muslim societies and cultures, as mentioned in Chapter 1.

21 The version of the *mawlid* used was by *Shaykh* al-Khatib Muhammad al-Madani. It is not composed by Bawa.

22 Richard Miller and Ruqaiyyah Lee-Hood, trans., *The Subhana Maulid: Maulidun-Nabi (Sal.)* (Philadelphia: The Fellowship Press, 1991, 2013), 26–7.

23 Ibid., 27.

24 Bawa also used to lecture after the *mawlid* recitations. To maintain this practice—after *mawlid* recitations, evening prayers, and dinner is served—readings are selected from Bawa's discourses and read aloud. *A Song of Muhammad*

(Philadelphia: The Fellowship Press, 1996) is one such example. During the readings, the use of different ritual languages is further highlighted by the use of Arabic, Tamil, and English. Tamil was spoken by Bawa and, as such, it is viewed as a sacred language among the members of the Fellowship. Some early members of the Fellowship studied Tamil enthusiastically in order to access Bawa directly. Arabic also came into use at the Fellowship in a similar manner. Tamil and Arabic, along with English, form the central liturgical languages particular to the Fellowship because of Bawa and his own Tamil identity.

25   Samuel Lewis was initially involved with the Theosophical Society. Lewis went on to travel and study, earning titles as a teacher in Zen Buddhism and Bhakti yogi. He eventually returned to America and taught "hippies" or the spiritual seekers in the San Francisco Bay area and began his work as a peace activist through the use of Sufism, especially through dance, which led to the formation of the "Dances of Universal Peace."

26   The tombs of Sufi saints are usually called *mazar* (shrine) although the names given to them may vary according to cultural context. For instance, tombs may be called a *dargah* (court or doorway), *zawiyah*, or *maqam* in Arabic.

27   His daughter Seyyedeh Dr Nahid Angha is the founder of International Association of Sufism, which maintains his legacy. Dr Angha is a human rights activist, women's rights activist, and Sufi leader and scholar in her own right, which is evident in her roles as the codirector and cofounder of International Sufi Women Organization. She is also the organizer of the annual Sufism Symposium and Songs of the Soul: Poetry and Sacred Music Festival. She has authored and translated many books including, *The Journey Seyr Va Soluk* (California: International Association of Sufi Publications, 1991) and *Principles of Sufism* (California: Asian Humanities Press, 1991).

28   Interview with author, residence of Michael Green, Coatesville, Pennsylvania, March 4, 2016.

29   The members referenced here are part of the Unionville branch, which formed in 1982 while Bawa was in Sri Lanka. Coatesville is a city in Chester County, Pennsylvania, and is about thirty-nine miles west of Philadelphia. The branch is also known as Unionville, the name of the unincorporated community in the region, and so Unionville branch is the same as Coatesville, which includes the *mazar* and farm.

30   Kabir asked me to use the name given by Bawa to him. Interview with author, Bawa Muhaiyaddeen *Mazar*, Coatesville, Pennsylvania, April 21, 2014.

31   Ibid.

32   Eleanor Finnegan, "*Hijra* and Homegrown Agriculture: Farming among American Muslim Communities" (PhD thesis, University of Florida, 2011); 123.

33   Ibid., 124.

34   Ibid.

35 On Sunday mornings, members have "Wisdom Meetings" at the welcome center where a video or an audio recording of Bawa's discourses is played. This is followed by an informal lunch, similar to meetings held in Philadelphia at the Fellowship house, that is, the meal is always vegetarian (to keep with Bawa's teachings) and usually South Asian cuisine prepared by members who volunteer to cook. During my visits, I have eaten *biryani* (mixed rice), *roti* (pita), *dhal* (lentils) curry, potato curry, and *kanji*, a traditional Sri Lankan rice soup that was a favorite of Bawa. These meetings and luncheons are open to everyone.

36 On the day of the *'urs*, amid all the changes due to the weather, members forgot to hand out the transliterated sheets to this song. As such, Ahamed Kabeer led a group of mainly non-Tamil members in singing this song. Everyone knew the chorus and joined in, but the main verses were sung more quietly.

37 The opening chapter of the Qur'an, the *Fatiha* (1:1-7), remains one of the most invoked chapters in Islamic piety, and as such, it is frequently referenced during daily *salat*. It is often compared to the Lord's Prayer in the Christian context. *Ya Sin* (36:1-83) has been referred to as the "heart of the Qur'an" as it affirms the power of Allah as the "Almighty, the Lord of Mercy" (36:6), the prophecy of Muhammad, and the messengers and the message of the Qur'an. And importantly it also signals the end times or the hereafter wherein judgment awaits.

38 During the *'urs* recitation, additional chapters of the Qur'an are also recited. They include the *Ad-Duha* or *the Morning Hours* (93), *Ash-Sharh* or The Solace (94), *At-Tin* or The Fig (95), *Al-'Alaq* or The Clot (96), *Al-Qadr* or Power (97), *Al-Bayyinah* or The Clear Proof (98), *Az-Zalzalah* or The Earthquake (99), *Al-'Adiyat* or The Coursers (100), *Al-Qari'ah* or The Calamity (101), *At-Takathur* or Rivalry in Worldly Increase (102), *Al-'asr* or The Declining Day (103), *Al-Humazah* or The Traducer (104), *Al-fil* or The Elephant (105), *Quraysh* or *Quraysh* Tribe (106), *Al-Ma'un* or Small Kindness (107), *Al-Kauthar* or Abundance (108), *Al-Kafirun* or The Disbelievers (109), *An-Nasr* or Succor (110), *Al-Masad* or Palm Fiber (111), *Al-Iklas* or The Sincerity (112, said three times), *Al-Falaq* or The Daybreak (113), and *An-Nas* or People (114).

39 Jonathan Granoff is the president of the Global Security Institute, senior advisor to the ABA's [American Law Association] Committee on Arms Control and National Security, and cochair of the ABA Blue Ribbon Task Force on Nuclear Non-Proliferation. He is a senior advisor to the Nobel Peace Laureate Summit and has served as vice president, and UN representative, of the Lawyers Alliance for World Security. Granoff met Bawa in the early 1970s and he is a current and active member of the Fellowship in Philadelphia where he plays an institutional role. For more on Granoff, please see Dickson's *Living Sufism in North America* (New York: SUNY, 2015).

40 M. R. Bawa Muhaiyaddeen, *The Tree That Fell to the West* (Philadelphia: The Fellowship Press, 2003).

41 This practice of burial *ad sanctos*, or being buried near sacred places such as tombs of holy figures, is seen across religious traditions such as in Christianity or Buddhism (Gregory Schopen, "Burial '*ad sanctos*' and the Physical Presence of the Buddha in Early Indian Buddhism: A Study of Archaeology of Religions," *Religion*, 17 (1987): 193–225). In Islam, there are some evidences of this practice, though it has not been thoroughly explored in scholarship to my knowledge. One of the challenges of this type of burial practice in Islam is that the dead must be buried soon after death, and usually within twenty-four hours. As such, it may not be possible to move a body to the desired location (i.e., near a saint's shrine) within this time frame, although this is not to say that this has not happened. Examples have occurred in the burials of royalty, such as the Mughal emperors and family members in South Asia, near shrines of Chishti Sufi saints. This practice is also evident at the Fellowship *mazar*. In my time at the *mazar*, I heard pilgrims ask Fellowship caretakers how one can secure a burial plot at the *mazar*. Fellowship caretakers often express to visitors that they must be members of the Fellowship to be able to be buried at the cemetery near Bawa's *mazar*.

42 Shoaib, interview with author, Bay and Bloor Plaza, in downtown Toronto, Canada, October 9, 2013.

43 Ibid.

44 Nur Sharon Marcus, interview with author at interviewee's home, Toronto, Canada, October 10, 2013.

45 Finnegan, "*Hijra* and Homegrown Agriculture," 119, 131.

46 M. J. Marzia, "It's so peaceful" on "Mazar of Bawa Muhaiyaddeen" Facebook group (April 16, 2017).

47 Muhammad Asim, "It is so nice" on "Mazar of Bawa Muhaiyaddeen" Facebook group (November 2016).

48 Interview with author, Bawa Muhaiyaddeen *Mazar*, Coatesville, Pennsylvania, April 21, 2014. I have used the name that Bawa gave Kabir, as per his request.

49 Ibid.

50 Kelly Pemberton, "Muslim Women Mystics and Female Spiritual Authority in South Asia Sufism," *Journal of Ritual Studies*, 18 (2004): 7.

51 William Rory Dickson and Merin Shobhana Xavier, "Négociation du sacré à Philadelphie: soufismes concurrents au sanctuaire de Bawa Muhaiyaddeen," *Social Compass*, 62, no. 4 (2015): 584–597.

52 On April 13, 2013, two bombs exploded during the Boston Marathon killing three people and injuring hundreds. The attacks were linked to Chechen brothers Dzhokhar and Tamerlan Tsarnaev. The search for these two bombers resulted in an intense manhunt that unfolded over several days and attracted the attention of all media networks in United States, most of whom immediately linked the bombers to foreign terrorist organizations. In the aftermath, no

such links were uncovered and the two men were found to have orchestrated the attacks on their own. At present Dzhokhar Tsarnaev is appealing his death sentence.

53 Khwaja Shamsuddin Azeemi is an editor of the magazine *Roohani Digest*, in Karachi and internationally. He is a student of Qalander Baba Auliya (Hasan Ukhra Syed Mohammad Azeem Barkhiya) who is connected to the tradition of Hazrat Abu Ayub Ansari, whose lineage (within the community) is traced to the Prophet Muhammad. His community is known as the Azeemia Sufi Order and they are based in Karachi, Pakistan. Qalander Baba Auliya was born in 1898 in Khorja, Buland Sheher in India. Khawaja Shamsuddin Azeemi was born in October 1927 in Saharanpur, India. It is his books (a total of forty-two thus far) that have gained him acclaim as a spiritual leader. His communities, known as Muraqba Halls, have grown internationally spanning across Europe, America, Russia, and Canada. For more on this community, please see: http://azeemiasilsila.org/khwaja_shamsuddin. php (accessed March 1, 2015).

54 Engseng Ho, *The Graves of Tarim: Genealogy and Mobility across the Indian Ocean* (Oakland: University of California Press, 2006), 7.

55 Ibid., 190.

56 Ibid., 7–8.

57 Ibid.

58 Thomas Tweed, *Our Lady of Exile: Diasporic Religion at a Cuban Catholic Shrine in Miami* (Oxford: Oxford University Press, 1997); Elaine Pena, *Performing Piety: Making Space Sacred with the Virgin of Guadalupe* (Berkeley and Los Angeles: University of California Press, 2011).

59 Annemarie Schimmel, *The Empire of the Great Mughals: History, Art and Culture* (London: Reaktion Books, 2004), 114.

60 Interview with author, Bawa Muhaiyaddeen *Mazar*, Coatesville, Pennsylvania, April 21, 2014. I have used the name Bawa gave Kabir, as per his request.

61 I was not able to access these discourses by Bawa, so I am not able to confirm Bawa's instructions to his communities.

62 The famous Bollywood and Oscar-winning singer and songwriter A. R. Rahman is a Hindu convert to Islam. He visited the *mazar* of Bawa while in New York on a musical tour of the United States. A. R. Rahman is an Indian composer, singer-songwriter, music producer, and musician. He has won two Academy Awards, two Grammy Awards, a British Academy of Film and Television Arts Award, a Golden Globe, and many more awards for his music and film scores. Carnatic, Hindustani, and Qawwali music heavily influences Rahman's music. His visit to the *mazar* was posted on a Bawa Muhaiyaddeen Facebook group, which has since become inaccessible.

63 Ho, *Graves of Tarim*, 61.

4: Women's Experiences in Bawa's Spaces

1 Scott Kugle, *Sufis & Saint's Bodies: Mysticism, Corporeality, and the Sacred Power in Islam* (North Carolina: University of North Carolina Press, 2007); Catharina Raudvere, *The Book and the Roses: Sufi Women, Visibility, and Zikr in Contemporary Istanbul* (Sweden: Bjärnums Tryckeri, 2002); Samuli Schielke, "Mystic States, Motherly Virtues, Female Participation and Leadership in an Egyptian Sufi Milieu," *Journal for Islamic Studies* (2008); Carla Bellamy, *The Powerful Ephemeral: Everyday Healing in an Ambiguously Islamic Place* (Berkeley: University of California, 2011); Joseph Hill, "'All Women are Guides': Sufi Leadership and Womanhood among Taalibe Bay in Senegal," *Journal of Religion in Africa*, 40 (2010).

2 Catharina Raudvere, "Knowledge in Trust: Sufi Women in Istanbul," *Social Compass*, 50, no. 23 (2003): 27.

3 Ibid., 47.

4 Ibid., 27.

5 There are many Sufi women who are active beyond formal Sufi communities and spaces. For instance, many Sufi women work in the academy and as translators of Sufi and Islamic texts including Laleh Bakhtiar, Gray (Aisha) Henry (Fons Vitae), Camille Helminski of the Threshold Society and Daisy Khan, the executive director of the American Society for Muslim Advancement (ASMA). The activist Dr Nahid Angha, who succeeded her father, the Shi'a Sufi Shah Maghsoud, currently leads the International Association of Sufism. The roles of Sufi women beyond the sacred space are often neglected in the study of women and Sufism in America. Exploring these voices and their contribution to North America would be an excellent contribution to the study of Sufism and women in America.

6 Audio discourse: Muhaiyaddeen, April 16, 1976.

7 Ibid.

8 Ibid.

9 Ibid.

10 Audio discourse: Muhaiyaddeen, August 24, 1979.

11 There are seventy verses of the Qur'an that refer to Maryam and her name is mentioned in thirty-four of these.

12 Ja'far al-Sadiq (765) is known as the sixth *imam* of the Shi'a Muslims. He is revered as a great scholar, jurist, and transmitter of *hadith* not only for Shi'a traditions but also for Sunnis and Sufis. The prominent Shi'a school of law, the Jafari School, is attributed to him. (Abu Hanifah, who created the Hanifi School of Law studied with Ja'far.) Two prominent Shi'a traditions of the Ismailis (Seveners) and the Ithna-Ashari (Twelvers) came from Ja'far's male children and their descendants. In Sufi circles, he is perceived as a *qutb*, or axial pole.

13 Farhana Mayer, trans., *Spiritual Gems: The Mystical Qur'an Commentary Ascribed by Sufis to Imam Ja'far al-Sadiq (d.148/765)* (Kentucky: Fons Vitae, 2011), liii.

14 Ibid., liv.

15 Kristen Zahra Sands, *Sufi Commentaries on the Qur'an in Classical Islam* (New York: Routledge, 2006).

16 Quoted in Margaret Smith, *Rabi'a: The Life and Works of Rabi'a and Other Women Mystics in Islam* (Oxford: Oneworld, 1994), 59. Rabi'a al-'Adawiya, born AD 717 in Basra, is often cited as the "first true saint of Islam" (Amila Buturovic, "Between the *Tariqa* and the *Shari'a*: The Making of the Female Self," in *Feminist Poetics of the Sacred Creative Suspicions*, edited by F. Devlin-Glass and L. Mcredden (Oxford: Oxford University Press, 2001), 144). She was likely around the age of 90 when she died in Basra, approximately AD 801 (Margaret Smith, *Rabi'a: the Life and Works of Rabi'a and Other Women Mystics in Islam* (Oxford: Oneworld, 1994), 22). Historical and current references to her by Sufis and scholars alike is a testament to her influence on Sufism. The biographer al-Munawi stated, "She was the most famous among them, of great devotion and conspicuous in worship and of perfect purity asceticism" (ibid.). That said, much of her life is based on hagiography rather than historical fact.

17 Quoted in Smith, *Rabi'a*, 21.

18 Henry Corbin, *Creative Imagination in the Sufism of Ibn Arabi* (New Jersey: Princeton University Press, 1969), 162.

19 Jamal Elias, "Female and Feminine in Islamic Mysticism," *The Muslim World*, 78 (1988): 217; Henry Corbin, *Alone with the Alone: Creative Imagination in the Sufism of Ibn Arabi* (New Jersey: Princeton University Press, 1998).

20 Elias, "Female and Feminine," 217; Sa'diyya Shaikh, *Sufi Narratives of Intimacy: Ibn 'Arabi, Gender and Sexuality* (Chapel Hill: The University of North Carolina Press, 2012); Stephen Hirtenstein, *The Unlimited Mercifier: The Spiritual Life and Thought of Ibn 'Arabi* (Oxford: Anqa Publishing, 1999).

21 Sachiko Murata, *The Tao of Islam: A Sourcebook on Gender Relationships in Islamic Thought* (New York: State University of New York Press, 1992).

22 Corbin, *Creative Imagination*, 145.

23 Ibid., 164.

24 Sand 2006, 108.

25 Sands, *Sufi Commentaries on the Qur'an in Classical Islam*, 108.

26 Sandrine Keriakos, "Apparitions of the Virgin in Egypt: Improving Relations between Copts and the Muslims?" in *Sharing Sacred Spaces in the Mediterranean: Christians, Muslims, and Jews at Shrines and Sanctuaries*, ed. Dionigi Albera and Maria Couroucli (Bloomington: Indiana University Press Bloomington, 2012).

27 Aliah Schleifer, *Mary the Blessed Virgin of Islam* (Louisville: Fons Vitae, 1997), 100.

28 Schielke, "Mystic States, Motherly Virtues," 102–103.

29 Bellamy, *The Powerful Ephemeral*, 6.

30 Ibid., 21.

31 Maryam Kabeer Faye in her autobiography, *Journey through Ten Thousand Veils* (New Jersey: Tughra Books, 2009), narrates her meetings and studies with many different mystical teachers and gurus, which culminated in Philadelphia with Bawa. She married Ahamed Kabeer, one of the *imam*s of the Fellowship *masjid*, but they later divorced. With the passing of Bawa she continued to encounter other Sufi *tariqa*s and she has now become a *shaykha*, and has been initiated into other orders, such as in the Senegalese *Tariqa Mustafawiyya* and her home serves as a *zawiyya*, or lodge in Philadelphia, which is located near the Fellowship. Furthermore, I do not enter into a discussion of the particularities of the white convert community members of the Fellowship, though this forms a small contingency of members in the Fellowship. Further study of converts to Islam in the Fellowship would be valuable to explore, especially in light of studies of convert Muslims in America. Zareena Grewal's study *Islam Is a Foreign Country: American Muslims and the Global Crisis of Authority* (New York: New York University Press, 2013) highlights that Sufi Islam has drawn especially European American female Muslim converts (222); whether this is the case in the Fellowship has yet to be determined.

32 Ahamed Kabeer was appointed as the Tamil *imam* for the Bawa Muhaiyaddeen Fellowship.

33 Interview with author, home of interviewee, Philadelphia, Pennsylvania, April 9, 2014.

34 Ibid.

35 Rosemary R. Corbett, *Making Moderate Islam: Sufism, Service, and the Ground Zero Mosque Controversy* (Stanford: Stanford University Press, 2016).

36 Interview with author, via Skype, May 16, 2014. This name is a pseudonym.

37 Ibid.

38 Ibid.

39 Ibid.

40 Amina Wadud is a visiting professor with the Center for Religious and Cross Cultural Studies at Gadjah Mada University in Yogyakarta, Indonesia, since she retired from her previous post as a professor of religion and philosophy at Virginia Commonwealth University. Her seminal scholarship has been on the progressive application of qur'anic exegesis in *Quran and Woman: Rereading the Sacred Text from a Woman's Perspective* (Oxford: Oxford University Press, 1999). Although she gave a *khutba* at Claremont Main Road Mosque in Cape Town, South Africa, she is remembered for leading *salat* with male and female congregants at the Episcopal Cathedral of Saint John the Divine in Manhattan in 2005, which resulted in death threats and made her famous (both negatively and positively) across the Muslim communities.

41 Interview with author, home of interviewee, Philadelphia, Pennsylvania, April 9, 2014.

42 Single males and females were not allowed to mix in the sleeping quarters. Bawa also arranged marriages between some of his male and female disciples. He taught that sexual relations was only to be practiced in the context of marriage, thus many children born into the Fellowship grew-up not being allowed to date or engage in sex before marriage. At the same time, he also taught some married couples to transcend sexual relations in their marriage. It appears that Bawa was traditionally bound by some aspects of South Asian Hindu-Islamic asceticism in his treatment of gender, sex and sexuality.

43 Marcia Hermansen, "What Is American about American Sufi Movements?" in *Sufism in Europe and North America*, ed. David Westerlund (London and New York: Routledge, 2004), 55.

44 Marcia Hermansen, "Sufism and American Women," *World History Connected* November 2006, http://worldhistoryconnected.press.illinois.edu/4.1/hermansen. html (accessed June 15, 2015), paragraph 13.

45 Interview with author, Starbucks, Toronto, Canada, May 2, 2014. This name is a pseudonym.

46 Rory Dickson, *Living Sufism in North America: Between Tradition and Transformation* (Albany: State University of New York Press, 2015), 167. Dickson interviewed Sufi leaders across America and asked them how they responded to gender norms and practices in their respective communities. Dickson found that gender roles and practices were dependent on the teachings and direction of each individual Sufi leader. For instance, when speaking of Zia Inayat Khan's Sufi Order International (now renamed the Inayati Order), Dickson labeled Hazrat Inayat Khan (the originator of the movement) an "innovator" for initiating two women— Rabia Martin in the United States and Zohra Mary Williams in England—to be the first leaders. In total, Khan only initiated four disciples to a level that authorized them to teach other student, and they were all women. Hazrat Inayat Khan also appointed his daughter, Noor un Nisa Inayat Khan (d. 1944), to lead the Sufi Order in America, but she would go on to become a British special operative agent, heroically finding intelligence against the Nazis during the Second World War. For this, please see the recent documentary *Enemy of the Reich: The Noor Inayat Khan Story* by Rob Gardner. Also see her books *King Akbar's Daughter: Stories for Everyone* (New York: Suluk Press, 2013) and *Twenty Jataka Tales* (Vermont: Inner Traditions International, 1985).

47 Julianne Hazen, "Contemporary Islamic Sufism in America: The Philosophy and Practices of Alami Tariqa in Waterport, New York" (PhD thesis, London: SOAS, University of London, 2011), 140; Corbett, *Making Moderate Islam*.

48 Aside from *mawlid* celebrations, *salat* and funerals are other times when those present are separated by gender in the Fellowship.

49 Marion Katz, "Women's *Mawlid* Performances in Sanaa and the Construction of 'Popular Islam,'" *International Journal of Middle East Studies* 40 (2008): 468.

50 Ibid. Although men were prominent participants during the *mawlid*s in Egypt,
    Samuli Schielke found that "the conventions regarding gendered spaces are
    significantly relaxed during the festival. Women are welcomed as customers in cafes
    that usually prefer to serve men only, while mosques and shrines where spatial
    separation of men and women is observed for most of the year become mixed
    spaces during the festival." Schielke, "Mystic States, Motherly Virtues."

51 Elias, "Female and Feminine," 218; Shaikh, *Sufi Narratives of Intimacy*.

52 Elias "Female and Feminine," 219. These factors presented limitations to the ways
    in which voices of Sufi women are captured in literary and scholarly traditions,
    especially from classical and formative periods in the study of Sufism. Voices of
    women in the history of Sufism have been noted through male Sufi writers of
    hagiographies or narratives of holy and exemplary peoples, such as the eleventh-
    century Persian mystic Abu 'Abd ar-Rahman al-Sulami. Rkia Cornell's *Early Sufi
    Women: Dhikr an-nisaw al-muta'abbidat as-Sufiyyat by Abu 'Abd ar-Rahman as
    Sulami* (Louisville, KY: Fons Vitae, 1999), a seminal translation of the eleventh-
    century Persian mystic Abu 'Abd ar-Rahman al-Sulami's *Dhikr an-niswa al-
    muta'abbidat as-Sufiyyat*, or *Early Sufi Women*, is one such example. It records many
    instances of Sufi women and their pieties, practices, and relationships both human
    and divine. Studies of women in classical Sufism also explore the nuances of Sufi
    practices and language in relation to their male counterparts.

53 Mayer, *Spiritual Gems*; Murata, *The Tao of Islam*; Shaikh, *Sufi Narratives of
    Intimacy*; Annemarie Schimmel, *My Soul Is a Woman: The Feminine in Islam*
    (New York: Continuum, 1997, 2003); Elias, "Female and Feminine"; Maria Dakake,
    "Walking upon the Path of God Like Men?: Women and the Feminine in Islamic
    Mystical Tradition," in *Sufism: Love and Wisdom*, ed. Roger Gaetani and Jean-Louis
    Michon (Bloomington: World Wisdom Press, 2006).

54 Laury Silvers suggests that one of the challenges in studying the role of women
    in Sufism has been the varying interpretations of the categories of "spirituality"
    or religiosity as it pertains to women. Silvers writes that the "sheer number of
    extant reports of men compared to women in the formative literature means that
    women are read as marginal to the development, transmission, and preservation
    of Sufi practices, knowledge, and teaching." Laury Silvers, "Early Pious, Mystic
    Sufi Women," in *The Cambridge Companion to Sufism*, edited by Llyod Ridgeon
    (New York: Cambridge University Press, 2015), 25.

55 Azad Arezou, "Female Mystics in Medieval Islam: The Quiet Legacy," *Journal of the
    Economic and Social History of the Orient*, 56 (2013): 73–81.

56 Elias, "Female and Feminine," 211.

57 Joyce Burkhalter Flueckiger, *In Amma's Healing Room: Gender and Vernacular
    Islam in South Asia* (Bloomington: Indiana University Press, 2006), 9.

58 Buturovic, "Between the *Tariqa* and the *Shari'a*," 144.

59 Laury Silvers, "Early Pious, Mystic Sufi Women," 48.

60 Schimmel writes that "Sufism, more than stern orthodoxy, offered women a certain amount of possibilities to participate actively in the religious and social life," recording examples such as in the Bektashi Order in Ottoman Turkey where female participation was popular, and on par with men, in Sufi ritual activities (*Mystical Dimension of Islam* (North Carolina: The University of North Carolina Press, 1975), 423).

61 The study of gender and Sufism has often been synonymous with women in Sufism. Scott Kugle is one example of a scholar who challenges this limitation in his study. *Sufis and Saints Bodies: Mysticism, Corporeality and Sacred Power in Islamic Culture* (Chapel Hill: University of North Carolina Press, 2007) explores both male and females' experiences in the path of Sufism. The text explores how same-sex love between male disciples was utilized by some historical Sufi personalities as a means to achieve love of God.

62 Elias, "Female and Feminine," 220.

63 Amila Buturovic, "Between the *Tariqa* and the *Shari'a*: The Making of the Female Self," in *Feminist Poetics of the Sacred: Creative Suspicions*, edited by F. Delvin-Glass and L. Mcredden (Oxford: Oxford University Press, 2001), 135.

64 Ahmed Sahab, *What Is Islam?* (Princeton: Princeton University Press, 2016), 517–18.

65 Ibid., 516.

66 Corbett, *Making Moderate Islam*.

67 Hermansen, "Sufism and American Women," no pagination.

5: *Swami* to *Qutb*: Bawa as *al-Insan al-Kamil*

1 Bawa M. R. Muhaiyaddeen, *Wisdom of the Divine (al-Hikmathul Jannath)* (Colombo: Serendib Sufi Study Circle 1988), i.

2 B. K. Narayan and Rajeev Sawhney, eds, *Dialogues of the Sufi Mystic Bawa Muhaiyaddeen* (New Delhi: Vikas Publishing House, 1999), 10.

3 Frank Korom explores the possible age of Bawa Muhaiyaddeen. See his contribution "Speaking with Sufis: Dialogue with Whom and About What?" in *Interreligious Dialogue and the Cultural Shaping of Religions*, edited by C. Cornille and S. Corigliano (Oregon: Cascade Books, 2012), 224–49.

4 M. R. Bawa Muhaiyaddeen, *The Tree That Fell to the West* (Philadelphia: The Fellowship Press, 2003).

5 Ibid.

6 Ibid.

7 Ibid., 31–9.

8   Ibid.

9   Quoted in Narayan and Sawhney, *Dialogues of the Sufi Mystic*, 9.

10 Muhaiyaddeen, *The Tree That Fell to the West*, 31–9, 91, 99.

11 Frank Korom, "Charisma and Community: A Brief History of the Bawa Muhaiyaddeen Fellowship," *The Sri Lanka Journal of Humanities*, 37 (2011): 21.

12 Mohamed Mauroof, "The Culture and Experience of Luminous and Liminal Komunesam" (PhD thesis, University of Pennsylvania, 1976), 23.

13 Ibid.

14 Ibid., 57.

15 In his dissertation, Mauroof further adds another category to understand Bawa as the "dramaturgical Bawa" (Mohamed Mauroof, "The Culture and Experience of Luminous and Liminal Komuesam," 57). An example of one of Bawa's statements for dramatic effect include "I am the lowest of the low" (ibid.).

16 Korom, "Charisma and Community"; Frank Korom "Speaking with Sufis."

17 Korom, "The Presence of Absence: Using Stuff in a South Asian Sufi Movement," *AAS Working Papers in Social Anthropology* (2012): 7.

18 Ibid.

19 Annemarie Schimmel, *And Muhammad Is His Messenger* (North Carolina: The University of North Carolina, 1985).

20 Titus Buckhardt, *Introduction to Sufi Doctrine*, trans, D. M. Matheson (Indiana: World Wisdon Inc, 1959), 123.

21 Muhaiyaddeen, *The Tree That Fell to the West*.

22 For more on Bawa's teachings on *al-insan al-kamil*, please see Merin Shobhana Xavier's "The *Insan Kamil* of Bawa: The Metaphysics of a Tamil Sufi *Sheikh*," *Sri Lanka Journal of Humanities*, 39 (2013): 51–63.

23 Louis Renou quoted in Jacqueline Suthren Hirst and John Zavos, *Religious Traditions in Modern South Asia* (London and New York: Routlege, 2011), 115.

24 Aya Ikegame and Jacob Copeman, eds, *The Guru in South Asia: New Interdisciplinary Perspectives* (London and New York: Routledge, 2012), 2.

25 The significance of charisma in religious authorities, such as prophetic figures and further routinization, was first developed by the sociologist Max Weber in his essay "The Three Types of Legitimate Rule (*Die drei reinen Typen der legitimen Herrschaft*)," *Preussische Jarbücher* 187, no. 1–2 (1922).

26 Carl Ernst, *The Shambhala Guide Sufism* (Boston: Shambhala, 1997); Carl Ernst and Bruce Lawrence, *The Chishti Order in South Asia and Beyond: Sufi Martyrs of Love* (New York: Palgrave Macmillian, 2002); Carl Ernst, *Refractions of Islam in India: Situating Sufism and Yoga* (London: Sage, 2016); Annemarie Schimmel, *Mystical Dimensions of Islam* (North Carolina: University of North Carolina Press, 1979); Joyce Burkhalter Flueckiger, *In Amma's Healing Room: Gender and Vernacular Islam in South Asia* (Bloomington: Indiana University Press, 2006); Yoginder Sikand, *Sacred Spaces: Exploring Traditions of Shared Faith in India*

(New York: Penguin, 2007); Carla Bellamy, *The Powerful Ephemeral: Everyday Healing in an Ambiguously Islamic Place* (Berkeley: University of California, 2011); Anna Bigelow, *Sharing the Sacred: Practicing Pluralism in Muslim North India* (New York: Oxford University Press, 2010).

27 Muhaiyaddeen, *The Tree That Fell to the West*. In Sri Lankan Tamil Hindu poems such as the *puram*, the deity of Murukan is mostly associated with, and revered for, his quality of *mara* (courage in warfare). *Puram* is genre of poetry found in the Tamil literary tradition that usually conveyed the actions of kings and their lives. These poems are treated as historically sound for the devotees who utilize them. For more discussion on *puram*, please see Norman Cutler's *Songs of Experience: The Poetics of Tamil Devotion* (Bloomington and Indianapolis: Indiana University Press, 1987), especially his chapter "Poems, Poets and Poetics."

28 Mount Kailasa sits northwest of the western Nepali, Indian, and Tibetan border. It holds religious significance for Hindus, Buddhist, Jains, and Bonpo, the indigenous people of Tibet. In Hindu cosmology, it is the residence of the god Shiva (god of destruction), his partner Parvati (Uma), their two sons Ganesa (god of success) and Karttikeya ("commander-in-chief" or Murukan in Tamil), and their two daughters Laksmi (goddess of social welfare) and Sarasvati (goddess of culture). Murukan, according to Tamil Hindu traditions, came to Sri Lanka to hunt in the jungles, but in the process, fell in love with Valli, and they lived together on Kataragama Hill (Wendy Doniger, *On Hinduism* (Oxford: Oxford University Press, 2014)). Buddhists revere it as "Kang Rinpoche" or the "precious jewel of the snows" that has the power to rid one of one's sins (T. D'Ancona, "A Sacred Trek Round Mount Kailash," *Mandala*, 64 (2001)). For Jains, it is the site in which their first Jain prophet reached enlightenment.

29 Mauroof, "The Culture and Experience of Liminous and Liminal Komunesam," 49.

30 Ibid., 50.

31 Paramahansa Yogananda, *Autobiography of a Yogi* (New York: Philosophical Library, 1946).

32 Idries Shah, *The Sufis* (New York: Doubleday and Company, 1964).

33 These included gurus such as Ram Dass and the infamous Chögyam Trungpa (d. 1987). Author of the popular book *Be Here Now* (1971), Ram Dass (born Richard Alpert in 1931) is an American spiritual teacher and prolific author. He is also a student of Hindu guru Neem Karoli Baba (d. 1973). He teaches via his website: http://www.ramdass.org (accessed August 12, 2014). Chögyam Trungpa Rinpoche (1939–87) was a Tibetan Buddhist meditation master and teacher in the lineage of Kagyu and Nyingma traditions. He was also the eleventh Trungpa tülku and founded the Shambhala organization. He arrived in the United States after a stay in England where he had married Diana Pybus. Known for teaching "crazy wisdom" and founding the Naropa Institute in Boulder, Colorado, his later life was riddled with scandals of drug and alcohol abuse and illicit sexual activities. He eventually died in Halifax, Nova

Scotia, where he moved the Shambhala headquarters. For more, see http://www. shambhala.org/teachers/chogyam-trungpa.php (accessed August 12, 2014).

34 Mauroof wrote "there was an exuberance of the 'love' principle in the American scenes of this story" (Mauroof, "The Culture and Experience of Luminous and Liminal Komunesam," 27–8).

35 Khair ul-Nissa, interview with author, office of the Bawa Muhaiyaddeen Fellowship, Philadelphia, Pennsylvania, April 18, 2014. This is her Arabic name.

36 For more on Hussein's experience during his pilgrimage to Mankumban, please see the subsection *Pilgrimages to Bawa's Spaces in Sri Lanka by Members of the Fellowship* in Chapter 2 of this book.

37 Follow-up interview with member via email, Toronto, Canada, December 3, 2013. This name is a pseudonym.

38 Rick Boardman, interview with author, home of interviewee Philadelphia, Pennsylvania, April 14, 2014.

39 Rahmat Bibi was introduced to Bawa when she was 19 years old and met him upon his return from Sri Lanka in 1978. She has asked that I use the name Bawa had given her.

40 Rahmat Bibi, interview with author, Starbucks, Philadelphia, Pennsylvania, April 3, 2014. I have used the name given to her by Bawa.

41 Muhaiyaddeen, *Asmā'ul Husnā*, 60.

42 While I was visiting the Matale branch of the Serendib Sufi Study Circle in Sri Lanka, devotees had painted portraits of Abdul Qadir al-Jilani (d. 1166) and Moinuddin Chishti (d. 1236) alongside a photograph of Bawa. When I asked the custodians of the Matale shrine about these photographs, they explained to me that both these Sufi masters had influenced Bawa. They added that Bawa painted the picture of Chishti's *dargah* in Ajmer, which further solidified Bawa's connection with the Chishti *tariqa* for this family of devotees. In stories that were relayed to me about Bawa's painting of Chishti's *mazar*, senior disciples explained that Bawa had a vision of this *mazar* and thus painted it from his memory of the vision even though he had never visited it. In my research of Bawa thus far, I have not come across any discussion on these connections as explained by Bawa himself.

43 Schimmel, *Mystical Dimensions of Islam*, 247.

44 Schimmel, *And Muhammad Is His Messenger*, 169.

45 His tomb in Baghdad is a popular site of pilgrimage.

46 Schimmel, *Mystical Dimensions of Islam*, 248.

47 Painting was completed by Bawa in 1978.

48 Translated by Dr Ganesan.

49 B. Muhaiyaddeen and Lex Hixon, "True Dimensions of *Dhikr*" (Philadelphia: WBAI Studio, CD, May 18, 1978).

50 Ibid.

51 In some discourses, Bawa alluded that Khidr taught him this concept. His first sighting near Kataragama, which is known in Sri Lankan Sufi traditions to be

associated with Khidr, is thought to support this connection. Other times, he has suggested this knowledge came from Abdul Qadir al-Jilani, since Bawa has also explained that he spent eleven years meditating at Dafter Jailani, which is dedicated to Abdul Qadir al-Jilani. Again, these are only speculations and the identity of this "guru" has yet to be confirmed.

52 Muhaiyaddeen, "True Dimensions of *Dhikr*."

53 God's qualities are sometimes referred to as the three thousand qualities of God; see Muhaiyaddeen, *Asmā'ul Husnā: The 99 Beautiful Names of Allah* (Philadelphia: The Fellowship Press, 1979).

54 Similar traditions of the "negation of the I," or self-annihilation, are also found in Tamil Sufi literature such as by the Sufi *Shaykh* Muhayyaddin Maluk Mudaliya, known as Kottar Gnaniar (1167–AH 1209). This negation of the ego-self, or the I, becomes the ultimate purpose of the *dhikr* and the achievement of this negation, according to Bawa, results in the realization of nondualism, the original state of all creation. Kottar Gnaniar makes a similar point. His main work is the *Meignana Thirupadattirattu* in the year AH 1316. In the introduction to this study, he had met a disciple of Hallaj who initiated and influenced him in the tradition of "*ana la-Haqq*" (M. Sahbdeen, *The Sufi Doctrine in Tamil Literature* (Madras: Basharath Publishers, 1986), 86). Bawa provided his own interpretation of the names recited in *dhikr*, phrase by phrase, in *Asmā'ul Husnā: The 99 Beautiful Names of Allah*, which was compiled by the Fellowship.

55 I have used the translations of the *surah*s as found in the *dhikr* pamphlet of the Fellowship to keep with their understanding of the recitation.

56 Michael Sells, *Early Islamic Mysticism: Sufi, Qur'an, Mi'raj, Poetic and Theological Writings* (New Jersey: Paulist Press, 1996), 45.

57 In the name of God, most merciful, most compassionate

Say: I seek refuge with the Lord of dawn
From the mischief of created things
From the mischief of darkness as it overspreads
From the mischief of those who practice secret arts
And from the mischief of the envious one as he practices envy.
Amin.

58 In the name of God, most merciful, most compassionate.

Say: I seek refuge with the Lord and Cherisher of mankind.
The king, or ruler of mankind
The God, or judge of mankind.
From the mischief of the whisperer of evil,
The same who whispers into the hearts of mankind.
Among *jinns* and men.
Amin.

59 For Bawa, these recitations have a deep esoteric significance. For instance,
    he explains the *surah* is the body. It is made of twenty-eight letters. They are
    the "*Alhamdu*" (Heart of Praise). The twenty-eight letters of the body are the
    Qur'an and that is the "*Suratul-Qur'an*" (the Inner Form of the Qur'an), which
    is the "*Suratul-Insan*" (the Inner Form of Man) (B. Muhaiyaddeen, *God His
    Prophets and His Children* (Philadelphia: Fellowship Press, 1978), 136). This
    pure life, driven by *iman*, is the manifestation of the human being's return to
    the beginning of all creation at which moment the soul was united with the
    Creator. It is also at this *maqam* (state) when the *qalb*, or "heart within the heart,"
    is in the state of Consciousness of Divine Analytic Wisdom where "the Heart
    and Throne of the True Believer" belongs to Allah that one is in a state of true
    iman (B. Muhaiyaddeen, *The Guidebook to the True Secret of the Heart*, Vol. 2
    (Philadelphia: Fellowship Press, 1976), 198). This inward reality is dependent on
    the vision of the *qalb* (heart).

60 B. Muhaiyddeen, *Morning Dhikr at the Mosque of Shaikh M. R. Bawa
    Muhaiyaddeen (Ral)* (Philadelphia: The Bawa Muhaiyaddeen Fellowship, 1996),
    6–9. I have kept the transliteration and translation as found in the original *dhikr*
    booklet so as not to create any confusion.

61 Afsar Mohammad, *The Festival of Pirs: Popular Islam and Shared Devotion in South
    India* (Oxford: Oxford University Press, 2013), 100.

62 Nur Sharon Marcus, interview with author, home of interviewee, Toronto, Canada,
    October 10, 2013.

63 Shoaib was introduced in Chapter 2. He is originally from Pakistan, but lives in
    Riyadh, Saudi Arabia, and visits Toronto and Philadelphia regularly. When I was
    in Jaffna in the summer of August 2013, some members of the Fellowship arrived
    in Sri Lanka for a pilgrimage to Bawa's *ashram* and Mankumban. Shoaib and his
    family were part of this group. I connected with Shoaib again in Toronto, a few
    months after our travels together in Sri Lanka, to understand his experience in
    Jaffna and relationship with Bawa.

64 Shoaib, interview with author, Bay and Bloor Plaza, downtown Toronto, Canada,
    October 9, 2013.

65 For more of these descriptions, as developed by Dr Ganesan and his editors, please
    see *The Resonance of Allah* (Philadelphia: The Fellowship Press, 2001), 710–12.

66 These discourses are gathered in the book, based on Bawa's lectures, *The Song of
    Muhammad* (Philadelphia: Fellowship Press, 1996).

67 Maroof, "The Culture and Experience of Luminous and Liminal Komunesam,"
    219. In her cosmological and metaphysical study, *Sufi Expressions of the Mystic Quest*
    (London: Thames and Hudson, 1976), Laleh Bakhtiar explains "unity of being"
    through the primal tenet of the Sufi expression "there is no god but God" (*La ilaha
    illa'Llah*) and "Muhammad is the Prophet of God" (Muhammad *rasula' Llah*) (9).
    The first expression, she writes, "expresses the concept of the Unity of Being which

annihilates all multiplicity, all separate entities [. . . while the second tenet] expresses the concept of the Universal Prototype (most often translated as the Universal Man)" (ibid.) underlining both unity in multiplicity and multiplicity in unity.

68 B. Muhaiyaddeen, *Asmā'ul Husnā: The 99 Beautiful Names of Allah* (Philadelphia: Fellowship Press, 1979). Throughout Bawa's spiritual teachings, he recalls the holy figures of the Abrahamic traditions as exemplars for humanity on their own paths to God. In relaying stories of prophets, such as Musa (Moses), Isa (Jesus), or Muhammad, Bawa used these prophetic figures as models for the journey of the *insan* to become *al-insan al-kamil*. He also incorporated exoteric (*zahir*) and esoteric (*batin*) interpretations of stories of the prophets. His retelling of the story of Khidr *nabi* and Musa, in *The Guidebook* (Philadelphia: Fellowship Press, 1976), 37–57, is such an example.

69 Rick Boardman, interview with author at interviewee's home, Philadelphia, Pennsylvania, April 14, 2014.

70 Mauroof, "The Culture and Experience of Luminous and Liminal Komunesam," 38.

71 It is in discussions of Bawa's philosophy and metaphysics that one begins to see similarities between Bawa's teachings and al-Jilani's philosophy, such as that of the "seven states." Elsewhere, Bawa also discusses colors and temperatures as notable in al-Jilani's own framework. Future studies should compare these two teachers and their traditions to explore the degree to which al-Jilani's teachings influenced Bawa and how they manifested in Tamil Sufism.

72 Ibid., 36.

73 Ibid., 219.

74 Musa Muhaiyaddeen also has a website on which his discourses are published and he speaks at various Sufi conferences across the world, such as the International Association of Sufism. Musa Muhaiyaddeen's website is http://www. thewitnesswithin.com (accessed June 7, 2014). He is the author of several books, such as the *Elixir of Truth: Journey on the Sufi Path*, Vol. 1 (Atlantic City, NJ: The Witness Within, 2013).

75 Musa Muhaiyaddeen, interview with author at the home of the interviewee, Philadelphia, Pennsylvania, January 5, 2014.

76 Interview with author, Starbucks, Toronto, Canada, November 18, 2013. This is a pseudonym.

77 In a discourse given by Bawa at St. Peter's Church in New York City on May 18, 1975, he explains that he is unlettered and unschooled. As usual, Bawa begins his discourses by first pleading for forgiveness from the audience for any shortcomings, stating "I do not know religions and philosophies. I am a very tiny man. I am smaller than an ant, I am still learning, and I am here to share with you some of what I have learned" (B. Muhaiyaddeen, "The Learning of an Ant Man" (New York City, 1975), audio-discourse). Bawa may be using imagery from the *Surah an-Naml* (27) or *The Ant*.

78 "Captain" was the name given to her by Bawa and the name that she requested
    that I use in my project. Interview with author, in the kitchen of the Bawa
    Muhaiyaddeen Fellowship, Philadelphia, Pennsylvania, April 8, 2014. *Hu* (He) is
    one of the names often recited during Sufi *dhikr*. The sound of *Hu*, often made from
    the back of one's throat, sometimes represents one's breath and so signifies that with
    every breath one recollects God, who is ultimate "Just He" (or He/She/It).

79 Muhaiyaddeen, *Asmā'ul Husnā*, 5.

80 Audio Muhaiyaddeen, May 18, 1975.

81 Ibid.

82 Muhaiyaddeen, *Asmā'ul Husnā*, 5.

83 Ibid., 11.

84 Ibid., 113.

85 Bawa M. R. Muhaiyaddeen, *God, His Prophets and His Children* (Philadelphia: The
    Fellowship Press, 1978); Muhaiyaddeen, *Asmā'ul Husnā*.

86 Here (T) signifies the term as Tamil. These elements represent various qualities and
    are associated with particular angelic, or prophetic, beings within the Abrahamic
    and Hindu traditions. Earth, which contains four hundred trillion ten thousand
    poisons is often represented with Adam and Eve (Paravadi) (T) and Hawwa. Water is
    connected with the *devi*, the spirit *Gangadevi*, or the archangel Mikael and contains
    one thousand and eight poisonous forces. Air is connected to the spirit *Vayubagavan*
    or the archangel Izrafil and contains two thousand one hundred and twenty-eight
    poisonous forces or energies. Finally, fire is associated with the spirit of *Akkinibagavan*
    or Izraeel, the archangel of death, and contains one thousand and eight poisonous
    forces that include *jinns* (spirits), fairies, and Satan, as well as arrogance, egoism, pride,
    and jealousy (Bawa Muhaiyaddeen, *The Guidebook to the True Secret of the Heart*, Vol.
    1 (Philadelphia: The Bawa Muhaiyaddeen Fellowship, 1976).

87 Bawa Muhaiyaddeen, *The Guidebook to the True Secret of the Heart*, Vol. 1
    (Philadelphia: The Bawa Muhaiyaddeen Fellowship, 1976), 102.

88 Ibid., 103.

89 Mauroof adds that the seventh state of consciousness was also associated with
    nur Muhammad and the sixth state was associated with *Qutb* Muhaiyaddeen and
    Murukan (Mauroof, "The Culture and Experience of Luminious and Liminal
    Komunesam," 87–8).

90 Muhaiyaddeen, May 18, 1975.

91 Ibid.

92 Muhaiyaddeen, *Asmā'ul Husnā*.

93 The *qalb* (heart), according to Sufis such as al-Hallaj (d. 922), is an essential
    physical and metaphysical feature of the human being. The early eighth-century
    mystic Hasan al-Basri (d. 728), framed spiritual "discernment" as "the science of
    hearts" (John Renard, *Historical Dictionary of Sufism* (Lanham, MD: Rowman &
    Littlefield, 2016), 134–5). The *qalb* is the "human faculty at the center of all spiritual

experience" and it contains the "innermost secret" or mystery (*sirr*), and thus the goal of Sufi discipline and contemplation is to "polish the mirror of the heart" (ibid.).

94 Buckhardt, *Introduction to Sufi Doctrine*; Toshihiko Izutsu, *Sufism and Taoism: A Comparative Study of Key Philosophical Concepts* (California: University of California Press, 1983); Julian Baldick, *Mystical Islam: An Introduction to Sufism* (London: I.B. Tauris & Co Ltd, 1989); William Chittick, *Sufism: A Beginner's Guide* (Oxford: Oneworld Books, 2000); William Chittick, *Ibn 'Arabi* (Oxford: Oneworld Publications, 2005); Caner K. Dagli, *Ringstones of Wisdom* (*Fusus al-Hikam*) (Chicago: Kazi Publication, 2004).

95 Chittick, *Sufism: A Beginner's Guide*.

96 Baldick, *Mystical Islam*.

97 Schimmel, *And Muhammad Is His Messenger*, 134.

98 Ibid., 135.

99 Baldick, *Mystical Islam*, 84.

100 Schimmel, *And Muhammad Is His Messenger*, 134. Fariduddin Attar of Nishapur (d.1220)—known for his hagiographies of Sufi saints and his seminal flight narrative *The Conference of the Birds*—understands this primordial manifestation of *Nur Muhammad* as the *Haqqia Muhammadiyya*, or the "Muhammadan Reality." This reality makes Muhammad the primordial creation which endows him with the role and status as the "Seal of the Prophets." Prophet Muhammad is signified as the "prototype of the prototype," *logos* (divine word) and, thus, the true *Qutb* (A. J. Arberry, *Sufism: An Account of the Mystics of Islam* (London: George Allen & Unwin, 1950), 93).

101 Muhaiyaddeen, July 25, 1983.

102 Maruoof, "The Culture and Experience of Liminous and Liminal Komunesam," 221, 247.

Conclusion

1 One such incident was the bombing of Lal Shabaz Qalandar's (d. 1275) shrine in Sindh, Pakistan, in February 2017 by ISIS. ISIS, which stands for the Islamic State in Iraq and Syria, also referred to as ISIL (Islamic State in Iraq and Levant), considers itself the Islamic State. The group has numerous branches globally, including in Yemen, Afghanistan, and the Philippines.

2 Shahab Ahmed, *What Is Islam? The Importance of Being Islamic* (Princeton: Princeton University Press, 2016).

3 Ibid., 124.

4 Robert Orsi, *Between Heaven and Earth: The Religious Worlds Peoples Make and the Scholars Who Study Them* (Princeton: Princeton University Press, 2005).

5 Ibid., 198.

6 Ibid., 204.

Bibliography

Abeydeera, Ananda. "Paths of Faith: Following the Blessed Footsteps of Adam to Ceylon." *Diogenses*, no. 159 (1992): 69–94.

Absoosally, Roshan. "Pictures of the Kuragala Islam Holy Site Demolition." May 17, 2013. https://www.colombotelegraph.com/index.php/pictures-of-the-kuragala-islam-holy-site-demolition/.

Ahmed, Shahab. *What Is Islam? The Importance of Being Islamic*. Princeton: Princeton University Press, 2016.

Albanese, Catherine L. *A Republic of Mind and Spirit: A Cultural History of American Metaphysical Religion*. New Haven, CT: London: Yale University Press, 2008.

Ali, Ameer. "The 1915 Racial Riots in Ceylon (Sri Lanka): A Reappraisal of Its Causes." *South Asia: Journal of South Asian Studies*, 4, no. 2 (1981): 1–20.

Ali, Ameer. "Kattankudy in Eastern Sri Lanka: A Mullah-Merchant Urban Complex Caught between Islamist Factionalism and Ethno-Nationalism." *Journal of Muslim Minority Affairs*, 29, no. 2 (2009): 183–94.

Ali, Ameer. "Muslims in Harmony and Conflict Plural Sri Lanka: A Historical Summary from a Religio-economic and Political Perspective." *Journal of Muslim Minority Affairs*, 34, no. 3 (2014): 227–42.

Alim, Tayka Shu'ayb. *Arabic, Arwi, and Persian in Sarandib and Tamil Nadu: A Study of the Contributions of Sri Lanka and Tamil Nadu to Arabic, Arwi, Persian, and Urdu Languages, Literature, and Education*. Madras and Colombo: Imamual Arus Trust for the Ministry of State Muslim Religious and Cultural Affairs, 1993.

Amarasingam, Amarnath. *Pain, Pride, and Politics. Social Movement Activism and the Sri Lanka Tamil Diaspora in Canada*. Georgia: University of Georgia Press, 2015.

Amarasingam, Amarnath, and Xavier, Merin Shobhana. "Caught between Rebels and Armies: Competing Nationalisms and Anti-Muslim Violence in Sri Lanka." *Islamophobia Studies Journal*, 7 (2016): 22–43.

Aminrazavi, Mehdi., ed. *Sufism and American Literary Masters*. New York: SUNY Press, 2014.

Ansaldo, Umberto. "Sri Lanka Malay and Its Lankan Adstrates." In *Creoles, Their Substrates and Language Typology*, edited by Claire Lefebvre, 367–82. Amsterdam: John Benjamins Publishing Co., 2011.

Appardurai, Arjun. *Modernity at Large: Cultural Dimensions of Globalization*. Minneapolis: University of Minnesota Press, 1996.

Arberry, A. J. *Sufism: An Account of the Mystics of Islam*. London: George Allen & Unwin, 1950.

Asiff, Hussein. *Sarandib: An Ethnological Study of Muslims of Sri Lanka.* Colombo: Asiff Hussein, 2007.

Aydin, Cemil, *The Idea of the Muslim World: A Global Intellectual History.* Boston: Harvard University Press, 2017.

Azad, Arezou. "Female Mystics in Mediaeval Islam: The Quiet Legacy." *Journal of the Economic and Social History of the Orient,* 56 (2013): 53–88.

Bakhtiar, Laleh. *Sufi Women of America: Angels in the Making.* Chicago: Kazi Publications, 1996.

Baldick, Julian. *Mystical Islam: An Introduction to Sufism.* London: I.B. Tauris & Co Ltd, 1989.

Barks, Coleman, and Green, Michael. *The Illuminated Rumi.* New York: Broadway Books, 1997.

Bass, Daniel. *Everyday Ethnicity in Sri Lanka: Up-Country Tamil Identity Politics.* London: Routledge, 2013.

Bastians, Dharisha. "Midweek Politics: The Battle for Sacred Ground." April 10, 2013, *Colombo* Telegraph, https://www.colombotelegraph.com/index.php/midweek-politics-the-battle-for- sacred-ground/.

Basu, Helene, and Werbner, Pnina, eds. *Embodying Charisma: Modernity, Locality and the Performance of Emotion in Sufi Cults.* London: Routledge, 1998.

Bayly, Susan. *Saints, Goddesses and Kings: Muslims and Christians in South Indian Society 1700–1900.* Cambridge: Cambridge University Press, 1989.

Bellamy, Carla. *The Powerful Ephemeral: Everyday Healing in an Ambiguously Islamic Place.* Berkeley: University of California, 2011.

Bennett, Clinton, and Ramsey, Charles M., ed. *South Asian Sufis: Devotion, Deviation, and Destiny.* NIPPOD edition. Bloomsbury Academic, 2014.

Bigelow, Anna. *Sharing the Sacred: Practicing Pluralism in Muslim North India.* New York: Oxford University Press, 2010.

Van Bruinessen, Martin, and Howell, Julia Day. *Sufism and the "Modern" in Islam.* London: I.B. Tauris, 2012.

Buckhardt, Titus. *Introduction to Sufi Doctrine.* Translated from French by D. M. Matheson. Bloomington, IN: World Wisdom Inc, 1959.

Buturovic, Amila. "Between the *Tariqa* and the *Shari'a*: The Making of the Female Self." In *Feminist Poetics of the Sacred Creative Suspicions,* edited by F. Devlin-Glass and L. Mcredden, 135–50. Oxford: Oxford University Press, 2001.

Chittick, William. *Sufism: A Beginner's Guide.* Oxford: Oneworld Books, 2000.

Chittick, William. *Ibn 'Arabi.* Oxford: Oneworld Publications, 2005.

Clothey, Fred W. "Pilgrimage Centers in the Tamil Cultus of Murukan." *The Journal of American Academy of Religion,* 40, no. 1 (1972): 79–95.

Cooke, Miriam, and Lawrence, Bruce B., eds. *Muslim Networks: From Hajj to Hip Hop.* North Carolina: The University of North Carolina Press, 2005.

Copeman, Jacob, and Ikegame, Aya, eds. *The Guru in South Asia: New Interdisciplinary Perspectives.* New York: Routledge, 2012.

Corbett, Rosemary R. *Making Moderate Islam: Sufism, Service, and The Ground Zero Mosque Controversy.* Stanford: Stanford University Press, 2016.

Corbin, Henry. *Alone with the Alone: Creative Imagination in the Sufism of Ibn Arabi.* New Jersey: Princeton University Press, 1998, 1962.

Cornell, Rkia. *Early Sufi Women: Dhikr an-nisaw al-muta'abbidat as-Sufiyyat by Abu 'Abd ar-Rahman as Sulami.* Louisville, KY: Fons Vitae, 1999.

Cornell, Rkia. "Sufi Women's Spirituality: A Theology of Servitude." *Voices of Islam vol. 2, Voices of the Spirit.* Edited by Vincent J. Cornell, 167–174. Westport, Connecticut and London: Praeger Publishers. 2007.

Dagli, Caner K. *Ringstones of Wisdom (Fusus al-Hikam).* Chicago: Kazi Publication, 2004.

Dakake, Maria Massi. "'Walking upon the Path of God Like Men?': Women and the Feminine in the Islamic Mystical Tradition." *Sophia: The Journal of Traditional Studies* 8, no. 2 (2002): 117–38.

Dakake, Maria Massi. "'Guest of the Inmost Heart': Conceptions of the Divine Beloved among Early Sufi Women." *Journal of Comparative Islamic Studies,* 3, no. 1 (2007): 72–97.

De Munck, V. C. "Sufi, Reformist and National Modes of Identity: The History of Muslim Village Festival in Sri Lanka." *Indian Sociology,* 28, no. 2 (1994): 273–93.

De Munck, V. C. "Islamic Orthodoxy and Sufism in Sri Lanka." *Anthropos,* 100, no. 2 (2005): 401–14.

De Silva, K. M. *A History of Sri Lanka.* Colombo, Sri Lanka: Vijitha Yapa Publications, 2005.

"Department of Census and Statistics Sri Lanka." http://www.statistics.gov.lk/page.asp?page= Population%20and%20Housing (accessed August 15, 2014).

Diaz, Marta Dominguez. "Shifting Field Sites: An Alternative Approach to Fieldwork in Transnational Sufism." *Fieldwork in Religion* (2011): 64–82.

Dickson, William Rory. *Living Sufism in North America: Between Tradition and Transformation.* PhD dissertation. Waterloo: Wilfrid Laurier University, 2012.

Dickson, William Rory. *Living Sufism in North America: Between Tradition and Transformation.* Albany: State University of New York Press, 2015.

Dickson, William Rory, and Xavier, Merin Shobhana. "Négociation du sacré à Philadelphie: soufismes concurrents au sanctuaire de Bawa Muhaiyaddeen." *Social Compass,* 62, no. 4 (2015): 584–97.

Dionigi, Albera, and Couroucil, Maria, eds. *Sharing Sacred Spaces in the Mediterranean: Christians, Muslims, and Jews at Shrines and Sanctuaries.* Bloomington: Indiana University Press, 2012.

Dressler, Markus, Geaves, Ron, and Klinkhammer, Gritt. *Sufis in Western Society: Global Networking and Locality.* New York: Routledge, 2009.

Dunn, Ross E. *The Adventures of Ibn Battuta: A Muslim Traveler of the 14th Century.* Berkeley and Los Angeles: University of California Press, 2012.

Eade, John, and Sallnow, Michael Jr., eds. *Contesting the Sacred: The Anthropology of Christian Pilgrimage*. London: Routledge, 1991.

Eaton, Richard. *The Rise of Islam and the Bengal Frontier 1204–1760*. Berkeley: University of California Press, 1996.

Einboden, Jeffrey. *Islam and Romanticism: Muslim Currents from Goethe to Emerson*. London: Oneworld Publications, 2014.

Eliade, Mircea. *The Sacred and the Profane: The Nature of Religion*. Florida: Harcourt, Inc. 1957.

Elias, Jamal. 1988. "Female and Feminine in Islamic Mysticism." *The Muslim World*, 78 (1988): 208–24.

Ernst, Carl W. *The Shambhala Guide to Sufism*. Boston: Shambhala, 1997.

Ernst, Carl W. *Refractions of Islam in India: Situating Sufism and Yoga*. London: Sage, 2016.

Ernst, Carl W., and Lawrence, Bruce B. *The Chishti Order in South Asia and Beyond: Sufi Martyrs of Love*. New York: Palgrave Macmillian, 2002.

Farhana Mayer, trans. *Spiritual Gems: The Mystical Qur'an Commentary Ascribed by Sufis to Imam Ja'far al-Sadiq (d.148/765)*. Kentucky: Fons Vitae, 2011.

Faye, Maryam Kabeer. *Journey through Ten Thousand Veils*. Somerset, NJ: Tughra Books, 2009.

Finnegan, Eleanor. "Cultivating Faith: The Relationship between Islam and Sustainable Agriculture in Rural Communities of American Muslims." In *Global Food Insecurity: Rethinking Agricultural and Rural Development Paradigm and Policy*, edited by Mohamed Behnassi, Sidney Draggan, and Sanni Yaya, 53–62. Netherlands: Springer, 2011.

Finnegan, Eleanor. "Hijra and Homegrown Agriculture: Farming among American Muslim Communities." PhD thesis. Florida: University of Florida, 2011.

Flueckiger, Joyce, Burkhalter. *In Amma's Healing Room: Gender and Vernacular Islam in South Asia*. Bloomington: Indiana University Press, 2006.

Foucault, Michel, "Des Espace Autres." In *Architecture/Mouvement/Continuité*, trans. Jay Miskowiec (1967/1984), 1–9.

Funk, Nathan C., Said, Abdul Aziz, et al., eds. *Peace and Conflict Resolution in Islam: Precept and Practice*. Lanham, MD: University Press of America, 2001.

Geaves, Ron. *The Sufis of Britain: An Exploration of Muslim Identity*. United Kingdom: Cardiff Academic Press, 2000.

Geaves, Ron. "The Bawa Muhaiyaddeen Fellowship." In *Encyclopedia of New Religions: New Religious Movements, Sects and Alternative Spiritualties*, edited by Christopher Patridge, 144. Oxford: Lion Publishing, 2004.

Geaves, Ron, and Theodre, Gabriel, eds. *Sufism in Britain*. London: Bloomsbury Press, 2013.

Geaves, Ron, Dressler, Markus, Klinkhammer, Gritt, eds. *Sufis in Western Society: Global Networking and Locality*. New York: Routledge, 2009.

Geertz, Clifford. *Islam Observed: Religious Development in Morocco and Indonesia.*
    Chicago: The University of Chicago Press, 1971.
GhaneaBassiri, Kambiz. *A History of Islam in America.* New York: Cambridge
    University Press, 2010.
Gilbert, Mitchell. *One Light: An Owner's Manual for the Human Being.*
    Philadelphia: One Light Press, 2005.
Godless, Alan. "Sufism, the West, and Modernity." http://islam.uga.edu/sufismwest.html
    (accessed March 31, 2017).
Goonasekera, Sunil. *Walking to Kataragama.* Colombo: International Center for Ethnic
    Studies, 2007.
Gottschalk, Peter. *Beyond Hindu and Muslim: Multiple Identity in Narratives from
    Village India.* New York: Oxford University Press, 2000.
Green, Nile. *Sufism: A Global History.* West Sussex: John Wiley & Sons, 2013.
Grewal, Zareena. *Islam Is a Foreign Country: American Muslims and the Global Crisis of
    Authority.* New York: New York University Press, 2013.
Grimes, Ronald L. "Defining Nascent Ritual." *Journal of the American Academy of
    Religion*, 50, no. 4 (1982): 539–55.
Grimes, Ronald L. "Jonathan Z. Smith's Theory of Ritual Space." *Religion*, 29, no. 3
    (1999): 261–73.
Haniffa, F. "Piety as Politics amongst Muslim Women in Contemporary Sri Lanka."
    Modern Asian Studies, 42 (2008): 347–75.
Hazen, Julianne. "Beyond Whirling and Weeping: Tasawwuf in America." *Polyvocia—
    The SOAS Journal of Graduate Research*, 3 (2011): 17–32.
Hazen, Julianne. "Contemporary Islamic Sufism in America: The Philosophy and
    Practices of Alami Tariqa in Waterport, New York." PhD thesis. London: SOAS,
    University of London, 2011.
Hazen, Julianne. *Sufism in America: The Alami Tariqa of Waterport, New York.*
    London: Lexington Books, 2017.
Hermansen, Marcia. "In the Garden of American Sufi Movements: Hybrids and
    Perennials." In *New Trends and Developments in the World of Islam*, edited by Peter
    Clark, 155–78. London: Luzac Oriental Press, 1997.
Hermansen, Marcia. "Literary Production of Western Sufi movements." In *Sufism in the
    West*, edited by J. Malik and J. Hinnells, 28–48. New York: Routledge, 2006.
Hermansen, Marcia. "Global Sufism: 'Theirs and Ours.'" In *Sufis in Western
    Society: Global Networking and Locality*, edited by R. Geaves, M. Dressler, et al., 26–
    45. New York: Routledge, 2009.
Hermansen, Marcia. "South Asian Sufism in the United States." In *South Asian
    Sufis: Devotion, Deviation and Destiny*, edited by Charles Ramsey, 247–68.
    New York: Continuum, 2012.
Hermansen, Marcia. "Sufism and American Women." *World History Connected*
    November 2006, http://worldhistoryconnected.press.illinois.edu/4.1/hermansen.
    html (accessed June 15, 2015).

Hill, Joseph. "'All Women Are Guides': Sufi Leadership and Womanhood among Taalibe Bay in Senegal." *Journal of Religion in Africa*, 40 (2010): 375–412.

Hirst, Jacqueline Suthren, and Zavos, John. *Religious Traditions in Modern South Asia.* London and New York: Routlege, 2011.

Hirtenstein, Stephen. *The Unlimited Mercifier: The Spiritual Life and Thought of Ibn ʿArabi.* Oxford: Anqa Publishing, 1999.

Ho, Engseng. *The Graves of Tarim: Genealogy and Mobility across the Indian Ocean.* Oakland: University of California Press, 2006.

Hughes, Aaron. *Abrahamic Religions: On the Uses and Abuses of History.* Oxford: Oxford University Press, 2012.

Inayat-Khan, Pir Zia, ed. *A Pearl in Wine: Essays in the Life, Music and Sufism of Hazrat Inayat Khan.* New Lebanon: Omega Publications, 2001.

Inayat-Khan, Pir Zia. "A Hybrid Sufi Order at the Crossroads of Modernity: The Sufi Order and Sufi Movement of Pir-o-Murshi Inayat Khan." PhD dissertation. Duke University, 2006.

Izutsu, T. *Sufism and Taoism: A Comparative Study of Key Philosophical Concepts.* California: University of California Press, 1983.

Jironet, Karin. *Sufism into the West: Life and Leadership of Hazrat Inayat Khan's Brothers 1927–1967.* Leuven: Peeters, 2009.

Kaptein, N. J. G. *Muhammad's Birthday Festival: Early History in the Central Muslim Lands and Development in the Muslim West until the 10th/16th Century.* Leiden: Brill, 1993.

Katz, Marion Holmes. *The Birth of the Prophet Muhammad.* New York: Routledge, 2007.

Katz, Marion Holmes. "Women's *Mawlid* Performances in Sanaa and the Construction of 'Popular Islam,'" *International Journal of Middle East Studies*, 40 (2008): 467–84.

Khan, Dominique-Sila. *Crossing the Threshold: Understanding Religious Identities in South Asia.* New York: I.B Tauris & Co Ltd, 2004.

Khan, Dominique-Sila. "Being One and Many among the Others: Muslim Diversity in the Context of South Asian Religious Pluralism." In *Diversity and Pluralism in Islam: Historical and Contemporary Discourses amongst Muslims*, edited by Zulfikar Hirji, 43–60. London: I.B. Tauris Publishers, in association with the Institute of Ismaili Studies, 2010.

Klem, Bart. "Islam, Politics and Violence in Eastern Sri Lanka." *Journal of Asian Studies*, 70, no. 3 (2011): 730–53.

Korom, Frank. "Charisma and Community: A Brief History of the Bawa Muhaiyaddeen Fellowship." *The Sri Lanka Journal of the Humanities*, 37 (2011): 19–33.

Korom, Frank. "Speaking with Sufis: Dialogue with Whom and about What?" In *Interreligious Dialogue and the Cultural Shaping of Religions*, edited by C. Cornille and S. Corigliano, 224–49. Oregon: Cascade Books, 2012.

Korom, Frank. "The Presence of Absence: Using Stuff in a South Asian Sufi Movement." *AAS Working Papers in Social Anthropology* (2012): 1–19.

Korom, Frank. "Longing and Belonging at a Sufi Saint Shrine Abroad." In *Islam, Sufism and Everyday Politics of Belonging in South Asia*, edited by Deepra Dandekar and Torsten Tschacher, 77–100. New York: Routledge, 2016.

Kugle, Scott. *Sufis & Saints' Bodies: Mysticism, Corporeality, & Sacred Power in Islam*. Chapel Hill: University of North Carolina Press, 2007.

Kugle, Scott, and Shaikh, Sa'diyya, eds. *Journal for Islamic Studies*, thematic issue: "Engaged Sufism," 26 (2006).

Kurukulasuriya, L. "Grandpass and the Tolerance of Religious Intolerance." *Colombo Telegraph*. http://www.colombotelegraph.com/index.php/ grandpass-and-the-tolerance-of-religious-intolerance/ (retrieved August 23, 2013).

Lewis, Franklin D. *Rumi: Past and Present, East and West: The Life, Teachings and Poetry of Jalal al-Din Rumi*. Oxford: Oneworld Publications, 2000.

Malik, Jamal, and Hinnells, John, ed. *Sufism in the West*. Oxon: Routledge, 2006.

Mandaville, Peter G. *Transnational Muslim Politics: Reimagining the Umma*. London: Routledge, 2003.

Mandaville, Peter G. *Global Political Islam*. New York: Routledge, 2007.

Marcus, George. "Ethnography in/of the World System: The Emergence of Multi-Sited Ethnography." *Annual Review of Anthropology* 24 (1995): 95–117.

Marcus, Sharon. *My Years with the Qutb: A Walk in Paradise*. Toronto: Self-published, 2005.

Mauroof, Mohamed. "The Culture and Experience of Luminous and Liminal Komunesam." PhD thesis. Pennsylvania: University of Pennsylvania, 1976.

McGilvray, Dennis. "Jailani: A Sufi Shrine in Sri Lanka." In *Lived Islam in South Asia: Adaptation, Accommodation & Conflict*, edited by Imtiaz Ahmad and Helmut Reifeld, 273–89. Berghahn Books: New York and Oxford, 2004.

McGilvray, Dennis. *Crucible of Conflict: Tamil and Muslim Society on the East Coast of Sri Lanka*. Durham, NC: Duke University Press, 2008.

McGilvray, Dennis. "A Matrilineal Sufi Shaykh in Sri Lanka." *South Asian History and Culture*, 5, no. 2 (2014): 246–61.

McGilvray, Dennis. "Islamic and Buddhist Impacts on the shrine at Daftar Jailani." In *Islam, Sufism and Everyday Politics of Belonging in South India*, edited by Deepra Dandekar and Torsten Tschacher, 62–76. London: Routledge, 2016.

McGilvray, Dennis, and Raheem, Mirak. *Muslim Perspectives on the Sri Lankan Conflict*. Washington: East-West Center Washington, 2007.

McKinley, Alexander, and Xavier, Merin Shobhana. "The Mysteries of the Universe: The Tamil Muslim Intellectualism of M. C. Sidde Lebbe." *South Asia: Journal of South Asian Studies* (2017): 1–18.

Metcalf, Barbara. *Islamic Revival in British India: Deoband, 1860–1900*. New Jersey: Princeton University Press, 2002.

Milani, Milad. "The Cultural Products of Global Sufism." In *Handbook of New Religions and Cultural Productions*, edited by Carole M. Cusack and Alex Norman, 659–80. Leiden, Boston: Brill, 2012.

Miller, Richard, and Lee-Hood, Ruq, trans. *The Subhana Maulid: Maulidun-Nabi (Sal.)* Philadelphia: Fellowship Press, 2013.

Mohammad, Afsar. *The Festival of Pirs: Popular Islam and Shared Devotion in South India.* Oxford: Oxford University Press, 2013.

Muhaiyaddeen, B. *Songs of God's Grace.* Philadelphia: Fellowship Press, 1973.

Muhaiyaddeen, B. *Dhikr Instructions Booklet.* Philadelphia: Fellowship Press, April 21, 1974.

Muhaiyaddeen, B. "The Learning of an Ant Man." New York City: Fellowship Press, audio-discourse, 1975.

Muhaiyaddeen, B. *The Guidebook to the True Secret of the Heart* (Vol. 2). Philadelphia: Fellowship Press, 1976.

Muhaiyaddeen, B. *God His Prophets and His Children.* Philadelphia: Fellowship Press, 1978.

Muhaiyaddeen, B. "Come Together and Search for God." Philadelphia: Fellowship Press, CD, 1978b.

Muhaiyaddeen, B., and Hixon, Lex. "True Dimensions of Dhikr." Philadelphia: WBAI Studio, CD, May 18, 1978.

Muhaiyaddeen, B. *Asmā'ul Husnā: The 99 Beautiful Names of Allah.* Philadelphia: Fellowship Press, 1979.

Muhaiyaddeen, B. "Change to *Insan Kamil*: The Direct Connection." Philadelphia: Fellowship Press, CD, 1979b.

Muhaiyaddeen, B. "Why We Recite Maulids." Philadelphia: Fellowship Press, February 7, 1982.

Muhaiyaddeen, B. "Talk to Executive Committee: As One Family, Look for the Truth. This Is God's House." CD, May 1, 1984.

Muhaiyaddeen, B. "With Iman Lets Search for the Treasure of the Heart." CD, May 27, 1984.

Muhaiyaddeen, B. *Islam & World Peace: Explanations of a Sufi.* Philadelphia: Fellowship Press, 1987.

Muhaiyaddeen, B. *Wisdom of the Divine (al-Hikmathul Jannath).* Colombo: Serendib Sufi Study Circle 1988.

Muhaiyddeen, B. *Morning Dhikr at the Mosque of Shaikh M. R. Bawa Muhaiyaddeen (Ral).* Philadelphia: The Bawa Muhaiyaddeen Fellowship, 1996.

Muhaiyaddeen, B. *Song of Muhammad.* Philadelphia: Fellowship Press, 1996.

Muhaiyaddeen, B. *The Resonance of Allah: Resplendent Explanations Arising from the Nur, Allah's Wisdom of Grace.* Philadelphia: Fellowship Press, 2001.

Muhaiyaddeen, B. *The Tree That Fell to the West: Autobiography of a Sufi.* Philadelphia: Fellowship Press, 2003.

Muhaiyaddeen, B. *The Map of the Journey to God Lessons from the School of Grace.* Philadelphia: Fellowship Press, 2006.

Muhaiyaddeen, Musa. *The Elixir of Truth: Journey on the Sufi Path.* Atlantic City: The Witness Within Inc, 2013.

Murata, Sachiko. *The Tao of Islam: A Sourcebook on Gender Relationships in Islamic Thought*. Albany: State University of New York Press, 1992.

Narayan, B. K., and Sawney, Rajeev, eds. *Dialogues of the Sufi Mystic Bawa Muhaiyaddeen*. New Delhi: Vikas Publishing House, 1999.

Neilesh, Bose. *Recasting the Region: Language, Culture, and Islam in Colonial Bengal*. Oxford University Press, 2014.

Numrich, Paul. *Old Wisdom in the New World: Americanization in Two Immigrant Theravada Buddhist Temples*. Knoxville: University of Tennessee Press/ Knoxville, 1999.

Orsi, Robert A. *Between Heaven and Earth: The Religious Worlds People Make and the Scholars who Study Them*. Princeton: Princeton University Press, 2005.

Pemberton, Kelly. "Women, Ritual Life, and Sufi Shrines in North India." PhD thesis. New York: Columbia University, 2000.

Pemberton, Kelly. "Muslim Women Mystics and Female Spiritual Authority in South Asian Sufism." *Journal of Ritual Studies*, 18 (2004): 1–23.

Pemberton, Kelly. "Women *Pirs*, Saintly Succession, and Spiritual Guidance in South Asian Sufism." *The Muslim World*, 96 (2006): 61–87.

Pemberton, Kelly. *Women Mystics and Sufi Shrines in India*. Columbia: University of South Carolina Press, 2010.

Pena, Elaine A. *Performing Piety: Making Space Sacred with the Virgin of Guadalupe*. Berkeley and Los Angeles: University of California Press, 2011.

Le Pichon, Chloë, Ganesan, Dwaraka, et al., ed. *The Mirror Photographs and Reflections on Life with M. R. Bawa Muhaiyaddeen*. Philadelphia: Chloë Le Pichon, 2010.

Pinkey, Andrea. "Prasada, the Gracious Gift, in Contemporary Classical South Asia." *Journal of the American Academy of Religion*, 81, no. 3 (2013): 734–756.

Ratnawalli, Darshanie. "What Paranavitana Said to McGilvray; 'Do Your Homework Son.'" *Colombo Telegraph*, 2015. https://www.colombotelegraph.com/ index.php/ what- paranavitana-said-to-mcgilvray-do-your-homework-son/.

Raudvere, Catharina. *The Book and the Roses: Sufi Women, Visibility, and Zikr in Contemporary Istanbul*. Sweden: Bjärnums Tryckeri, 2002.

Raudvere, Catharina. "Knowledge in Trust: Sufi Women in Istanbul." *Social Compass*, 50, no. 23 (2003): 23–34.

Raudvere, Catharina, and Stenberg, Leif. *Sufism Today: Heritage and Tradition in the Global Community*. New York: I.B. Tauris, 2008.

Ridgeon, Lloyd, eds. *The Cambridge Companion to Sufism*. Cambridge: Cambridge University Press, 2014.

Rozehnal, Robert. *Islamic Sufism Unbound: Politics and Piety in Twenty-First Century Pakistan*. Palgrave MacMillan, 2009.

Sahabdeen, A. M. M. *The Sufi Doctrine in Tamil Literature*. Sri Lanka: Abdul Majeed Mohamed Sahabdeen Trust Foundation, 1986.

Sands, Kristin Zahra. *Sufi Commentaries on the Qur'an in Classical Islam*. New York: Routledge, 2006.

Schielke, Samuli. "Snacks and Saints: Mawlid Festivals and the Politics of Festivity, Piety and Modernity in Contemporary Egypt." PhD thesis. University of Amsterdam, 2006.

Schielke, Samuli. "Mystic States, Motherly Virtues, Female Participation and Leadership in an Egyptian Sufi Milieu." *Journal for Islamic Studies*, 28 (2008): 94–126.

Schimmel, Annemarie. *Mystical Dimensions of Islam*. North Carolina: The University of North Carolina Press, 1975.

Schimmel, Annemarie. *And Muhammad Is His Messenger*. North Carolina: The University of North Carolina, 1985.

Schimmel, Annemarie. *My Soul Is a Woman: The Feminine in Islam*. New York: Bloomsbury Academic, 2003.

Schleifer, Aliah. *Mary the Blessed Virgin of Islam*. Louisville, KY: Fons Vitae, 1997.

Schmidt, Leigh Eric. *Restless Souls: The Making of American Spirituality*. California: University of California Press, 2012.

Schomburg, Susan Elizabeth. " 'Reviving Religion': The Qadiri Sufi Order, Popular Devotion to Sufi Saint Muhyiuddin 'Abdul Qadir al-Gilani and Processes of 'Islamization' in Tamil Nadu and Sri Lanka." PhD thesis. Cambridge: Harvard University, 2003.

Schönbeck, Oluf. "Sufism in the USA: Creolisation, Hybridisation, Syncretisation?" In *Sufism Today: Heritage and Tradition in the Global Community*, edited by Catharina Raudvere and Leif Stenberg, 177–88. London: I.B. Taurus, 2009.

Schopen, Gregory. *Bones, Stones, and Buddhist Monks: Collected Papers on the Archaeology, Epigraphy, and Texts of Monastic Buddhism in India*. Hawai'i: University of Hawai'i, 1997.

Sedgwick, Mark, *Western Sufism: From the Abbasids to the New Age*. Oxford: Oxford University Press, 2017.

Sells, Michael. *Early Islamic Mysticism: Sufi, Qur'an, Mi'raj, Poetic and Theological Writings*. New Jersey: Paulist Press, 1996.

Shah, Idries. *The Sufis*. New York: Doubleday and Company, 1964.

Shaikh, Sa'diyya. *Sufi Narratives of Intimacy: Ibn 'Arabi, Gender and Sexuality*. Chapel Hill: The University of North Carolina Press, 2012.

Sikand, Yoginder. *Sacred Spaces: Exploring Traditions of Shared Faith in India*. New York: Penguin, 2007.

Silvers, Laury. "Early Pious, Mystic Sufi Women." In *The Cambridge Companion to Sufism*, edited by Llyod Ridgeon, 24–52. New York: Cambridge University Press, 2015.

Singh, Shukdev. *The Bijak of Kabir*. New York: Oxford University Press, 2002.

Sirriyeh, Elizabeth. *Sufis and Anti-Sufis: The Defence, Rethinking and Rejection of Sufism in the Modern World*. Richmond, UK: Curzon Press, 1999.

Smith, Jane I. *Islam in America*. Columbia: Columbia University Press, 2010.

Smith, Jonathan Z. *Map Is Not a Territory: Studies in the History of Religions*. Leiden, the Netherlands: E. J. Brill, 1978.

Smith, Jonathan Z. *To Take Place: Toward Theory in Ritual*. Chicago: University of Chicago Press, 1987.

Smith, Margaret. *Rabi'a: the Life and Works of Rabi'a and Other Women Mystics in Islam*. Oxford: Oneworld, 1994.

Spencer, Jonathan, ed. *Sri Lanka: History and the Roots of Conflict*. London: Routledge, 1990.

Spencer, Jonathan, Goodhand, Jonathan, et al. *Checkpoint, Temple, Church and Mosque. A Collaborative Ethnography of War and Peace*. London: PlutoPress, 2015.

Taji-Farouki, Suha. *Beshara and Ibn 'Arabi: A Movement of Sufi Spirituality in the Modern World*. Reprint edition. Oxford: Anqa Publishing, 2010.

Thiranagama, Sharika. *In My Mother's House Civil War in Sri Lanka*. Pennsylvania: University of Pennsylvania, 2011.

Thurlkill, Mary F. *Chosen among Women: Mary and Fatima in Medieval Christianity and Shi'ite Islam*. Indiana: University of Notre Dame Press, 2007.

Tschacher, Torsten, and Dandekar, Deepra, eds. *Islam, Sufism and Everyday Politics of Belonging in South Asia*. London: Routledge, 2016.

Turner, Victor. *The Ritual Process: Structure and Anti-Structure*. Chicago: Aldine Publishing, 1969.

Turner, Victor. "Dramatic Ritual/Ritual Drama: Performative and Reflexive Anthropology." *The Kenyon Review*, New Series, 1/3 (1979): 80–93.

Turner, Victor, and Turner, Edith. *Image and Pilgrimages Culture: Anthropological Perspectives*. New York: Columbia University Press, 1978.

Tweed, Thomas A. *Our Lady of Exile: Diasporic Religion at a Cuban Catholic Shrine in Miami*. Oxford: Oxford University Press, 1997.

Tweed, Thomas A. *Crossing and Dwelling: A Theory of Religion*. Cambridge, MA: Harvard University Press, 2008.

Uwise, M. M. *Muslim Contributions to Tamil Literature*. Kilakkarai: Fifth International Islamic Tamil Literary Conference, 1990.

Van Bruinessen, Martin, and Howell, Julia Day, eds. *Sufism and the "Modern" in Islam*. New York: I.B. Taurus, 2007.

Vàsquez, M. A. "Studying Religion in Motion: A Networks Approach." *Method and Theory in the Study of Religion*, 20 (2008): 151–84.

Webb, Gisela. "Tradition and Innovation in Contemporary American Spirituality: The Bawa Muhaiyaddeen Fellowship." In *Muslim Communities in North America*, edited by Y. Haddad and J. Smith, 75–108. Albany: State University of New York Press, 1994.

Webb, Gisela. "Teaching with Pictures: Three Paintings of Bawa Muhaiyaddeen." In *Windows on the House of Islam*, edited by J. Renard, 290–6. Berkeley: University of California Press, 1998.

Webb, Gisela. "Third-Wave Sufism in America and the Bawa Muhaiyaddeen Fellowship." In *Sufism in the West*, edited by J. Malik and J. Hinnells, 86–102. New York: Routledge, 2006.

Webb, Gisela. "Negotiating Boundaries: American Sufis." In *The Cambridge Companion to American Islam*, edited by J. Hammer and O. Safi, 190–207. New York: Cambridge University Press, 2013.

Werbner, Pnina. *Pilgrims of Love: The Anthropology of a Global Sufi Cult.* Bloomington: Indiana University Press, 2004.

Werbner, Pnina. "Transnationalism and Regional Cults." In *The Cambridge Companion of Sufism*, edited by Llyod Ridgeon, 282–300. Cambridge: Cambridge University Press, 2015.

Werbner, Pnina, and Basu, Helen. "The Embodiment of Charisa." In *Embodying Charisma: Modernity, Locality and the Performance of Emotion in Sufi Cults*, edited by Pnina Werbner and Helen Basu, 3–28. London: Routledge, 1998.

Wright, John B. 2007. "Sri Pada: Sacred Pilgrimage Mountain of Sri Lanka." *Focus on Geography*, 50, no. 2 (2007): 1–6.

Xavier, Merin Shobhana. "The *Insan Kamil* of Bawa: the Metaphysics of a Tamil Sufi Sheikh." *The Sri Lanka Journal of Humanities*, 39 (2013): 51–63.

Yogananda, Paramahansa. *Autobiography of a Yogi.* New York: Philosophical Library, 1946.

Yohannan, John D. "Emerson's Translations of Persian Poetry from German Sources." *American Literature*, 14, no. 4 (1943): 407–20.

Index